The Business of Bigotry

Civil War America

Caroline E. Janney and Aaron Sheehan-Dean, editors

This landmark series interprets broadly the history and culture of the Civil War era through the long nineteenth century and beyond. Drawing on diverse approaches and methods, the series publishes historical works that explore all aspects of the war, biographies of leading commanders, and tactical and campaign studies, along with select editions of primary sources. Together, these books shed new light on an era that remains central to our understanding of American and world history.

A complete list of books published in Civil War America is available at https://uncpress.org/series/civil-war-america.

The Business of Bigotry

John Van Evrie's Nineteenth-Century Racist Media Empire

MICHAEL E. WOODS

The University of North Carolina Press
Chapel Hill

Set in Minion Pro by Westchester Publishing Services

Library of Congress Cataloging-in-Publication Data
Names: Woods, Michael E. author
Title: The business of bigotry : John Van Evrie's nineteenth-century racist media empire / Michael E. Woods.
Description: Chapel Hill : The University of North Carolina Press, [2026] | Includes bibliographical references and index.
Identifiers: LCCN 2026018200 | ISBN 9781469696751 cloth | ISBN 9781469696768 paperback | ISBN 9781469695747 epub | ISBN 9781469696775 pdf
Subjects: LCSH: Van Evrie, John H., 1814–1896 | Racism in the press | Press—United States—History—19th century | Publishers and publishing—United States—History—19th century | Racism against Black people—United States—History—19th century | BISAC: HISTORY / United States / Civil War Period (1850–1877) | SOCIAL SCIENCE / Discrimination
Classification: LCC PN4888.R3 W66 2026
LC record available at https://lccn.loc.gov/2026018200

Cover art reprinted from John Van Evrie, *Negroes and Negro "Slavery": The First an Inferior Race: The Latter Its Normal Condition*, 3rd ed. (New York: Van Evrie, Horton & Co., 1863).

For product safety concerns under the European Union's General Product Safety Regulation (EU GPSR), please contact gpsr@mare-nostrum.co.uk or write to the University of North Carolina Press and Mare Nostrum Group B.V., Doelen 72, 4831 GR Breda, The Netherlands.

for Beth

Contents

Acknowledgments

It is humbling to reflect on all the people who helped me research and write this book. I am grateful to everyone who shared their time, energy, and expertise with me. Thank you.

Librarians and archivists across North America provided indispensable assistance in chasing down leads and accessing materials—even during the pandemic-related disruption. I offer sincere thanks to those mentioned here and to their colleagues as well: Kristin Rodgers (Health Sciences Library, Medical Heritage Center, Ohio State University); Tamara Jones (Ward M. Canady Center for Special Collections, University of Toledo); Katherine A. Neidig (Detre Library and Archives, Senator John Heinz History Center); Timothy Engels and Robin Wheelwright Ness (John Hay Library, Brown University); Autumn Haag and Melinda Wallington (Department of Rare Books, Special Collections, and Preservation, University of Rochester); Irene Martin (Local History and Genealogy Department, Toledo Lucas County Public Library); Dawn Eurich (Special Collections, Detroit Public Library); Elise DeAndrea (Archives & Special Collections, SUNY Upstate Medical University); Sara Pezzoni (Special Collections, University of Texas at Arlington); Tutti Jackson (Ohio History Connection); Jay Osborne (Local History and Genealogy Division, Central Library of Rochester and Monroe County); Christine Ridarsky (Rochester Public Library); Bill Keeler (Rochester Historical Society); Kathleen Britton (Rochester Medical Museum and Archives); R. Bruce Colburn (St. Luke and St. Simon Cyrene Episcopal Church, Rochester); Laura Haskell and Brianne Barrett (American Antiquarian Society); Abbie Weinberg (Folger Shakespeare Library); Bradford Brown and Elizabeth Bloodworth (Bradley University); Brandon Moblo (Warren Hunting Smith Library, Hobart and William Smith Colleges); Gina Modero, Mariam Touba, and Crystal Toscano (New-York Historical Society); Tara Craig (Rare Book and Manuscript Library, Columbia University); Marvin J. Taylor (New York University); Eric Nystrom (Arizona State University); Carmel Wilkes (National Archives and Records Administration, Washington, DC); Tim Rives (National Archives and Records Administration, Kansas City); Timothy H. Horning (University Archives, University of Pennsylvania); Daniel Williams (Archives, Special Collections, and Digital Initiatives, Mercer University); Lynn Heidelbaugh (Smithsonian National Postal Museum); Kathy Shoemaker (Stuart A.

Rose Manuscript, Archives, and Rare Book Library, Emory University); Karlyn Marcantonio (Connecticut Historical Society); Aryn Glazier (Dolph Briscoe Center for American History, University of Texas at Austin); Tim Ribaric and Edith Williams (Brock University); Susan Krueger, Lee Grady, and Emily Noffke (Wisconsin Historical Society Archives); Hang Nguyen (University of Iowa Special Collections Department); Anne Causey (Albert and Shirley Small Special Collections Library, University of Virginia); Matthew Guillen and Kate Weis (Virginia Museum of History and Culture); Victoria Duncan and Laura Eliason (Indiana State Library); Haley Walton (Duke University Libraries); Kyle Ainsworth (Stephen F. Austin State University); Jessica Tubis (Beinecke Rare Book and Manuscript Library, Yale University); Genevieve Coyle (Manuscripts and Archives Repository, Yale University); Robert F. Hancock (American Civil War Museum); Desirée Butterfield-Nagy (Fogler Library, University of Maine); Carley C. Altenburger (Winterthur Museum, Garden and Library); Melissa Murphy (Baker Library, Bloomberg Center, Harvard Business School); Michelle Miller and Christopher Schnell (Abraham Lincoln Presidential Library and Museum); Randi Beem and Andrew Pack (J. Murrey Atkins Library, University of North Carolina–Charlotte); Karen Martin (Huntington Historical Society); Alexia Loumankis (Bora Baskin Law Library, University of Toronto); Jayne Ptolemy (Clements Library, University of Michigan); and all the librarians and library staff at Marshall University and the University of Tennessee, Knoxville.

Many thanks to my colleagues in the history departments at Marshall and Tennessee for intellectual and moral support throughout the process. Thank you to department chairs Dan Holbrook and Greta Rensenbrink, and department heads Ernie Freeberg and Susan Lawrence, for all your support. Special thanks to Monica Black, Rob Bland, Tom Coens, Luke Harlow, Bill Mercer, Laura-Eve Moss, and Tore Olsson for insightful conversations about the book, and to everyone who participated in the University of Tennessee history department's faculty research colloquium where I presented some early findings. Heartfelt thanks to Mary Beckley, Kim Harrison, and Bernie Koprince for all their assistance. We miss you, Kim. I am also deeply grateful to several graduate research assistants for their diligent work: thank you to Amanda Deanda, Roraig Finney, and John Morden (University of Tennessee) and to Laura Earls (University of Delaware) for help in accessing and processing key sources.

Colleagues on multiple continents shared conversations, insights, and research materials with me, for which I am deeply indebted. Many thanks to Stuart Anderson-Davis, Thomas Balcerski, Robert Bonner, Michael Brown, Lyndsay Campbell, Shaun Creighton, Karolyn Smardz Frost, Sarah Gronningsater, Randall Hall, Richard John, David Kramer, Brian Luskey, Nicole Saffold Maskiell, Lawrence McDonnell, Kerby A. Miller, Mark Neely, John

Newmark, Elizabeth Pryor, Cara Rogers, Jason Stacy, Melissa Stein, Tara Strauch, Elizabeth Varon, Jonathan Daniel Wells, Andrew Wiley, Christopher Willoughby, and Donald Yacovone. Special thanks to the intrepid members of the political history writing group for their incisive comments on early drafts: Erik Alexander, Matt Mason, Rachel Shelden, Adam Smith, and Frank Towers.

For thoughtful questions and insightful feedback on my preliminary work on this project, I am grateful to fellow panelists and audience members at several conferences, including the Society of Civil War Historians; the American Political History Conference; the Electocracy in America and the Atlantic World Conference (Kinder Institute, University of Missouri); Interdisciplinary Nineteenth-Century Studies; Rothermere American Institute (University of Oxford); the Society for Historians of the Early American Republic; the Nineteenth-Century Studies Association; and the Symposium on the 19th Century Press, the Civil War, and Free Expression (University of Tennessee, Chattanooga). For opportunities to share work and receive feedback, I am also grateful to the Washington Early American Seminar (University of Maryland); the Massachusetts Historical Society; Centre College; the American History Research Seminar, Rothermere American Institute; and the History Club and the Honors and Scholars Program at the University of Tennessee, Knoxville.

For indispensable financial support, I wish to thank the University of Tennessee, Marshall University, the West Virginia Humanities Council, Indiana University's Lilly Library, the American Philosophical Society, and the American Council of Learned Societies.

My gratitude extends to everyone at the University of North Carolina Press who helped make this book a reality. Special thanks to Mark Simpson-Vos, Tara Jordan, Alyssa Brown, Valerie Burton, Emily Spangenberg, Lindsay Starr, Dawn Durante, and Kylie Haggen; to series editors Caroline E. Janney and Aaron Sheehan-Dean; and to both anonymous readers. I also thank Abigail Michaud and everyone at Westchester Publishing Services.

Finally, I offer love and thanks to my family. Since I began this project, we have mourned terrible losses and celebrated great joys, and I am profoundly grateful that we are in this together. I love you all. Special thanks to Jennifer and Rick for everything. And the biggest of thank-yous to Beth and the friends who live in our hearts.

The Business of Bigotry

Introduction

Joseph Addison Turner was limping badly, but he had almost arrived. The journey from Putnam County, Georgia, to New York City would have exhausted a hardy traveler—which he was not. The spare Georgian's lined face and hobbling gait made him look much older than thirty-four. But his mind was keen. The bone infection that felled him in adolescence and nearly took his leg had given him time to read and think. He would never be a dashing soldier, but he could fight with his pen. Convinced that newspapers and magazines were the "great weapons of the nineteenth century," he mortgaged his land and laborers to finance a periodical called the *Plantation*. Turner had grand plans for his quarterly. He would distribute it nationwide. He would annihilate the abolitionists. He would rout the Republicans and their lanky, log-splitting leader. He would print it—alas—in New York. Was it embarrassing to produce the *Plantation* in downtown Manhattan? Perhaps, but it made good sense: Low production costs, high print runs, and convenient transportation meant wider circulation. Plus, there were friends here. There were people who shared his cause and commitment, who agreed that cotton was king and that white freedom required Black servitude. With the manuscript for the *Plantation*'s September 1860 issue tucked under his arm, Turner ignored his throbbing leg and continued down Nassau Street toward the five-story stone building where he would meet one of those friends.[1]

As Turner stepped inside, he saw why New York was the nation's print media capital. Nothing in Putnam County could compare. On the ground floor, clerks and accountants hunched at their desks, scribbling away at letters and ledgers. Their names never appeared in print, but no enterprise of this scale could spare them. One floor down, workers folded and wrapped newspapers for delivery to every state and territory in the Union. Deeper underground, a caloric engine powered two printing presses that churned out copies for fifty thousand weekly subscribers. Turner headed upstairs, not to the top floor, where twenty typesetters bent over their toilsome tasks, but the one just below. He entered the editorial office, the brains of the operation, where the proprietors penned columns and plotted strategy. Here, Turner exulted, "Southern visitors are always sure of a cordial reception."[2] Whatever other New Yorkers thought of the shambling planter-journalist, he found camaraderie here. This was the headquarters of the *New York Day Book*. And this was where he finally met John H. Van Evrie.

Who was this Manhattan media magnate? Historians frequently quote passages from Van Evrie's prolific writings to illustrate the depravity of proslavery racism.[3] They have not misinterpreted him. Van Evrie was one of America's vilest villains. But in the massive literature on Civil War–era politics and print culture, he is regularly seen but not really *known*. He left no collection of papers, wrote no memoir, changed the spelling of his surname, and lied about his past, as when he told Turner he was born in New York.[4] This elusiveness has discouraged deeper analysis of his career. One scholar, inspired by parallels between Van Evrie's views and Nazism, commenced a book-length study during World War II but eventually abandoned the chase.[5] So, while his words echo in histories of his time, Van Evrie remains in the shadows. Brief sketches have partially illuminated him, but some are bedeviled by errors. He has been misidentified as a Southerner, for instance, and mischaracterized as a successful physician.[6] In fact, he was a Canadian immigrant who started writing after driving his medical practice into bankruptcy.

Why is Van Evrie's abominable career worth a book? It is not for the novelty of his ideas; he was evil, but not an evil genius. He probably did write "more words in defense of slavery than any other American," but his corpus is tediously repetitive and derived mainly from more original thinkers.[7] For this reason, intellectual historians have largely ignored him and focused on more innovative "scientific" racists like Samuel George Morton and Louis Agassiz and more creative proslavery theorists like George Fitzhugh and James Henry Hammond.[8] But Van Evrie is significant for other reasons.[9] Matthew Frye Jacobson called him a "publicist" whose "singular contribution to the scientific discourse of race involved not substance but simply volume."[10] Tali Mendelberg posited that he was "the most widely cited racist author of the 1860s."[11] George M. Fredrickson dubbed him "the first professional racist in American history."[12]

These observations remind us that racism has more than an intellectual history; it has a political history, a communications history, and a business history as well. *These* are the histories illuminated by Van Evrie's story. This book uses his life, written corpus, and publishing company to analyze connections between party politics, racist ideologies, and print media across the Civil War era. These histories cannot be understood in isolation. Ideologues needed party backing and media platforms to maximize their influence; newspaper editors relied on political patrons to remain solvent; office seekers needed friendly journalists to propagate their platforms and energize voters.

Although not a traditional biography, this book uses Van Evrie's career to untangle these threads. It offers a business history of a political publishing enterprise and a political history of proslavery print media, told through the life of the man who popularized the phrase *white supremacy.* That slogan's origin in an 1865 *New York Day Book* advertising campaign is a striking example of how Van Evrie braided partisan politics, financial interests, and racist ideas to build his business of bigotry.

Van Evrie's story is instructive both for its uniqueness and its typicality. He was certainly a singular figure. Born in Canada and educated in New York, he practiced medicine in Ohio and tasted combat as a surgeon in the Mexican-American War. After returning in 1848, Van Evrie spent seven years in Washington, DC, transforming himself from an obscure physician into a prominent proslavery propagandist. Convinced that polygenism—the notion that human races are distinct species descended from separately created original pairs—proved that God designed Black people for servitude and that he should propagate this idea to save the Union, Van Evrie devoted himself to writing, editing, and publishing. Between 1855 and 1879, he lived in Manhattan and made the *New York Day Book* the foundation of his "great Proslavery publishing concern."[13] Backed by Southern enslavers and New York merchants who wanted to preserve their lucrative commerce in cotton, he preached proslavery Unionism before the Civil War, proslavery reconciliation during the conflict, and violent resistance to Reconstruction. Only business failure halted his printing press.

Throughout his public career, Van Evrie strove to unite white Americans across divisions of region and class in support of slavery as a national boon. To that end, he labored to mold the Democratic Party in his own image. By his own metric, his failures outweighed his triumphs. He did not prevent the Civil War, thwart emancipation, or unify white people within a Democratic Party that met his standards. But because his single-minded campaign spanned the Civil War era, Van Evrie's singular story reveals stubborn continuities and strategic adaptations over a period of violent revolutionary change.[14] In particular, it highlights three themes. One is the tension between ideology and partisan allegiance, a theme that reverberates throughout the career of a lifelong Democrat who partnered with proslavery Whigs and routinely denounced Democratic Party leaders for subordinating principles to electoral advantage. Historians have traced in detail the conflicts between pragmatists and purists that roiled antislavery politics.[15] Van Evrie's complicated relationship with politicians of the Democratic Party reveals a fascinating parallel on the other side. Van Evrie's efforts to become a party spokesman, campaign strategist, and ideological gatekeeper sometimes inspired, but often aggravated, party insiders. Attention to this persistent friction complements recent studies of Democrats' fierce intraparty conflicts that raged amid the Civil War era's disorienting partisan upheaval and profound political change.[16]

Second is the depth of sectional division throughout the period. Van Evrie believed that slavery underpinned national prosperity, liberty, and unity, and his career illuminates national complicity in the sin of enslavement. But his career also underscores the salience of sectional conflict.[17] Determined to convert white Northerners, Van Evrie tailored his proslavery arguments for them and thus necessarily diverged from Southern allies who increasingly infused their own proslavery politics with regional separatism. This variance culminated in the rupture of 1861, when secession wrenched proslavery nationalism into Confederate hands, but it persisted throughout Reconstruction, not least in Van Evrie's sparring with the Southern Lost Cause promoters he criticized for denying slavery's centrality to the Confederate project. Determined to purge sectionalism from American politics, Van Evrie unwittingly illuminated, and sometimes collided with, regional differences.

The third theme is proslavery propagandists' ability to harness the communications revolution to their agenda. Scholars often celebrate technological innovations such as the railroad, telegraph, and rotary printing press for allowing ideas to move more quickly and cheaply.[18] Studies of proslavery responses to these developments, meanwhile, often cast them as purely defensive, with reactionaries resisting the torrent of abolitionist publications by murdering journalists, blocking postal deliveries, and strangling free speech.[19] This censorship was enormously important, but so is the story of how proslavery publishers and authors capitalized on the opportunities afforded them by the suppression of their opponents. By exploring how one advocate of slavery and scientific racism championed his cause, this book uncovers the communications revolution's sinister side.[20] Van Evrie, like Turner, believed that printing technology had unleashed an enormous power to shape public opinion, and he worked to appropriate it for himself. Confident that he could wield that power with decisive skill, Van Evrie fancied himself a national hero who would rescue a slaveholding Union from all enemies, foreign and domestic.[21] He relentlessly pursued this goal throughout the Civil War era, adapting his prose and adopting new tactics as circumstances shifted but rejecting all calls for moderation. Because Van Evrie operated from a Northern communications hub and with Northern readers in mind, his story extends other studies of Northern racism by illuminating how proslavery propaganda was produced, disseminated, and consumed among white Northerners.[22]

Of course, Van Evrie was hardly alone in assuming that print media could mold mass opinion. He disagreed with Frederick Douglass, William Lloyd Garrison, and Horace Greeley about most things, but not about the importance of the press. Thus, while Van Evrie's uniqueness makes him grotesquely fascinating, he is also instructive as a representative figure. As a case study of the Civil War–era press, this book uses Van Evrie and his publishing company to elucidate the business and politics of publishing. To persuade voters, influence elected officials, and achieve his heroic ambitions, Van Evrie had to maintain solvency. And while his effort to run a Northern proslavery publishing house was unusual, his basic struggle—to market his wares, recruit readers and advertisers, and turn a profit—was well-nigh universal. Yet this struggle remains relatively neglected. Studies of Civil War–era newspapers often focus on the major Northeastern dailies, such as the *Herald* and the *Tribune*, because they foreshadowed the twentieth-century rise of professional independent journalism.[23] But most mid-nineteenth-century papers were not forerunners of the modern *New York Times* or *Washington Post*; not all roads led to Bob Woodward and Carl Bernstein. Eighty percent of American newspapers in 1860 were still scrappy partisan sheets.[24] As a weekly political paper that relied on patronage, subscription dues, and private financing, Van Evrie's *Day Book* was more typical than the mammoth *Tribune*, whose offices were next door. The story of how Van Evrie kept his company afloat while trying to maximize his partisan influence and ideological impact reveals much about how nineteenth-century political print media *worked*.

It is primarily a story about business and politics. Technology-focused accounts of the communications revolution obscure the fact that cranking out newspapers or pamphlets mattered little if no one bought them. An ideologue whose political influence depended on his business success, Van Evrie's career reveals the intricate intertwining of marketing printed materials, promoting political campaigns, and promulgating ideas. All political newspaper editors had to align their business interests with their partisan loyalties and ideological aims. For Van Evrie, this meant pushing Democrats to adopt his unyielding proslavery stance while maximizing revenues from readers, advertisers, and patrons. Sometimes these efforts aligned, as in his 1865 "white supremacy" campaign. Other times, they did not, as in his catastrophic course during the 1872 presidential election. But the constant need to balance material, party, and ideological imperatives shaped Van Evrie's entire career, including his most sinister successes and disastrous defeats. He remained a professional racist only as long as his message was marketable.[25]

Unearthing the political and business history of nineteenth-century publishing requires thinking differently about print media. Historians understandably focus on content, with political historians devoting particular attention to editorials. From this angle, newspapers appear as vehicles for promoting ideology, and whether they shaped or reflected reader opinion, they are important as texts. Yet nineteenth-century Americans did not engage with print media in quite the same way; they could not conjure newspapers on computer screens or swiftly search them for juicy quotations. Instead, they encountered newspapers as *things*, physical objects with price tags—as consumer goods. Newspapers were produced, advertised, and sold in a competitive marketplace where ideology and partisanship shaped consumer preferences. By attending as closely to how Van Evrie hawked his wares as to his repetitious editorials, this book explores a Civil War–era media environment where the bottom line mattered as much as the party line.

Charting the production and movement of Van Evrie's words informs our interpretation of his message. His overtures to the white working class seem rather duplicitous when we discover that the *Day Book* adopted a pathbreaking strategy for breaking a printers' strike. His crusade to convert opinion in the North appears less straightforward when we learn that most of his readers lived in the South. His most famous contribution to the racist lexicon, the phrase "white supremacy," takes on greater significance when we notice that, although he first used the expression in an 1856 editorial, it did not catch fire until he spotlighted the slogan in an 1865 advertising campaign.

Tracing the dissemination of Van Evrie's virulent catalog means following money and people as well as ideas, and it illuminates the central place of print media in nineteenth-century social and political networks.[26] This approach yields important insights into the proslavery political campaign to which Van Evrie dedicated his life. Consider an account from Willow Grove in Delaware. According to Ezekiel L. Cooper, the *Day Book* was unknown there until 1859, when T. C. Rogers left a copy on the counter at Cooper's general store. Shoppers perused its columns, and many rushed to subscribe.[27] Unable to access the *Day Book* as a disembodied text, as modern readers can, Cooper's customers encountered a physical sample when Rogers introduced it into a center of public life. Given his background, it was almost certainly no accident. Thomas Cooper Rogers was born in Maryland and named after a South Carolina nullifier. Educated at the University of Pennsylvania, he became a physician and a vocal promoter of polygenesis. When he visited Cooper's store, Rogers was fresh off a tour lecturing on "Ethnology or the Negro a Distinct Species."[28] His strategic deployment of the *Day Book* advanced his broader campaign to spread proslavery ideas in his community.

Rogers, an Ivy League professional who leveraged his influence on behalf of slavery, was typical of the promoters who spread Van Evrie's publications through local networks. Careful study of Van Evrie's grassroots marketing campaigns reveals hundreds of individuals like Rogers who placed the Manhattan propagandist's materials in their neighbors' hands, either individually or through the immensely important institution of the subscriber club. Most were educated and affluent, and a striking number lived in small towns or rural enclaves. The *Day Book* was most actively promoted in both the North and the South by those with considerable material interests at stake in preserving slavery. In their case, at least, proslavery views were broadcast from above. Newspapers like Van Evrie's bound readers in political networks that stretched vertically as well as horizontally; the imagined community of *Day Book* readers was patently hierarchical.[29] And while Van Evrie's promoters were more prominent than most readers, evidence about his supporters offers intriguing surprises. Historians of popular nineteenth-century racism have focused on the white urban working class.[30] But racism has never been limited to the unskilled or poorly educated. Indeed, Van Evrie's keenest supporters tended to be wealthier, more deeply rooted, and more highly skilled than their neighbors. His work was financed by Southern capital and publicized by planters, merchants, and officeholders, who integrated *Day Book* marketing into everyday social and political activities. Thousands of eager readers consumed his publications, which permeated the Civil War–era United States. His intertwined political and promotional campaigns were not elite conspiracies but they did operate from the top down.

Yet his message was not imposed unilaterally; rather, Van Evrie forged reciprocal relationships with patrons and promoters. Proslavery politicians, Southern enslavers, and Northern merchants relied on him to champion their interests and popularize their cause. Van Evrie in turn needed them to bankroll his business and market his wares. His publishing firm operated within interlocking political, economic, and social networks that were rooted in slavery. Uncovering these networks illuminates the entrenched interests that confronted antislavery activists. As legal historian Cynthia Nicoletti has observed, without seriously studying "those who espoused . . . views that we now find distasteful," it is "almost impossible to answer the question of why history looks the way it does."[31] Heroes cannot be understood without a sober accounting of the villains.

Van Evrie developed and depended on a nationwide web of influencers who tried to beat the abolitionists in a nineteenth-century information war. Using technologies and marketing strategies common to most publishers, Van Evrie promoted a distinct brand of proslavery that braided polygenism with American nationalism and celebrated slavery as the foundation of national prosperity and white men's democracy. Through the *Day Book* and his other works, Van Evrie propounded and monetized a venomous worldview that he believed would preserve a slaveholding Union. With shrilly repetitive rhetoric, shrewd self-promotion, and unwavering faith in his own heroism, he energized a malevolent empire of proslavery activists who adapted but never acceded to the unfinished revolution wrought by the Civil War.[32]

Chapter 1
Origins

They moved north through the forest, bringing what they could carry and leaving everything they had known. Refugees from a republic's violent birth, they followed paths later used by more famous freedom-seeking fugitives. Their ordeal continued after reaching British soil. David Van Every enlisted in a Loyalist unit and waged the first of his two wars against the United States. Sarah Van Every, pregnant with their child, trekked on to the grim camp where she delivered a son whom she named for her husband. David Jr. grew up to fight his own battles and raise his own family, including another boy born into a war-torn world. But young John would defy family tradition and return to the United States. David and Sarah never suspected that they were fleeing the nation their grandson would love and defending the empire he would loathe.[1]

John Van Every's Loyalist ancestry and Canadian upbringing brim with irony. His forebears fled to what abolitionists deemed the "Refuge for Americans escaping from abuse and cruel bondage in their native land!"[2] Raised in Upper Canada (now Ontario) by unwavering enemies of the United States, Van Every was a ferocious American nationalist. Descended from stalwart British subjects, he was a paranoid Anglophobe. From his pedigree, Van Every might seem no more destined to become an American proslavery propagandist than a Cistercian monk or an adviser to the czar.

But Van Every's background is more illuminating than incongruous. Neither his racism nor his politics were anomalous in Upper Canada. He inherited proslavery ideas from relatives who were as keen on slavery as any of their American cousins. What separated Van Every from his kin—and, later, from Confederates—was not proslavery racism but national loyalty. And even this departure was not abnormal, for he had neighbors, teachers, and role models who admired the American republic and regarded its citizens as exemplars, perhaps even future compatriots. The Upper Canada of Van Every's youth was neither a bastion of British conservatism nor a paragon of racial progress. It was, rather, a school where lessons about racial hierarchy, mass politics, and the power of print media were taught every day.

Few details from Van Every's early life survive, but attention to context helps explain the contours of his career. Born into a family known for human trafficking, he needed no proslavery tutoring from Americans. Brought up by veterans and refugees, he accepted the utility of violence. Raised in a polity animated by fiery journalism, he grasped the pen and press as political weapons. Reared amid imperial upheaval, he embraced Anglophobic conspiracy theories. And, coupled with his later experiences in Mexico, his Canadian background clarifies his peculiar proslavery worldview, which blended nationalist zeal with an international perspective. Van Every saw slavery neither as a regional sin nor the foundation of Southern separatism, but as the basis of US democracy. Obsessed with alleged British perfidy and Mexican degeneracy, he defended American slavery as a democratic redoubt in a global clash against aristocracy. Van Every's Canadian origins shaped rather than stifled the proslavery American nationalism that he promoted through the Civil War and Reconstruction.

Dutch brothers Myndert and Carsden Van Iveren moved to Beverwyck (now Albany) in 1653. Their descendants intermarried with British settlers who entered the Hudson River Valley after New Amsterdam became New York. Among Myndert's great-grandchildren was McGregory, born in 1723 and named for Patrick McGregory, a Scottish army officer and family friend. Perhaps influenced by his namesake or his British wife, Mary Wilcox, McGregory's imperial devotion ran deep. He anglicized his surname, henceforth Van Every. And it was his branch of the family that stood by the crown—and carried their name into Canada.[3]

In 1776, war reached McGregory's Hudson Valley. A fertile source of provisions and a tempting avenue for invasion, the valley was divided between a staunch Loyalist minority and a Patriot majority determined to ferret out traitors. They soon targeted McGregory. Vigilant patriots arrested him twice as a British sympathizer, seized his livestock, and forced two of his sons, David and Benjamin, to join a New York Line regiment. They shared their father's loyalties and deserted, later fleeing with their families to Oswego, where they enlisted in a Loyalist unit. Three younger brothers followed, as did McGregory, who volunteered in 1781. Thus, six of John Van Every's ancestors rallied to the king's colors as members of Butler's Rangers.[4]

Despised by Patriots as barbarians, Butler's Rangers waged a fiercely personal war. Based at Fort Niagara and led by landowner and fur trader John Butler, the Rangers and their Native American allies swept across New York and Pennsylvania, raiding Patriot settlements and making places like Cherry Valley bywords for brutality among their outraged foes. Butler considered them retribution for attacks on Indigenous villages perpetrated by rebels determined to starve adversaries they could not conquer. A few Black Loyalists fought under Butler's command; John Van Every's ancestors served in a multiethnic unit. But some Rangers were longtime enslavers, and others captured enslaved people to sell north of the border.[5]

Military exploits were part of a larger story of violence and suffering that encompassed the noncombatants who congregated at Niagara. British leaders, tired of running army installations as "a nursery for women and children," sent them down the St. Lawrence River to hastily built and poorly supplied barracks, where twenty people squeezed into little more than seven hundred square feet.[6] Sarah Van Every arrived at the Machiche camp in early 1780 and gave birth to David Jr. in late July. Another child, a little girl, accompanied her and then vanished from the rolls; she might have died. Quebec governor Frederick Haldimand insisted that the "discontented and troublesome" refugees were well treated. They certainly were vocal: In 1781, a group of Machiche women, all tied to Butler's Rangers, petitioned to return to Fort Niagara. Many did so the following year, including Sarah and David.[7]

The Van Everys faced a clouded future at war's end in 1783. Reports of retaliation dashed hopes for returning home; one Loyalist who visited his parents in Orange County was tarred and feathered.[8] According to Butler, his veterans "would rather go to Japan than go among the Americans where they could never live in peace."[9] British strategists, who envisioned them as the nucleus of a colony that would counterbalance the newly independent United States, offered discharged soldiers land on the Niagara Peninsula, including two hundred acres to noncommissioned officers like David, who had made sergeant, and fifty acres for each additional family member. By 1784, over six hundred Rangers and their families had accepted these terms. Among them were McGregory, David, Sarah, and David Jr.[10]

In the afterglow of confederation in 1867, Canadian nationalists forged the Loyalist saga into an origin myth that featured the United Empire Loyalists, as they were designated in 1789, carving civilization out of the "wild woods." Their colony was a bulwark of British imperialism, the heart of an Anglophone Protestant Canada, and a beacon of racial benevolence.[11] In this light, Upper Canada (so named in 1791) seems unlikely to produce John Van Every. But its early history was neither simple nor isolated. Historians have long known that the border was porous; as one noted in 1940, the United States and Canada "spill[ed] great waves of men and women into each other's territories," making North America "a continent where international boundaries have been disregarded by restless humans for almost two centuries."[12]

Upper Canada's principal resource was land, and it attracted Americans like a magnet. After extracting concessions from the Mississauga people, the Crown offered enormous tracts to prospective farmers. For two decades after

1785, Upper Canada's non-Indigenous population grew more than 10 percent per year, topping 45,000 by 1805. Most came from the United States. By 1812, four in five non-Indigenous Upper Canadians were US-born migrants (dubbed Late Loyalists) or their children. Following the war that commenced that year, colonial authorities deterred American immigration. But the interwar influx ensured that young John Van Every had many American neighbors.[13]

Those neighbors brought practices that Canadian nationalists preferred to forget. Most notable was slavery, which gave some Loyalists and Late Loyalists alike an edge in a labor-hungry environment. One was McGregory Van Every, who cleared eight wooded acres in his first year at Niagara. It was tough work for a man over sixty, but Jurden, his "slave or negro servant," sweated with him.[14] Jurden's legal status is ambiguous, but other early settlers, including Butler himself, compelled enslaved people to fell trees, mind children, and do other essential labor.[15]

A brutal event in 1793 marked the beginning of slavery's end in Upper Canada—and implicated the Van Every family in human trafficking. It started when Adam and William Vrooman decided to sell Chloe Cooley to someone in New York. The brothers and an accomplice tied Cooley and forced her onto a boat, crossed the Niagara River, and, while she "screamed violently and made resistance," delivered her to a buyer. Witnesses identified their abettor as "one *Vanevery*."[16] It is unclear which of John's ancestors this was, but his grandfather David had ties to the Vrooman family.[17] Outraged by this cruelty, lieutenant governor John Graves Simcoe demanded an abolition law, but it was an uphill battle: Six of the sixteen colonial legislators were enslavers, and Simcoe had no mass movement behind him. The assembly ultimately outlawed importing enslaved people and stipulated that children born to enslaved mothers would become free at age twenty-five. Those currently enslaved in Upper Canada would remain so until they died.[18]

Abolition's progress was painfully slow. Newspapers in Upper Canada advertised slave sales into the nineteenth century, and transactions persisted into the 1830s.[19] Freedom-seekers fled from Upper Canada to Detroit and New York.[20] Britain's Slavery Abolition Act finally took effect in 1834, but many schools, churches, and taverns remained segregated. Black people built communities in Upper Canada, but formal equality collided with racist practices.[21] And since John Van Every moved away the year slavery was outlawed, Upper Canada was slave territory for the entire time he lived there.

Renewed warfare hardened the US–Upper Canada divide. Aptly called a civil war in the borderland, the War of 1812 inflamed enduring hostility in the battle-scarred Niagara region.[22] The Van Everys escaped the worst because

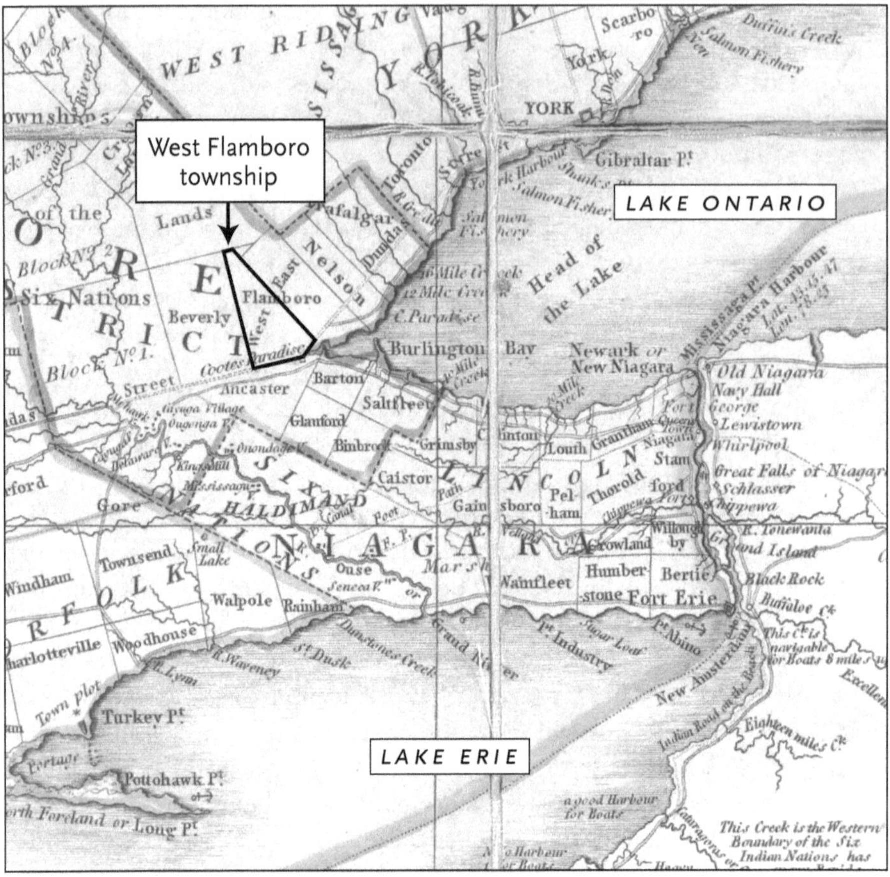

Map of Upper Canada in 1818, during John Van Every's childhood, including his home township of West Flamboro (Flamborough), located immediately west of the head of Lake Ontario. Courtesy of the Toronto Public Library.

they had already relocated further west. But two generations of Van Every men, including John's father and grandfather, battled American invaders whom they never stopped hating.

As outsiders flocked to the Niagara Peninsula, the Van Everys leveraged their United Empire Loyalist status to claim real estate further inland. One after another, McGregory's descendants moved to an area west of Lake Ontario, centered on the township of West Flamborough. David's brothers Andrew and Peter received land there in 1794.[23] In 1802, David secured eight hundred acres near West Flamborough and built a stately oak home.[24] That April, David Van Every Jr. claimed two hundred acres as the child of a Loyalist.[25] Thus established, he married Sarah Eliza Jones in October.[26]

The Van Everys left Niagara just in time. Provoked by naval impressment, clashes with Native Americans, and dreams of conquering Canada, the US

Congress declared war on Britain in June 1812. Some of the fiercest combat occurred on the Niagara Peninsula, the target of American invasions in 1812, 1813, and 1814. The first was the most decisive. In October 1812, US troops crossed the Niagara River, expecting American-born locals to welcome them as liberators. British leaders feared mass defections and braced for disaster but found a hero in General Isaac Brock. Rallying the resistance, Brock led regulars, Canadian militia, and Native American allies to victory at Queenston Heights, where a sharpshooter's bullet made him a martyr. Brock's widely quoted but likely apocryphal dying exhortation—"Push on, brave York volunteers"—nourished the legend that plucky militia forces had single-handedly thwarted the invasion.[27]

John Van Every's father was probably among the brave Yorkers. An 1824 land petition indicates that David Jr. served as a "Flanker" in the 1812 campaign.[28] According to Brock's recommendation, each militia regiment featured two elite flank companies that received special training under professional officers. David Jr.'s unit, the Second Regiment of York Militia, sent its flank companies into action at Queenston Heights, where Brock immortalized them in his reputed final words.[29] And while scholars have debunked the militia myth, David Jr. venerated his fallen commander. Two years after the battle, he named a son Isaac Brock Van Every.[30]

David Jr.'s service ended in 1812, but his father, a lieutenant in the same regiment, remained in uniform as the war devolved into cycles of atrocity and reprisal. In 1813, American soldiers burned Upper Canada's capital of York and the village of Newark. British raiders retaliated by burning Lewiston and Buffalo. Thereafter, regulars, militia, and partisan bands roamed widely, attacking neighbors and settling scores.[31] David Sr. saw it all up close. Stationed at the stronghold of Burlington Heights in 1813, he rounded up recruits and coordinated local defense.[32] The following summer, he went east to hunt traitors and passed near the village of St. David's shortly after US soldiers razed it.[33]

By war's end, the peninsula was devastated. An American visitor could not find "a house or barn but what was burnt or the inside destroyed" and expressed feeling "ashamed of my own countrymen."[34] Upper Canadians felt strongly about Americans, too. In 1820, a traveler found that "the Inhabitants here hate the Yankies as the Devil, and wish to have another opportunity of shooting a few of them."[35] David Sr. carried his hatred to the grave. A youngster who met the elderly veteran recalled that "Grandfather Vanevery, a relic of Butler's Rangers . . . never tired of telling anecdotes and exploits" from his wars. A generation after 1812, he was still "'down' on the Americans and on President Madison in particular."[36]

John Henry Van Every entered a family that revered British heroes, reviled American enemies, and relished violent resistance. His mother, Sarah Eliza, delivered him in October 1814; presumably, Isaac Brock was his twin.[37] The boys arrived three months after the clash at Lundy's Lane and three months before Andrew Jackson prevailed at New Orleans. But why did John reject his father's idols? A close look at his world reveals likely influences on his worldview.

Van Every received enough schooling to begin studying medicine at nineteen. Following years of neglect, Upper Canada invested in education after the war, though quality remained uneven. Parents had organized most schools before 1812, but the instructors had poor reputations for ineptitude and disloyalty. Laws enacted in 1816 and 1824 funded public schools and required instructors to be British subjects or swear oaths of allegiance. But the low pay—some positions offered only five pounds per year, while artisans could make fifteen times more—relegated teaching to novices, many of them recent American arrivals. The year Van Every turned fourteen, one observer fretted that Upper Canadian youth were being corrupted by "persons from the United States who are unacquainted with the principles of the British Constitution or its jurisprudence, & who inculcate on their pupils a greater love for a republican Government than that of a monarchy."[38] Memoirs by Van Every's contemporaries confirm the prevalence of American instructors; some even used Noah Webster's nationalistic spelling book.[39] Whatever anti-American messages Van Every heard at home, he might have learned very different lessons in school.

Upper Canada's ruling class blamed nefarious American ideas for the debates that raged during Van Every's early life. His political consciousness developed amid conflicts between a tight-knit oligarchy and its diverse critics. Early Upper Canada was dominated by administrators, professionals, and merchants, known collectively as the Family Compact, who enjoyed cozy ties to the British-appointed lieutenant governor and whose power extended downward through webs of patronage. They valued imperial loyalty, paternalistic bonds between rulers and the ruled, and deference to the crown and the Anglican Church. They reflexively denounced critics as pro-American seditionists set on abandoning Britain and unleashing democratic misrule. But they never silenced dissent, and while popular unrest peaked in the rebellion of 1837–38, it grew from protests that rocked Upper Canada as Van Every matured in the 1820s and early 1830s. Many early reformers wanted to strengthen the popularly elected Legislative Assembly by giving it the power of the purse and greater authority over the lieutenant governor. Others demanded popular elections for members of the Legislative Council and colonial representation in Parliament. Some embraced American-style self-government. But all promoted "responsible government," the slogan that galvanized dissent.[40]

Reformers used petitions, public meetings, parades, and election-day festivities to energize mass protests. Consider the boisterous career of Robert Gourlay. Born in Scotland and inspired by British radicals like William Cobbett, he moved to Upper Canada in 1817. Appalled by corruption and anti-American policies that he blamed for discouraging immigration and stifling economic growth, Gourlay urged residents to convene, catalog local problems, and petition for investigations into mismanagement of colonial affairs. The Family Compact reacted ferociously, trying Gourlay twice for seditious libel, outlawing his township meetings, and horsewhipping him in the streets of Kingston. In 1819, he was banished from the colony. But Gourlay had shown how to stir mass political action.[41] He also inspired Van Every's kin: among those who signed a petition at the West Flamborough meeting were Andrew Van Every (David Sr.'s brother) and Andrew Jones, John Van Every's maternal grandfather.[42]

United Empire Loyalists might seem like natural conservatives, but the Van Everys had reasons to crave reform. As historian Maya Jasanoff has noted, Loyalists valued self-government and resisted elite domination.[43] Memories of Sarah's suffering at Machiche probably sharpened her family's aversion to arrogant and inept governance. They also may have been motivated by religion. Dissenters, particularly Methodists, sought to transform a society dominated by Anglicans, who reserved for themselves vast swaths of public land and sole authority to solemnize marriages.[44] Like other settlers, the Van Everys used multiple churches. John Van Every's parents were (by necessity) married in an Anglican church.[45] David Sr. donated money to build a Presbyterian church in 1794.[46] But many Van Everys were Methodists, whose camp meetings roused rural dwellers.[47] McGregory and Mary were buried in what became a large family plot at the Warner Methodist Burying Ground, site of Upper Canada's first Methodist church.[48] The 1851 Canadian census lists as Methodists some of John Van Every's closest living relatives, including his younger brother Hugh.[49]

Whatever their inspiration, reformers used a thriving print culture to disseminate their ideas. Young John Van Every witnessed Upper Canada's transformation from media backwater into battleground, a process that fueled and fed on political conflict. A turning point came in 1821. Before then, print journalism was dominated by the staid and government-subsidized *Upper Canada Gazette*. But in 1821, several smaller sheets began printing Legislative Assembly debates. The effect was stunning. Readers rushed to buy periodicals that offered timely political news, and the number of publications multiplied; there were four newspapers in the colony in 1812, but by 1836 there were at least thirty-eight papers published in twenty-one communities. Mass politics and mass media thrived synergistically as political news encouraged newspaper readership and newspaper coverage broadened access to political information.[50] Van Every learned that writers and printers could exert immense influence.

No one taught this lesson more vividly than William Lyon Mackenzie. The Scottish-born firebrand emigrated to Upper Canada in 1820 and founded the *Colonial Advocate* newspaper four years later. From the start, he wielded his newspaper like a cudgel against the Family Compact. In Mackenzie's acerbic editorials, the lieutenant governor was a "jackal" whose "minions" strangled the economy. The government was "an aristocracy of office holders, men nearly above all law" who enjoyed "a monopoly of religion, law, legislation, indeed everything in their grasp."[51] The echoes of Jacksonian rhetoric were intentional. Although Mackenzie sharply criticized slavery, he admired Andrew Jackson, championed hardy producers against parasitic elites, and extolled the United States as a model of good government. Opponents denounced him as a reckless demagogue and sacked his office, destroying his printing press and hurling his printing type blocks into Lake Ontario. Undaunted, Mackenzie won a Legislative Assembly seat in 1828. He demanded accountability in public finance, autonomy within the British Empire, adoption of a written constitution, popular election of local magistrates, establishment of a nonsectarian university, and improved public education. Emulating Gourlay, he solicited petitions and personally carried them to Britain in 1832. After repeated expulsions from the Assembly and threats against his life, Mackenzie was elected mayor of Toronto (formerly York) in 1834.[52] Van Every's views of Mackenzie are unknown, but if anyone stands out as a likely role model, it was the crusader who fused journalism with politics, lauded American republicanism, and defied the colonial aristocracy.

Seventeen-year-old John Van Every entered the media marketplace—and first saw his name in print—by serving as a sales agent for a struggling literary periodical, the *Canadian Casket*.[53] In hindsight, this was a portentous step. But his first career was in commerce, not journalism. As a small-town merchant, he resembled the local commercial notables who later promoted his newspaper throughout the United States.

John went into business with his uncle, Samuel Henry Van Every, in the promising hamlet of Paris. Founded in 1829 by Hiram Capron, an American transplant, the community grew at the forks of the Grand River twenty miles west of West Flamborough. Capron touted its rich potential, envisioning diversified manufacturing, bountiful harvests, and bustling trade.[54] Samuel arrived soon after and established one of Paris's first stores.[55] By September 1830, John, not quite sixteen, had joined the business, most likely as a clerk. He also began cosigning promissory notes with which Samuel bought goods from merchants in Montreal and York.[56] When Samuel died a year later, the enterprise fell into his nephew's inexpert hands.[57]

The youthful proprietor stayed afloat for two years, but he had little aptitude for business, a failing that would later sink his publishing company. To stock his shelves and purchase a town lot, he borrowed over $2,200 from several lenders, including Hiram Capron, who recorded the debts in his day book. But John Van Every gave up by mid-1833. With Capron as intermediary, he surrendered his assets to the York firm of Gamble & Birchall and asked them to satisfy his other creditors.[58] Evidently assuming that the slate was clean—or perhaps trying to elude the moneylenders—Van Every vanished until he reemerged in Rochester, New York, as a medical student.

Not yet nineteen, Van Every had suffered the first of three financial failures that punctuated his life. Each crisis triggered a change of course; this one jolted him into an American medical career. What explains this choice? Perhaps it was personal tragedy or recent events. Van Every's mother and older sister both died in 1819, probably from epidemic influenza.[59] Two years before he departed for Rochester, cholera struck Upper Canada and killed some five hundred people in York alone.[60] These calamities and the local shortage of physicians might have inspired a youth seeking professional security.[61]

Van Every's decision to move to the United States is easier to explain. Canada's only medical school, Montreal Medical Institution, was more than four hundred miles away, and most Upper Canadian physicians studied either in Great Britain or the United States, often after an apprenticeship with a local doctor.[62] This worried local elites who feared that they would return with "unfriendly" ideas from American schools that were "pervaded with pernicious politics."[63] Yet Van Every may not have planned to return. He might still have been dodging creditors. Moreover, Upper Canadian medical licensing boards still prized liberal learning, including in the classics, which he would not receive at his rough-and-tumble medical school.[64] Nor did he emigrate alone: Isaac Brock, his illustriously named brother, accompanied him and launched a successful mercantile career.[65] Whatever his intentions, there is no evidence that John ever saw Upper Canada again.

John Van Every surfaced in an 1834 Rochester city directory as a "student of medicine."[66] It was a promising place for reinvention. Named for Nathaniel Rochester, a wealthy Marylander who moved to the area in 1810, the town at the falls of the Genessee River was booming thanks to abundant waterpower, fertile soil, and the Erie Canal. It was a bustling community of strangers; the population had swelled from around fifteen hundred in 1820 to over nine thousand people in 1830, and when Van Every arrived, nine in ten residents had lived there for less than seven years. Led by Thomas Hart Rochester and other descendants of the town's founder, locals were building churches and voluntary societies to tame the tumult.[67]

With its breakneck growth, brash exuberance, vibrant diversity, and churning conflict, Rochester epitomized Van Every's adopted country. American politics were as contentious as those in Upper Canada and hinged on debates over sovereignty and power, growth and opportunity, exclusion and belonging. In 1834, President Andrew Jackson and fellow Democrats were waging a war on the Second Bank of the United States that would shape American politics for a generation, while their critics, newly dubbed Whigs, had coalesced in opposition. Partisan competition was passionate and sometimes violent, particularly when alcohol and ideology inflamed election-day confrontations.[68]

As in Upper Canada, newspapers competed in a raucous marketplace that energized political activity. Van Every arrived at a watershed moment for American journalism. Earlier newspapers depended on wealthy patrons and offered commercial and political news principally to elite readers. In 1833, however, Benjamin Day introduced the *Sun*, a New York newspaper that featured accessible prose, sensational stories, and an attractive cover price of one cent. Imitators multiplied as the business model of the penny press—which relied on advertising and mass circulation—took off. Improvements in printing and papermaking technology enabled large print runs and low prices, which made newspapers a staple of American print culture.[69] Foreign visitors marveled at their ubiquity. One concluded that the number of US newspapers "baffles all computation." He praised the "knowledge and useful information" they imparted to far-flung readers, lauded cheap postage as a beneficial government subsidy, and heralded the press as the most powerful of all "instruments . . . for the emancipation of the human mind."[70]

Yet newspapers were not divorced from politics. A few urban dailies in the Northeast subsisted on advertising revenue, but they were not the norm. From small-town weeklies to big-city sheets, most American newspapers remained closely tied to partisanship. The political parties of the 1830s depended on newspaper editors to communicate with voters. Newspapers advertised political rallies and broadcast stump speeches, legislative debates, and convention proceedings. They endorsed candidates, encouraged voter turnout, and printed the tickets that voters deposited in ballot boxes. Without newspapers, the machinery of American politics would have ground to a halt. In turn, editors, who usually operated on shoestring budgets, depended on elected officials. Without cash payments, public printing contracts (which paid editors to print laws and other official documents), and lucrative public offices, newspaper proprietors would have failed even more often than they did. Thus, while the *Sun* anticipated a future of political independence, another development of the 1830s revealed enduring interconnections between journalists and political patrons: Andrew Jackson's elevation of editors like Francis Blair and Amos Kendall to key positions in his administration.[71] As in Upper Canada, politics permeated the press—and vice versa.

But in one crucial respect, Van Every's new home was strikingly different: slavery. Outlawed in Upper Canada by imperial fiat, slavery was booming in the United States, simultaneously forging connections and sharpening divisions between regions. Tension between national complicity and sectional conflict would shape Van Every's career. No place dramatized that dynamic more vividly than his future home of New York City, which was already emerging as the hub of American commerce and print media. On the one hand, the city, like the rest of the state, had abolished slavery. In the colonial era, one in five New Yorkers had been enslaved, forced to build everything from agricultural improvements to the barricade that gave Wall Street its name. A 1799 abolition law mandated an agonizingly gradual process akin to Upper Canada's. Only in 1827 was slavery finally dismantled.[72] On the other hand, the expansion of cotton cultivation in the 1820s and 1830s deepened Manhattan's entanglement with slavery. Planters in Alabama, Mississippi, and Louisiana depended on New York bankers for credit, which they used to purchase land and laborers. Meanwhile, merchants profited from the increasingly lucrative Southern trade, which channeled exports and imports through Manhattan. Their ships carried cotton to Europe, returned with manufactured goods, and sailed south to repeat the cycle. Already in 1822, cotton accounted for 40 percent of the value of New York exports. By 1860, a New Yorker could declare that the city "belongs almost as much to the South as to the North."[73]

Local hostility toward abolitionists ran deep. In July 1834, as Van Every settled into Rochester (itself a hotbed of antislavery activity), anti-abolitionist violence erupted in Manhattan. It was fueled by a vitriolic press, including James Watson Webb's *Courier and Enquirer*, which spread rumors about abolitionist support for interracial sex and slave revolts and about the perfidious intentions of visiting Britons like George Thompson, allegedly the ringleader of a monarchical plot against the Union. Furious white New Yorkers attacked the homes and businesses of prominent abolitionists and Black residents for several days until the militia put them down.[74] Van Evrie would regularly rehash this mixture of proslavery racism and Anglophobia.

Yet the rioters' abundant targets reflected the vibrancy of New York's Black community and abolitionism's powerful presence in the city. Black New Yorkers and white allies created schools, churches, and charities. The nation's first Black newspaper, *Freedom's Journal*, was published in New York in 1827. Six years later, white merchant and abolitionist Arthur Tappan launched the *Emancipator*, and before year's end, the American Anti-Slavery Society established its headquarters at 143 Nassau Street, a stone's throw from the future site of Van Every's office. Conflict raged in New York through the Civil War and beyond. The city was not a proslavery monolith but a battleground over racial slavery's role in an ostensibly egalitarian republic.[75]

Two decades later, Van Every charged headlong into this battle. A descendant of enslavers and kidnappers, he waved the proslavery banner even after emancipation. Raised amid contests over imperial governance in a land where slavery was toppled by British elites, he spun conspiracy theories about abolitionism's foreign and aristocratic roots. Yet if his proslavery worldview was already congealing before he reached Rochester, his medical training added one key component: the poisonous doctrine of polygenesis.

Chapter 2

Medicine

John Van Every's earliest surviving composition is an 1836 letter urging his chemistry professor to cancel the term's last four lectures. Writing on behalf of their classmates, Van Every and a coauthor lamented the "feeble health" of Professor Edward Cutbush, a former naval surgeon and seasoned educator. "However much we may desire the benefit of your instruction," both "personal esteem" and "the common principles of humanity" compelled them to "beg that you will terminate your duties for the remainder of the course."[1] Were they truly concerned or simply eager to cut class? The letter allows both readings; its efficacy is unknown. But it is instructive for two reasons. First, Van Every's peers selected him to write it. Seventeen years before his first publication, his Geneva Medical College companions entrusted their case to his pen. Second, the possibly facetious note indicates a rather indifferent student. Van Every never actually finished his degree and struggled for a decade to make a living practicing medicine. Written by a mediocre scholar, the 1836 note foreshadowed its author's transformation from physician to polemicist.

Yet medicine was more than a professional dead end. Van Every gained notoriety as a propagandist, not a healer, but his medical background shaped his public image and written work. He flaunted his medical training to brand himself as an evidence-driven expert. Despite lacking a degree, Van Every deployed "Dr." and "MD" to credentialize himself as "a scientific student of the question of races."[2] And while his bigotry almost certainly predated his exposure to the canonical works of allegedly scientific racism, it was no coincidence that, among all the varieties of proslavery ideology, he embraced the polygenist argument that races were separately created species, each with a naturally ordained social role. As a physician, Van Every inhabited a community deeply enmeshed in practices of slavery and theories of racial difference. Physicians spearheaded the development and dissemination of polygenism because it allowed them to leverage anatomical expertise into professional and political clout. Convinced that polygenism revealed God's plan for humanity, Van Every made it the cornerstone of his politics. Medicine thus influenced him long after he left the field, providing the scaffolding for his worldview and the basis for his claim to intellectual authority. Van Every was a popularizer of existing ideas rather than a novel thinker, but his medical background, like his Canadian roots, shaped his career as a professional racist.

Van Every entered medicine as the protégé of one of Rochester's leading citizens, Anson Colman. Born in 1795, Colman moved to Rochester in 1817 and, two years later, married Nathaniel Rochester's daughter Catherine. Ensconced in the upper crust, Colman built a stellar career in medicine and public service. He helped organize the Monroe County Medical Society in 1821. Soon after, he served the village of Rochester as a trustee. And when cholera struck North America in 1832, Colman trekked to Montreal to study the local response; his report helped Rochester authorities prepare for the scourge.[3] Meanwhile, he and Catherine raised five children. Colman's correspondence reveals his close bond with the eldest, Sophia, whose education he prioritized and who helped run the household during his long absences.[4] Catherine's letters, meanwhile, expressed disgust with South Carolina nullifiers and sympathy for the "Poor Degraded Affricans" they enslaved.[5] It is just possible that Colman encountered Van Every during his Canadian travels. However they met, the youngster was studying with him by 1834. Van Every had found the first of the formidable patrons who nurtured his career.

The following year, Colman accepted an invitation to teach medical jurisprudence and botany at a newly founded medical school forty-five miles southeast of Rochester; Van Every tagged along but never formally enrolled. Geneva Medical College (GMC), situated on the shore of Seneca Lake, was part of a wave of small proprietary schools created after 1810 to satisfy the enormous demand for physicians. State chartered but poorly resourced, GMC, like its numerous peers, offered few of the amenities found at institutions like the University of Pennsylvania. Lacking many opportunities for clinical observation or laboratory experimentation, GMC pupils relied on textbooks and two years of lectures—actually two iterations of the same sixteen-week curriculum—for training. After twice attending courses in anatomy and physiology, the principles and practice of surgery, materia medica and botany, obstetrics, medical jurisprudence, chemistry, and the institutes and practices of medicine, GMC students could write a thesis and claim their degrees. Critics denounced these alleged diploma mills for having "depressed" the "standard of professional excellence" to the level of "unqualified aspirants."[6] Yet if their abundance triggered a pedagogical race to the bottom, the schools also offered rudimentary training to a wider range of pupils. The lecture course cost only $55, and with room and board, one could complete the entire program for $200.[7] GMC students probably absorbed as much as students at comparable institutions and departed with basic knowledge of the heroic therapies such as bleeding and purging, which were then predominant in mainstream medicine. GMC made the profession more accessible.[8] Eventually, female students could enroll: In 1847, GMC accepted Elizabeth Blackwell, who became the first woman to earn a medical degree in the United States.[9] But the college still barred African Americans like James McCune Smith, whose rejection compelled him to study in Scotland before launching his career as a physician and abolitionist.[10] The only Black individuals Van Every saw at GMC were service workers, including the janitor, Anthony Jupiter.[11]

GMC's curriculum reflected the interweaving of medicine and racism. Some textbooks ignored race, but others presented it in terms of immutable hierarchies that experts could divine through comparative anatomy.[12] One anatomical text linked craniological features to intellectual prowess and ranked "Europeans" far above "negroes" on this score.[13] A physiology book sketched three "Varieties of Mankind"—Caucasian, Mongolian, and Ethiopian—each descended from one of Noah's three sons. The author lumped them all within one species but emphasized their dissimilarities and opined that Black people's "less perfect organization" relegated them to "a middle place between the Caucasian and the ourang-outang."[14] Even the author who damned slave trading and slavery as "an iniquitous traffic and a cruel tyranny" extrapolated from "differences of [physical] organisation" a "striking inequality in the developement of the moral and intellectual faculties."[15]

These 1830s texts reflected the erosion of an environmentalist view of racial difference under the onslaught of more rigid biological theories. Most GMC textbooks endorsed monogenism, which placed humans in a single species and attributed phenotypical variation to environmental influences, principally climate.[16] But, like growing numbers of their contemporaries, some authors doubted that environment alone could explain the ostensibly vast physical and mental disparities between groups. Robley Dunglison, author of a physiology text, identified racial types in ancient statuary and suggested that racial differentiation was as old as humanity itself. How, he asked, could the "Caucasian and Ethiopian varieties . . . have originated from the same source" when their dissimilarities were so pronounced and primeval? He dutifully conjectured that a single human species had been divided into races by environmental or divine interventions.[17] But his questions betrayed frustration with a theory that seemed incapable of explaining either the antiquity or the profundity of racial divergence.

Polygenists offered an alternative hypothesis that proved horribly seductive for a host of intellectual, professional, and political reasons. In the second quarter of the nineteenth century, polygenists transformed academic thinking about human origins and diversity and, by so doing, presented proslavery propagandists with ostensibly conclusive scientific arguments.

OF THE

MEDICAL INSTITUTION

OF

GENEVA COLLEGE.

GENEVA, N. Y.

1836–7.

Cover page of the *Circular of the Medical Institution of Geneva College* published in 1836–37 while John Van Every studied there under Dr. Anson Colman. Courtesy of the Geneva Medical College Collection, Archives and Special Collections, SUNY Upstate Medical University.

To wavering monogenists who wondered if external forces created multiple races during the span of human history, then estimated at only a few thousand years, polygenists answered *no*. Rather, there had been separate creations of several original pairs. Each pair produced a race fitted to its surroundings and endowed with different physical, intellectual, and moral traits. The races therefore constituted distinct species within one genus. And since racial differences dated from creation, they were immutable. It was this premise that gave Van Every's proslavery racism a razor's edge. Environmental monogenism fostered racist narratives of nonwhite peoples' degeneration from a primordial white archetype, but it also emboldened self-styled philanthropists to envision racial uplift. Polygenists, however, believed racial traits were fixed at creation and therefore unchangeable. Relations between races could shift over time; for many polygenists, this was the driving force of history itself. But since progress for putatively inferior races was impossible, polygenists argued, social systems must be designed to suit their strengths and weaknesses.[18]

Polygenist ideas had percolated in Europe and North America for centuries, but they surged in the antebellum United States. Precursors to polygenism included the pre-Adamite theory of Isaac La Peyrère, a seventeenth-century French writer who hypothesized that some modern peoples descended from humans created before Adam and Eve.[19] In *Notes on the State of Virginia* (1785), Thomas Jefferson pondered plural creations and perpetual racial differences. "I advanced it therefore as a suspicion only," he wrote, "that the blacks, whether originally a distinct race, or made distinct by time and circumstances, are inferior to the whites in the endowments of both body and mind."[20] Van Every emblazoned this passage on the title page of his first book, thus claiming Jefferson as polygenism's founding father.[21] But other theorizers were more confident than the master of Monticello. In 1799, Englishman Charles White concluded that "various species of men were originally created and separated" into distinct biological zones.[22] Americans soon boarded the polygenist bandwagon. In 1830, Charles Caldwell denied "the original unity of the human race," but he softened the blow by insisting that plural creations better fit scripture. Given humankind's short history, as delineated in biblical genealogies, there was not enough time for environmental conditions to produce distinct races.[23] Nine years later, Samuel George Morton of Philadelphia launched the polygenist American School of Ethnology with the publication of the first of his notorious skull studies. He held that cranial capacity determined cognitive ability and varied widely between races, whose skull measurements remained constant over time.[24] Josiah Nott of Mobile, Alabama, piled on in the 1840s, picking quarrels with Christian monogenists and contributing his own proslavery pronouncements to the polygenist canon.[25] When Van Every entered the fray in the early 1850s, polygenism was poised for triumph.

White, Caldwell, Morton, and Nott shared a revealing commonality: All were physicians or surgeons. Early-nineteenth-century doctors were hungry for professional prestige and protective of their intellectual cachet. Beset by rival healers such as midwives, herbalists, and sundry medical sectarians, and mistrusted by many laypeople horrified by heroic treatments, orthodox physicians strove to bolster their status. They promoted stricter licensing laws and formed professional organizations, including the American Medical Association in 1847.[26] But they also dove into debates about racial differences. Whether genuinely curious about anatomy and disease, determined to justify oppression, or simply eager to prove the relevance of their erudition, medical researchers vaulted into academic quarrels that had urgent political ramifications. Polygenism attracted physicians because its claims both relied on and demonstrated the value of anatomical knowledge. And regardless of whether they accepted polygenism's contested conclusions about human origins, antebellum medical practitioners generally agreed that racial differences were tangible and immutable. As historian Christopher D. E. Willoughby notes, "Racial thinking underwrote the professionalization of medicine in the United States."[27] Connections between medicine, racism, and slavery were especially sinister in the South, where physicians like James Marion Sims exploited enslaved people's legally vulnerable bodies to conduct research that rationalized their bondage.[28] But even in New York, medicine and racism were deeply entwined. In his penchant for polygenism and his underlying faith in the scientific validity of race, Van Every shared much with his professional peers.

Debates over slavery, dispossession of Indigenous people, and imperial expansion accelerated the spread of polygenist ideas beyond academia. Confronted by intrepid abolitionists and determined to reconcile slavery with egalitarian ideals, many proslavery propagandists hailed polygenism as proof that slavery's virtue was settled science. When Pennsylvania-born Samuel George Morton died in 1851, the *Charleston Medical Journal* opined: "We of the South should consider him as our benefactor, for aiding most materially in giving to the negro his true position as an inferior race."[29] Polygenism remained controversial even among slavery's defenders because of its religious implications. However, white Christians who balked at the notion of plural creations might still be convinced that God designed some people to rule and others to serve.[30] A proslavery writer with religious sensibilities, medical credentials, and a willingness to soft-pedal the specifics of human origins potentially could persuade them.

Van Every thus matured during a crucial period in the histories of medicine, ostensibly scientific racism, and conflict over slavery. By the 1830s, some medical practitioners used polygenism to enhance their authority and demonstrate the relevance of their expertise. Simultaneously, slavery's champions welcomed polygenism as a weapon against abolitionists. In this atmosphere, Van Every began to systematize the racism bequeathed by his slave-trafficking ancestors. His exact status at Geneva Medical College is obscure. He earned no degree and never appeared on student rosters, although he attended lectures—and tried to skip them.[31] But by joining the medical profession when he did, he gathered the intellectual components for his polygenist worldview. He flaunted fraudulent credentials, but medicine deeply imprinted his thinking and, later, his brand.

Proslavery crusading lay in Van Every's future when he ventured out from Geneva. Anson Colman's death in 1837 might have forced him to abort his studies, either for financial reasons or because he attended GMC as Colman's guest. Regardless, two things were clear. One was Van Every's attachment to his mentor; he informed classmates of Colman's passing and witnessed the execution of Colman's will.[32] The other was his readiness to move again. In spring 1838, Van Every headed west.

He commenced the next chapter of his restless life in northwestern Ohio's Maumee River Valley. Colman might have inspired this choice, as other physicians in Colman's orbit discussed relocating there in the late 1830s.[33] Van Every moved with Chauncey Matthews, a New Yorker who had apprenticed with Colman and graduated from GMC.[34] They settled in Maumee City, located ten miles upstream from Toledo, near the site where US troops defeated British and Native American forces at the Battle of Fallen Timbers in 1794. Locals blamed the low and soggy terrain, nicknamed the Great Black Swamp, for the region's insalubrity. The regular outbreaks of malaria and typhoid fever, which kept some prospective migrants at bay, may have attracted Van Every and Matthews with the prospects of plentiful patients and fees.[35] In June 1838, they rented an office on Detroit Street and offered their services as "Physicians and Surgeons."[36]

Van Every suffered a rocky start when, one month after arriving, he misplaced a surgical kit and had to advertise the loss in hopes of recovering it.[37] But thereafter he built a respected practice. In 1840, he was appointed to Maumee City's new Board of Health.[38] Two years later, he impressed Daniel Drake, Ohio's leading physician and founder of the state's first medical school. When Drake passed through while researching western diseases, he interviewed Van Every about the terrible fever epidemic of 1838 and recorded the young doctor's prescription of heavy bleeding, cathartics, and quinine.[39] Van Every also drew attention from the federal government, which paid him eighty dollars for attending to a group of Ottawas before their forced expulsion from Ohio. When Van Every later pontificated about Native Americans, he wrote both as a racist theorizer and as a hired accomplice in the process of dispossession.[40] His career peaked in 1842, when he helped establish the Maumee Valley Medical Association.[41]

The same year, Van Every visited Rochester to marry Sophia Elizabeth Colman, his lamented teacher's eldest daughter. Seven years his junior, Sophia got to know him during his stint under her father's tutelage, and they apparently continued courting after he moved away. On January 24, 1842, with Thomas H. Rochester, Sophia's esteemed uncle, among the witnesses, they exchanged vows in St. Luke's Episcopal Church.[42]

It was a logical match, given Van Every's close ties to the Colmans, but partisanship made it complicated. He had been a staunch Democrat since 1837, when, as he later recalled, President Martin Van Buren's battle to divorce the government from banks "made a profound impression on my mind, and I became an earnest sincere and devoted Politician."[43] Thereafter, he dabbled in Ohio politics. During the boisterous presidential contest of 1840, Van Every drafted a statement of principles for his local Democratic organization.[44] The following year, he served on the resolutions committee at a county convention.[45] Ohio Democrats, like Geneva medical students, trusted Van Every's pen to express their sentiments. But he had married, as he later put it, into Rochester's "Whig aristocracy."[46] Two of Sophia's uncles were especially active partisans: Nathaniel Thrift Rochester was elected assessor of Rochester's Third Ward in 1838, and Thomas H. Rochester, Sophia's former guardian, served as treasurer of Monroe County's Whig Central Committee during the hard-fought 1844 presidential race.[47] Political polarization did not prevent the wedding in 1842, but it soon poisoned the family circle.

The newlyweds settled in Maumee City, where their finances collapsed as their household grew. Sophia likely became pregnant in autumn 1842 because their first child, Catherine Rochester Van Every, was born on July 9, 1843.[48] Meanwhile, John petitioned for bankruptcy in December 1842.[49] That the Bankruptcy Act of 1841, which allowed him to file for relief, was a Whig measure did not stop him; partisan purity was a luxury he could not afford.[50] The bankruptcy proceedings reveal that old debts from Canada still haunted him and that he had accumulated new obligations as well. On top of the roughly $2,200 he owed to Canadian creditors, Van Every borrowed more than $400 from Rochester acquaintances, including his brother Isaac, and around $1,000 from lenders in Ohio and Illinois. With liabilities topping $3,600 and assets of only $931.92, the expectant father was in trouble.[51] He must have felt relieved when his bankruptcy petition was granted, although he retained only $118 in household goods and relied on Chauncey Matthews to pay $8.42 in court fees.[52]

Among the personal property shielded from Van Every's creditors was a small library that revealed Sophia's influence in their home. Anyone envisioning shelves of racist tomes will be surprised by the inventory. Most volumes were Romantic poetry compilations and devotional texts, with a sprinkling of historical works, including *Memoirs of the Life and Correspondence of Mrs. Hannah More*—a British antislavery activist—and *History of Woman in England*, a forward-thinking study by Hannah Lawrance, who advocated women's equal education.[53] These books reflected the reading habits of an educated woman from the Northeast and, along with her subscriptions to religious publications, offer our only insight into Sophia Van Every.[54]

Whatever he thought of his wife's literary tastes, John Van Every hoped her kin would resuscitate his career. In spring 1844, he moved back to Rochester with Sophia and little Catherine, expecting that Sophia's relatives would help him build a thriving practice.[55] But it was an awkward time for a Democrat to seek assistance from prominent Whigs: 1844 was a presidential election year. Sophia's relations rallied behind Henry Clay, the Whig icon making his third White House bid, while Van Every backed James K. Polk. The election turned on a razor-thin margin in New York and revealed mounting conflict over slavery and territorial expansion, particularly after Polk and the Democrats endorsed annexing the slaveholding republic of Texas. Sophia's relatives undoubtedly agreed with Northern anti-annexationists like New York *Tribune* editor Horace Greeley, who skewered Democrats for yielding to "the ultra Slavery prejudices of the South—the new fanatics enlisted by Calhoun & Co. for a crusade to extend and consolidate Human Bondage."[56] But Van Every proudly followed ex-president Andrew Jackson on all national issues, "especially Texas," thereby aligning himself with the Tennessee cotton planter who deemed annexation vital to protecting the South from Britons scheming to "govern Texas, and introduce abolition on our confines."[57]

Van Every's in-laws tried to change his politics with financial leverage. He recalled arriving in Rochester "dependant upon my wife's friends . . . for a favorable introduction into practice." He also felt pressure from Sophia, who was "brought up, and accustomed to" an elevated "social position" in her hometown. Sophia's wealthy family apparently offered him introductions to elite clients if he supported Clay. But if he "interfere[d] with our interests," they asked, "can you suppose we will advance yours." Amid election-year tension, Van Every "was placed in a position where strong convictions of duty and equally strong motives of self interest conflicted."[58] Even allowing for his customary self-aggrandizement, it was a tough spot for a recent bankrupt tempted by social acceptance and professional succor. One local antislavery activist confirmed Van Every's account, noting that he was given "strong inducements . . . from family connexions" to abandon the Democrats.[59]

Van Every refused. He later boasted that since "every thing that a great & Patriotic party had struggled for, for forty years were at hazard," he would not prioritize his "insignificant interests" over victory.[60] A neighbor confirmed that he remained "an unwavering and consistent" Democrat throughout the campaign, in which Polk ultimately prevailed.[61] The consequences were exactly as Van Every anticipated. Sophia faced "humiliation" and was "treated as a renegade" by friends and family. John's "Professional interests" were ruined.[62] The episode undoubtedly left an indelible impression on him. He would not always maintain such stubborn independence; one day, a leading ex-Whig discovered that Van Every could be bought. But while clashes with in-laws, in which class resentment magnified party rivalry and policy disputes, did not determine his Democratic allegiance, they undoubtedly gave his partisanship a keenly personal edge. As an editor, Van Every regularly sparred with Democrats over party doctrine, but he reserved his harshest invective for enemies who resembled the kinfolk who snubbed him after Clay's defeat.

Van Every always chased support from powerful patrons. Anson Colman jump-started his medical career; years later, he beseeched Jefferson Davis for help, even after the Mississippian became president of the Confederacy. Not surprisingly, he turned to James K. Polk for aid in 1845. That spring, Van Every repeatedly asked the new president for a diplomatic post in Paris, hoping to extend his medical studies and earn a credential that might win clients in Rochester.[63] Paris hospitals offered the best hands-on clinical training available to American physicians, hundreds of whom traveled there to learn from French researchers' pioneering empirical studies.[64] Polk never responded, thus becoming the first, but not the last, Democratic president to deny Van Every a patronage plum.

Personal tragedy compounded Van Every's woes in November 1845, when Sophia died giving birth to their second child, who also perished.[65] Thirty-one years old, with poor professional prospects and a toddler to raise, Van Every needed all the help he could get. Fortunately for him—and his child—the Rochesters took in Catherine. Just as he had done with Sophia after Anson Colman passed away, Thomas H. Rochester made young Catherine Van Every his ward. She maintained contact with her father and later followed him in altering the spelling of her surname, but spent the rest of her days in Rochester, living with her great-uncle until his death and then with other members of her mother's renowned family. She imbibed the Rochesters' spirit of charity and civic duty and supported numerous benevolent and religious causes. When she died in 1922, local reporters recited her illustrious maternal ancestry but never mentioned her perfidious father.[66]

Not long after ignoring Van Every's pleas, Polk inadvertently rescued the failed physician by leading the nation into war. Van Every would find the conflict immensely profitable, both for his pocketbook and his persona. Military service sharpened his ugly worldview, steered him from medicine to politics, and enhanced his personal brand.

Chapter 3

Mexico

John Van Every loved giving unsought advice to prominent politicians. Eager to display his acumen, he flashed his phony credentials. But the decisive episode in his intellectual autobiography was his very real stint in Mexico. Consider the public letter he addressed to President Andrew Johnson in December 1865. It focused on emancipation and Reconstruction, using polygenist precepts to assail the Republicans. But Van Every opened by recalling his military adventures: "During the Mexican war, I became profoundly interested in the mongrel population of the great cities of that country," he wrote, claiming that generations of intermixture had left "scarcely a single white man, Indian, or Negro, to be seen among a hundred thousand people." Alarmed that abolitionists were "rapidly impelling us in the same direction that had so broken down the barriers of race and deteriorated the grand old Spanish conquerors, I naturally, as a physiologist, became profoundly interested in the momentous subject" and spent fifteen years researching the "specific character and natural relations of the human races."[1] Van Every revealed little about himself during his public career, hiding his Canadian roots and financial woes. But his war service in Mexico, like his medical training, featured in his marketing materials. One advertisement for the *New York Day Book* boasted that its editor "has given several years of his life to a scientific examination of the question of races. Beside this, however, he enjoyed rare advantages, as a surgeon in Gen. Scott's army during the war with Mexico, to observe the effect of the mixture of the races in that distracted country." This made his writings "worthy of more than ordinary attention."[2] The war was the pivot of Van Every's self-spun origin story, providing the impetus for his crusade and a prop for his authority.

There is no reason to doubt the war's galvanizing effect. Immediately afterward, he abandoned medicine and launched his venomous second career as a writer. Van Every was deeply racist before he visited Mexico. But it was precisely because he carried racism alongside his surgical kit that his encounters with *mestizaje* had such a profound influence. Primed to view his enemies through a polygenist lens, Van Every saw what he expected to see in Mexico. Upon returning to a country fracturing over slavery's future, he wove his self-taught wartime lessons into the proslavery argument that he proclaimed for the next quarter century. Military service accentuated the international outlook of his proslavery nationalism, informing the comparative analysis in which he made Mexico a cautionary tale about the perils of racial mingling. He was not the only American to pronounce this view. But he used his firsthand experiences to add urgency to his assertions. Years before politicians and pundits warned against the "Mexicanization" of American *politics* during the 1876 presidential election's tumultuous finale, Van Every made warnings about the "Mexicanization" of the American *population* a cornerstone of his case that Black enslavement safeguarded white purity and American democracy.[3]

The war with Mexico underscored racism's pervasiveness in American political culture and its instability as a foundation for consensus on policy. Southern racists yearned to expand slavery into conquered Mexican territory—except for those who resisted a land grab that would bring more nonwhite people under the Stars and Stripes. Northern racists denounced the proslavery war—except for those who welcomed imperial expansion as long as they could keep Black people, enslaved or free, out of the captured territory. Some racists fantasized about uplifting their Mexican neighbors by marrying Mexican women to white men. Others, like Van Every, recoiled from such reveries. In going to war, the struggling physician joined a nationalist enterprise that inflamed the sectional conflict he spent the rest of his career trying to extinguish.[4]

Van Every opposed restricting slavery's geographic expansion but considered Mexican people more significant than Mexican land. Trained to regard races as distinct species, he despised the signs of racial mixture that surrounded him during his short, violent encounter with Mexico's citizens. He departed the country bearing a horror story that he would tell and retell in pamphlets, editorials, and books: Interracial sex had doomed Mexico to degeneracy, and abolition would trigger a similar catastrophe in the United States. Mexico was Van Every's proving ground for theories seeded in Canada and nurtured in New York and Ohio, as well as the setting for a marketable autobiographical anecdote. By 1848, Van Every had developed a twisted mythology in which Black slavery safeguarded white democracy from foreign and domestic foes hell-bent on ruining the Union.

Van Every's earliest surviving racist screed is a March 1846 letter to Senator John C. Calhoun of South Carolina. Penned in Rochester and sent to the man who crowned slavery a "positive good," the note recorded Van Every's thinking before his departure for Mexico and anticipated much of his published work.[5] He wrote to solicit Calhoun's views on the prospect of equal Black suffrage in New York. Under the state's 1821 constitution, Black men could vote only if they owned $250 in freehold property, a provision that disenfranchised all but a few hundred of them. But the issue was revived when a convention was called to rewrite the state constitution. Led by abolitionists, Liberty Party activists, and some Whigs, including *Tribune* editor Horace Greeley, a campaign to eliminate the racist property requirement gained steam.[6]

Writing three months before the convention met in Albany, Van Every deemed the equal suffrage initiative "the most dangerous movement that has ever occurred in this country." He blamed it on devious Whigs, presumably including his in-laws, and their "convenient Allies" in the Liberty Party, who schemed to "give the Whig monopoly party a complete ascendency" in New York. With the state's thirty-six electoral votes, the Whigs could then secure a lock on the presidency. Meanwhile, Democrats slept at their posts. "Democratic politicians and papers have scarcely alluded to the subject," he carped, "and when they have done so it has been in a shuffling and noncommital manner." Van Every claimed to be the "only Democrat" in Rochester who "dare openly *oppose* it." And yet the stakes for white Northerners were enormous. If Black voters placed New York in the Whig column, the Whigs would impose "a great National Bank Protective Tariff etc etc" and consolidate political and economic power in the hands of Northeastern elites. Were it not for Southern enslavers, their "natural allies," the Northern masses would have fallen into poverty and oppression long ago. Knowing this, Whigs and abolitionists connived to end slavery, "the great Protection of the Northern laborer" and the "chief corner stone of our Republican edifice." Indeed, "the great cause of liberty" teetered on the brink because it depended on "the preservation of this purity of the Anglo Saxon race and our present well balanced Federative Sistem."[7]

Calhoun never replied, but the letter is illuminating. It establishes the intensity of Van Every's proslavery racism before he left for Mexico; his experiences there confirmed his existing views of white "purity" and Black enslavement. It also continued his habit of seeking support from powerful Southerners. Calhoun, like James Polk, ignored him, but later efforts proved more fruitful. Additionally, it shows how early Van Every's understanding of race, slavery, and national politics had coalesced. Written seven years before his first publication, nine years before he joined the *Day Book*, and eleven years before he became its proprietor, Van Every's letter to Calhoun sketched the major themes of his embryonic career. Preservation of slavery and what was not yet called white supremacy, he argued, was a national imperative, not a sectional project. Southern enslavers and Northern laborers must combine against the titans of the Northeast, he insisted, and white Northerners should protect themselves by preserving slavery. In time, he would forge this into a rebuttal of the politically potent "Slave Power" theory that Calhoun's kind were greedy aristocrats who harmed rather than helped common whites. Finally, while Van Every, still seething at his in-laws, was clearly a zealous partisan, he also roasted timid Democrats. Already in 1846, he sensed a tension that shaped his public career: the Democratic Party was essential to executing his policy agenda but rarely met his ideological standards.

Van Every probably rejoiced when New York voters rejected the equal suffrage amendment by a vote of 224,336 to 85,406.[8] And yet his personal prospects were still poor. By the end of 1846, he was a thirty-two-year-old widower whose career had stalled amid bankruptcy and family feuding. But just two months after he appealed to Calhoun, Van Every discovered that President James Polk had thrown him a lifeline.

On May 11, 1846, Polk told Congress that Mexican troops had "invaded our territory and shed American blood on American soil."[9] Friction between the republics had intensified since the US annexation of Texas, until Polk forced the issue by sending soldiers into the disputed region between the Nueces River and the Rio Grande. When the Mexican cavalry killed eleven of them in late April, Polk seized the pretext to conquer the region between Texas and the California coast that Mexico had refused to sell. Despite sharp Whig criticism, Congress quickly declared war. Polk sent columns westward into New Mexico and southward across the Rio Grande, where they smashed Mexican forces at Monterrey in September 1846 and at Buena Vista the following February. Yet Mexico's government would not capitulate. Seeking to land a knockout punch, Polk directed General Winfield Scott to assail the Mexican capital from the east. In March 1847, Scott's army executed an amphibious landing at Veracruz and then marched westward along the path of conquistadors toward Mexico City.[10]

Meanwhile, Van Every dedicated his medical knowledge to Manifest Destiny. Over opposition from Whigs and Calhounites, Congress in February 1847 approved raising ten new army regiments.[11] A recruiting station for the Fifteenth US Infantry Regiment opened in Toledo, Ohio, where Van Every had returned, and he took a job inspecting volunteers.[12] The thoroughness of these examinations varied, but physicians aimed to ensure that recruits were minimally fit for duty. Enlistees needed to be free of contagious disease, have healthy limbs and eyes and enough teeth to bite open cartridges, and have no history of head injuries that "might produce occasional insanity."[13] They also had to be white. The ties between medicine, racism, and nationalism were obvious here, as was the sloppiness of racist thinking. Men of color were barred from Mr. Polk's Army, but although very dark-skinned volunteers were easily identified and rejected, men of mixed ancestry were harder to spot. Inspectors like Van Every attempted to triangulate between complexion, skull shape, and hair texture to screen them out, but applying ostensibly objective racial categories proved trickier in practice than in theory and often depended on aesthetic judgments or gut feelings. There were embarrassing failures. One Virginia recruit raised doubts in his examining physician but was accepted for service; a few weeks later, an angry planter arrived to reclaim him as both his property and his son. So much for slavery as a safeguard against so-called amalgamation. Lapses like these prompted publication of revised guidelines for medical examiners, warning that "soldiers would not tolerate the mixed breed as comrades" and citing lessons from the Mexican-American War to prevent future blunders.[14] But from the start of his national service, Van Every stood sentinel against racial blending.

The physical examination reflected the society that produced it. Jingoistic journalists denounced Mexicans as an "imbecile, effete . . . race," mere "reptiles in the path of progressive democracy" who "must either crawl or be crushed."[15] US commentators blamed intermixture for making Mexico's modern inhabitants inferior to their ancestors. Theirs was a "degenerate mixed race," a "mongrel race," and, according to an antislavery Ohio Whig, a "sad compound of Spanish, English, Indian, and negro bloods" that yielded "a slothful, indolent, ignorant race of beings."[16] Soldiers carried these views to the front. George Meade, a junior officer destined for fame at Gettysburg, believed that "listless" Mexicans fought poorly because their Spanish blood had mingled "with the Indian and negro race."[17] A war correspondent described the Mexican soldier as a "degraded being" descended from multiple races who exhibited the "evil qualities of each."[18] Combat hardened prejudices and unleashed cycles of atrocity and reprisal. US soldiers blamed Mexican guerrillas' racial traits for their hit-and-run tactics and retaliated by killing civilians, looting property, and destroying churches, thereby inspiring renewed resistance.[19] Battlefields became laboratories for racist science. A Cincinnati ethnologist cited skulls gleaned from Palo Alto's gory ground as proof of the "very coarse organization, rather animal than intellectual," of the Mexicans.[20]

American racism led in diverse, sometimes divergent directions on policy questions. Some of the most virulent invective came from Whig and Calhounite leaders who resisted Democrats' voracious imperial appetites, especially the idea, which gained traction in 1847, of annexing all of Mexico. Calhoun would take the sparsely inhabited northern area already under US occupation but opposed "incorporating into our Union any but the Caucasian race," and certainly not the "impure races" crowded into the Mexican heartland.[21] More adamant was Edward C. Cabell, a Florida Whig who asked how Congress could "convert the black, white, red, mongrel, miserable population of Mexico—the Mexicans, Indians, Mulattoes, Mestizos, Chinos, Zambos, Quinteros—into free and enlightened American citizens."[22] As Van Every later found, racism worked better as a goad than a unifying force.

In the spring of 1847, however, he was hoping to continue with the army. He accompanied the Fifteenth US Infantry to New Orleans, where he received one hundred dollars for his medical services in transit.[23] Then he shipped out with them to Mexico, expecting to be commissioned as an assistant surgeon.[24] His hope was not unrealistic, given the army's chronic shortage of medical personnel. At the war's onset, the Army Medical Department had only 71 staff members to care for 7,500 regulars. The Ten Regiment Bill authorized one surgeon and two assistant surgeons for each new regiment, but even on paper, the medical officers were stretched thin: Some 250 medical officers were scattered across an active force of 50,000 soldiers. In fact, half or more of these slots remained vacant, and field hospitals exacerbated the problem by poaching surgeons from regiments on campaign.[25] The result was a catastrophe of suffering and death. Diarrhea, malaria, and dysentery ravaged volunteers and regulars, killing nearly 11,000 soldiers and making the Mexican-American War the deadliest conflict in US history as measured by soldier mortality rate. An Illinoisan described his comrades as "the most sickly, enfeebled set of men I ever saw." Soldiers had to choose between visiting filthy, understaffed field hospitals or fending for themselves. One soldier who survived his first hospital stay vowed never to return; after being wounded in action, he sneaked away rather than submit to military medicine.[26]

After reaching General Scott's army in July, Van Every sought his commission with help from Colonel George Washington Morgan, commander of the Fifteenth US Infantry.[27] The request was denied for unstated reasons, but on August 2, Van Every signed on as a civilian contractor, pledging to "perform the duties of an Assistant Surgeon, agreeably to the Army Regulations," in exchange for a monthly salary of one hundred dollars.[28] This was a common arrangement, particularly in mid-1847, when regular surgeons struggled to care for thousands of patients languishing in camps and field hospitals.[29] Meanwhile, Scott itched to press on to Mexico City. After generals Gideon Pillow and Franklin Pierce arrived with reinforcements, Scott consigned convalescent soldiers to the hospital in Puebla and resumed his westward march on August 7.[30] Among those left in the lightly garrisoned city was civilian surgeon John Van Every.

Nestled amid volcanoes and boasting elegant edifices, bustling markets, and a temperate climate, Puebla impressed many US soldiers stationed there. Assistant surgeon Robert Hagan expressed a typical opinion when he praised its amenities and damned its residents: "The city is well built and contains many public buildings of rich architecture and beautiful appearance," he wrote shortly after Scott decamped, "but the inhabitants, generally speaking are a miserable looking set."[31] A Virginian agreed, marveling at the "splendid" cathedrals and rating the residents "little better" than "savages."[32] The city was also an important link in the line of communications between Scott's army and Veracruz. When Scott moved against Mexico City, he left Brevet Colonel Thomas Childs, a West Pointer and veteran of the War of 1812's Niagara campaign, to hold Puebla with around 450 soldiers. Madison Mills, a surgeon already indignant over being assigned to manage the Puebla hospital, feared the worst. "This force is by far too small," he fretted soon after Van Every's arrival. "If the Mexicans attack us they can use us up very quick. . . . We shall some day meet with disaster."[33]

Meanwhile, Mills tried to care for nearly 2,000 patients. "The sick are crowded on us without preparation on our part," he complained on August 10. After being promised seasoned assistants, he received only "citizen surgeons" who were too "*green*" to be "familiar with the details of service."[34] One of them was John Van Every, or in Mills's creative variation, "Van Everez of Rochester, N.Y." Along with colleagues identified only as I. E. Stevens of Boston, Smith of Illinois, Samuel L. Barbour of Georgia, Glover Perin of Ohio, Owen of Kentucky, and Allen of Texas, Van Every and his exasperated superior set to work.[35] Mills resolved to keep the hospital's inmates "properly quartered physicked and fed," but swore never to undertake a similar task.[36]

Mills and many colleagues disliked the civilian contract surgeons, and Van Every's lack of military experience was indeed glaring.[37] By mid-August, he had been attached to the army for only three months, in Mexico for two, and in Puebla for a little over a week. There is scant record of his activities, but he likely spent his days diagnosing illnesses, dispensing medicine, and attempting to mind the hundreds of soldiers under his supervision. His only known patient was John W. Dodd, a Hoosier who enlisted in the Fourth Indiana Volunteers in the spring of 1847. Dodd, who also tripped over Van Every's surname, seemed content with the care provided. "My health is quite good," he wrote in a letter home, "with the exception of the sore throat and mouth which, though better, does not seem inclined to leave me immediately. I am going through a course of medicine, which of course makes me irritable, weak and out of humor at times. Doct Van Avery, who is my physician says it is nothing, and that it will pass off in a short time. I associate no danger with it, but it has troubled me for a long time and is very inconvenient."[38] Whether Van Every craved more active duty or preferred his situation at Puebla is unknown, but he probably relished the prospect of regular pay.

Service in the Puebla garrison certainly seemed quieter than in Scott's field army. Pushing toward Mexico City, Scott's forces fought costly battles at Contreras and Churubusco in August, then at Molino del Rey and Chapultepec in September. Their comrades in Puebla waited anxiously, straining to distinguish fact from fiction, including the rumored destruction of Scott's army.[39] They also watched Mexican incursions around Puebla grow larger and bolder. On August 22, Mills reported that "guerrillas have been hovering about the city for the last ten days," although he insisted that "we are not concerned."[40] He was more alarmed the next day, however, noting that 4,000 Mexican cavalry had massed nearby and briefly entered the city, reaching the main plaza at night.[41] Thereafter, he recorded the steady escalation of nighttime forays by regular and irregular forces. Mexican soldiers drove off livestock, killed pickets, and occasionally shelled buildings the Americans used as barracks and hospitals.[42] These menacing maneuvers, especially the nocturnal guerrilla attacks, provoked jumpy US soldiers who often considered them proof of innate inferiority. When locals became "very saucy" after Scott's main force left town, one volunteer recalled, he and his comrades seized and flogged several of them. Thereafter, they posted heavy nighttime guards, but the enemy "had not the courage to charge or show any fight, or show their yellow, beggaring faces."[43] Anticipating an attack, Childs concentrated his troops in three citadels, including the imposing Cathedral de San José, now a heavily fortified hospital where Mills, his assistants, and their patients braced for the assault.[44]

The hammer fell on the night of September 13. Mexican general Joaquín Rea entered Puebla in force, encircled the US strongholds, and barricaded the streets. For several days and nights, Rea's troops maintained a barrage that did comparatively little damage but rattled the Americans' nerves and disrupted their sleep. When Childs refused to surrender on the sixteenth—Mexico's independence day—Rea assailed the Cathedral de San José and urged local citizens to help him crush the invaders. General Antonio López de Santa Anna arrived with reinforcements on September 22, hoping to trap Scott's army by capturing Puebla and severing his connection to the coast, but Childs was defiant. Low on food and outnumbered, he armed every convalescent soldier who could fight; Mills's assistants shouldered muskets as well.[45]

The siege lasted almost a month. Theodore Laidley, a West Pointer from western Virginia who handled Childs's artillery, described the ordeal to his father:

> We have had a long & fatiguing time of it—for twenty eight days they were continually firing at us, the balls were whizzing through the air

Siege of Puebla, Began Sept. 13th. Ended Oct. 12th. 1847, lithograph published in 1850 by G. Warren Smith & Company. The fortified Cathedral de San José, which housed the military hospital defended by John Van Every, his fellow surgeons, medical staff, and convalescent soldiers, appears on the far left. Courtesy of Special Collections, University of Texas at Arlington Libraries.

> where ever you went. It required us to be constantly on the watch, many of us did not sleep, scarcely at all, during the night, sometimes nod a little lying beside our guns. For more than a month I did not have my clothes off to sleep. Of course, cut off from the city & from every body else we had to take a soldier's fare, bread & meat which last article gave out before reinforcements arrived. However we would have held out much longer before we would surrender to Santa Anna's eight thousand, though we had only some six hundred at either of the three separate posts and many of them were convalescents not worth the third of a well man.[46]

The pressure eased in early October when Santa Anna pulled troops out of Puebla to confront a US relief column marching westward from Veracruz. The approaching Americans defeated Santa Anna at Huamantla on October 9, 1847, and reached Puebla three days later, where they fought a vicious street battle before driving the remaining Mexican soldiers away. Madison Mills watched with dismay as the victors got drunk, looted stores, and caroused in clothing stolen from women and priests. Their commanding officer was

General Joseph Lane, an Indiana politician fated to play a brief but important role in Van Every's public career.[47]

Colonel Childs celebrated by congratulating his troops on "the happy termination of the siege" and naming many of those who held Puebla for twenty-eight grueling days. Van Every merited no specific mention, but Childs thanked Mills "and his able assistants" for their "valuable services" as both surgeons and combat soldiers.[48] Van Every never published an account of the siege, a curious silence given the vastness of his written corpus and his contemporaries' tendency to weave grand reputations out of the thinnest threads of martial glory. But it was probably the most perilous month of his life. "The siege," wrote one survivor, "will forever stand in the memory of every soldier who participated in it, as one of the most surprising events in the history of the Mexican war."[49]

Van Every's final eight months in Mexico were anticlimactic but productive. He remained in Puebla until June 1848, toiling at the hospital while US and Mexican negotiators hammered out the Treaty of Guadalupe Hidalgo, which was signed in February but not proclaimed until July 4. Hospital duty involved frantic labor and grinding tedium, but it was an instructive interlude. Van Every witnessed a striking example of print media's enormous importance. Americans ran numerous newspapers in occupied Mexico, including the Puebla *Flag of Freedom*, which appeared on October 20, 1847, and continued until February 1848. The weekly sold for five cents per copy and was printed with equipment seized from Mexican publishers. It was unique in being managed by active-duty soldiers, not civilian journalists, who worked out of an office near the Cathedral de San José.[50] After watching comrades launch a newspaper almost as soon as the smoke cleared from Puebla, any lingering doubts Van Every may have entertained about the power of the press were likely dispelled.

Flag of Freedom's columns also reflected the brutal complexity of the occupation and the occupiers. The editors routinely reported and denounced American soldiers' atrocities against Puebla's civilians, including the killing of a pregnant woman by three soldiers who were attempting to steal blankets from her household.[51] They indulged in casual racism, printing advertisements for minstrel shows and anecdotes featuring Black people speaking in caricatured dialect.[52] But they also celebrated marriages between white American men and Mexican women, sometimes calling them "annexations," a metaphor that implied both unequal power dynamics and the uplift of ostensible inferiors.[53] Van Every likely read these announcements with disgust, but he studiously ignored them in his later diatribes. In his accounts, so-called amalgamation was prewar Mexico's besetting sin, not a wartime occurrence, and served to distinguish Mexicans from white Americans, not bring them together. Unwilling to admit that some of his fellow citizens applauded Mexico's "whitening" through intermarriage, he spent a quarter of a century urging them to protect the purity of their blood.[54]

It was also probably in this period that Van Every made the ethnological observations that he later weaponized against abolitionists. He joined a slew of arrogant visitors who indicted racial intermixture for Mexico's alleged economic decay, social degeneracy, and failure in self-government. Brantz Mayer of Baltimore spent several years during the early 1840s as secretary to the American legation in Mexico and published extensively about the country before and after Van Every's visit. One could expect nothing from "the unenlightened Mixed Races" of Mexico, Mayer proclaimed, particularly those descended from "a medly mosaic" of progenitors. "The hope of Mexico must . . . repose in the whites alone," he wrote.[55] Thomas Jefferson Farnham reached similar conclusions during his travels in California: The "law of Nature" against racial "mingling" had doomed the Mexicans to "fade away" before advancing Anglo-Saxons.[56] When Van Every began publishing in the early 1850s, readers were familiar with his basic ideas.

As we will see, however, Van Every, like many proslavery polygenists, used his Mexican musings for different ends. Farnham and his ilk denigrated *mestizaje* to rationalize Manifest Destiny. Van Every supported territorial expansion, too, but he prioritized domestic politics. Mexico mattered to him most as a negative example of racial intermingling, and he used his sojourn there to intervene authoritatively in polygenist proslavery politics. Racial mixture horrified polygenists because they regarded it as the crossing of separate species. Thus, while monogenists, like the *Flag of Freedom*'s editors, might celebrate intermixing as a mechanism for uplift, polygenists denounced it as abnormal.[57] Yet mixed-race people presented a serious empirical problem. Like mules (a comparison embedded in the term "mulatto"), they were supposed to be infertile, one of many physical and mental deficits that Josiah Nott and other polygenists attributed to interracial "hybrids." When confronted with evidence of fertility, these authors tied themselves in knots trying to prove that eventually, perhaps in a generation or two (or however long it took), the pitfalls of "amalgamation" would appear. Critics pounced on this weak spot. But polygenists' obsessive attacks on hybridization countered the notion that a "whitened" slave population might eventually be manumitted. If mixing caused deterioration rather than improvement, it could never warrant abolition.[58]

Van Every shared polygenists' politics but prioritized political application over theoretical precision. Degeneration of the body politic mattered more to him than degeneration of actual bodies. Not coincidentally, he wrote most extensively about Mexico—and most frequently used the term "mongrel," an epithet commonly applied to Mexicans in the 1840s—during Reconstruction, when the Fifteenth Amendment produced electoral "amalgamation." He was a political advocate first and a scientific theorist second. We will see that, just as he sidestepped debates over human origins, he avoided quarrels over declining fertility. This is one reason why *intellectual historians* of racism usually ignore him; he added little to polygenist doctrine and chided those, like Nott, who courted controversy. But Van Every's tactical evasiveness made him more important in the *political and business history* of racism. He found that popularizing polygenist theories was more profitable than wrangling over minutiae. Thus, he more closely resembled the politicians who used Mexico to score points in conflicts over race and slavery in the United States. Leaving Nott to battle irate theologians and skeptical scientists, Van Every joined proslavery officeholders like Jefferson Davis, who proclaimed the importance of preserving slavery intact and bloodlines unsullied. Thank goodness your "Puritan fathers . . . kept pure the Caucasian blood which flowed in their veins," Davis told a Maine audience, for "therein is the cause of your present high civilization, your progress, your dignity and your strength." We must "remain unmixed," he warned: "In our neighbors of Southern and Central America we have a sufficient warning; and may it never be our ill-fortune to learn by experience the lessons taught by their example."[59]

Davis was a fellow Mexican-American War veteran and became Van Every's steadfast patron. And while they did not meet in Mexico, Van Every's army stint stands out as the first time he lived and worked closely with white Southerners. Prior to 1847, there is no evidence he ever traveled south of the Great Lakes region, or that Southern politicians ever responded to his letters. But in Puebla, he fought alongside Southern soldiers and physicians. Three of the assistant surgeons working for Madison Mills (a New Yorker) hailed from slave states. Only Samuel L. Barbour of Georgia can be positively identified, but he could have provided firsthand testimony from the planter class. Barbour's father was a major enslaver in Jasper County, where in 1850 he held seventy-seven people in bondage.[60] Van Every did not need Barbour to teach him that slavery was a positive good. But he might have been the first of many Southerners who embraced Van Every as a kindred spirit.

Van Every's journey from Upper Canada to New York to Ohio to Mexico infused his proslavery worldview with nationalist fervor, partisan passion, and a global outlook. His upbringing in a colony where British officials imposed abolition whetted his Anglophobia. His long residence in free states primed him to regard slavery as a national boon, not a regional peculiarity, and to defend it as an American nationalist rather than a Southern sectionalist. Bitterly personal conflicts with Whigs fired his partisan zeal. Service in Mexico heightened his revulsion against racial intermingling and convinced him that white Americans must avoid the biological disaster of abolition. These themes formed the core of Van Every's message in the 1850s, across the war years, and throughout Reconstruction. Van Every adapted his terminology but never his tenets. Rigid consistency was the basis of his brand—until a sudden swerve sent his career off the rails.

As he sailed home in the summer of 1848, Van Every's faith in slavery's transcendent importance was fully developed. But making a career promoting an idea requires more than mere belief. Somewhere between Puebla and New Orleans, Van Every resolved to abandon medicine and reinvent himself as a writer. Thus began a three-decade career notable for ruthless focus, shameless self-promotion, and tireless dedication, all born of the conviction that he must unite white Americans behind slavery before it was too late. Van Every fancied himself a hero, not for what he had done in Mexico, but for what he would do for the Union.

Chapter 4

Transformation

Antebellum Americans hungered for heroes. Nagged by self-doubt as the republic passed into their hands, they mourned the demise of their Revolutionary forebears. "We look around with anxious and eager eye," John Quincy Adams observed in 1836, "for *one* of that illustrious host of Patriots and heroes" who won American independence. Alas, after James Madison's death, Adams eulogized, "We look around in vain."[1] They exalted past heroes in the hope of inspiring new ones. Hence the naming of towns and counties after departed luminaries. Hence the founding of historical societies and the writing of historical treatises. Hence the bestowal of illustrious monikers on children, whether named for foreign notables or homegrown "patriot-heroes." Simon Bolivar Buckner (b. 1823), Napoleon Bonaparte Brown (b. 1834), George Washington Morgan (b. 1820), and Winfield Scott Hancock (b. 1824) were living testaments to the Romantic fixation on heroes.[2]

Implicit in this "hero worship" was a theory of history best articulated by that term's inventor, Thomas Carlyle. First delivered as a series of lectures in 1840 and published the following year as *On Heroes, Hero-Worship, & the Heroic in History*, Carlyle's thesis was straightforward: History "is at bottom the History of the Great Men who have worked here." Extraordinary individuals propelled human progress as "the modellers, patterns, and . . . creators" of everything done by "the general mass of men." Great Men appeared in different guises over the ages. Long ago, they were worshipped as gods or venerated as prophets, while more recent civilizations knew them as poets, priests, authors, or kings. But in every era and in every form, they revealed to lesser mortals what Carlyle unhesitatingly capitalized as Truth.[3]

As technological marvels brought printed words to more people with greater speed and at lower cost than ever before, Carlyle readily attributed godlike influence to writers. Thus, he devoted his fifth lecture to "The Hero as Man of Letters." Inspired by eternal truths just like his ancient precursors and newly empowered to transcend time and space with his words, the "Man-of-Letters Hero," Carlyle believed, "must be regarded as our most important modern person." He might seem an unlikely hero, living in a hovel and sporting ink-spattered clothes. Nevertheless, the "true Literary man" was the "world's Priest," able to preach "to all men in all times and places" and thus to "accomplish *miracles*" through the power of persuasion. The modern author-hero guided his contemporaries like a "sacred Pillar of Fire."[4]

Carlyle inspired literary strivers who yearned for greatness. Horace Greeley, who commenced his career with the New York *Tribune* the same year that *On Heroes* appeared in print, praised Carlyle's "glorious volume" and fancied himself a man-of-letters hero who elevated his fellow citizens by expounding great truths.[5] Indeed, while Carlyle's prose smacked of Victorian smugness, contemporaries had good reason to agree with him. In an age when rotary presses, railroads, and telegraphs sent words flying across continents, even the humblest of scribblers could attain deific influence. Consider abolitionist editor William Lloyd Garrison. Living on bread and water in his cramped office under the eaves at No. 10 Merchants Hall, Garrison personified Carlyle's scruffy hero. Within months of its appearance in 1831, Garrison's *Liberator* so alarmed proslavery Southerners that they put a price on the Bostonian's balding head.[6] Two decades later, Harriet Beecher Stowe stirred Northerners' consciences with a novel, first serialized in an antislavery newspaper and then published in two volumes in 1852. Abraham Lincoln never claimed that *Uncle Tom's Cabin* started the Civil War, but white Southerners attested to its force by restricting its circulation and penning proslavery novels in response.[7] Scores of antebellum authors, editors, and publishers sallied forth to convert disciples and bend the arc of history. Proslavery prophets like James D. B. De Bow and Robert Barnwell Rhett clashed with abolitionists like Garrison and Frederick Douglass. But they all believed that gifted individuals could wield the power of written words.

John Van Every shared their faith. Whether inspired by Carlyle, examples from his youth, or both, he had heroic ambitions. Upon returning from Mexico, Van Every labored to become an author-hero who would save his adopted country by illuminating the ostensibly transcendent truths of race. Certainly, he was a committed racist before his Mexican campaigns and postwar ethnological inquiries. But these experiences, and the context in which they occurred, motivated him to devote his life to disseminating a racist brand of American nationalism. Van Every returned to a country shaken by political conflict over slavery. Settling in Washington, DC, he spent seven years in a slaveholding city where debates over slavery's future ripped the fabric of national unity. This upheaval inflamed his heroic aspirations. Drawing on his medical training and flaunting his scientific credentials, Van Every embraced the polygenist American School of Ethnology as it reached the zenith of its popularity. He also cultivated a network of patrons, including influential Southern politicians who provided financial and logistical support. Laboring in an atmosphere of political discord and academic racism, Van Every commenced a career that would outlive Reconstruction. In the process, he adopted a new purpose and persona, marking the transformation by changing the spelling of his surname. In the crucible of sectional strife and racist reaction, Van Every the frustrated physician became Van Evrie the prophetic propagandist.

In 1853, Van Evrie shouted his way into the cacophonous public sphere. Blending racist science with strident nationalism and Anglophobic conspiracy mongering, he targeted a broad but perceptibly Northern audience with his core message: Slavery must live so that the white man's republic could thrive. He spent the next quarter century hammering on this theme, often amplifying the volume but seldom varying the tune. The story of Van Evrie's self-remaking is, therefore, essential to understanding his later career, for it was in these years that he became a professional racist.

The brig *Tasso* carried Van Every from Veracruz to New Orleans and back into civilian life.[8] When he reached the Crescent City on July 9, 1848, the country was technically at peace but trembling with upheaval. Movements of all sorts were accelerating. Within two weeks of Van Every's homecoming, activists convened at Seneca Falls to proclaim that all women and men are created equal. In August, the *New York Herald* announced the discovery of gold in California; within a year, a hundred thousand people had poured into the recently conquered province. Mass migration quickened a global cholera outbreak that killed millions, including James K. Polk. Yet in the summer of Van Every's return, perhaps nothing captivated the attention of more Americans than revolution abroad and sectionalism at home.

Fueled by crop failure, government repression, nationalist ardor, and class strife, revolution swept through Europe in 1848. First in France, where a new republic rose atop another shattered monarchy, and then across the continent, liberal and radical insurgents assailed the old regimes. Within a year, counterrevolutionary armies in most countries had suppressed the dissenters and restored conservative governments. Nevertheless, the Springtime of Nations bequeathed a potent legacy. Revolutionaries won some victories: Serfdom was abolished in Austria and Hungary, for instance, and constitutional monarchy supplanted absolutism in Denmark. Even failed revolutionaries enjoyed acclaim, including those forced into exile, such as Hungary's nationalist hero Lajos Kossuth and the German Forty-Eighters who fled to America and joined the antislavery movement. But reactionaries regained ascendancy in most of Europe, including France, where President Louis-Napoleon Bonaparte soon followed his uncle's example and crowned himself Emperor. Throughout the 1850s, Napoleon III and his counterparts across Europe cracked down on radicals and crafted new rationales for preserving the status quo.[9]

Meanwhile, a different specter haunted the United States: disunion. The war that swelled American nationalism and sent Van Every marching through Mexico also fanned smoldering conflicts over slavery and expansion. Fearing the consequences, Ralph Waldo Emerson predicted that "Mexico will poison us."[10] The controversy fostered forms of antislavery politics that were compatible with racism but also attracted the mass following that eluded more egalitarian abolitionists. When David Wilmot, a Pennsylvania Democrat, offered his famous amendment to a military appropriations bill in August 1846, intending to bar slavery from all conquered Mexican territory, he acted on behalf of free white Northerners, not enslaved Black Southerners. Indeed, he defended his eponymous proviso as a means to "preserve to free white labor a fair country" where workers "of my own race and own color" would not be disgraced by "association with negro slavery."[11] But by framing the conflict over slavery's expansion as a struggle between Northern workers and Southern aristocrats, the Wilmot Proviso catalyzed mass antislavery activism, roiled party politics, and rattled the Union.[12]

Wilmot introduced his proviso before Van Every departed for Mexico, and by the time Van Every returned stateside, its momentous political impact was already evident. Van Every's homecoming coincided with another fierce presidential canvass. Earlier that spring, Whigs and Democrats convened to select their candidates. Whigs chose Louisiana war hero Zachary Taylor, while Democrats tapped Lewis Cass of Michigan. When neither party endorsed the Wilmot Proviso, disaffected Northerners bolted from both parties and founded the Free Soil Party. With an old Jacksonian Democrat, Martin Van Buren, atop their ticket and Whig stalwart Charles Francis Adams in the vice presidential slot, the Free Soilers had forged a portentous antislavery coalition. Their platform advocated Wilmot's Proviso and appealed to Northern class resentment, vowing "to maintain the rights of free labor against the aggressions of the slave power"—the widely used term for the South's planter aristocracy—"and to secure free soil for a free people."[13] The belief that slavery undergirded a selfish Southern ruling class was spreading, even among racists, and its partisan expression presaged a revolution in Northern politics.[14] Proslavery Southerners, disinclined to distinguish between moderate and radical opposition to slavery, sounded the alarm. Shortly before the election, Senator Jefferson Davis of Mississippi deprecated the "storm of anti-slavery agitation," warning that the Free Soil program would someday give Northerners enough states to abolish slavery by constitutional amendment and urging Southern whites to unite against this "war upon your rights." Ominously, he stated that passage of the Wilmot Proviso would justify secession.[15]

The Free Soil ticket carried only 10 percent of the popular vote and zero states, but the tempest unleashed in 1848 raged for years thereafter. Portents of disunion appeared in rapid succession. In February 1849, Davis and a large minority of his Southern colleagues signed John C. Calhoun's "Southern Address," which called for sectional solidarity in defense of "our peculiar institution."[16] That December, disputes over conquered Mexican territory provoked another legislative showdown. Congressional members from the South threatened to secede if Congress passed the Wilmot Proviso or admitted California as a free state. As debate thundered deep into 1850, members of Congress hurled insults, brandished weapons, and spoke of civil war. Moderates patched together the Compromise of 1850 in September, but it infuriated proslavery and antislavery partisans alike. Antislavery Northerners loathed the Fugitive Slave Act, which compelled their complicity in slave catching, while proslavery Southerners fumed over California statehood and restrictions on slave trading in the District of Columbia. Thereafter, clashes between slave hunters and antislavery activists stoked further controversy and primed the intense Northern response to *Uncle Tom's Cabin*. As slavery's violence spilled into their communities, thousands of Northern readers sympathized with Eliza, whose bloody footprints marked her desperate dash across the half-frozen Ohio River.[17]

Living in Washington, DC, Van Every was close to the action. He later bragged of having been "in frequent, almost daily, intercourse" with congressional representatives from the South during the early 1850s, and he likely witnessed legislative clashes firsthand.[18] Perhaps he saw the House of Representatives erupt into a brawl over choosing a speaker. Maybe he heard Senator William Seward of New York declare that a "higher law than the Constitution" condemned slavery or Representative Robert Toombs from Georgia swear that if Northerners barred slavery from California, "*I am for disunion*."[19] An avid reader and debater, Van Every undoubtedly talked politics in Washington's boardinghouses, hotels, and taverns. His home, after all, was both the epicenter of political controversy and contested ground in battles over slavery's status in the District. Intense sectionalism catalyzed Van Every the physician's transformation into Van Evrie the propagandist. The uneasy truce that prevailed when he published his first works in 1853 was frequently punctuated by bitter words and violent deeds. In America as in Europe, revolutionary fervor had been repelled but not vanquished.

With reckonings only postponed, intellectual ferment surged in the years after 1848. It was a prolific period for aspiring author-heroes. European and American societies had been shaken by revolution and reaction, prompting analysts to revisit basic questions: How do human societies work? What would an ideal society look like? Writers wielded pens and printing presses as weapons in a renewed struggle to understand the past and mold the future.

In Europe, where theological justifications for social hierarchy and political authority were battered by waves of revolution, theorists turned to ostensibly more scientific frameworks. For some, particularly those on the political left, the key was social class. Banished from Prussia for joining the 1848 upheaval, including serving as editor of the *New Rhineland News*, Karl Marx fled to London, where he toiled to expand his influence in print. By the early 1850s, Marx had commenced his study of political economy, which ultimately yielded *Capital* (1867), as well as his more prolific journalistic work, including several years as a correspondent for Greeley's *Tribune*. In Marx's materialist view, class conflicts propelled historical change and necessarily underpinned political analysis and activism.[20]

Others, especially on Europe's reactionary right, grounded their analysis in race. No one in the post-1848 era expounded racial determinism more stridently than Joseph Arthur de Gobineau. A French aristocrat who had been relatively moderate before 1848, Gobineau was horrified by revolutionary mayhem, which left him embittered against democracy and ready to embrace authoritarianism as a bulwark against chaos. Yet even as he defended aristocracy, he framed his analysis in explicitly racist terms, as reflected in the title of his *Essay on the Inequality of the Human Races* (1853–55). For Gobineau, history was the story of conflict among "black," "yellow," and "white" races. The rise and fall of societies reflected the ascent, decadence, and decline of white groups that had established every civilization, from India, Egypt, and Rome to China, Mexico, and Peru. Gobineau's whites were uniquely capable of greatness but also doomed to deteriorate if they mixed with other races. Since every society's destiny hinged on its racial inheritance, superior peoples' propensity to mingle with inferiors meant that civilization's decay was inevitable.[21]

This pessimism did not diminish Gobineau's popularity among scientific racists exhilarated by the intellectual currents of the 1850s. Even in America, which Gobineau criticized for egalitarianism and openness to crossing European bloodlines, the aristocrat's ideas met a warm reception. Shortly after Gobineau's *Essay* appeared in French, Josiah Nott hired Henry Hotze (later a Confederate propagandist in Europe) to translate it; they published the heavily edited result as *The Moral and Intellectual Diversity of Races* in 1856. This project demonstrated the scavenger nature of racist ideologies, particularly among American writers eager to co-opt European ideas. Gobineau was a monogenist, and although convinced of Black inferiority, he was lukewarm on slavery. Nott and Hotze simply omitted unwelcome portions of the *Essay*, added a polygenist appendix, and dedicated their scissors-and-paste job "to the Statesmen of America" as a refresher course on proslavery science. Astonished, Gobineau resented the Americans "who believe that I am encouraging them to bludgeon their Negroes . . . but who are unwilling to translate the part of the work which concerns them."[22]

This arrogation of Gobineau's work reflected the brazen conceit of mid-nineteenth-century American scientific racists, particularly the polygenists of the American School of Ethnology (ASE). The years from the late 1840s to the Civil War marked their golden age. Marx had a few American disciples during this period, but among leading American intellectuals, race, not class, was the key to social and political analysis, and polygenists within the ASE's orbit claimed unique expertise on the subject. Polygenism had lurked in American thought for decades, from Jefferson's conjectures to the more confident work of physicians like Charles Caldwell and Samuel George Morton in the 1830s. Although it remained controversial because of its heterodox religious implications, polygenism proliferated in the 1840s, and after 1850, its popularity soared. This was partly due to bravado. Josiah Nott's notoriety took off with the publication of major works in 1844 and 1849, in which he nettled Christian thinkers by disparaging the Bible's account of human origins.[23] Certainly, this "parson skinning" delighted those who shared Nott's belief in the supremacy of modern science over ancient superstition.[24] But other advocates lent greater respectability to polygenism. Chief among them was a Swiss celebrity-scientist whose conversion to polygenism in 1850 accelerated the theory's rise to intellectual prominence.

Born in Switzerland in 1807, Louis Agassiz enjoyed an elite education and made his name as an expert on freshwater fish. Among his mentors was Georges Cuvier, a monogenist who used fossilized remains to argue for the permanence (rather than evolutionary mutability) of species. After Cuvier died of cholera in 1832, Agassiz continued his work and produced a renowned study of fish fossils in 1843. Blending geology, comparative anatomy, and taxonomy with ichthyology and paleontology, Agassiz's magnum opus cemented his reputation as a brilliant interdisciplinary scholar. And while his early work did not explore human origins, it did prefigure his acceptance of polygenesis. Agassiz theorized that plant and animal species occupied distinct zoological provinces, with each species created to thrive in one environment. Only humans flourished in multiple provinces. But Agassiz's belief in the unity of humankind weakened after he moved to Boston in 1846.[25]

Agassiz arrived amid swelling sectionalism and with his own finances in tatters. But he soon landed an appointment as professor of zoology and geology at Harvard and further padded his pocketbook by delivering public lectures. While on tour, Agassiz made friends who transformed his thinking about race and slavery. One was Samuel George Morton, who dazzled Agassiz with his skull collection. Another was Robert W. Gibbes, a South Carolina physician who tempted Agassiz to visit by promising him an opportunity to examine African-born enslaved people. While in Columbia in 1850, Agassiz had some of the captives photographed. The result was a viciously exploitive photo collection rediscovered in 1976 at Harvard's Peabody Museum of Archaeology and Ethnology. Agassiz sought to document, with modern technology, the allegedly self-evident truths of racial difference. Of course, his eyes saw exactly what he was prepared to see, and his swift descent into polygenism was more visceral than cerebral. Shortly after his arrival in the United States, Agassiz was already privately expressing his aversion to Black people. The more he interacted with "this degraded and degenerate race," he told his mother, "the more . . . impossible it becomes for me to repress the feeling that they are not of the same blood as we." Subsequent theorizing cloaked these sentiments in the garb of scientific objectivity.[26]

As the mid-nineteenth-century crisis peaked and Van Every passed his third year in Washington, Agassiz threw his intellectual weight behind the ASE. In March 1850, he visited Charleston to attend the annual meeting of the American Association for the Advancement of Science. Participants included such prominent polygenists as Josiah Nott; Samuel S. Kneeland, a skull measurer from Boston; and Peter A. Browne of Philadelphia, known for his microscopic study of hair. As monogenists squirmed in their seats, Agassiz delivered his paper. While he allowed that all human races were superior to animals, he insisted on their plural origins, with each race designed for its own zoological province. Thus, they were separate species whose creations were not all recorded in the Bible. The paper provoked massive backlash, but Agassiz addressed his pious critics in a series of articles in which he championed free inquiry and urged Christians to support polygenesis because it recognized divine creation of fixed species. The only alternative, he maintained, was to graft evolutionary change onto the Book of Genesis. Polygenism remained controversial, but Agassiz's conversion gave proponents an edge. Proslavery propagandists were delighted. "With Agassiz in the war," exulted Nott, "the battle is ours." Agassiz's later collaborations with Nott reinforced the alliance between natural science and proslavery polemics.[27]

By the early 1850s, polygenism was all the rage in America. It lent scientific legitimacy to the nation's blend of white men's egalitarianism and strict racial hierarchy because plural creations implied disparate abilities. As separate species, the races allegedly had varied physical, moral, and intellectual endowments, with lesser beings divinely ordained to serve their superiors. Perhaps nowhere were these political implications expressed more emphatically than in an 1851 volume published by John Campbell as *Negro-Mania: Being an Examination of the Falsely Assumed Equality of the Various Races of Men*. A compendium rather than an original work, the book reflected polygenism's proliferation: It was now possible to compile five hundred pages of extracts from polygenist texts. It also demonstrated the theory's seductive appeal to erstwhile radicals. Campbell was an Irish-born Chartist who, as recently as 1848, had denounced capitalism and inequality and championed workers of all colors. Three tumultuous years later, Campbell assailed abolitionists and derided Black people as lazy nonproducers. In *Negro-Mania*, "a text book for white men," Campbell presented polygenism as irrefutable proof of Black inferiority and the impracticability of an egalitarian multiracial society. "No dark race of men has ever been equal to a white race," he insisted, and "the two cannot exist together in the same community on terms of equality." For Campbell, polygenism dissolved the paradox of racial subordination in an egalitarian nation: no one could equalize what God had made unequal—and no one should try.[28]

The atmosphere during Van Every's Washington years was heavy with political conflict and reactionary racism. Later, he spotlighted this interlude in advertisements for his publications, bragging that he had "given several years of his life to a scientific examination of the question of races."[29] His writings showcased extensive reading in European and American scientific racism, including canonical texts from the ASE. But devouring these tomes did not automatically launch his infamous career. The circumstances in which he read them were crucial. Absent the threat of disunion, Van Every might have remained a consumer of racist treatises; it was sectional conflict that spurred him to write. As Van Evrie, he would forge white unity based on what he deemed was scientifically grounded proslavery patriotism.

Still, making a literary living would be difficult. Carlyle's prototypical man-of-letters hero lived in squalor, and certainly people like William Lloyd Garrison achieved much on a shoestring budget. But Van Every returned from Mexico with little more than his army pay and a bogus medical degree. The army pay amounted to $1,186.65, a healthy sum but not enough to live on indefinitely.[30] With the degree, he could have started a new medical practice, but his first venture had spiraled into bankruptcy. To launch a literary career, Van Every needed an income stream that would afford him time to write. Authorial finance was shifting in this period from a patron-client model to a mass-marketing model, with writers increasingly relying on broad sales rather than a few deep pockets.[31] But for an unpublished aspirant, elite patronage was essential to make a start. Van Every, who had cultivated patrons since medical school, secured this support by networking with Southern members of Congress. Setting a pattern that would persist throughout his public life, Van Every inaugurated his writing career as a paid propagandist for the Slave Power.

Expansion of the federal bureaucracy provided opportunities for employment. During his Washington years, Van Every worked periodically as a clerk in the General Land Office (GLO), an agency housed within the Department of the Interior that later evolved into the Bureau of Land Management. Antebellum state formation and capitalist development depended on an army of clerks—in 1855, some 14,000 in New York City alone—who copied documents, balanced ledgers, and kept the wheels of governance and commerce turning. This unglamorous labor could provide a stepping stone to self-employment, so aspiring clerks flocked to cities, chasing the financial and social capital necessary for upward mobility into economic independence. Good penmanship and a well-placed connection often sufficed to secure a post. And while Van Every, who turned thirty-four during his first autumn in Washington, was older than most clerks, he otherwise fit the profile as an unmarried white man with a decent education and burning ambition. Fortunately for Van Every, federal clerkships multiplied at midcentury. The federal payroll was tiny by modern standards, but executive departments expanded to handle the work of governing a rapidly growing nation. In 1849, the GLO employed 64 clerks; by 1853, the number had swelled to 105.[32]

Van Every never landed a permanent clerical position, but given his authorial aspirations, it is unlikely that he wanted one. Instead, he worked intermittently for the GLO under the provisions of a May 1848 House resolution that ordered the preparation of maps detailing which public lands had been surveyed and sold.[33] Since the maps were updated for each session of Congress, the project regularly created demand for extra clerks, and Van Every was hired repeatedly in the early 1850s. He worked on the mapping project continuously between October 1850 and March 1851, earning one hundred dollars per month, and again for another month, this time earning ninety dollars, in 1852 or 1853.[34]

How did a proud Democrat land a job in President Millard Fillmore's Whig administration? Influential benefactors usually paved the way in these situations, and although it is unclear who sponsored his earliest clerical employment, he likely received assistance from Southerners. Van Every's standing among powerful Southern politicians is evident in a chilling letter written by his staunchest patron, Jefferson Davis of Mississippi. A senator until 1851 who returned to Washington in 1853 to head the War Department, Davis appreciated Van Every's proslavery crusade. In October 1854, after Van Every was an established author, Davis sought to secure for him another interim position, this time in the Patent Office. So, he composed a letter to Interior Secretary Robert McClelland. Davis introduced Van Evrie (as he now styled himself) as "a devotee to truth and a powerful advocate of sound principles" and "the author of a powerful and learned essay on the negro race and negro Slavery" who "labored to beat down fanaticism and treason by facts and philosophy." Van Evrie needed financial assistance to continue his campaign, Davis added. Would McClelland please give him a job copying patent reports?[35]

By 1854, Van Evrie had impressed Southern politicians so much that some lobbied to give him a federal subsidy to write proslavery propaganda. The Interior Department's contingent expenses for 1854–55 and 1855–56 do not list him among the clerks, so Davis's request likely went unfulfilled.[36] But when Van Every, as he was known then, worked on his first publication in 1850, a similar effort by Davis or another Southern patron probably landed him employment in the General Land Office. And whether disbursed by the army or the GLO, federal funds sustained Van Every as he crafted his first contributions to the pernicious library of proslavery polygenism.

Chapter 5

Propagandist

Eighteen fifty-three was a banner year for racists. In most narratives of sectional strife, the year slinks by softly between the 1850 showdown and the Kansas struggle that exploded in 1854. But for racists who weaponized science, 1853 was decisive because numerous projects seeded during the crises of the mid-nineteenth century now bore poisonous fruit. Early in the year, Louis Agassiz lectured on polygenism in Charleston, Mobile, and New Orleans.[1] That spring, Josiah Nott and George R. Gliddon began selling subscriptions to their magnum opus, *Types of Mankind*, and quickly secured more than five hundred backers who pledged five dollars per copy. By the time they finished the manuscript in August, the book, destined to be the epitome of American polygenism, was already a financial success.[2] And in June and July, the first two volumes of Joseph Arthur de Gobineau's *Essay on the Inequality of the Human Races* appeared in Paris.[3] The field was crowded when John Van Evrie—as he now called himself—burst onto the scene. Despite the competition, Van Evrie commanded the attention of friends and foes alike.

Van Evrie's first two publications foreshadowed his career as a Democratic partisan and steadfast ally of Southern planters. In June 1853, he published an essay entitled "Negroes and Negro Slavery" in the inaugural issue of the *Monthly Democratic Review*, a Washington, DC–based Democratic periodical launched to support President Franklin Pierce's administration.[4] The following month, he published "Slavery Extension" in *De Bow's Review*. Founded in 1846 by New Orleans editor James D. B. De Bow, *De Bow's Review* promoted Southern economic development and slavery, printing articles by leading proslavery propagandists, including polygenist Louisiana physician Samuel A. Cartwright and the incomparably reactionary George Fitzhugh of Virginia. De Bow botched Van Evrie's surname, printing it as Van Evne, but nonetheless introduced him to an eager audience of Southern planters and merchants.[5] Together, the essays assailed the twin pillars of popular antislavery: the defense of free soil and hostility to the Slave Power. Thus, while Van Evrie's earliest writings ingratiated him to white Southerners, they also initiated his long campaign to convert white Northerners through a regionally calibrated proslavery appeal.

Given the clashes over the Wilmot Proviso, "Slavery Extension" was the more timely article, though it was less original. Van Evrie denounced free soil as one of many Northern "delusions," comparable to the Salem witch trials, spirit communication, and the Seneca Falls Convention. Free soil grew from a still greater delusion "that the negro is a black white man." Van Evrie recycled this slogan whenever he summarized the polygenist critique of antislavery: Abolitionists and their political kin, including Free-Soilers, erroneously assumed that racial distinctions were skin deep. In fact, he asserted, Blacks and whites were unalterably different in physiology, morality, and intellect. As separate species, they were created for different climates. Crudely echoing Louis Agassiz's claims about zoological provinces, Van Evrie insisted that "the negro is as much a product of the tropics as the orange or the banana," so Black people could thrive—and labor profitably for white masters—only in tropical regions. Migration patterns supposedly proved this. Since arriving in North America, Black people had begun congregating in the Deep South, leaving Canada and the Northeast comparatively white. What Free-Soilers condemned as proslavery imperialism was a "healthy and normal" process that must continue into Mexico and the Caribbean. The alternative was catastrophe. If the South's Black population kept growing without any outlet, Blacks would turn to "crime, robbery, insurrections, to violence and blood." Genocidal white retaliation would end in Black people's "complete and total destruction." Claiming the philanthropic high ground, Van Evrie concluded that "the cry of . . . no more extension of slavery, is tantamount to no more room for the blacks, and *death to the negro*."[6] This was a shrill argument, but not a novel one. Even without polygenism, proslavery writers had long insisted that restrictions on slavery's expansion would trigger a race war.[7] Van Evrie simply added a scientific gloss to a proslavery cliché.

More enduringly influential was "Negroes and Negro Slavery," which received far more attention and established themes that Van Evrie would harp on for decades. Presented as the first installment of a larger volume, "Negroes" in fact laid the foundation for both of Van Evrie's books and the bulk of his voluminous proslavery editorials. He repeatedly revised the original essay, so its evolution reveals his sinister mind at work as he maneuvered to convince white Northerners to oppose abolitionism. Van Evrie believed that the "slavery question *must be understood* at the North" or the Union would perish.[8] The development of his "Negroes" essay illuminates how he crafted an appeal to Northern readers.

Monthly Democratic Review editor Ovid F. Johnson presented Van Evrie's essay as the introduction to a forthcoming book, also entitled *Negroes and Negro Slavery*. Later, Van Evrie explained that friends had convinced him to publish the book in installments rather than wait to release the complete volume.[9] Ironically, this was exactly how Harriet Beecher Stowe had published *Uncle Tom's Cabin.* Van Evrie's motivation was probably financial. By the 1850s, many authors opted for serialization followed by full publication because they could double their royalties, a tantalizing prospect for any cash-strapped writer.[10] Johnson also gave Van Evrie his unearned title of "Doctor" and touted the "several years" he spent compiling the "authentic materials" for the project. Having established the author's credentials, Johnson praised the significance of his findings. Deploying "absolutely overwhelming" evidence, Van Evrie would silence the "noisy" abolitionists by "subvert[ing] the very foundation of their creed."[11]

Van Evrie's essay foregrounded his fundamentally political interpretation of polygenism. He celebrated the insights of scholars like Agassiz but criticized them for underselling the value of their work; theories of plural origins were mere antiquarianism if not put to practical use. Properly applied, however, science could resolve political disputes by illuminating the unique social role for which each human species was created. Scientific illiteracy, Van Evrie argued, led radicals to demand racial and gender equality. To accede to either one would flout "all the laws of organic existence" and make "a rapid stride towards barbarism." Behind these demands lurked even more sinister forces. American abolitionists were merely the "dupes" of the "enemies of Democratic progress"—namely, British monarchists who proclaimed the unity of humankind to destroy slavery under the guise of philanthropy. They also fomented "hybridism"—racial mixing—which, Van Evrie insisted, would corrupt the United States just as it had undermined Mexico. Meanwhile, British aristocrats lorded over their compatriots, racial equals trapped in unnatural degradation by enforced ignorance and standing armies. In building their societies on the artificial hierarchy of class, Europeans had created monstrosities. The United States, on the other hand, aligned its social structure and political system with the biological concept of race. Only abolitionists, feminists, and other "Americans so debauched by Britishism" doubted it. But the delusion would vanish once white Americans understood that nature "forever places the Negro in subordination to the Caucasian."[12] Adding his own patriotic gloss to the final page of Van Evrie's article, the *Monthly Democratic Review*'s editor printed a facsimile of the original manuscript of Francis Scott Key's "The Star-Spangled Banner."[13]

The first iteration of "Negroes and Negro Slavery" gave polygenism a ringing endorsement, but even a sympathetic reader might have questions. What evidence was there for the plurality of human species? Why had Britain launched an abolitionist onslaught against the United States? Why should nonslaveholders protect enslavers' property rights? Didn't Southern planters resemble the Old World aristocrats Van Evrie despised? And why was *slavery*, not some other system of racial hierarchy, so important to the Union and its nonslaveholding white majority? Van Evrie yearned to tackle these questions in a longer version of his essay that he hoped to publish through the Smithsonian Institution. Among the regents was his patron Jefferson Davis, who probably encouraged Van Evrie to submit his manuscript for consideration. Ultimately, the Smithsonian published a study of North American snakes instead, a decision that still rankled Van Evrie when he recounted the story sixteen years later.[14]

Having failed to secure a federal imprimatur for his work, Van Evrie relied on private publishers to produce the enlarged essay. He had lived among white Northerners for thirteen years. They had been his in-laws and neighbors; his teachers and classmates; his colleagues and patients. They comprised his imagined audience as he expanded the "Negroes" article into a more combative and carefully calibrated pamphlet that differed from the original version in both tone and content. It presented the pseudoscientific case for polygenism with ostensibly more precise (if revealingly inconsistent) data, but mainly it developed a provocative argument about the origins of abolitionism. The result was a memorable piece of propaganda, brimming with scientific racism but leavened with an elaborate conspiracy theory through which Van Evrie upended the Slave Power argument and cast Southern planters as the guardians of white American freedom. Van Evrie was an unoriginal scientific theorist, but each revised edition revealed his diabolical cleverness as polemicist and advertiser.

Baltimore publisher J. D. Toy printed the first pamphlet edition of *Negroes and Negro Slavery; The First, an Inferior Race—The Latter, Its Normal Condition*. The lengthy title encapsulated Van Evrie's argument that polygenism proved the divine origins and scientific truth of Black people's fitness for servitude. Van Evrie also burnished his credentials. The cover identified him as an MD, bolstering his claims to scientific objectivity. Four blurbs on the inside cover served a similar purpose. Praise from Jefferson Davis and James D. B. De Bow reassured Southern whites about Van Evrie's soundness. Meanwhile, endorsements from Daniel S. Dickinson, a former New York senator, and the *New York National Democrat* provided sectional balance and strengthened his nationalist appeal. After the 1850 secession scare, Northern whites needed to know that Van Evrie spoke as an American patriot, not as a Southern separatist.

Van Evrie also added a preface in which he competed for the hearts and minds of Northerners by offering his work as a response to "a certain famous or *in*famous negro novel": *Uncle Tom's Cabin*. He presented himself as Stowe's antithesis. He was the rational, objective, male expert, laboring to correct misconceptions spread by an emotional, biased, female scribbler who "represent[ed] her negro characters as white people." Reusing his catchphrase, he denied that "the negro is a black white man, or that Southern Slaves are people like ourselves are." Far from inflicting the "suffering" depicted by Stowe, slavery gave the African race "a greater measure of happiness than ever before known in its history." Speaking as a modern scientist, Van Evrie proclaimed it was "time that the popular fallacy in regard to the negro was exploded," and he posed as the author-hero who could do it. Then he spelled out his polygenist thesis in capital letters: "The negro . . . is not a black white man, or a man merely with a black skin, but a DIFFERENT AND INFERIOR SPECIES OF MAN," permanently inferior to whites, and "designed by the Almighty Creator" for servitude. It followed that "so-called slavery" was "a natural relation" between superior and inferior species and was vital to "the order, progress, and general well-being of the superior one, and absolutely essential to the very existence of the inferior race."[15] After summarizing these points in the initial pamphlet, Van Evrie promised he would issue additional monthly installments until the four-hundred-page work was complete.

Much of the pamphlet's polygenist content was identical to the original essay, though Van Evrie did attempt to enhance its scientific precision. He added craniological data to strengthen his claim that granting Blacks the same duties and privileges as whites violated divine dictates revealed through anatomy. Tellingly, his figures fluctuated between editions; whether because of authorial bungling or printer error, the J. D. Toy pamphlet listed Black brains as measuring sixty-five to seventy cubic inches, while subsequent editions claimed sixty-five to seventy-five.[16] So much for empirical rigor. But the most important revisions had less to do with science than with politics. The key innovation in the revised edition was a direct attack on the Slave Power argument, in which Van Evrie hailed Southern planters as defenders of American democracy against an international conspiracy.

Van Evrie had sketched this idea in his letter to John C. Calhoun and alluded to it in the original *Monthly Democratic Review* essay. But he expanded it in the pamphlet editions, contending that abolitionism was not only dangerous to the Union but in fact a plot of entirely foreign and antidemocratic origin. He argued that vengeful British aristocrats commenced an assault on slavery soon after the American Revolution in order to crush democracy, safeguard their class privileges, and grind the poor through the machinery of finance and industrial capitalism. They targeted slavery for two reasons. First, they hoped to destroy the Union, a plan that nearly succeeded in 1850. Second, they knew that US slaveholders were "the originators of Democratic institutions on this continent." From George Washington to James Polk, Southern planters nourished American democracy by enlarging its territorial reach, refining its ideals, and empowering white workers. In sum, he argued, "every thing great or beneficial in our national history" came from Southern enslavers. Meanwhile, foes of democracy, from Alexander Hamilton to John Quincy Adams, plotted to erect a British-style class system by chartering a national bank, restricting territorial expansion, immiserating wage laborers, and using abolitionism to attack "the founders and true defenders of Democratic institutions." In this account, Samuel Johnson's observation that enslavers were the "loudest yelpers" for American independence was not proof of hypocrisy but a point of pride. Abolition would "annihilat[e]" the class that produced Jefferson, Jackson, and Calhoun and would therefore "be the greatest misfortune that could happen to mankind." Slavery made the Union the world's last bastion of democracy, so its ruin was the object for which "British aristocracy and European monarchists, their tools and instruments all over, everywhere, openly or covertly labor incessantly."[17]

Van Evrie turned the Slave Power thesis on its head. Far from supporting an aristocracy, slavery protected democracy by sustaining the only class that could defend common whites against the capitalists who conspired to oppress them. Attacks on slavery were attacks on democracy itself and could only be explained as part of a foreign plot against America's uniquely free institutions. Van Evrie extended the slavery-democracy connection far beyond two common themes of proslavery demagoguery: the psychological claim that Black servitude made white men feel equal, and the economic claim that slavery protected white workers from Black competition. For Van Evrie, slavery was the *only* safeguard for American democracy because it fostered a cadre of leaders who understood that class hierarchies among whites were unnatural and that white men must live as equals. In this view, protecting slavery was both patriotic and a matter of self-preservation.

Van Evrie's pamphlet also directly appealed to Anglophobia. After the American Revolution, whites of all regions regularly lambasted British enemies, whom they used as a negative reference point in forging a national identity. Anglophobia resonated especially powerfully in the South after slavery's abolition in the British Empire in 1834. For James H. Hammond, John C. Calhoun, and other Southern partisans, British abolitionists were hypocrites who diverted attention from their own downtrodden white laborers. They were imperialists who schemed to destroy competitors by undermining slavery in the United States and the Texas Republic. And they were rivals who contrived to demolish the Union by fanning sectional conflict. There was nothing new about proslavery Anglophobic rhetoric; indeed, by the 1850s it was, in the words of one historian, "shopworn."[18] But Van Evrie deployed it to persuade nationalistic Northerners.

What Van Evrie omitted from *Negroes and Negro Slavery*, moreover, was as important as what he included. As they grew more aggressive in the 1850s, Southern proslavery propagandists espoused ideas likely to alienate Northern readers. Van Evrie eschewed these arguments. Unlike polygenist provocateur Josiah Nott, for example, he did not needle pious Christians. In Van Evrie's view, scientists were interpreting God's will through polygenism, and he never claimed that polygenism displaced Biblical truth. Rather, he melded science and Christianity in his argument that Black people were natural slaves. Through frequent references to a "Creator," Van Evrie ventriloquized a proslavery God whose creations were perfectly suited to their roles. Abolitionists who demanded unnatural equality were the real heretics.[19]

Van Evrie also refused to make invidious regional comparisons. By the 1850s, many Southern proslavery writers argued for the superiority of their society, claiming that slavery was better than wage labor, Northern workers were more degraded than Southern slaves, and the South boasted a superior civilization. Some, like George Fitzhugh, even announced that white Northern workers would be better off as slaves; others bragged that white Southerners were racially superior to their Northern rivals. But Van Evrie rejected sectional chauvinism. He never deemed Northern society a failure. He never insulted Northern whites as mudsills.[20] And he flatly rebuked Southerners who claimed that Black slaves fared better than white operatives. Their "vital mistake" was comparing different species—truly confusing apples and oranges—and forgetting that Blacks and whites were designed for different purposes.[21] Race was all-important. Northern and Southern whites were racial equals; slavery was for racial inferiors. And while slavery was limited to regions where Black people thrived, it benefited the whole country. Thus, Van Evrie's defense of slavery never veered into Southern nationalism. Seeking to strengthen the Union, not inspire secession, he promoted slavery as an *American* institution and denounced abolitionism as a *foreign* scheme. He courted self-respecting Northerners disturbed by the turmoil of 1850—although this strategy would leave him ill-prepared for the crisis unleashed a decade later.

Van Evrie continued polishing *Negroes and Negro Slavery*, publishing a second edition with J. D. Toy and a final version with a New York printer. Most changes involved branding and marketing rather than content, but they demonstrated his penchant for self-promotion. Three features of the New York edition stand out. First, he added new endorsements. Two came from Southern politicians—J. Wofford Tucker and Thomas L. Clingman—and the third from Dr. Samuel Cartwright, a New Orleans physician who diagnosed enslaved people's freedom-seeking tendencies as a disease called drapetomania. Second, he placed scare quotes around *Slavery* in the title, using a sarcastic flourish to enliven a pet theory. Because nature decreed bondage for

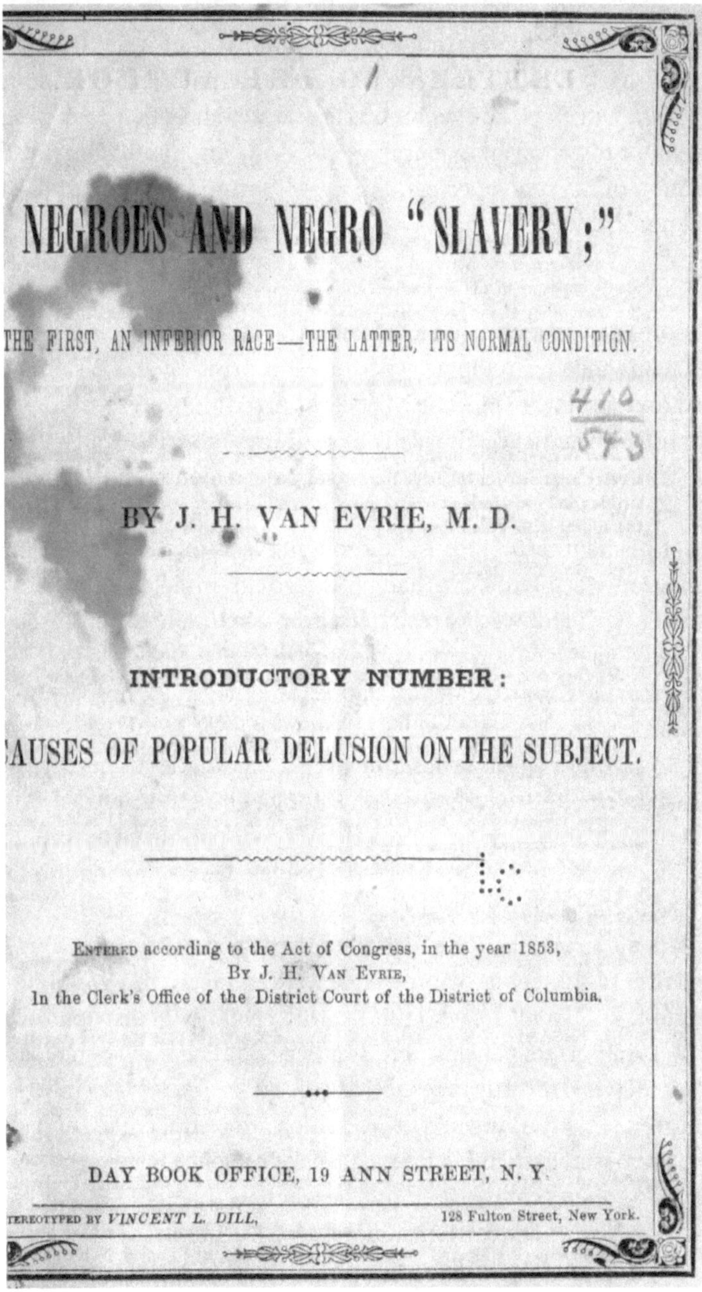
NEGROES AND NEGRO "SLAVERY;"

THE FIRST, AN INFERIOR RACE—THE LATTER, ITS NORMAL CONDITION.

410
543

BY J. H. VAN EVRIE, M. D.

INTRODUCTORY NUMBER:

CAUSES OF POPULAR DELUSION ON THE SUBJECT.

ENTERED according to the Act of Congress, in the year 1853,
BY J. H. VAN EVRIE,
In the Clerk's Office of the District Court of the District of Columbia.

DAY BOOK OFFICE, 19 ANN STREET, N. Y.

STEREOTYPED BY *VINCENT L. DILL,* 128 Fulton Street, New York.

Cover page of the final edition of John Van Evrie's breakthrough pamphlet, *Negroes and Negro "Slavery"* (1853), printed at Nathaniel Stimson's *New York Day Book* office.

Black people, he argued, it was not really slavery at all. He put the word in quotation marks for the rest of his career, making it part of his brand, a signature that marked each Van Evrie production. Finally, he found a printer in the *New York Day Book*, the venomous proslavery sheet that soon became the foundation of his publishing empire. Personally and professionally, the *Day Book* edition of *Negroes and Negro "Slavery"* portended Van Evrie's ascent to national notoriety.[22]

It took more than an active pen to become an author-hero; words had to reach readers. And while technological advances in printing and distribution unshackled texts from the plodding pace of horses and sailing ships, they did not guarantee an audience. But Van Evrie, always more innovative in promoting polygenism than developing the racist canon, contrived to broadcast his message as widely as possible. Combining authorial strategies with the resources of his Southern patrons, he brought *Negroes and Negro "Slavery"* to readers nationwide. By 1855, he had produced no miracles—Americans were more acutely divided over slavery than ever—but he had impressed admirers, provoked enemies, and won some converts.

Van Evrie maximized his work's appeal by making it broadly accessible. Here, a comparison to Nott and Gliddon's *Types of Mankind* is instructive. Readers unfamiliar with Amunoph IV or zygomatic arches likely found *Types*—all seven hundred pages—rather tough going. In contrast, while Van Evrie's writing had a scientific veneer, he avoided specialized terminology and confined his prose to a brisk thirty-two pages. He also made it affordable. *Types of Mankind* sold for five dollars at a time when skilled workers earned two dollars a day and unskilled laborers perhaps half as much. But *Negroes* cost just twenty-five cents.[23] Some readers even received it gratis, thanks to Washington, DC, sponsors who funded its free national distribution.[24]

The most important patrons were Southern politicians who mailed *Negroes and Negro "Slavery"* directly to recipients around the country. Members of Congress enjoyed the "franking privilege," which allowed them to send materials through the postal system for free. Eager to influence voters, they exercised this power so often that by the 1850s, nearly half the mail leaving Washington, DC, traveled under congressional frank.[25] And just as Van Evrie's elite Southern backers had sponsored composition of the *Negroes* essay, they used their franking power to subsidize its distribution. Some sent it to individual readers. Congressional representative John A. Quitman, for instance, disseminated the pamphlet during the fiercely contested 1856 presidential election. Naturally, he sent it to Mississippi constituents, but he also gifted copies to correspondents from Missouri to New York.[26] Other patrons funneled the pamphlet to newspaper editors, whose printed notices aided Van Evrie's marketing efforts. South Carolina fire-eater Laurence Keitt sent *Negroes and Negro "Slavery"* to editors in Abbeville, Lancaster, and Greenville, who gave it favorable reviews and valuable publicity.[27] Some editors printed lengthy extracts from the pamphlet, allowing readers to sample Van Evrie's work at no extra cost.[28] By 1856, these efforts had brought the *Negroes* pamphlet before a wide swath of the reading public.

Responses to *Negroes and Negro "Slavery"* followed predictable patterns that reflected the failure of Van Evrie's loftiest ambitions. He did change a few minds, and his devotees echoed his hope that the pamphlet would save the Union by demolishing abolitionism. But no single voice could unite a deeply polarized nation. Instead, proslavery and antislavery partisans took positions on Van Evrie's work that aligned with what they already believed. Van Evrie leveraged his esteem among proslavery propagandists into a lengthy career, but he could not stem the surge of popular antislavery that soon produced the Republican Party.

Southern reviewers read *Negroes* with delight. Channeling Thomas Carlyle, some hailed Van Evrie as a man-of-letters hero destined to transform Northern views of slavery. "There are times in the history of national politics," wrote a Mississippian, "that a single pen or a single tongue, fired with eloquence and logic, and inspired by the very spirit of truth, has wielded an influence so great as to turn the tide of public opinion, or change the policy of an Empire." Such was Van Evrie, author of "the ablest, most logical and lucid exposition and vindication" of slavery ever written.[29] Some Southern editors regretted Van Evrie's Biblical heterodoxy, but this did not smother their enthusiasm for his "most able defence of the institution of Southern Slavery."[30] Especially zealous promoters urged readers to help Van Evrie spread the proslavery gospel among benighted Northerners. A Mississippian deemed the pamphlet a "great work" and exhorted every "Southern man" to donate money, through his member of Congress, to Van Evrie's crusade.[31]

Similarly positive reviews came from a range of Washington, DC, newspapers. The *Daily Union*, a Pierce administration organ, endorsed the prediction that, if widely circulated, *Negroes and Negro "Slavery"* "could not fail to quiet the northern mind on the subject of southern negro slavery."[32] A few months later, the *National Intelligencer*, a Whig publication, deemed *Negroes* the most interesting recent work on slavery and encouraged Van Evrie to finish his book, reckoning that he could contribute more than any previous author "toward removing the most prominent cause of excitement and ill-feeling between the two great sections of our country."[33] Sympathetic Washington Whigs and Democrats alike believed heroism was within Van Evrie's reach.

Northern reviews were more divided. Moderates largely ignored the pamphlet, leaving proslavery and abolitionist partisans to debate it. Among the former, none surpassed the *New York Day Book* in promoting Van Evrie's fame. In a widely reprinted review of dubious objectivity, since the *Day Book* had printed the pamphlet's final edition, the editors applauded Van Evrie for unmasking abolitionism as a British plot and showing that slavery was "founded on the fact" of "natural inequality."[34] *Day Book* editors subsequently published several articles vindicating Van Evrie's "unassailable" thesis and scourging his detractors for swallowing the fallacy that "the negro, in everything but the color of his skin, is a white man."[35]

Abolitionists excoriated Van Evrie and his defenders. Setting an enduring pattern, they toggled between mocking Van Evrie's scientific pretensions and denouncing his barbaric politics. Frederick Douglass dismissed the *Day Book* editor as "shallow" and Van Evrie as "pompous," and denied that any abolitionist claimed that "the negro is a white man." Rather, abolitionists agreed with the Declaration of Independence that all men were equal.[36] As we will see, *Negroes* incited a ferocious editorial duel between Douglass and his *Day Book* rivals. Other antislavery writers blasted Van Evrie for ignoring slavery's brutality. Racial differences aside, did God authorize enslavers to "deprive the negro of education, to separate the wife from the husband and the husband from the wife, to rob the parent of his children, to ignore the ordinances of marriage, and to transform a man into a chattel?"[37] Blending outrage and derision, an Indianan skewered Van Evrie's acolytes for cribbing lines from his "picayune pamphlets."[38] Although they scorned his shoddy science, antislavery authors never assumed that everyone would see through Van Evrie's lies. A correspondent for *Frederick Douglass' Paper* deemed him an "infidel" and a "consummate blockhead," but warned that his pamphlet was circulating widely in western New York. Even in the Burned-Over District, an antislavery bastion, some people believed Van Evrie's "sophistries."[39]

How persuasive was Van Evrie's early proslavery proselytizing? Published responses suggest that he preached most effectively to the choir and did more to fuel existing polarization than to transform public opinion. Private reflections generally concur, but with some important caveats. Sympathetic readers welcomed Van Evrie into the proslavery pantheon. Consider Samuel Morse, whose contributions to telegraphy underscore the links between the communications revolution and proslavery politics. After reading an extract from *Negroes* in the *Day Book*, Morse requested a copy of the pamphlet and saluted Van Evrie's effort to make polygenism palpable to Northern Christians, deeming polygenist arguments "*impregnable*" because they were "founded on God's truth as clearly set forth in the Bible."[40] But some doubted Van Evrie's prospects for success. William O. Goode, a member of

Congress from Virginia, considered polygenism a "curious & interesting subject to the learned and inquisitive" and praised *Negroes* for outlining a fruitful agenda for "investigation and discussion." But he groused that no new installments had appeared by early 1855 and surmised that Van Evrie had abandoned the project. "The *work* has not been continued beyond the Pamphlet which you have read," he informed his father-in-law, for the "North is in a furor against the theory—& the *Readers* of the South do not exist in numbers to justify the publication."[41] Van Evrie had not actually thrown in the towel, but Goode's skepticism was reasonable, given that the completed *Negroes and Negro "Slavery"* volume would not appear for another six years.

Goode could not know that Van Evrie had persuaded some readers that slavery was natural. Proslavery Southerners needed little convincing on this point, of course, while abolitionists rejected it. But huge numbers of white Northerners were both racially prejudiced and uncomfortable with slavery, and it was among them that Van Evrie's propaganda could make a difference. A long reflection by John L. O'Sullivan reveals polygenism's devastating power to persuade. Born in 1813 to an American father and a British mother, O'-Sullivan founded the *United States Magazine and Democratic Review* in 1837 and commanded considerable influence, as shown in his popularization of the term "Manifest Destiny." An ardent expansionist who rejected abolitionists as radicals, O'Sullivan nevertheless once believed in the "Unity of the Human Race" and that Black people's "inferiority" was "merely temporary and accidental." From this, he had concluded that slavery was "wrongful oppression" and violated "the essential American Idea" of equality. But during scientific racism's banner year of 1853, he changed his mind. As he explained to Senator Stephen Douglas, O'Sullivan now accepted "the truth of that doctrine of *original diversity of species*, which has of late years been placed in a strong light by Agassiz, Van Amringe, Smith, Nott, Van Evrie, and others." He regarded "slavery to the superior race" as "a better as well as more natural relation" for Black people. And while a shelf of polygenist texts had persuaded O'Sullivan, Van Evrie's influence stood out when O'Sullivan used one of the ex-physician's catchphrases to describe his blunder: "I used to assume . . . that the Negro was merely a Black white man," he wrote, but now he deemed slavery "a great blessing."[42] Van Evrie failed to convert the nation in one heroic effort, but he added his quotable prose to a flood of propaganda that could numb guilty consciences and persuade wavering Northern whites that slavery was a positive good.

Van Evrie knew white Northerners best and soon returned to them. By late 1855, the transformation from physician to polemicist complete, he relocated to New York City. The main draw was the *Day Book*. In a letter to Jefferson Davis, Van Evrie explained his decision. "The slavery question *must be understood* at the North," he wrote, and "the New York Day Book talks right out on this Subject—it explains this thing to the people—it Shows that negro slavery is right." But it needed help. As "*the only paper* in the North" that was sound on slavery, it was isolated and financially fragile. Southern politicians, the Pierce administration, and the Democratic Party should provide patronage, Van Evrie urged, while he assisted by writing editorials.[43] This was a decisive step. Whatever he thought about the reception of his initial work, Van Evrie was not looking back. The propaganda war over slavery would not be won in a single battle, so he dug in for a siege. His headquarters was the office of the newspaper whose fate henceforth would be entwined with his own.

Chapter 6

Launch

The *New York Day Book* was infamous long before it came under John Van Evrie's control, although detractors were divided over what it was infamous *for.* Some rebuked its proslavery politics, others its partisanship. But many ridiculed the paper's finances. One deemed it a scruffy rag that "earns a scanty subsistence at the New-York Customs-House."[1] Why did critics consider this a devastating critique? And, if true, what does it reveal about the *Day Book*'s place in New York?

Antebellum tourists flocked to the intersection of Broad and Wall Streets, but not to see the New York Stock Exchange. Instead, they visited a Greek Revival building erected in 1842 to serve as the US Custom House for the Port of New York. Within this "showy edifice," noted one observer, "more than two thirds of the entire revenue of the United States is collected, where five thousand vessels are entered and cleared in a year, and where nearly two hundred millions of exports and imports are annually passed through their accounts." Despite its poor ventilation and cramped floor plan, the Custom House drew enormous crowds.[2]

People came for many reasons. Peddlers hawked snacks, tobacco, and newspapers. Merchants and mariners transacted business. Others either had or coveted a customs job. There was plenty of work to do: The nation's busiest port handled mountains of goods that had to be measured, counted, valued, tabulated, and paid for. Supervised by a presidentially appointed collector, the Custom House employed legions of deputy collectors, auditors, cashiers, bookkeepers, appraisers, clerks, guards, messengers, warehouse hands, weighers, measurers, gaugers, inspectors, and night inspectors.[3] But not everyone on the payroll spent much time on the job. Some positions existed to repay favors or recruit allies. For just as collectors processed millions of dollars in customs duties, they also handled vast quantities of the currency of antebellum politics: patronage. In an era when political parties rose on the scaffolding of patronage networks and the lure of public employment kept party loyalists in line, the Custom House was as much a hub of political power as of commerce.

By the 1850s, the Custom House had been a locus of party building for over a generation. First under William Crawford, treasury secretary for presidents James Madison and James Monroe, and then under President Andrew

Jackson, collectorships became prizes awarded to loyal lieutenants who packed the payroll with party stalwarts, donated campaign funds, and hustled for votes. Theoretically, rotation in office prevented incumbents from creating fiefdoms. Practically, it placed collectorships at the heart of the spoils system. Patronage ties between the White House and custom houses gave structure to the national political parties themselves.[4]

Given the enormous sums of money flowing through custom houses and the primacy of loyalty in appointments, the system became notorious for corruption. Partisans prowled for scandal and pounced on rivals' wrongdoing. After Democratic appointee Samuel Swartwout fled to England with $1 million filched from the New York Custom House, Whigs launched a congressional investigation and reaped the benefits in 1840 by capturing the presidency for the first time.[5] Two decades later, congressional Republicans led by Pennsylvania's John Covode spotlighted the New York Custom House in their probe into President James Buchanan's administration. They uncovered numerous vignettes of venality, including one involving William M. Browne, editor of the Democratic *Journal of Commerce*. Browne was hired at the Custom House by Buchanan-appointed collector Augustus Schell, but he never came to work. Republican investigators explained that this was a typical scheme: Appoint party hacks to remunerative positions during campaign season and immediately grant them leave to work full-time at electioneering. "This employment of the servants and moneys of the government in aiding elections," concluded the indignant Republicans, "is a palpable violation of law, and subversive of the rights and interests of the people." The report added a weapon to the Republican arsenal in time for Abraham Lincoln's presidential run.[6]

So, when John Van Buren—son of perhaps the wiliest wire-puller of all—denounced the *Day Book* for earning "a scanty subsistence at the New-York Customs-House," he meant no compliment.[7] Neither did the Maine editor who claimed that it "receives its sustenance from the New York Customs House."[8] In one phrase, critics indicted the *Day Book* for blind partisanship, fawning dependence, and felonious greed. Its editor was the servant of crooked masters, too unprincipled to speak his own mind and too untalented to earn his own living. But antebellum editors always slung mud at each other. What do these aspersions reveal about the *Day Book*, the mainstay of Van Evrie's poisonous career?

The accusations were truthful when made but are most revealing as synecdoche. In the mid-1850s, Custom House patronage salvaged the *Day Book*'s finances and brought it into the Democratic fold. But its roots in New York's commercial world ran much deeper. As a business venture, political mouthpiece, and media product, the *Day Book* flourished in a Northern city with close economic ties to the South. Nurtured by merchants and politicians determined to maintain a slaveholding Union that profited their city, the *Day Book* appeared in 1848, the same year that Van Evrie settled in Washington, DC. When he joined its staff seven years later, it was already a notorious proslavery journal. But the *Day Book*'s path twisted and turned—and its story presents some puzzles. Infamous for proslavery propaganda, the paper was founded by an antislavery activist. Best known as a Democratic organ, the *Day Book* first rose to prominence as a Whig journal. Closely tied to Northern merchants, the paper circulated more widely in the South. Only in the context of ruthless professional competition, wrenching political realignment, and the relentless pressures of the newspaper business does the story make sense. The *Day Book*'s early development, the subject of this chapter and the next, is essential to understanding Van Evrie's tenure with the North's most malicious proslavery paper.

Visitors who strolled from the Custom House up Nassau Street would, in ten minutes, reach the intersection of Spruce Street and Park Row. To the north was City Hall. To the west was Broadway. And all around stood four- and five-story brick buildings housing the businesses that, by 1860, comprised the city's largest industry. The signs gave them away: *Times*, *Herald*, *World*, *Tribune*. This was Newspaper Row. And at Park and Spruce, the offices of the city's leading papers clustered around Printing House Square.[9]

The area drew tourists, travel writers, and artists because it showcased the major dailies: the upstart *Times*, the mighty *Tribune*, and the colossal *Herald* with its world-leading 77,000 daily subscribers.[10] Despite their impressive circulations, prolific steam printing presses, and formidable news-gathering networks, these behemoths alone did not enable New York to produce nearly a third of the nation's publishing output.[11] In the shadows of these giants scurried smaller fry: scrappy, often short-lived enterprises that survived on job printing—one-time orders like broadsides or flyers—and their own publications, usually low-circulation weeklies. By the 1850s, scores of modest firms carved out market share by producing periodicals that served audiences defined by occupation, faith, ethnicity, or politics. Specialization meant fragmentation: subscribers chose the news they wanted and thereby sustained the myriad minor papers that lived and died in a harrowing media marketplace.[12]

Historians often attribute New York's publishing dominance to geographic and institutional advantages. Certainly, robust water and rail transportation, early establishment of regular packet service to Europe, extensive telegraphic networks, and the Associated Press all gave New York publishers an edge.[13]

But they also needed labor. By 1860, New York's publishing industry employed over five thousand people. As high-tech presses multiplied, much of the work formerly performed by expert printers fell to poorly paid unskilled laborers.[14] Yet before the printing stage, other workers, culturally elevated but professionally precarious, generated the content. In antebellum New York, much of this creative work was done by hordes of aspiring author-heroes inhabiting a literary underworld that was more squalid than bohemian. Passably educated but lacking entrée into the belletristic elite, hack writers lived hard and worked sporadically, cycling between feverish output, enforced idleness, and intoxicated languor. Seedy and cerebral, mercenary and idealistic, this reserve army of scriveners attracted recruits with the lure of literary triumph in the republic's cultural capital. As novelist Elizabeth Drew Stoddard told young journalist Manton Marble, New York was *the* place for "literary vagabonds."[15]

Some wandering wordsmiths did well. The career of George Goodrich Foster reveals the symbiosis between writer and milieu. Probably born in Vermont around 1814, Foster dabbled in journalism and poetry before wandering through Pittsburgh, Mobile, and St. Louis. Along the way, he edited newspapers, promoted Whig and nativist politics, played flute in a theater orchestra, and dreamed of returning east. By 1848, he had settled in New York and signed on with Horace Greeley's *Tribune*, where he captivated readers with word sketches of his nighttime rambles through the slums. A resident-observer of New York's netherworld, Foster chronicled with sympathetic candor the sin and suffering endemic in the city's poorest wards. Compiled in an 1849 volume entitled *New York in Slices*, the vignettes documented harsh truths, and readers wanted more. Foster responded with *New York by Gas-Light* (1850), which earned him the nickname "Gaslight," an allusion to the flickering nocturnal cityscape he captured in prose. Yet success brought neither contentment nor stability. Foster moved to Philadelphia and was arrested for forgery. After a brief incarceration, he returned to journalism and married Julie de Marguerites, an opera singer and music critic, before dying in April 1856.[16]

Few vagabonds equaled Foster's success, but many shared his failings. Take Samuel J. Anderson. Born in Georgia around 1811, Anderson snagged an impressive series of appointments: private secretary to Governor George W. Crawford of Georgia, a War Department chief clerkship under President Zachary Taylor, and a deputy sheriff's post in New York City. His Confederate sympathies led to his incarceration in 1861, however, and after his release, Anderson drifted, just another face in the crowd of underemployed litterateurs. He dabbled in atheism and Lost Cause apologetics, wrote sycophantic letters to fallen Confederate luminaries, and subsisted on hack work for newspapers. Eventually, he landed a job in the city comptroller's office and leaked evidence that helped topple Boss Tweed in 1871. That same year, Anderson made his first suicide attempt when he slashed his throat with a razor. Broke and despondent, he moved to Atlanta and tried to wheedle money from former Confederate general Robert Toombs. After exhausting Toombs's patience, Anderson penned a self-serving note, bit down on a revolver barrel, and fired.[17]

Somewhere between Foster's celebrity and Anderson's self-annihilation was the turbulent career of A. F. Banks. The author of an 1883 Beadle dime novel, he left few other traces outside the diary of Thomas Butler Gunn, an English-born writer and artist who caroused with Walt Whitman and Thomas Nast. A swollen, bearded man who reeked of cheap beer and tobacco, Banks irked his companions in both good times and bad. While employed on Wall Street, he flaunted his cash and bragged about his next book. After being fired and losing his book deal, he begged for charity. When another author thrashed Banks in a nighttime brawl on Broadway, Gunn hoped that the experience would chasten him. It did—briefly. But Banks relapsed. He resented other writers' success, angled for work at the *Tribune*, mooched off mistresses, and marveled at how crinolines concealed signs of pregnancy. Gunn wrote him off as "improvident, cracked, deboshed, good-humored, egotistic, offensive, the greatest of bores," and predicted that he would "die in a garret and be buried by contribution."[18]

These were the self-promoting and self-destroying scribblers who filled the mediocre pages that poured from Manhattan presses. Foster, Anderson, and Banks followed different paths but had much in common. They were white men with enough education to make headway as writers and secure other work when needed. They brimmed with desire and entitlement. And all three, during their long careers in the literary demimonde, wrote for the *New York Day Book*.

Dr. David Francis Bacon was an unlikely entrant into this rowdy world when he founded the *Day Book* in 1848. Born to pious New Englanders, he imbibed their reformist spirit, but his flesh was weak. He binged on alcohol. He squandered money. And as he went to ruin, a rival wrested the *Day Book* from his shaky hands. Soon, the newspaper that Bacon launched as a vehicle for progress veered into proslavery propaganda.

Bacon's parents dreamed of spreading Yankee virtues across the nation. First as missionaries to Native Americans in Michigan and then as settlers in Ohio's Western Reserve, they sought to build outposts of New England civilization, new cities upon hills to inspire the world. Babies arrived regularly, but the Bacons were more prolific than prosperous and eventually retreated to Connecticut. Amid this disappointed idealism, David Francis was born in 1813. His father died four years later.[19]

Leonard, David's elder brother by eleven years, became his primary paternal figure. Educated at Yale and Andover Theological Seminary, Leonard championed numerous causes, including colonization: the scheme to transport free-born and formerly enslaved Black Americans to Africa. When founded in 1817, the American Colonization Society (ACS) was led by Upper South enslavers. Over time, however, colonization's center of gravity moved to the Northeast, where white reformers hoped to dismantle a sinful institution and spread Christianity in Africa. Two events heralded this shift: the appointment of Congregationalist minister Ralph Randolph Gurley as ACS secretary in 1825 and the nearly simultaneous publication of Leonard Bacon's July 4, 1825, sermon *A Plea for Africa*. Bacon denounced slavery for scourging the bodies, dulling the intellects, and blighting the souls of enslaved people, but he and Gurley shrank from immediate abolition. They believed in Black people's humanity but could not envision an integrated free society. They presumed to know what was best for Black people on two continents but ignored Black neighbors who wanted to remain in their homes.[20]

Leonard saw in pro-colonization journalism an outlet for his younger brother's energy and an opportunity to counter the immediate abolitionists, who were expertly using the press to denounce the ACS. In 1834, Leonard established a weekly colonizationist organ, the *Journal of Freedom*, and installed his twenty-one-year-old brother as editor.[21] David Francis soon left to study at Yale, where he earned a medical degree in March 1836, but he remained committed to colonization. Three months after graduation, he applied for the position of colonial physician in Liberia. "I have for several years steadfastly maintained the determination to make Africa the scene and the occasion of the best efforts of my best days," wrote Dr. Bacon, and he pledged "to do my utmost for the interests of the society and colony."[22] His flurry of follow-up letters showed that Bacon wanted the Liberian post more than anything in the world.[23]

Bacon sailed to Liberia immediately after receiving the prized appointment, but his two years there were profoundly disillusioning.[24] The colony, he reported, was impoverished and ravaged by disease. Established colonists robbed and abused recent arrivals. Worst of all, ACS agents speculated in slave trading, shipping African captives "to be worked and whipped to death on the sugar plantations of Cuba."[25] First in private letters to Leonard and later in exposés reprinted by abolitionists like William Lloyd Garrison and Frederick Douglass, David Francis unmasked ACS criminality.[26]

Bacon returned in 1839 disgusted with the ACS but brimming with vitality—he was not yet twenty-six—and moral fervor. His new passion was politics. Bacon plunged into Whig campaigning, hailing Henry Clay as the champion of light, truth, and the protective tariff. He exchanged letters with leading Whigs, including former president John Quincy Adams.[27] In 1844, he gained notoriety by crowning Whigs, not Democrats, as Thomas Jefferson's true political heirs.[28] Allies praised his partisanship as "ardent and uncompromising," while foes ridiculed it as "violent" and "hare-brained."[29] But everyone saw his sincerity.

For diehard partisans, journalism offered one way to make a living while serving the cause. Given Bacon's experience with the *Journal of Freedom*, it was logical for him to identify newspaper work as "just what I have been seeking for eight years"—ever since his dispiriting departure from Liberia.[30] So, a few months ahead of Van Evrie, Bacon swapped the lancet for the pen. On January 3, 1848, as politicians girded for the presidential campaign, Bacon unveiled the *New York Day Book*. From an office in the converted South Baptist Church building at 84 Nassau Street, a few blocks southwest of Printing House Square, Bacon unwittingly laid the foundation for Van Evrie's proslavery crusade.[31]

The *Day Book*'s name reflected its mercantile emphasis, which persisted through all its later evolutions. It referred to a standard tool for double-entry bookkeeping: Merchants and clerks used day books to record transactions as they occurred, later transferring the data to ledgers for tracking profits and losses.[32] Day books were so ubiquitous that they became a metonym for their users, much like plows for farmers or anvils for blacksmiths. Thus one member of the Odd Fellows fraternal order imagined others leaving work to attend lodge night: "The physician, turning from his well cared for patients; the lawyer, leaving his papers and his clients; the accountant, securely locking up his day book and ledger; the student, quitting his abstruse studies, all wend their way to the genial lodge room."[33] And since day books contained the freshest records, the name was perfect for a newspaper. Other papers used monikers like "chronicle," "journal," or "transcript" to flaunt the currency of their contents; Bacon made a similar point, and added an allusion to New York's bustling commerce, by choosing "day book." Indeed, a century before Alan Barth called news the "rough draft of history," Governor Alexander Ramsey of Minnesota Territory proclaimed that "newspapers are the day books of history."[34] Along with its waggish motto, "Principle and Interest," the *Day Book*'s name affirmed its Whiggish dedication to lively content, timely commercial news, and moral rectitude. And since nine-tenths of New York's merchants were Whigs, Bacon targeted a robust local subscriber base.[35]

The *Day Book* immediately attracted attention. One fellow editor deemed Bacon's sheet a "promising" journal. A more exuberant observer, writing just twelve days after the *Day Book* commenced publication, named it "one of the most interesting dailies ever published in this city."[36] By year's end, Bacon had snagged his first three congressional subscribers, all Whigs: Green Adams (Kentucky), Andrew S. Fulton (Virginia), and Washington Hunt (New York).[37]

The *Day Book* punched above its weight thanks to Bacon's unique background and lofty connections. In July 1848, he printed his shocking chronicles of ACS-backed slave trading. These articles thrilled abolitionist editors, who devoted considerable column space to reprinting them. Bacon was no abolitionist, but this, they shrewdly noted, only made his exposé more devastating.[38] Later, during a cholera outbreak, editors copied Bacon's expert commentary on the terrifying disease.[39] Yet, in the presidential election year of 1848, it was Bacon's political content that made the biggest splash. His cleverest move was to republish a sensational letter written to Edmund P. Gaines by Whig frontrunner and eventual nominee Zachary Taylor. The "Gaines Letter" put the *Day Book* on the journalistic map.

Taylor's letter, like his presidential prospects, stemmed from his service in the Mexican-American War. After commanding and winning the Battle of Monterrey in September 1846, Taylor accepted an extended armistice and lingered in northern Mexico, despite intense pressure from President James K. Polk, a Democrat, to press southward. Seething, Taylor penned a letter to Gaines, a fellow officer, in which he justified the armistice and accused Polk of withholding supplies and reinforcements.[40]

Back home, Bacon and other Whigs resented Polk's attacks on Taylor as politically motivated. Bacon was also an intimate friend of Edmund and Myra Clark Gaines, who consulted him on everything from their daughter's education to Myra's remarkably protracted, fifty-seven-year legal battle over her father's estate.[41] When Gaines showed him Taylor's letter, Bacon recognized its value and, with Gaines's blessing, gave it to the *New York Express*, which printed a slightly redacted version on January 22, 1847. It caused an immediate sensation: Rival Manhattan papers reprinted the letter in their evening editions, and other journals, from *Niles' Weekly Register* to the *Weekly Arkansas Gazette*, published it soon after. Bacon's role in the leak quickly became public knowledge as well.[42]

Weeks after launching the *Day Book*, Bacon printed an unexpurgated version of the Gaines letter.[43] It revealed few new facts but garnered widespread attention by reviving a controversy whose significance rose with Taylor's presidential prospects. Scores of papers reprinted the letter, tantalizing readers with headlines about "suppressed passages" finally seeing daylight. Crucially, they identified its source as the "paper edited by Dr. Francis Bacon, who brought before the public the famous letter of Gen. Taylor to Gen. Gaines."[44]

Yet all was not well in the *Day Book* office. Timely leaks and shocking exposés boosted visibility but did not guarantee viability. Editing a newspaper meant running a business, and Bacon struggled to keep creditors at bay. Between money troubles and alcoholic demons, his proprietorship was tenuous—and a usurper waited in the wings.

Deft prose and political passion were necessary but not sufficient for success in antebellum journalism. Editors needed money. Bacon struggled from the start and never secured enough advertising revenue, subscription sales, and political patronage to achieve financial stability. Already in November 1848, he struggled to meet payroll expenses and anticipated suspending publication. Indeed, Bacon's finances were so disordered that his landlord cut off his credit for board.[45] A few days later, Bacon reported that benefactors had pledged $500 to sustain him until subscription revenue increased.[46]

The recovery was only temporary, however, and Bacon's fortunes collapsed the following summer. In an August 1849 letter to his brother Leonard, David projected optimism but added a long list of liabilities, including $600 for office rent, which reflected acute anxiety. Nor could he conceal the truth revealed in his ragged penmanship. Formerly inelegant but tidy, it had devolved into a loose scrawl, likely because of worsening alcohol abuse.[47] Then his creditors began hounding Leonard.[48] Alarmed and ashamed, David hinted that another loan might enable him to right the ship. Like a gambler begging for one more throw of the dice, David hoped to escape what he aptly called "the frequent and complicated pecuniary embarrassments of this desperate newspaper enterprise."[49]

While Bacon floundered, a villain lurked nearby. He appeared in one of David's reports: "Mr. Stimson seems to think now that the Day-Book will survive."[50] His judgment impaired by liquor, wishful thinking, or both, Bacon never suspected that this false friend would betray him and transform the paper into the proslavery organ that propelled John Van Evrie's career.

Nathaniel R. Stimson was another Northerner who dabbled in antislavery politics and stumbled into journalism. Born in Greene County, New York, in 1815, he moved to New York City and clerked for Arthur and Lewis Tappan, the silk merchants who bankrolled the abolitionist press and cofounded the American Anti-Slavery Society.[51] According to one source, Stimson shared their views. During the horrific anti-abolition riots of 1834, Stimson allegedly risked death to carry food to George Thompson, a British abolitionist sheltering in the Tappans' store.[52] Yet Van Evrie later claimed it was Stimson's experience with the Tappans that "first conceived that mortal hatred to Abolitionism which finally became a part of his very being."[53] Both stories could be true: Stimson might have changed his mind about slavery while working for the Tappans. If so, he changed it completely.

Stimson eventually entered business for himself, but his aspirations crumbled under the grinding depression that followed the Panic of 1837. A venture with John V. Richardson and John C. Van Epps dissolved as the partners quarreled over paying debts and dividing their property.[54] Two years later, Stimson filed for bankruptcy under the same statute that Van Evrie used in Ohio.[55] Stimson subsequently founded a new silk and dry goods firm in Brooklyn.[56] But by 1848, it had closed and Stimson pivoted into journalism.[57]

How Stimson connected with Bacon is obscure, but their relationship quickly soured, and, in August 1849, Stimson departed to start his own newspaper. Perhaps he despised Bacon's antislavery stance. Maybe he smelled blood as creditors closed in and Bacon reached for the bottle. Whatever his thinking, Stimson was not simply a fledgling leaving the nest: The name of his paper and the location of his office issued a direct challenge to his old boss. Stimson set up shop at 82 Nassau Street, adjacent to Bacon, and called his paper the *Merchant's Day Book*. A bemused New Orleans correspondent correctly predicted "terrific warfare" between them.[58] Indeed, their professional duel soon spilled into the courtroom. Later that month, Stimson sued Bacon for libel (a legal weapon commonly wielded by editors), and Bacon responded in kind in October.[59] But the countersuit commenced amid Bacon's professional death throes. Swamped by debts topping $10,000, Bacon could not compete with the ruthless upstart who had all but stolen his newspaper's name from the masthead. The very day his own libel suit appeared in the press, Bacon closed the *Day Book* and retreated into medicine, eventually finding work as resident physician at the Astor House Hotel.[60] Stimson used the *Merchant's Day Book* name for another year, but by late 1850, he had claimed the *New York Day Book* moniker as the spoils of victory.[61]

When a census taker visited his home that year, Stimson seemed to have prevailed. Not yet thirty-five, he lived in Queens with his wife Helen and three small children. Their household also included three Irish adults, likely servants.[62] Yet his firm was capitalized at only $8,000, relied on a manual printing press, and employed sixteen hands whose monthly wages totaled $500, while subscriptions brought in only $583. Could Stimson channel his simmering anti-abolitionism into a product capable of surviving in the vicious arena of New York journalism?[63]

Chapter 7

Survival

Not everything changed when Nathaniel R. Stimson purloined the *New York Day Book* from its hapless founder. Along with the newspaper's name, Stimson preserved its commercial focus and Whig allegiance. Stimson's key employees were also Whigs, including George "Gaslight" Foster, the former *Tribune* columnist and ardent admirer of Henry Clay.[1] As the paper gained traction, it became universally recognized as a Whig organ; two-thirds of its congressional subscribers in 1851–52 were Whigs.[2] Yet Stimson's Whiggery differed significantly from David Francis Bacon's. Bacon supported the party's antislavery wing, led in New York by Senator William H. Seward and the wily editor Thurlow Weed. Stimson joined many merchants in backing the conservative anti-abolitionist wing, known in New York as "Silver Grays." Northern Whigs were approaching an explosive rupture.[3]

Their discord intensified at midcentury amid mounting sectional conflict. Like Van Evrie, who was then studying politics and polygenism in Washington, DC, Stimson watched politicians lob insults, hurl threats, and debate Union-saving nostrums in the tense summer of 1850. Sewardites cheered as their champion indicted slavery for violating a "higher law than the Constitution," while Silver Grays lauded Daniel Webster as a patriotic peacemaker.[4] Stimson, like Van Evrie, responded to the strife by redoubling his commitment to a proslavery Union. Tracing this story requires keeping Stimson and the *Day Book* at center stage. In the uneasy aftermath of the Compromise of 1850, Stimson found the scoop of a lifetime. In one infamous editorial, he carved out the proslavery niche that defined the *Day Book*'s business model and political agenda. Thereafter, Stimson built the paper into the ideal mouthpiece for Van Evrie's brand of polygenist proslavery nationalism.

The 1850 crisis horrified Stimson's readers. Open any copy of the Stimson-era *Day Book* and the contents evoke his target audience: Southern cotton planters and New York merchants. If Van Evrie fixated on the political interdependence of Southern planters and the Northern working class, Stimson focused on the economic interdependence of Southern planters and Northern business leaders. Consider the issue of January 19, 1852. Like most antebellum papers, it comprised four pages, with the first and last devoted to advertisements. In the *Day Book*, advertisements catered to the affluent. Ads for upscale theaters, stylish clothiers, and elegant hotels promised cosmopolitan New Yorkers the pleasures of conspicuous consumption. Shipping schedules, including for the New York–Liverpool line, spotlighted global trade. Notices from insurance brokers, attorneys, and bankers connected merchants to the professionals who kept commerce humming. Other listings appealed to prosperous Southerners. Ads for imported "Fancy Goods"—perfume, brandy, and fine fabrics—ran alongside announcements from merchants who specialized in "the Southern trade" and supplied the crude tools and coarse cloth that maintained enslaved people's basic subsistence.

Pages two and three featured content tailored for this audience. The lead editorial in that January 19 issue touted Daniel Webster's presidential aspirations. A letter from Boston correspondent "G. B." echoed this appeal, hailing Webster's Seventh of March speech—which had delighted friends and enraged foes of slavery by endorsing the Fugitive Slave Bill—and lauding him as "the champion of the Constitution and the supporter of the compromise." News items emphasized Manhattan happenings and commercial intelligence: an announcement for a poetry recital at the Mercantile Library Association, updates on local real estate deals, and analysis of the financial implications of the new French constitution. On page three, readers found stock quotes, commodity prices, and appraisals of Manhattan's business climate. Opera reviews, a regular *Day Book* feature, exemplified its highbrow cultural content.[5]

Stimson's paper *attracted* Southern planters and New York merchants with its commercial news and proslavery editorials. But it also *connected* these readers by facilitating interregional communication. Stimson solicited advertisements from merchants who specialized in the Southern trade, boasting that the *Day Book* had the largest Southern circulation of any New York paper.[6] Van Evrie later followed suit with appeals "To Business Men," in which he trumpeted the *Day Book*'s advantages for New York merchants, "especially those engaged in the southern trade."[7] Southerners also used the *Day Book* to communicate, placing ads for plantations and slave auctions that ran alongside dry goods notices and shipping timetables.[8] Given its large circulation in the South and among New Yorkers who traded with the South, *Day Book* editors aptly deemed the paper "the organ of that [Southern] trade in the great metropolis of the Union."[9]

Yet this boast inadvertently revealed a vulnerability in Stimson's business model and his political and economic vision. Like generations of later historians, Stimson understood the importance of the economic ties between New York and the cotton South. But the 1850 crisis underscored the fragility of the political framework within which that trade operated. Economic links did not guarantee political harmony. Political estrangement, even short of disunion, could upset the flows of cotton and credit that made so many fortunes in Manhattan and Mississippi. From conversations with merchant neighbors and the elite Southerners who visited New York every year, Stimson sensed the political strain on their economic relationship.

Consider white Southern views of New York merchants. Even if he discounted the secession rhetoric that reverberated across the South in 1850 as mere gasconade, Stimson had reason to fret about commercial disruptions. Whenever sectional conflict intensified, Southerners decried Manhattan's commercial predominance and called for direct trade between Southern ports and Europe. In the late 1830s, riled by abolitionist activism and insurrection scares, Southern planters and merchants held a series of commercial conventions that promoted direct trade. The cotton states, proclaimed delegates to the 1837 Augusta convention, "never can be practically independent and enjoy the full measure of the bounties which Providence has so abundantly provided for them" until their commerce was "carried on by our own merchants." They never should have let outsiders divert cotton into the "circuitous route" through Manhattan. Profits skimmed by New York merchants resembled tribute levied by a "foreign jurisdiction." In a deliberately provocative appeal, the Augusta assemblage urged white Southerners to shatter "the shackles of our commercial dependence" on New York.[10]

These calls reverberated again after New Orleans editor James D. B. De Bow revived the direct-trade discussion in a series of *De Bow's Review* articles in 1847.[11] Amid endless wrangling over slavery in the territories, white Southerners fantasized about waging economic warfare against the North. Whether this meant temporary boycotts or sustained direct trade with Europe, as envisioned at an Old Point Comfort, Virginia, convention in July 1850, dreams of commercial autonomy enchanted many enslavers just as Stimson launched a newspaper devoted to cross-sectional partnership. And these visions persisted after the Compromise of 1850. Though outright secessionists were defeated, fresh calls for boycotts echoed across the South, nourished by antipathy for what South Carolina representative Isaac Holmes called the "wealthy and overgrown city of New York."[12] For white Southerners agitated by antislavery and envious of Yankee prosperity, New York merchants' central role in cotton trading looked less like complicity and more like parasitism.

Meanwhile, New York merchants were neither unified nor secure in their power. Some, to be sure, were devoted to a system that remained extremely lucrative through the 1850s. Cotton cultivation kept expanding, most dramatically in Texas, and Southern-oriented merchants continued to make a killing. Rattled by the midcentury crisis, they and their allies in the press exalted compromise and condemned abolitionists as lunatics. New York's "merchants, men of business, and men of property," screamed the *Herald*, "should frown down the meetings of these madmen, if they would save themselves!"[13] After the passage of compromise legislation in September, these merchants, led by Moses Taylor and Henry Grinnell, organized the Union Safety Committee to enforce Northern compliance. This involved everything from backing pro-compromise candidates to raising legal funds for an enslaver seeking to recover Henry Long, an alleged fugitive apprehended in New York, whose own attorney's fees were paid by the New York Anti-Slavery Society. This merchant subcommunity promoted increasingly reactionary politics to maintain the Union and keep Southern commerce flowing through their harbor.[14]

Other merchants doubted that their future pointed to the South. Some sensed that commerce in the West would soon challenge the Southern trade's supremacy. First by water, once the Erie Canal was completed in 1825, and then by rail, bounteous flour, lumber, and meat from the Northwest entered New York's commercial orbit. By the 1850s, growing numbers of merchants specialized in this trade, exporting western commodities and importing finished goods for sale in Cleveland, Detroit, and Chicago. California's Gold Rush lured their attention even farther west as ballooning Pacific Coast demand energized New York's economy. Others invested in manufacturing. Shipbuilding, garment-making, and other industries financed by merchant capital took off in the 1850s. By 1860, New York ranked first and Brooklyn (still a separate municipality) fifth among American cities in value of manufactured goods, and the metropolitan area produced nearly 15 percent of the country's industrial output. Industrialization weakened merchants' political dominance, both by swelling the ranks of a restive working class and by driving a wedge between merchants—who valued free trade and sectional harmony—and manufacturers, who welcomed protective tariffs and were less deferential to the Slave Power.[15] Political divisions between North and South *and* within New York City frightened those who hoped that the Compromise of 1850 would safeguard a proslavery Union.

Against this backdrop of anxious interdependence and mutual mistrust, Stimson stormed into national headlines. On October 15, shortly after the compromise measures became law, *Day Book* readers encountered an article with a clumsy title and an explosive message: "New York Merchants and the South—Their Relation to Each Other, and Their Duty to the Union." Addressing Southern planters, politicians, and journalists, Stimson announced that "you are deceived by your own merchants." New York was a "den of deception and trickery" where business leaders fattened on Southern trade while supporting antislavery fanatics like Seward and Greeley. He advised boycotting specific merchants until they stopped assailing the labor system that underwrote their profits. And he named names, listing a dozen merchants, Southern trade specialists all, with secret antislavery sympathies. "Don't be startled, Mr. Southern Press," Stimson concluded, with a teasing allusion to future revelations. "The Day-Book has not half done."[16]

Stimson's sizzling exposé was widely reprinted and acutely polarizing. Antislavery editors reviled him as an opportunistic publicity hound. The *National Era*, which soon serialized *Uncle Tom's Cabin*, denounced the *Day Book* as a "contemptible Black Mail concern," while an antislavery Ohio Whig decried the "palpable injustice" of Stimson's ambush.[17] The article became so notorious that critics could refer to the *Day Book* as "the paper that lately sold itself to slaveholders" without further explanation.[18] Years later, they remembered how the *Day Book* had "sprung up out of the miasmatic filth of the Compromise of 1850, like a toad-stool on a manure heap."[19] Less quotable but potentially more damaging was a rebuttal published by the New York *Courier and Enquirer* and reprinted in antislavery periodicals, which highlighted Stimson's political background and condemned him as a rank extortionist. Addressed to proslavery Southerners, the editorial urged them to ignore the slanderous *Day Book*. It recalled Stimson's past ties to Arthur and Lewis Tappan, the abolitionist silk merchants, and claimed that he planned to profit from the exposé by wooing Southern subscribers and blackmailing Northern victims. According to "one of the best known gentlemen in our city," Stimson had "stated . . . *that it was his intention to attack the most distinguished persons in the City to make his paper known; and he attempted to extort money from him under a threat of being denounced!*"[20]

Ecstatic Southern editors ignored these warnings and encouraged readers to embrace the *Day Book* as an ally operating behind enemy lines, a proslavery organ lodged in the heart of the nation's communication network. A Missourian applauded Stimson's "spirited and fearless" stance, while a Mississippian jeered merchants' panicked reaction to the indictment.[21] Some editors who favored boycotting Northern newspapers made an exception for the *Day Book*, which had "taken, upon the Slavery question, a bold, fearless and determined stand for the South." For planters who needed New York commercial news, the *Day Book* was the only suitable option.[22]

Southern responses undoubtedly lifted Stimson's spirits. They portended a boost in subscriptions and showed that Southern fans appreciated his business model and political agenda. The *Day Book* would not only connect Southern planters to Northern merchants; it would also preserve their economic partnership by strengthening its political foundation. More than a tawdry bid for Southern patronage, the article was an attempt to police New York's fractious merchant community. It announced that mere acquiescence to the Compromise of 1850 was not enough. Stimson would solidify the alliance between New York and the cotton states by advocating slavery as a positive good in order to dissuade Southerners from pursuing direct trade or disunion.

Hereafter, he would espouse a fiery proslavery ideology and demand that local merchants toe the line.

Stimson thus tied the *Day Book*'s future as a commercial newspaper to the success of its political campaign to make proslavery a national creed. He proclaimed himself the guardian of a partnership buffeted by political strife, Northern diversification, and Southern separatism. That partnership depended on preserving political harmony, which Stimson concluded must rest on the positive good of slavery. This meant mass conversion of white Northern opinion. Stimson's campaign continued to evolve, most notably after he hired Van Evrie in 1855, but already in late 1850 Southern proslavery zealots recognized the *Day Book* as a kindred spirit.

Stimson had charted a perilous course. If he pushed too hard against wayward merchants, he risked alienating local supporters and undermining the Union by stoking the fears of white Southerners. Pull back too far, however, and he might lose Southern favor. Eventually, his political project *did* fail, the economic link *did* break, and secession *did* nearly pull the *Day Book* down with the Union. But this was in the unknowable future when Stimson rushed to capitalize on his new notoriety as a Manhattan man with proslavery principles.

Stimson's gambit initially produced predictable results. Profits from Southern celebrityhood mitigated losses from the Northern backlash, but the *Day Book* remained precarious because the material demands of newspaper proprietorship were unrelenting. He soon discovered that public patronage might be the only basis for financial stability.

Eager to burnish his reputation, Stimson embarked on a widely publicized tour of Southern cities in the winter of 1850–51. While visiting Petersburg, Wilmington, Savannah, and Augusta, he circulated a *Day Book* prospectus titled "A Southern Press in New York."[23] Speaking through the Southern editors who chronicled his journey, Stimson announced his intention to improve his proslavery propaganda by seeing the institution firsthand. En route, he penned a series of letters, published in the *Day Book* and reprinted in *De Bow's Review* and other Southern periodicals, that echoed the core clichés of positive good ideology: Contented slaves lived better than Northern laborers; manumission was impossible; Northern do-gooders should help needy neighbors instead of meddling in the South.[24] He also wanted to drum up subscriptions, a goal that colleagues in the South supported. Upon Stimson's arrival, a Savannah editor welcomed him as a "staunch friend of all Southern interests" and advised readers to take the *Day Book*.[25] A Wilmingtonian added that because the paper had "lost ground at home by its advocacy of Southern rights," it merited "the patronage of the South."[26]

Stimson's Southern sojourn was a triumphal march through a region where his proslavery views were an asset rather than a liability. But his finances remained tenuous. *Day Book* circulation languished at two thousand subscribers. At $5 each, they generated only $833 in monthly revenue.[27] Desperate, Stimson visited Washington to seek President Millard Fillmore's aid. Unable to secure an interview, Stimson wrote a plaintive letter recounting his immense personal investment in the *Day Book*, bemoaning the Northern backlash against his merchant exposé, and pleading for a job in the New York Custom House.[28] Fillmore ignored him. By fall 1851, Stimson was begging the Union Safety Committee for money.[29] Facing a hostile hometown audience and a pitiless media marketplace, Stimson needed patronage. But those with the most to give, including a president from his own party, were less than generous.

Stimson found hope in the upcoming presidential contest. He knew that the Whigs would clash over the nominee, with Silver Grays confronting Sewardites in New York. If Stimson backed a candidate who could win the nomination and prevail in the general election, he could gorge on printing contracts and other goodies that would flow from the public trough. And, like many other New Yorkers, he picked Daniel Webster as his man.

Conservative business leaders in the Northeast had idolized Webster for years and now rallied to him as a Union candidate who could conciliate the South and crush antislavery agitators. Formerly a Massachusetts senator and now secretary of state, Webster thrilled his acolytes with his support for compromise legislation in 1850 and subsequent calls for rigorous enforcement of the Fugitive Slave Act and retaliation against Whig dissenters. New Yorkers concerned about Southern trade flocked to his standard. Three weeks after the March 7 speech, Manhattan merchants gifted Webster a gold chain to honor his Unionism. Eleven months later, another contingent upped the ante by presenting him with a carriage and a team of horses. By 1852, many merchants agreed that with Webster atop the ticket, "the triumph of the Whig party would be assured."[30]

Stimson was one of Webster's earliest and warmest advocates. He plastered Webster's name on the *Day Book* masthead in January 1852, organized rallies to promote his nomination, and briefly ran a second paper, the *New York Unionist*, as a Webster campaign sheet.[31] He also assailed Whig rivals. He condemned Sewardites as fanatics whose pretended Unionism was "trash."[32] Supporters of military hero Winfield Scott were either covert abolitionists or ignorant dupes. Like many conservative Whigs, Stimson detested Scott's evasiveness on the Compromise of 1850 and worried that his nomination would lead New York merchants to vote for Franklin Pierce, the Democrat running on a pro-compromise platform.[33] After Scott triumphed at the party's Baltimore convention, Stimson defiantly endorsed Webster as an independent candidate and spent the fall promoting Webster's "Independent Union Whig Ticket." Alas, Webster's death nine days before the election hurt his chances. Nevertheless, Stimson *still* touted the Webster ticket, which, after all, featured plenty of breathing and electorally viable candidates for state offices.[34]

The results confirmed his fears. Pierce trounced Scott in the Electoral College vote count, 254 to 42. Forced to choose between party loyalty and conservative Unionism, multitudes of Manhattan merchants defected to the Democratic Party, lifting Pierce to the largest New York City majority of any presidential candidate in twenty years. Stimson relished the repudiation of antislavery "fanaticism," but he was not ready to change parties.[35] As a perceptive *National Era* author recognized, Stimson longed to rebuild Whiggery "on a pure Conservative basis" and defend "the rights of the South" as a Whig.[36] Stimson continued soliciting a Custom House job until the end of the Fillmore administration, sharply criticized Pierce's early presidency, and identified as a Whig throughout 1853.[37] When hiring new staff, he favored Whigs, including Rushmore Horton, a Websterite who became an assistant editor in early 1854.[38] And when Stimson did contemplate realignment, he expressed far less interest in becoming a Democrat than in building a new party. In mid-1853, he drafted a platform that blended Whiggish and Democratic ingredients with a dash of nativism: protective tariffs and internal improvements, cheap public lands for farmers, and stricter naturalization laws.[39] Amid these reveries, however, Stimson also had to keep the *Day Book* afloat as sectionalism soared and the Whig Party staggered toward dissolution.

In 1853 and after, as Whigs debated their future and as the first pamphlet edition of Van Evrie's *Negroes and Negro Slavery* circulated nationwide, Stimson sustained the newspaper that would catalyze Van Evrie's career. Material necessity eventually induced a partisan shift, but Stimson also relied on stunts and stratagems to boost the *Day Book*'s visibility, entice subscribers and advertisers, and cut costs. In the process, he burnished the paper's reputation for unpredictability and deepened its dedication to proslavery politics.

Stimson's response to a labor dispute kept people talking about the *Day Book*. Skilled typesetters and printers were among the most militant industrial laborers. Their struggle was defensive: As proprietors (who increasingly were not former printers themselves) took over the production process, they deployed new technology that allowed them to hire less-skilled workers and slash wages. In a grim preview of his famous slogan, Horace Greeley advised printers to go West and farm rather than remain "slaves" of their employers. But many stayed and fought. In 1850, they formed the New York Printers' Union (NYPU), which braided radical rhetoric about "perpetual antagonism between labor and capital" with bread-and-butter demands, including a uniform wage scale that would lift their incomes and prevent proprietors from replacing them with unskilled operatives.[40]

Rampant inflation triggered an early 1853 showdown between Stimson, who previously accepted the union pay scale, and the NYPU. Pinched by rising prices, printers demanded a raise. Stimson refused. When unionized workers walked out of the *Day Book*'s composing room, he published an editorial blasting them as greedy ingrates out to squeeze the last dime from their employers.[41] He then suspended publication while he trained new compositors, all young women. Soon, Stimson peddled the paper as a champion of "the working girls," a dozen of whom set type in his office. By August, associate editor T. D. Curtis declared the experiment a success, reporting that the "girls," who ranged from twelve to twenty years old, were quick learners and deft workers. They also worked cheaply, earning twenty-eight cents per thousand ems of type, while the NYPU wanted an increase from thirty-two to thirty-four cents per thousand.[42]

The episode became a Rorschach test for observers' views of gender and labor. Pioneering women journalists, like the editors of the Providence *Una*, hailed Stimson's new employees as harbingers of a "revolution" that would make typesetting an all-female job.[43] (When Stimson misogynistically mocked a women's rights convention, however, they swiftly condemned his hypocritical posturing as a benefactor of working women.[44]) Other editors agreed that this was a "new era," but they were keener on cutting wages than empowering women.[45] For critics, that was precisely the problem: Uninterested in the "elevation of women," Stimson wanted them to work "at prices lower than males would do it, and less than they ought to accept."[46] Some onlookers simply gawked at the spectacle, which evidently titillated the editor who described the "nimble fingers of the girls . . . kiss[ing] the type with great rapidity."[47] Meanwhile, Stimson kept the women on the payroll and opened a female typesetting school that produced fifty graduates by 1857.[48] It was a revealing chapter in the history of a newspaper that later claimed to champion workingmen.

Stimson also promoted himself by feuding with rivals. Antebellum America's editorial wars were nasty, brutish, and prolonged, but they could be mutually beneficial by allowing participants to win admirers through public clashes against well-chosen enemies. Consider Stimson's row with self-emancipated orator, author, and editor Frederick Douglass. Douglass first noticed the *Day Book* in 1853, when he accused Stimson of being motivated not by "love for slavery" or even "malice towards the blacks," but sheer self-interest.[49] Douglass continued studying proslavery texts while working on his second autobiography, *My Bondage and My Freedom*. Alarmed by proslavery perversions of science, Douglass took aim at polygenesis.[50] His labors culminated in a July 1854 speech that rebuked ostensibly objective researchers who unfailingly found, "in the character of the oppressed, a full justification for his oppression."[51]

Stimson and Douglass were on a collision course, and Van Evrie's *Negroes and Negro "Slavery"* caused the final smash. In September 1855, Stimson (who soon hired Van Evrie to his staff) published a fawning review of the pamphlet and rehashed its claims: No one could make "the negro" a white man; slavery was scientifically sound; abolitionism was a British plot.[52] Out of hundreds of *Day Book* articles, Douglass, troubled by proslavery science and forewarned about Van Evrie's popularity, replied to this one. He hurled the personal insults typical of editorial brawls, mocking Stimson as "shallow" and possessed of "a very poor order of intellect." But he also refuted Stimson's and Van Evrie's arguments. No one ever asserted that Blacks were white, he mused. "God forbid! We profess to be *men*" entitled to the rights enshrined in the Declaration of Independence. As for cant about separate species, clearly neither Stimson nor Van Evrie had visited Virginia, where enslaved people's light complexions reflected generations of so-called mixing. Douglass urged upon Stimson "either the cultivation of his mental and his moral nature, or his immediate departure from the country for his country's good."[53]

The scathing column sparked a two-month row. Douglass lampooned Stimson's sloppy grammar, touchy bravado, and obsession with "hybrids."[54] He derided the *Day Book*'s small circulation, rejoicing that most Americans were "blissfully ignorant" of its existence and positing that it lived on the largesse of those who had "hired" Stimson "to do the dirty work of the proslaveryites at the North." Stimson struck back, likening the "delusion" of racial equality to witchcraft and spiritualism and blasting his detractors' ignorance about Black people and slavery, a curious charge to aim at Douglass.[55] Douglass nicknamed Stimson "Hybrid," ridiculing his refusal to recognize the unity of humankind.[56]

Douglass landed more punches, but both men likely profited from the scrap. Douglass advanced his campaign against polygenesis by confronting two of its leading promoters. Stimson, meanwhile, piggybacked on Douglass's fame, which swelled with the publication of *My Bondage and My Freedom* that August. The eight-week feud with a Black activist provided a golden opportunity to grow his brand as a proslavery nationalist who battled the abolitionists on their own turf. Southern admirers appreciated that the *Day Book*, "although published in the very midst of the abolitionists, hurls defiance in their teeth and battles for the cause of Southern Rights."[57] Readers of the Stimson–Douglass exchange saw this for themselves.

It took more than stunts to salvage the *Day Book*'s finances. Stimson had long chased the holy grail of political patronage; in 1854, he seized it with desperate greed. This was a decisive moment in the newspaper's history. It marked an abrupt partisan reversal. Hereafter, the *Day Book* maintained an enduring, if often uneasy, alliance with the Democratic Party. It also facilitated Van Evrie's hiring, a key step in his career. Finally, the partisan shift reflected a broader realignment that mirrored the rise of the Republican Party. Just as antislavery Northerners of all parties were coalescing under the Republican banner, many proslavery Northern Whigs and Democrats aligned themselves with an increasingly reactionary Democratic Party. Frederick Douglass took notice. "A fraternization is going on," he warned. "The Silver Gray Whig shakes hands with the Hunker Democrat. . . . They are of one heart, one mind, and the union is natural and perhaps inevitable."[58] The *Day Book* staff represented this convergence in microcosm, as Stimson and Rushmore Horton, who were Whigs, joined Van Evrie, a Democrat, to defend a slaveholding Union. As two elements of Northern proslavery politics fused in the crucible of sectionalism, they found a powerful advocate in the *Day Book*. Meanwhile, Stimson, politically adrift and financially vulnerable, secured the paper a new partisan home.

Stimson's negotiations with Democrats may have commenced in 1852. That August, George Foster sent a panicked letter to Whig editor and Seward ally Thurlow Weed, reporting the *Day Book*'s pending sale to New York's Democratic General Committee. The deal was allegedly brokered by Augustus Schell, a corporate lawyer, railroad executive, and Tammany Hall Democrat who recently had become committee chair and later served as collector at the New York Custom House. According to Foster, Schell planned to run the paper as an "independent Webster organ" to siphon votes away from Scott in New York and the South. Given the *Day Book*'s audience, it was ideal for the job. The only alternative was for Scott's friends to buy the paper and keep it in the Whig mainstream. Stimson urged Weed to respond within three days, or it would be too late.[59]

No other sources confirm Foster's story. Perhaps it was genuine, and the deal between Stimson and Schell fell through. Alternatively, Foster and Stimson may have conspired to peddle their struggling paper to the highest bidder, playing Whigs off Democrats by warning each that the *Day Book* would be sold to the other. Whatever the truth, part of Foster's prediction came true. The *Day Book* backed Webster's doomed candidacy to the bitter end but remained aloof from the Democrats through 1853. Only in 1854, as the Kansas struggle erupted and President Franklin Pierce scrounged for allies, did Stimson's bargaining with the Democrats bear fruit.

The process began in January 1854 when Stimson hired David Augustus Wright as an assistant editor. Born in Connecticut in 1820, Wright studied at Columbia and Yale before entering the newspaper business.[60] He was an ardent Pierce devotee, and while Stimson still habitually hired Whigs (Horton came aboard soon after), Wright's arrival opened a channel to the administration. Wright promised that if Stimson made the *Day Book* a Democratic organ, he would receive $10,000 in cash, patronage preferment, and government printing contracts—sweeteners that typically clinched alliances between editors and politicians. Stimson, who was "as poor as a rat," eagerly consented.[61] For his part, Pierce hoped to reconcile two factions of New York Democrats: the "Softs," who favored rapprochement with the prodigal Democrats who had bolted to the Free Soil Party, and the "Hards," who did not. The *Day Book*, which supported the Kansas-Nebraska Bill, was ideologically closer to the Hards, while Pierce enjoyed warmer support from the Softs. By making the *Day Book* an administration organ, Pierce hoped to unify New York's fractious Democrats behind him.[62]

Wright's proffered deal may have fallen through, but there were other irons in the fire. In February, New York customs collector Herman J. Redfield advised William L. Marcy, Pierce's secretary of state, to award the *Day Book* a contract to publish federal laws. Editors coveted these agreements, which delivered steady revenue streams. In case Marcy doubted the paper's solvency, Redfield touted Stimson's shrewd decision to slash labor costs by hiring women, a move Redfield believed every publisher should imitate.[63] Thus began the cooperation between the *Day Book* and the Pierce administration, and the party switch soon followed. By midsummer, Stimson had rebranded his paper as a Pierce organ and a champion of the Soft faction of the New York Democratic Party.[64]

Subsequent payoffs sealed Stimson's conversion. Marcy funneled printing jobs to the *Day Book*, opening a torrent of State Department patronage that flowed unimpeded through December 1856.[65] James Guthrie's Treasury Department provided similar support.[66] And in October 1854, Pierce delivered the plum Stimson had craved since 1850: a connection to the Custom House. That month, deputy collector John Mumford joined the *Day Book* as assistant editor.[67] Mumford was an ideal liaison between the Pierce administration, New York's elite, and the *Day Book*. Born into a prominent merchant family, he had worked in the Custom House since 1838, stumped for Pierce in 1852, and served on the New York State Democratic Committee in 1853. He also had journalistic experience from his years editing the *New York Standard*.

His brief tenure on Stimson's staff enhanced the paper's credibility among Democratic readers.[68] New York City Democrats followed suit by making the *Day Book* their official mouthpiece in December 1854.[69] That same month, Redfield and other local notables, including the city postmaster, publicly endorsed the *Day Book* and asked congressional Democrats to promote it.[70] Democrats welcomed Stimson with open arms and deep pockets.

Stimson was now a Democrat. Ideologically, it was no great leap, as Pierce's acolytes shared his zeal for the Compromise of 1850 and the property rights of enslavers. Politically, Stimson had few palatable alternatives. The Whig Party had imploded following its shellacking in 1852, the American Party was obsessed with immigration, and the Republican Party was an antislavery foe. Financially, the Pierce administration resuscitated his business, even if his "scanty subsistence" drew sneers.[71] If Stimson ever regretted the switch, he never admitted it. Nor was he the only Whig to follow this path. James Brooks, later notorious as a Manhattan Copperhead, was a Whig who shunned the Democrats until the Civil War. George B. McClellan, the sluggish Union general and 1864 Democratic presidential nominee, was a Whig whose "conservative views" nudged him into the Democratic Party in the late 1850s.[72] Stimson was one of many who changed parties in search of institutional power, public influence, and material gain. They reshaped the Democratic Party while savoring its succor. And the *Day Book*'s complex relationship with the party endured for the next quarter century.

The Pierce administration may have played no direct role in Van Evrie's hiring, but the president and the propagandist had much in common. Both were Northern men with Southern sympathies. They shared a powerful friend in Jefferson Davis, Van Evrie's patron and Pierce's secretary of war. Both served under Winfield Scott in Mexico and might have crossed paths in Puebla. Van Evrie first published "Negroes and Negro Slavery" in the inaugural issue of the *Monthly Democratic Review*, a Pierce-backed Washington journal. Pierce might have admired Van Evrie and helped bring him to New York. Certainly, Stimson's party switch, which Pierce's administration paid for, made it easy for a stalwart Democrat like Van Evrie to join the *Day Book* in 1855. Hereafter, the fates of the paper and the propagandist would be inseparable.

Six months later, Van Evrie wrote another editorial insisting that Black slavery and white democracy were mutually necessary. American society, he proclaimed, must respect the "natural law of white supremacy and negro subordination."[73] He buried the line in a long, tediously didactic article. Readers might have missed it as they scanned for news from Bleeding Kansas. But it took root in the author's mind, a sprout that would yield bitter fruit.

Chapter 8

Apprentice

Van Evrie's arrival cemented the *Day Book*'s status as the North's leading proslavery newspaper. Thereafter, a publication that previously wove proslavery politics into commercial news coverage now fixated on a racist proslavery message. Anticipating this, some of Nathaniel Stimson's friends counseled against employing Van Evrie, whose zealotry was evident in *Negroes and Negro "Slavery."*[1] But Stimson wagered that firebrand editorials would attract more readers than they repelled, and Van Evrie's influence grew steadily. An August 25, 1855, *Day Book* editorial parroted his trademark denial that "the negro, in everything but the color of his skin, is a white man."[2] Three weeks later, the paper announced that "arrangements" had been made with "gentlemen competent to deal" with slavery "in all its phases, scientific as well as social and political."[3] By late September, the *Day Book* was running editorials cribbed from Van Evrie's previous work, and soon his telltale quotes appeared around the word *slavery*.[4] Thus began Van Evrie's two years on staff, during which he used the *Day Book*'s editorial columns to amplify themes from his early writings. The symbiosis between professional racist and proslavery rag had commenced.

Van Evrie also began an apprenticeship in the newspaper business. Stimson could teach him little about polygenesis, but Van Evrie now discovered the practical challenges of newspaper proprietorship. He encountered patronage trouble and the fickleness of public support. He faced problems of audience as he worked to sway Northern opinion through a newspaper that circulated mainly in the South. He confronted explosive sectionalism, which threatened to rupture Manhattan merchants' ties to cotton growers and made it increasingly difficult to sustain a nationalist case for slavery. Always, his task was to achieve political goals by reaching the right audience with the right message, while keeping the business alive. These difficulties vexed Van Evrie for the rest of his career.

Stimson's business model influenced the novice editorialist. Adopting Stimson's focus on planters and merchants, Van Evrie muffled his earlier appeals to workers and, for the next half-decade, stressed the shared interests of Northern and Southern elites. Thus, even as he infused the *Day Book* with a relentless proslavery message, he also adapted to its target audience. This approach outlived Stimson by several years; not until wartime did Van Evrie return to his roots. Proslavery politics came in multiple forms, and, while he learned the business of publishing, Van Evrie followed his teacher's lead. Yet by late 1857, the *Day Book* was in serious trouble as Stimson staggered toward an early grave.

Day Book content narrowed after Van Evrie's arrival. Consider the lead editorials published in the presidential election years of 1852 and 1856. Of those printed in 1852, nearly one-quarter (24 percent) focused on slavery or racism. They made Stimson's antipathy for abolitionism crystal clear, but he also covered temperance, foreign policy, and other major issues. Four years later, Van Evrie fastened the paper's editorial attention on slavery and polygenesis with his customary single-mindedness. Of the lead editorials printed in 1856, fully 85 percent focused on racism or slavery. Current events in Kansas contributed to this shift. But it also reflected Van Evrie's belief that slavery was "THE GREAT ISSUE."[5]

Day Book editorials changed qualitatively as well. Stimson demonized abolitionists, praised slavery, and urged sectional rapprochement for the sake of the Southern trade. But he said little about polygenesis, democracy, or British conspiracies. After Van Evrie arrived, these themes permeated the *Day Book*'s columns. Throughout 1856 and 1857, he unleashed a torrent of editorials drawn directly from his *Negroes* pamphlet. Many insisted that Black people comprised a separate and unequal species whose natural subordination to whites was not slavery at all.[6] Others proclaimed that democracy depended on slavery and hailed Southern planters as paladins of white men's equality.[7] Some recycled Van Evrie's conspiracy theory about abolitionism's foreign origins and monarchist aims.[8]

Van Evrie routinely flirted with self-plagiarism. If he "wrote more words in defense of slavery than any other American," his corpus was bloated by repetition.[9] Rather than widen his range, Van Evrie bombarded *Day Book* readers with fixed precepts. Slavery was ordained by science and religion. Slavery underpinned white freedom. Slavery demanded patriotic protection. Rigid consistency was a source of persuasive power. As fresh events roiled politics in the late 1850s—Bleeding Kansas, the *Dred Scott* decision, the Lecompton Constitution, John Brown's raid—Van Evrie's messaging never wavered. Whether speaking to Manhattan merchants startled by Southern separatism, cotton planters menaced by abolitionism, or Unionists from all quarters who feared civil war, he prescribed the same remedy: white Americans must embrace slavery as a national boon.

Van Evrie also used the *Day Book to* cultivate his own reputation. He placed sarcastic quotation marks around the word *slavery*, weaving his trademark into the *Day Book*'s house style.[10] The paper regularly advertised Stimson's

1853 edition of *Negroes and Negro "Slavery"* (which remained in print three years later).[11] Lest readers balk at the twenty-five-cent cover price, the paper ran testimonials from satisfied customers, including one who lauded it as "the best thing I have ever seen upon the subject."[12] As Van Evrie harnessed the *Day Book* to his dreams of author-heroism, he blurred the line between author and venue; their fortunes were inseparable.

These efforts dovetailed with Stimson's proslavery nationalist crusade, which he advanced by opening the *Day Book*'s pages to Southern writers seeking national audiences accessible through New York publications. Antebellum editors constantly reprinted each other's material, and because New York papers operated from the nation's communications hub, their content reached far-flung readers with lightning speed as it was recopied across the country.[13] Thus, proslavery Southerners found in the *Day Book* a doubly powerful ally: It both espoused their cause and amplified their voices. In November 1857, the *Day Book* printed a proslavery essay by Dr. Samuel Cartwright of New Orleans, an early champion of Van Evrie's work who diagnosed enslaved people's flight as a medical malady.[14] Extracts from the article soon appeared in newspapers from Massachusetts to Iowa.[15] Cartwright's was one of a spate of *Day Book* articles penned by Southern doctors who endorsed polygenism as proof of slavery's beneficence.[16] Southern physicians had long used racist science to assert their authority, and Stimson helped them preach polygenist proslavery on a national stage.

Especially important was Stimson's dissemination of Southern accounts of Bleeding Kansas. News from the territory filled thousands of newspaper columns with starkly polarized coverage that arguably did more than any other topic to inflame sectional hostility. Indeed, its influence echoes in the term "Bleeding Kansas" itself, coined by Horace Greeley's *Tribune*.[17] The *Day Book* reached only a fraction of Greeley's readership, but Stimson published correspondents who countered free-soil reportage with proslavery narratives. In April 1856, Stimson printed a note from a self-styled "Border Ruffian" who described fellow proslavery settlers as "free, generous, brave and open-hearted," defending "home, country, friends, and the institutions of our fathers" against corporate-sponsored antislavery "bullies."[18] In October, he published an update from a Kansas correspondent who denounced free-soil militia as bandits preying on innocent Southern homesteaders.[19]

Then, in early 1857, the *Day Book* ran a long letter from Jefferson Buford, a proslavery crusader whose career entwined with Van Evrie's. Born in South Carolina, Buford was practicing law in Alabama when, alarmed by news of antislavery emigrants streaming into Kansas from New England, he organized a proslavery battalion to oppose them. He recruited several hundred volunteers and marched west under banners proclaiming "Kansas, the Outpost" and "The Supremacy of the White Race." The latter slogan borrowed from the *Day Book*. In May, Van Evrie had used the obscure phrase "white supremacy" in an editorial; the following month, while soliciting donations, Buford asked listeners if they were ready to "surrender white supremacy in the South." If not, they must hold Kansas, lest the dominoes fall from west to east as abolitionists toppled Missouri, Arkansas, and beyond. Buford was an avid *Day Book* fan. His January 1857 letter from Missouri brimmed with praise for the newspaper, as well as optimism about the future of slave-grown hemp in Kansas. By printing Buford's screed, the *Day Book* boosted an early imitator of the slogan Van Evrie would popularize a decade later.[20]

The *Day Book* also vindicated proslavery violence in Washington, DC. In May 1856, outraged by Senator Charles Sumner's rebuke of proslavery expansionists, South Carolina representative Preston Brooks caned him on the Senate floor. The assault aroused intense indignation among Northerners, including some Democrats.[21] But not *Day Book* writers. Two days after the assault, Van Evrie proclaimed that Sumner "was served just right."[22] He flogged the issue through the summer, scourging Republicans for idolizing Sumner and castigating efforts to expel Brooks from the House.[23] Brooks reciprocated by taking a *Day Book* subscription and penning a personal thank-you note "for the liberal and gentlemanly comments you have been pleased to make upon the collision between Mr. Sumner and myself."[24]

Yet while the *Day Book* battled antislavery behemoths like the *Tribune*, its relationship with proslavery Southerners was not always congenial. Hindsight clarifies the source of friction: In the South, proslavery commitments were nurturing a separatist impulse inimical to Stimson and Van Evrie's reactionary Unionism.[25] As these varieties of proslavery politics diverged in the late 1850s, the *Day Book*'s nationalist campaign strained against Southern sectionalism. The rupture was still years away when Van Evrie joined the paper, but he glimpsed the widening rift.

Consider the *Day Book*'s tortured response to Southern proslavery propagandists who disparaged the North. Van Evrie, eager to win Northern converts, eschewed invidious sectional comparisons. But many Southern ideologues flaunted slavery as a badge of sectional superiority. Few stirred more controversy—or put the *Day Book* in a more difficult bind—than George Fitzhugh. A Virginian who bemoaned the Enlightenment, scoured socialist tracts for proof of wage labor's brutality, and argued that slavery best harmonized labor and capital, Fitzhugh taunted defenders of "mere negro slavery" and deemed bondage a boon for all workers "without regard to race or color."[26] Fitzhugh's brand of proslavery was eccentric, but by indicting "the Failure of Free Society," it channeled the South's burgeoning separatist spirit.[27] For Stimson and Van Evrie, this was a problem. Fitzhugh's fulminations validated claims that the Slave Power imperiled white freedom, and meshed easily with secessionist schemes that threatened interregional trade and the Union. His vitriol weakened bonds that the *Day Book* labored to protect. When Fitzhugh's magnum opus *Cannibals All!* appeared in 1857, Van Evrie wrote a convoluted review that attempted to reconcile Fitzhugh's scorching illiberalism with his own worldview. British society was a failure, Van Evrie agreed, but the North was sound. Slavery was a boon, Van Evrie agreed, but only for Black workers. In seeking common ground, Van Evrie dodged Fitzhugh's most provocative ideas. He ignored Fitzhugh's rebuke of race-based proslavery, overlooked his contempt for democracy, and meekly refused to "controvert his philosophy or main position." This dithering effort to appease a rival proslavery propagandist foreshadowed the rupture of 1861.[28]

Still more portentous were *Day Book* discussions of slavery and commerce. Stimson rode the merchant exposé to minor stardom in 1850, but he had goaded a dangerous creature: Southern hostility to Manhattan's commercial power. Thereafter, Stimson tried to cage this beast. He used the threat of Southern economic separatism to coerce Manhattan merchants into a proslavery stance, while cajoling Southern readers to trust the New Yorkers who dominated the cotton trade. During his apprenticeship, Van Evrie saw how delicate this balancing act could be.

Despite the backlash against his 1850 article, Stimson continued passing judgment on local merchants, separating the sheep who accepted proslavery truths from the goats who strayed into antislavery heresy. In the tense run-up to the 1856 election, amid Southern threats to secede over a Republican victory, Stimson printed two new lists: one of the "substantial and respectable" merchants who held a proslavery Union meeting on Wall Street; the other of the "ranting, noisy abolitionist" merchants who hosted Republican orators.[29] Clearly, Stimson wanted to intimidate antislavery dissenters. But this was also a defensive move spurred by fear of economic estrangement and political separation. Stimson feared the Southern movement for commercial independence. He recognized that sectional strife kindled suspicion, resentment, and dreams of direct Southern trade with Europe. He wanted Northern readers to understand this, so his reportage on Southern commercial conventions always connected the dots between Northern antislavery and Southern retaliation.[30]

Meanwhile, Southern subscribers scrutinized Northern commercial circles for signs of antislavery contamination. Stimson noted that they regularly demanded updated lists of politically objectionable merchants.[31] Their questions about whether antislavery merchants advertised in his pages alarmed him so much that he published a disavowal in early 1857. Proclaiming that he never *solicited* advertisements from abolitionists, Stimson made a tacit confession by pledging never to *accept* advertisements from them in the future.[32] Forced to choose between losing Southern subscribers or Northern advertisers, Stimson pandered to the Southern readers who refused to exempt even the *Day Book* from suspicion. Van Evrie, who took over the business ten months later, saw the difficulty of satisfying the paper's interlinked but potentially antagonistic audiences.

He and Stimson tackled this problem by regularly printing two types of editorials. In one, they harangued New York merchants about the moral and commercial evils of abolitionism. Stimson issued a prototypical appeal in 1852, exhorting "we of the North," who profited "from an extensive commerce in the productions of slave-holding States," to repudiate abolitionism as insulting to the South, dangerous to the Union, and rotten for business.[33] Like Democrats' wartime warnings that emancipation would inundate the North with cheap Black labor, these articles insisted that white Northerners had a material stake in slavery. But unlike the later pronunciamentos, which targeted wageworkers, these antebellum jeremiads addressed the mercantile community in which the *Day Book* was rooted. The emphasis on business rather than labor came naturally to a commercial journal famous for hiring scabs. Van Evrie continued in this vein in the late 1850s. Days after purchasing the *Day Book*, he declared that no one had more interest in preserving slavery than merchants. The editorial, which included his trademark references to "slavery," signaled that Van Evrie would continue policing Northern merchants' politics by teaching them that slavery was the basis of their wealth.[34]

In the second type of editorial, the *Day Book* gently parried Southern calls for commercial autonomy. A typical specimen, published in 1857, extolled the potential of New Orleans as a commercial conduit between North America and the tropics. Left implicit was that the Crescent City would *not* supplant New York as the link between North America and Europe. Gotham would remain the vital intermediary between suppliers and consumers of cotton. Forging ahead, the editorialist (likely Van Evrie) decried the delusions, propagated by British malefactors, that racial difference was skin-deep and that Black people suffered in bondage. This article encapsulated the *Day Book*'s antebellum mission: Flatter Southern pride, smother commercial rivalry, and bury sectional strife beneath racist praise for slavery as a national boon.[35] A similar editorial published under Van Evrie's proprietorship echoed these points. Southern cities could thrive on trade with Latin America, especially if slavery were reinstituted there, but New York would "remain the great emporium and centre of European and American exchange."[36] Like the rejoinder to Fitzhugh, these articles gingerly steered Southern whites away from separatism.

Stimson strove to bolster Southern confidence and rebuke wayward Northern merchants. But the *Day Book*'s wary replies to Fitzhugh and the direct traders reflected the growing difficulty of defending slavery on nationalist grounds. As more Northerners criticized slavery as a sectional evil and more Southerners valorized it as a sectional blessing, Stimson doubled down on his proslavery nationalist project. Yet warnings abounded that this was neither a stable political position nor a secure basis for financial success. The *Day Book* remained the North's preeminent proslavery newspaper, but it upheld an increasingly awkward position.

Meanwhile, in their bid to run a partisan Democratic newspaper, Stimson and Van Evrie notched major victories but yielded disappointing returns. The 1856 presidential election, the first since his conversion, gave Stimson a loyalty test. He aced it. Although he initially endorsed Franklin Pierce's renomination, Stimson rallied behind Democratic nominee James Buchanan, proving that his party commitment transcended fealty to any single patron.[37] Thus, the old Whig, whose 1852 Daniel Webster campaign outlived its candidate, now redeemed his Democratic pledges. Aided by Van Evrie and Rushmore Horton, Stimson melded the *Day Book*'s proslavery nationalist crusade with partisan politicking, lauding Buchanan's Democrats exactly as he had praised Webster's Whigs: as guardians of a slaveholding Union. Yet Buchanan's triumph brought little reward, raising the familiar question of whether a Northern proslavery newspaper could survive.

Participants sensed the enormous stakes of the 1856 presidential race. The three-sided contest pitted Buchanan, an impressively credentialed Pennsylvanian, against former president Millard Fillmore (atop the American Party ticket) and John C. Frémont, the celebrity explorer of the West who was tapped by the Republicans. All three campaigned as saviors of the republic. Democrats denounced Republicans as abolitionists who would drive the South to secede. Republicans denounced Democrats as minions of the planter oligarchy. Nativists denounced both as unpatriotic. Many contemporaries rejected Van Evrie's prescriptions, but few doubted his diagnosis: "We are rapidly approaching a crisis," he opined in June 1856, "the greatest crisis in our history or in the history of free institutions."[38]

Stimson's team churned out editorials praising Buchanan as a Union-loving patriot and damning Republicans as abolitionist puppets of the British aristocracy. They also wrote, printed, and distributed other appeals that infused Democratic electioneering with proslavery Unionism. Ex-Whig Rushmore Horton contributed the campaign biography. Within four weeks of Buchanan's nomination, he produced a four-hundred-page hagiography extolling Buchanan's private virtues and public service. Horton closed with a paean to white unity, Black subordination, and proslavery American nationalism:

> All good and reasonable men must therefore be convinced that the peace, prosperity, and safety of twenty millions of the happiest, freest, and most advanced white men, with their noble structure of republican government, cemented by the blood, the sufferings, and treasures of their ancestors, should not be sacrificed—nay, not even jeopardized for the supposed interests of three millions of the African race, who, whatever may be their present condition, are certainly better off than any other three million of their own race of which we have any knowledge.

Recycling the logic that had drawn him to Webster, Horton urged whites to "unite once more the bonds of fraternal feeling between all sections" and elect "the consistent statesman, the pure patriot, and the honest man, JAMES BUCHANAN."[39] Democratic notables, including Buchanan's running mate John C. Breckinridge, praised Horton's effort.[40]

Meanwhile, *Day Book* staff rebranded *Negroes and Negro "Slavery"* as a campaign text. Van Evrie was a longtime Democrat, but he wrote *Negroes* as a nonpartisan cure for sectional division. Now Stimson repurposed it to support Buchanan, printing thousands of fresh copies alongside other campaign materials, including South Carolina Senator A. P. Butler's rejoinder to the recuperating Charles Sumner. The price: twelve and a half cents per copy or seven dollars for one hundred.[41] Democrats mobilized to put the pamphlet in voters' hands. From an obscure Ohioan who requested an extra copy to share with friends to members of Congress, including Mississippi representative John A. Quitman, who mailed it to recipients nationwide, partisans disseminated *Negroes* as a definitive rebuttal of Republican antislavery appeals.[42]

Did Van Evrie, Horton, and Stimson speak for the Democratic Party? During and after the Civil War, contemporaries debated whether Van Evrie was a party advocate or a rogue agent. The *Day Book*'s affiliation was no less significant in 1856. Throughout the campaign, Republican and abolitionist editors quoted the paper to tar Democrats as tools of the Slave Power. Their argument was simple: The *Day Book*'s proslavery pronouncements unmasked the Democratic Party as the champion of a reactionary ideology that endangered every American's freedom.[43] The effort peaked in late summer and fall, when Republican editors pounced on *Day Book* commentary that veered toward Fitzhugh's class-based proslavery doctrine. After describing the miseries of Manhattan's impoverished white children, the editorial offered a solution: "Sell the parents of these children into SLAVERY. Let our Legislature pass a law that whoever will take these parents and take care of them and their OFFSPRING in sickness and in health . . . *shall be legally entitled to their service*" for life. Dozens of Republican papers reprinted this extract, spotlighting its origin in a Northern Buchanan mouthpiece and pairing it with similar remarks by Southern Democrats. The warning was clear: Enslavers controlled the Democratic Party, and only Republicans could thwart its atrocious agenda.[44] In broadsides, legislative resolutions, and speeches, antislavery activists quoted the passage through the end of the Civil War.[45] Probably no other *Day Book* excerpt was condemned as widely. It was a godsend to critics of Van Evrie's claims that Southern planters were freedom-loving democrats, and that Black slavery undergirded white equality.

Why did Van Evrie give his foes such a gift? How could a Northern opponent of the Slave Power theory blunder so badly? In fact, he did not. Republicans found the passage in an 1850 Senate speech by Louisiana Democrat Solomon W. Downs, who quoted from a Stimson editorial, published in the *Merchant's Day Book*, entitled "A Remedy for Northern Pauperism."[46] Inspired by the want and degradation that moved George G. Foster to chronicle New York's slums, Stimson transmuted white hardship into a vindication of Black enslavement. He echoed a gripe common among Southern partisans: Northern busybodies should care for their own poor instead of censuring the South, where workers lived well. These notions, when expressed through a modest proposal for enslaving destitute whites, graded into Fitzhugh's brand of proslavery. That Stimson entertained these ideas is doubly revealing. First, it shows that promoters of varied proslavery arguments united against common foes. Stimson's comments haunted Van Evrie in 1856, but their distinctive versions of proslavery did not preclude their partnership. Second, it reconfirms that Stimson's *Day Book* was not a labor paper and did not presume to speak for the Northern masses. He aligned with the merchants and bankers enriched by Southern trade. Only later, under Van Evrie's proprietorship and amid the financial and political strain of war, would this change. Until then, the editor of a commercial journal could vindicate Black bondage by imagining white servitude.

Van Evrie battled the backlash against Stimson's old article with deflection and demagoguery. In September, he blasted Republicans for asserting that the *Day Book* advocated white enslavement and then quickly claimed victory, despite their persistent attacks.[47] Just before the election, he announced that a vote for Buchanan was a vote for white men's democracy. Enslavers were natural allies of white Northerners; bondage was the "normal condition" of Blacks; only "traitors to their race" or the "miserable dupes" of foreign schemers could advocate something as "hideous and impious . . . as negro freedom."[48] Thus, he responded by amplifying his standard racist and nationalist appeals. As Northern whites clashed over slavery, Van Evrie insisted that it safeguarded white privilege, while antislavery activists argued that it jeopardized white freedom. For now, other Democratic editors kept mum, neither defending nor disavowing the *Day Book*. They would not always be so patient.

Buchanan carried most of the South and enough Northern states to prevail. Yet if Democrats were content with the *Day Book*, the reverse was not true. Commencing a quarter-century struggle over party orthodoxy, Van Evrie blamed Buchanan's poor free-state showing on Northern Democrats who chose evasive moderation over strident proslavery. Rather than "explode the lies of the anti-slavery party," he thundered, they had embraced centrism and denied that their party advocated slavery. Four years hence, he warned, if Democrats did not "explode this delusion" of slavery's wickedness, the party and the Union would crumble.[49] Confronted by a vibrant antislavery movement, Van Evrie refused to tack toward the political center. He took his stand on slavery as a positive good. Like Stimson, he regarded it as the Union's bedrock, and he excoriated Democrats who failed to join him.

Democratic patronage policies proved similarly disappointing. After Buchanan's inauguration in March 1857, the flow of printing contracts and other federal support dried up. Notwithstanding Stimson, Horton, and Van Evrie's campaign efforts, the new president, offended by their criticism of some early appointments, deprived the *Day Book* of a valuable revenue stream by making the *News* his New York mouthpiece.[50] The *Day Book* was not dying: Between July 1855 and August 1856, its circulation increased from six thousand to thirty thousand, likely because of election excitement.[51] But the loss of patronage stung, and it was only one of several blows that battered the *Day Book* as Stimson's health deteriorated in 1857.

Despite the cold shoulder, Van Evrie found much to celebrate in Buchanan's presidency. Shortly after the inauguration, when the Supreme Court ruled against Dred Scott's bid for freedom, Chief Justice Roger Taney's opinion enshrined proslavery nationalism in law. Holding that Scott could not sue because he was Black, and thus could not be a US citizen, Taney dismissed antislavery constitutionalism and foreclosed debate on race and citizenship. Van Evrie loved it. In a spate of repetitive editorials, he lionized Taney and exulted that the Court had joined God and nature in rendering the "*fact*" of Black inferiority as "eternal as time and indistructible as creation."[52] In 1860, he published Taney's opinion alongside a polygenist piece by Samuel Cartwright, combining in one tract the leading legal and scientific rationales of the time for racial slavery. In his introduction, Van Evrie hailed *Dred Scott* as second only to the Declaration of Independence as the "most momentous event that has ever occurred on this continent."[53] He deemed the Constitution as construed by Taney the basis for a perpetual slaveholding Union and clung to this position long after Southern secessionists decided otherwise.

Soon after Taney boosted their spirits, however, things began to unravel for Van Evrie and Stimson. Like most Americans, they were blindsided by the economic panic that struck in late summer 1857. Cascading bank failures, stock market losses, and business closures shook the nation and hit Manhattan especially hard. Newspaper proprietors felt the pinch and numerous papers shut down. The *Day Book* stayed afloat, in part because Southerners, who comprised a majority of its subscribers, escaped the worst of the panic and continued paying their dues. But Stimson's firm was reeling: Northern advertising and subscription revenues plunged as businesses curtailed expenses, and he had to sell Southern banknotes at a steep discount to nervous local bankers. He begged Southern readers to renew early and pay in gold.[54]

One industry that still thrived was gambling. Turning to the South for revenue, Stimson began running advertisements for a lottery operated in Augusta, Georgia, by Swan & Company.[55] Lotteries had been ubiquitous in colonial, Revolutionary, and early republic America. Often run by private entities under state license, they helped pool capital for everything from education to infrastructure. By 1830, New York hosted around 160 lottery vendors, with annual revenues exceeding $1.5 million. But lotteries drew fire from religious reformers, and many states began outlawing them, including New York in 1833. Thus, while Swan & Company operated legally in Georgia, Stimson violated New York law by printing advertisements and announcing winning numbers. He was indicted in October 1857.[56]

Stimson and the *Day Book* were in peril. He was unlikely to be incarcerated, but court costs and fines could drain his purse and sink his business. Responding through an editorial, he and Van Evrie accused district attorney A. Oakey Hall of partisan bias. Hall was a "red-mouthed Black Republican" who targeted the *Day Book* because, they hissed, he "hates the South and everything southern as heartily as the devil hates holiness."[57] They sustained this barrage of criticisms for a month and refused to pull the Swan advertisements.[58] Hall, in truth, was no partisan hack. A Whig-turned-Republican, he studied law in New Orleans under Democrat John Slidell and later served as district attorney and then New York mayor as a Tammany Hall Democrat. His anti-lottery crusade was linked to a reelection campaign meant to woo back voters who were outraged by his bid to pin a high-profile murder on an indigent widow. The ploy failed—Hall lost and did not regain his post until he ran as a Democrat in 1864. However, the episode unnerved Stimson, whose bluster betrayed his anxiety.[59]

As fall turned to winter, the *Day Book* was foundering. Federal patronage had evaporated. Advertising and subscription revenues were falling. The proprietor faced indictment and a serious cardiac ailment. But Van Evrie was about to encounter a golden opportunity.

Chapter 9
Proprietor

It was a mild November afternoon, but Nathaniel Stimson wasn't enjoying the warmth. He was dying. As he grabbed a handrail to steady himself at Manhattan's South Ferry terminal, he probably sensed that his time was short. Stimson had been sickly throughout his forty-two years, and heart palpitations had confined him to bed over the weekend. What preoccupied him as he waited to cross the East River? He likely worried about Helen and their four children, including twelve-year-old Horatio, who had accompanied him into the city. Or perhaps he couldn't concentrate on anything. When the ferry arrived, Stimson was barely conscious. A fellow passenger helped him aboard and accompanied him to the Brooklyn terminal, where he transferred to the Long Island Railroad that would carry him home to Cypress Hills. He never made it. Shortly after departing, the train entered the Cobble Hill Tunnel; when it emerged at the other end, Stimson was dead. Horatio, traveling in a different car, was spared the shock of watching his father die, but soon the family faced the grim challenge of survival.[1] Meanwhile, fellow journalists debated Stimson's legacy. Van Evrie lauded his patriotism, while antislavery editors coolly noted the passing of "an unblushing advocate of Human Slavery."[2] He remained divisive even in death.

Stimson's demise marked a crisis and an opportunity for his assistant editors. He left behind an enterprise struggling under loss of patronage, legal jeopardy, and financial distress. But his death allowed Van Evrie and Rushmore Horton to purchase the newspaper they had managed for two years. Now Van Evrie could freely chase his dream of author-heroism. Now slavery's self-anointed savior could steer the business, as well as the editorial page, as he saw fit. The results were remarkable. With the *New York Day Book* as the foundation, Van Evrie, Horton & Co. built a publishing house that churned out editorials, pamphlets, and books that amplified Van Evrie's polygenist proslavery nationalism. By 1861, thanks to shrewd business maneuvers, strategic activism, and aggressive marketing, their "great Proslavery publishing concern" was flourishing.[3] Whether it could save a splintering Union was more doubtful.

On December 19, 1857, the Baltimore *Sun* observed: "Since the death of N. R. Stimson, Esq., the New York Day Book has passed into the hands of Dr. J. Van

Evrie, Horton & Co."[4] Accurate but incomplete, the notice elided the private drama that brought the *Day Book* under Van Evrie's control. Stimson had established the paper's reputation but never stabilized its finances, and his death coincided with an economic crisis. Ironically, this was ideal for his successors, who purchased the business on astonishingly generous terms.

Two weeks after Stimson died intestate, his assets and debts passed to his widow, Helen.[5] A single woman with four young children, she had every reason to sell the *Day Book* quickly. By disposing of it, she could raise cash and offload an enterprise that some mourners blamed for driving her husband to his grave.[6] But how much could she get? In 1855, one observer estimated the *Day Book* was worth $6,000; subsequent increases in circulation may have boosted its value.[7] Yet Helen sold out to Van Evrie and Horton for just $2,500, to be paid in weekly installments of $10. She might have asked for more; Benjamin Wood, brother of defeated New York mayor Fernando Wood, reputedly offered $16,000. Why did Helen sell to Van Evrie, Horton & Co. for a "trifle"?[8] Maybe she wanted the business to stay in friendly hands. Maybe she trusted Van Evrie to carry on the *Day Book*'s mission. Maybe Wood's offer was apocryphal, and $2,500 was the top bid. Whatever Helen's motives, Van Evrie and Horton purchased the *Day Book* for a song.

Van Evrie announced his ownership with arrogance verging on messianism. On December 16, he declared that Van Evrie, Horton & Co. would operate the paper from its current office at 17 Ann Street, around the corner from Printing House Square. Its content would not change, since the paper's "political character," particularly regarding slavery, had already been under Van Evrie's "direct management" for two years. "Dr. Van Evrie . . . has devoted a number of years to an investigation of this, the greatest question of the day, and his mode of dealing with it has called out an extent and degree of popular approbation from all parts of the country . . . that is as flattering as it is unexpected." His expertise was indispensable. Northerners were "laboring under a frightful delusion," propagated by Britons, that slavery was unjust. Misinformation could destroy the country, so it was imperative that Northerners "be enlightened on this momentous subject." Van Evrie would do it. And despite slumping ad sales and dependence on cut-rate subscriptions, he would never relent. To help him, readers should spread the word and propel the *Day Book* to 100,000 subscribers. Braiding heroic posturing with an appeal for subscriptions, Van Evrie took the helm.[9]

Soon after, he clarified his close but complex ties to Manhattan business leaders and the Democratic Party. He addressed the former in an editorial response to a local subscriber who urged him to make the paper more "acceptable" to New York's "business community." This meant adding market reports, daily lists of hotel arrivals, and other merchant-oriented news. The writer also begged Van Evrie to moderate his politics, stressing that Manhattanites admired his talent but choked on his extremism. Could he meet them halfway? While "a paper can never be made fully acceptable to the people of the free States that advocates the institution of slavery," Northerners could be convinced to "tolerate" the rights of enslavers. Nothing more could be asked of those who regarded slavery with "repugnance."[10]

Van Evrie's reply reiterated two familiar themes: He needed money, and he loved slavery. Providing timely business coverage required paying large fees to join news services like the Associated Press. He could not do this "without capital," he complained, though he pledged "to render our daily in due time, such a paper as the business community will have no excuse for not patronizing." Thus, he maintained the *Day Book*'s commercial character. But he also vowed to preserve its proslavery stance. "There would be no point," he insisted, "no sense in the Day Book, and in fact no use of publishing it if we should abandon the ground we have assumed on the so-called slavery question." Sectional strife stemmed from one issue: Was slavery right or wrong? Constitutional hair-splitting and partisan tactics aside, it was a moral question. Van Evrie's job was to convince white Northerners that slavery was ordained by God and science. He would run the *Day Book* as a proslavery commercial journal. Prevarication would mean abandoning his heroic mission.[11]

Two days later, Van Evrie defined the *Day Book*'s relationship with the Democratic Party in similar terms. He recollected the paper's cozy ties to President Franklin Pierce's administration and the subsequent loss of patronage. But dallying with Democrats mattered far less than enlightening Northern opinion. "This paper," he explained, "does not claim to be a 'party organ' in the sense usually accorded to that term." It existed not to promote any leader or faction but to unmask antislavery as a delusion. Other Northern Democrats might cower before public sentiment. They might even banish the *Day Book* from the party. But its new proprietors would not falter. Proud Democrats but not partisan drones, they would never countenance perversions of principle. Just as he presented the *Day Book* as a proslavery commercial journal, in that order, Van Evrie proclaimed it a proslavery Democratic paper. He exhorted Democrats to uphold proslavery Unionism, but he would never submit to their dictates.[12] Van Evrie followed this course for the next twenty-two years—with one exception.

Little of what Van Evrie published in his first two years as proprietor was surprising. He rehashed his usual fare about slavery as the natural relationship between superior and inferior species, Black servitude as the basis for white democracy, and abolitionism as a British plot.[13] He admonished New York merchants about the dangers of abolitionism and cautiously critiqued Southern calls for direct trade.[14] He tantalized readers with extracts from his promised book-length edition of *Negroes and Negro "Slavery"*.[15] He printed Southern-authored work, including a proslavery essay by Edmund Ruffin.[16] And, of course, he intervened in political debates.

Predictably, Van Evrie sided with Jefferson Davis, James Buchanan, and other proslavery Democrats in the struggle over the Lecompton Constitution. In attempting to foist a fraudulent but impeccably proslavery state constitution on Kansas Territory, Buchanan and the Lecomptonites collided with Republicans and most Northern Democrats, including Stephen Douglas, in a struggle that rattled the Democratic Party. Van Evrie avoided a complete rupture with Douglas, the North's most popular Democrat, hoping that he would relent. But for now, Van Evrie pulled few punches. He denounced Douglas's pet doctrine of popular sovereignty as a "wretched humbug" that failed to safeguard enslavers' property rights, citing it as proof that Northern Democrats were truckling to antislavery sentiment. Douglas himself was a selfish demagogue who had "taken the fatal step that leads into the abyss of Abolitionism."[17] These attacks on Northern Democrats suited Van Evrie's ideological commitments and reliance on Southern patrons. As he confided to Davis, his main goal was to "drive the Northern Democrats from their skulking places" and on to "victory over Abolitiondom."[18] And since he believed every political debate must be settled by considering first principles, the Lecompton dispute offered another opportunity to affirm that "white equality and negro subordination must be accepted as the normal order of American society, and Democracy and 'slavery' understood as they are in fact, the twin sisters of American civilization."[19]

Van Evrie was pouring old wine into new bottles, but bottles mattered because marketing was as important as content. During his apprenticeship, Van Evrie focused on writing editorials. Now, as proprietor, he had to run a company. He delegated many daily operations to Rushmore Horton, who excelled as a business manager.[20] Together, they enlisted investors, recruited subscribers, and improved advertising and distribution. Within two years, they had prepared their enterprise to survive secession and civil war. Thus, while the early years of their proprietorship generated predictable content, their energetic management secured the stability that had eluded Stimson. And because they achieved this without federal largesse, their firm was not reliant on public patronage. Van Evrie and Horton had learned how to run an independent, proslavery commercial paper and were poised to produce the extensive catalog of publications that flowed from their presses during and after the Civil War.

Buchanan's withdrawal of patronage showed that federal aid was a fickle boon, but private investment could bolster newspaper finances regardless of presidential whims or election outcomes. Nothing did more to strengthen the *Day Book* than capital from a single investor: George Washington Olney Jr. A South Carolinian, Olney joined the parade of Southern patrons who backed Van Evrie throughout his career. The *Day Book* germinated in Northern soil, but Southern money fertilized its rapid growth in the late 1850s.

The *Day Book* welcomed Olney in June 1858. Introducing him as a cosmopolitan "gentleman of liberal attainments," Van Evrie promised that his new partner had an "abiding confidence in the generous patriotism of the North" and shared the *Day Book*'s proslavery nationalism. Indeed, the paper's cross-sectional ownership exemplified the "harmony of sentiment and feeling on the distracting question of 'slavery'" that Van Evrie promoted nationwide.[21] But Olney brought money as well as regional diversity. He purchased a one-third share of the business and thus claimed a spot on the masthead, which henceforth named Van Evrie, Horton, & Olney as proprietors.[22]

Olney was a Southern man with Northern connections, a son of Carolina and grandson of New England. Born in Charleston, he was not quite thirty-three when he sank a slice of his family's mercantile fortune into the *Day Book*. The elder George W. Olney, son of a Revolutionary War hero, was born in Rhode Island and moved to Charleston after the War of 1812. He prospered by selling slave-grown staples, married a Massachusetts woman, and raised a large family. By 1850, he owned $5,000 in real property and had seven children, including George Jr., the eldest, who clerked for him; the household also included four enslaved people. Tall and fair with light brown hair and blue eyes, George the younger headed north and earned a law degree at Harvard in 1855. After touring Europe, he began a long journalistic career by investing in the *Day Book*.[23]

Southern cash launched the newspaper on a soaring trajectory that continued until secession. It immediately rescued Van Evrie and Horton from the crushing debt and poor credit bequeathed to them by Stimson.[24] But it also allowed them to invest in the future by relocating to a large brownstone building at 40 Ann Street, on the corner of Nassau Street and close to Printing House Square. And it financed other improvements. First, Van Evrie and Horton nearly doubled the paper's physical size and added an evening edition. To fill column space and maximize the timeliness of their coverage, they hired correspondents, invested nearly $2,000 into telegraphic news services, and added new features such as daily reports on the grain, cotton, and money markets and a daily updated bank note table that listed discount rates for paper money issued by banks nationwide. They also cut the annual prepaid subscription rate to five dollars, making the *Day Book* (they claimed) New York's cheapest daily.[25] Soon after, they sank several thousand dollars into a cylinder printing press powered by a caloric engine and bought a second

"Grand Procession of Wide-Awakes at New York on the Evening of October 3, 1860," *Harper's Weekly*, October 13, 1860. Like other 1860s-era illustrations of Printing House Square, this one shows the *Day Book* office, adjacent to the *Tribune*'s headquarters and near the other leading New York papers, including the *Times*. Courtesy of the Library of Congress.

cylinder press in 1860.[26] These improvements boosted circulation and elicited modest local and state patronage. By 1860, New York City's Common Council had selected the *Day Book* to print its proceedings, and the state's Board of Supervisors had awarded it a contract to print state laws.[27] Van Evrie and Horton rode this momentum all the way to Printing House Square. In May 1860, they announced their move to a five-story office at 162 Nassau Street, adjacent to the *Tribune* and near the other major daily newspapers.[28] The journalist who predicted "warm times when two such opposing elements as the Tribune and the Day Book come into such close contact" was right: Van Evrie had moved next door to—and leased the space from—his nemesis, Horace Greeley.[29] But the *Day Book* had arrived.

With these investments, Van Evrie redeemed his promise to run a proslavery commercial newspaper that championed Manhattan's Southern trade. Each time he unveiled an upgrade, he reiterated his commitment to, and solicited support from, elite New Yorkers. In May 1858, he boasted that daily market reports would make the *Day Book* "very acceptable to merchants and business men generally," alluding to his pledge to earn their custom.[30] Three months later, he bragged that the paper circulated widely among New York's "very best mercantile and commercial houses" and urged business readers to protect their interests by backing his efforts. Abolitionism threatened the national unity that had "made this commercial emporium what it is." Since the *Day Book* could prevent sectional schism and economic ruin, it deserved the "complete confidence and support of the business community of New York."[31] The following year, he emphasized his service to Northern and Southern elites alike, but challenged the former to step up their contributions. New York subscribers, he enthused, "doubtless represent *nine-tenths* of the southern business of the city," while Southern subscribers "represent *nine-tenths* of the productive wealth of the southern States." But he needed some of that money. Southerners contributed by taking a majority of *Day Book* subscriptions. Now, the merchants who made New York "the great commercial emporium of the South" were "bound . . . to extend the same support and encouragement," for they had an "identical" interest in preserving slavery. "If the persons in New York engaged in southern trade and dependent upon the continuation of negro 'slavery' or subordination . . . *will support such a paper by their advertising*, it can be done."[32] These appeals reaffirmed that the *Day Book* was not geared toward laborers but toward the planters and merchants who were making a killing on cotton. Van Evrie targeted a broader constituency when he insisted that Black slavery underpinned white democracy. But his business depended on deep pockets. In the late 1850s, it was propertied readers whose interests he promoted, whose news coverage needs he served, and whose stake in slavery he deemed most urgent.

Van Evrie lamented that advertising revenue lagged circulation, but increases in *Day Book* subscribers were striking. He claimed that subscriptions doubled within three months of the paper's June 1858 enlargement.[33] Circulation surged over the next two years, with weekly subscriptions rising from 20,000 to 30,000 between June and September 1859, and topping 40,000 at year's end.[34] By mid-1860, the *Day Book* ranked second among the city's weeklies and evening dailies.[35] And since New York was the nation's news hub, the paper was positioned for maximum influence. Indeed, a South Carolina subscriber, whose home state boasted such fiery proslavery journals as the *Charleston Mercury*, raved that the *Day Book* was "calculated . . . better to advance southern rights than any paper South."[36] Judging by its swelling subscriber list, thousands of other readers were equally excited about its prospects.

Subscribers did not materialize unbidden. Van Evrie and Horton enticed them with shrewd marketing. Neither novel nor unique, their promotional strategies exemplify how proprietors survived the hypercompetitive nineteenth-century media marketplace.

Occasionally, they pounced on opportunities to recruit readers en masse. One appeared in 1859, when John Mitchel, proprietor of the *Southern Citizen*, rededicated himself to Irish independence. Ulster-born Mitchel espoused Irish nationalism from youth. During the Great Famine, which he denounced as genocide, he established the *United Irishman* newspaper to promote revolution and land redistribution. Mitchel was convicted of treason and exiled to Tasmania but escaped to America and settled in Tennessee. Still politically zealous, he now sided with power—the Slave Power. Through the *Southern Citizen*, which he founded in Knoxville in 1857 and later relocated to Washington, Mitchel championed slavery as a positive good, lauded the African slave trade, and preached Southern nationalism. But, like most newspapers, the *Southern Citizen* struggled financially. When war erupted in Europe in summer 1859, Mitchel decided to return home and strike anew for Irish nationhood. Before departing, he sold his subscriber list to Van Evrie, an ally against British imperialism who had defended Mitchel in print, and arranged for the *Day Book* to finish all current *Southern Citizen* subscriptions. Mitchel's parting gift was a warm endorsement: In a public letter to Charleston slave-trade agitator Leonidas Spratt, he praised the *Day Book* as "a very staunch southern paper." Van Evrie now probably reached more Southern subscribers than any other editor in the North.[37] His task was to retain Southern support while steering proslavery zeal away from regional separatism.

Van Evrie and Horton chased other windfalls by asking proslavery luminaries for assistance. Antebellum politicians often kept lists of constituents to whom they dispatched speeches, pamphlets, and newspapers. This system had already boosted Van Evrie's career when John Quitman and other sympathetic politicians sent copies of *Negroes and Negro "Slavery"* to their contacts. During an 1859 subscription campaign, Van Evrie and Horton privately asked congressional allies for their mailing lists, intending to distribute free samples of the *Day Book*. Their most prominent target was Senator James H. Hammond of South Carolina, whose "mudsill" speech the previous year had outraged many Northern whites by likening the subordination of wage workers and slaves. Few slavocrats were more monstrous, but Van Evrie sought to swell circulation by capitalizing on Hammond's connections.[38]

Usually, however, new readers arrived in smaller groups of ten or twenty, as Van Evrie and Horton relied on newspaper clubs for marketing and distribution. Now largely forgotten, subscriber clubs enlisted readers to promote newspapers through their own networks. These clubs predated US independence, but they proliferated after 1852, when Congress authorized a cheap bulk rate of a half cent per ounce for packets of periodicals delivered to one destination. Shrewd editors offered discounted dues to groups of subscribers who shared a post office. Newspaper clubs thus fostered camaraderie among neighbors who supported the same news source. In a fragmented media marketplace, where consumers chose periodicals that suited their political views, religious faith, or economic interests, forming a subscriber club was both a thrifty strategy and a means of self-identification and group bonding. It was also a grassroots political activity that transformed consumers into advertisers. By soliciting friends, clients, and neighbors, they recruited supporters and funds for the media mouthpieces that championed their favorite causes.[39]

Stimson first promoted *Day Book* clubs during an 1855 subscription drive in which he offered a gold watch to the largest club organizer. "Let every democrat who desires the success of his principles," he urged, "make an effort to get up a club and forward on the names." He also encouraged postmasters to drum up subscribers and mailed free copies of the May 12 issue to postmasters around the country. This was a savvy move. By this time, Stimson had switched parties, and with Franklin Pierce's presidency in its third year, postmasters comprised a national network of Democratic loyalists. Since post offices were hubs of social life and political activity, postmasters were strategically positioned to sell periodicals. Weekly subscriptions cost $2 per year, but members of clubs of ten paid only $1.50 and members of clubs of twenty only $1.[40] The campaign paid off: weekly *Day Book* subscriptions grew by a factor of five between July 1855 and August 1856.[41]

Soon after taking over, Van Evrie and Horton launched their own club campaign, and circulation more than doubled by August 1858.[42] Thereafter, Van Evrie and Horton regularly promoted club formation as a means for readers to support the Democratic Party and their favorite paper. These efforts peaked in May 1860 when, in his announcement of the *Day Book*'s move to Printing House Square, Van Evrie enumerated the 167 largest subscriber clubs, specifying their location and size.[43] The list reveals patterns in *Day Book* support and underscores the importance of clubs in attracting readers. Together, the largest clubs encompassed 6,424 people, accounting for 16 percent of the *Day Book*'s 40,000 weekly subscribers. Median membership was 38.5 subscribers, with the smallest numbering 20 subscribers and the largest, located in Olney's hometown of Charleston, reached 110. Tied for second place with 80 subscribers were clubs in Mayfield, Kentucky, and Rusk, Texas; the fourth largest, in Gonzales, Texas, boasted 78 subscribers. Van Evrie acknowledged that his subscriber base was heavily Southern, and this was reflected in the club data. All but nineteen of the clubs were in slave states, with one in Nebraska Territory and eighteen in free states. Texas contained the most clubs (thirty-one), trailed by four other cotton states: Arkansas (eighteen), Alabama (seventeen), Mississippi (sixteen), and Georgia (fourteen). Among the free states, Indiana led with ten large clubs, followed by Pennsylvania (five) and Michigan (four). Southern predominance was not driven by the exigencies of rural distribution, for clubs flourished in cities like Charleston, New Orleans, Mobile, Wilmington, and Savannah.

Most club organizers were local notables who used their influence to recruit readers and disseminate proslavery doctrines. Because Van Evrie regularly published letters from club organizers, scores of them can be identified in the census and other sources. An examination of 83 individuals who founded *Day Book* subscriber clubs between 1855 and 1860 illuminates the local promoters who peddled Van Evrie's proslavery propaganda during a period of escalating conflict. *Day Book* subscriber campaigns were not quite astroturfed movements, but they bore a distinctly top-down stamp.

Antebellum organizers resided in twenty-eight states and territories, with a Southern tilt in their geographic distribution. Forty-nine, or nearly 60 percent, lived in slave states, and thirty-four in free states or territories. Given that white Southerners accounted for less than a third of the nation's white population, they were highly overrepresented, but their share of the club organizers probably reflected the regional distribution of *Day Book* readers.

More striking are the founders' wealth and occupational profiles. The mean free-state club organizer held $3,115 in real property and $2,092 in personal property at a time when skilled workers earned around a dollar a day. Among the club organizers, nine were merchants (the largest occupational bloc), with farmers, artisans, and professionals (physicians, attorneys, and ministers) contributing another dozen. Around 15 percent were postmasters, suggesting that the *Day Book*'s postal marketing strategy was successful. Southern club organizers were even wealthier, owning on average $12,314 in real property and $18,921 in personal property. Nearly three-quarters of them were enslavers, with an average of twelve enslaved people in their households. Twenty-two were farmers or planters; six merchants, eleven professionals, three printers, and two postmasters also formed clubs.

Prosperous and well-connected club organizers had motive and opportunity to promote Van Evrie's virulent ideology. Southern enslavers eagerly disseminated a newspaper that vindicated slavery as the basis of national prosperity, white liberty, and social order. Some organizers also led other proslavery initiatives. Curtis W. Jacobs, for instance, owned three plantations on Maryland's Eastern Shore and enslaved forty-three people. Unnerved by a rash of escapes and John Brown's raid on Harpers Ferry, Jacobs organized a *Day Book* club in late 1859, weeks before sponsoring legislation to ban manumissions and either expel or enslave Maryland's large free Black population.[44] The late 1850s were an especially uneasy time for enslavers like Jacobs. They feared abolitionism and enslaved people's resistance, of course. But they also worried that soaring inequality and class resentment might spread antislavery among poor whites. As they scrambled to fortify mass support for slavery, some turned to the *Day Book*. Henry P. Hill, a Georgian who enslaved eight people, organized a *Day Book* club in 1858 to enlighten his neighbors about their "true position" in the slavery controversy.[45] Early the next year, Alabama planter John G. Johnson bragged about violently dispersing an illicit dance attended by enslaved people and poor whites. He cheered Van Evrie's efforts to instill in all whites a sense of superiority—and, by organizing a club, helped spread that message.[46]

Northern organizers' motivations were equally compelling. A quarter were born in Southern states, suggesting that historians have correctly identified interregional migration as a propagator of proslavery ideology in the free states.[47] Many were Democratic zealots, often officeholders, who backed the party's proslavery wing amid the intraparty conflicts of the late 1850s. David H. Rowland served in the Michigan legislature before founding a *Day Book* club in 1855, while Joshua Parsons had been a state legislator and town clerk in Maine.[48] Dismayed by internal quarrels, they relished the *Day Book*'s hardline proslavery stance and formed clubs to convert their neighbors. William J. Stewart of Indiana established a twelve-member club in early 1860 to stiffen the spines of "milk-and-water and doubtful Democrats" in the area.[49] The numerous merchants among Northern club founders may also have been motivated by hostility to industrialists and the Republican Party that championed their interests. In the late 1850s, a long era of free trade and merchant domination of the economy was waning, and Republicans' protectionist program promised to hasten its end. In time, this would allow manufacturers to take over the distribution and marketing of finished goods, undercutting merchants' local economic power. The *Day Book*'s free-trade editorials and overt appeals to merchants encouraged them to view it as their ally.[50]

Club organizers were also positioned to promote *Day Book* readership by connecting their neighbors to the print network that led to Van Evrie's office. The planters, merchants, and postmasters who predominated among club founders all linked their communities to the outside world. Planters ginned humbler neighbors' cotton and exported it with their own. Merchants extended credit, shared market news, and brought a world of goods to isolated hamlets. Postmasters kept print material flowing to their neighborhoods and monitored what their customers were reading, as they were legally bound to list subscriptions in their record books.[51] The people best able to form *Day Book* clubs were the same local elites who had the most to gain from promulgating Van Evrie's ideas.

Given the founders' motives and opportunities, it is worth exploring how clubs were established. Did club formation reflect camaraderie? Certainly, it often did. When Alabama physician Andrew Denny created a *Day Book* club with a dozen friends in 1858, for instance, the process was voluntary and all members were of similar status.[52] But other organizers simply submitted lists of recipients, along with their subscription fees, without consulting the new subscribers, who received a dose of proslavery propaganda whether they wanted it or not. Mississippi Unionist Levi H. Naron noted that his neighborhood "was flooded by the New York *Day Book*" amid spiraling sectionalism in 1860. "Persons would not subscribe for it, no matter what their politics," he explained, but "it would be sent to them for six months," prepaid by "Southern capitalists."[53] Following the Union debacle at Bull Run in July 1861, rumors of a similar campaign swept the North, where Confederate sympathizers allegedly stockpiled copies of the *Day Book* "for gratuitous distribution" as part of a subversion campaign.[54]

Often, the dynamics of club organization fell somewhere between chummy fellowship and elite imposition. Consider the case of a growing *Day Book* club in western Missouri. Organizers O. B. Pearson and William B. Sappington sent in several lists of names in 1858 as they persuaded additional people to take the paper. It was hard work: Subscribers were not rushing to sign up, but the Missourians labored to "convince them."[55] And they were well-positioned to do so. Pearson was a planter with more than $33,000 in property—including twenty-eight enslaved people, town lots, and a store—and a major donor to the local Methodist Episcopal Church.[56] Sappington was worth nearly $100,000, enslaved thirty-eight individuals, and had invested heavily in the local branch of the Bank of Missouri. His son-in-law later served as Missouri's governor during the secession crisis. Sappington may have learned the hard sell from his father, a physician who peddled Sappington's Anti-Fever Pills throughout the Mississippi River Valley.[57] And if their persuasive powers failed, Sappington and Pearson could apply other pressure: calling in loans, denying credit, or refusing patronage. When powerful people promoted *Day Book* clubs, it was difficult for their humbler neighbors to say no.

Whether born of comradeship or coercion, subscriber clubs allowed Van Evrie to leverage local networks to maximize his circulation and energize Democratic voters. Few institutions better reveal how newspapers braided ideology and partisanship with business than the clubs that helped double *Day Book* readership between 1858 and 1860, and would continue to facilitate Van Evrie's marketing and mass mobilization deep into Reconstruction.

Chapter 10

Savior

It was no accident that *Day Book* readership soared alongside sectional tensions. Boosters more easily sold a proslavery paper when the subject dominated American politics. Hence, one of the ironies of Van Evrie's career: While he strove to smother sectionalism with proslavery nationalism, sectional conflict fueled demand for his product. What was good for Van Evrie's business was bad for his political project. This dynamic eventually alienated Unionists, who accused him of profiting at their expense. But in the three years before secession, Van Evrie monetized the turmoil with a series of political interventions that grew his personal brand and the *Day Book*'s subscriber list, particularly among Southerners. Although he presented the paper as an antidote to sectional rancor and portrayed himself as a national savior, Van Evrie leaned further to the South than ever before, in both editorial content and subscriber base.

High-profile rivalries were good for business. Nathaniel Stimson had tangled with Frederick Douglass, and Van Evrie had confronted Harriet Beecher Stowe. Now, he confronted Hinton Rowan Helper. Born in North Carolina, Helper began writing after a disappointing trek to California's gold mines. A censorious proslavery publisher piqued his fury against the Slave Power and inspired him to write *The Impending Crisis of the South* (1857) and *Compendium of the Impending Crisis of the South* (1860). Presenting himself as a loyal Southerner and class-conscious yeoman, Helper advocated abolition and freedpeople's deportation in order to liberate common whites from planters' repressive rule. Helper was the anti-Van Evrie: a Southerner whose work sold best in the North, and an antislavery author who held that Black servitude exacerbated inequality among whites. Shared racism notwithstanding, Van Evrie and Helper battled for the hearts and minds of the nation's nonslaveholding white majority.[1]

Helper's firebrand publications stoked conflict. Republicans lauded him as a champion of downtrodden Southern whites, echoed his arguments in Congress, and adopted *Impending Crisis* as a campaign text in 1860. For proslavery Southerners, Helper was a nightmare. Never certain of nonslaveholders' loyalty and appalled by Northern praise for a man who condoned violent resistance to slavery, Southern elites outlawed the distribution of Helper's work and hurried to rebut his class-based critique.[2] James D. B. De Bow responded with *The Interest in Slavery of the Southern Non-Slaveholder* (1860), while Southern politicians cranked up the demagoguery. Jefferson Davis swore that, in the South, "white men have an equality . . . which cannot exist where white men fill the position here occupied by the servile race."[3]

Van Evrie, accustomed to battling the Slave Power's Northern critics, promptly attacked the Southern heretic. In April 1858, he dismissed *Impending Crisis* as a "silly book" that was packed with "stupendous lies" and "unworthy of notice."[4] But he kept noticing Helper—and reviling him. In "What the Abolitionists Are Doing," he shared with "the people of the South" information gleaned from antislavery newspapers, including a plan (printed in Horace Greeley's *Tribune*) to distribute *Impending Crisis* across the slave states. Amid spiking Southern fears of subversion, Van Evrie posed as a sleepless sentinel.[5] He also countered Helper's class critique, insisting that nonslaveholders in the South presented a "united front" against abolition.[6] When Helper lectured in New York, Rushmore Horton organized protests against "fanatical and misguided people" who opposed "the best interests of our common country."[7] And when Van Evrie's book-length *Negroes and Negro "Slavery"* finally appeared in print, Southern enthusiasts praised it for exposing Helper's "fallacy" and hoped it would circulate as widely as *Impending Crisis*.[8] Undaunted, Helper publicly mocked the "snivelling, servile, little *Day Book*."[9] Thus two racist loudmouths clashed over slavery's place in their country.

While assailing a Southern dissenter, Van Evrie also nurtured the alliance between Manhattan and the cotton states, which had been strained by the Panic of 1857. The panic's disparate impact inflamed sectional rivalries by intensifying Northern hostility toward the Slave Power and emboldening Southern dreams of economic autonomy and political independence.[10] In the North, Republicans broadened their appeal with a blueprint for economic recovery that included homestead legislation, infrastructure investment, and tariff protection. Southern opposition confirmed Republican criticism of the Slave Power as a venal oligarchy that would consign Northern workers to poverty. Slavery, according to a standard Republican indictment, waged "an aggressive war" against the "interest of the free states."[11] With thousands unemployed and hundreds of businesses ruined, the Panic of 1857 lent urgency to this message.

In the South, which escaped the worst of the slump, the panic bolstered separatist confidence while underscoring regional dependence on Northern intermediaries. Proslavery pundits cited Northern distress as proof that slavery was superior to wage labor. And at a moment when the cotton kingdom thrived while commerce and manufacturing withered, claims that the global economy danced to a Southern tune seemed plausible. No one blended these two themes more provocatively than Senator James H. Hammond of South

Carolina. In March 1858, he proclaimed that the South, with its harmonious social system and bountiful cotton, was prepared to go it alone. Blessed by an enslaved "mudsill" class, immune to "speculative bubbles," and ready to withhold its staple crop until "England . . . topple[d] headlong and carr[ied] the whole civilized world with her," Hammond's cotton kingdom appeared all-powerful.[12] The speech infuriated Northern workers, who reappropriated Hammond's epithet and organized Mudsill Clubs to support Republicans.[13] Yet his bravado masked the bitterness of Southern planters and merchants who strained against Northern economic power. Cotton might be king, but exports still passed through Manhattan, where bank failures dramatized the perils of what a Charlestonian deemed the "unnatural and colonial dependency of our commercial community on New York."[14]

While Republicans appealed to Northern pride, and as haughty resentment festered in the South, Van Evrie labored to maintain a proslavery Union. Alarmed that Republican protectionism was winning converts, he devoted more column space to vindicating free trade.[15] He also ratcheted up the rhetoric about the North's dependence on slave-grown staples. New York, he argued, was "indebted to the southern States for her unrivalled position as the great commercial metropolis of this vast country."[16] The same went for "every city, town, and hamlet" along the northeastern Atlantic coast.[17] Van Evrie grew increasingly dogmatic on this theme and rebuked anyone who suggested that dependency was mutual, declaring that "New York commerce is founded almost entirely upon the products of the southern States." He wanted to convince Northern business leaders of their stake in slavery. "Strike a blow at southern production," he warned, "and you destroy the market for northern goods, wares and merchandise."[18] But his portrayal of Manhattan's Southern trade now looked less like a partnership and more like vassalage. He sounded like Hammond. Fittingly, he printed an extract from "Cotton Is King" on the *Day Book*'s front page, recommended it to "every merchant in New York," and echoed Hammond's claim that the "commerce of this country comes mainly from the South." Never mind that the Carolinian had taunted Northern workers. Never mind that his speech reeked of sectional chauvinism. What mattered for Van Evrie was that the "social system at the South" was the basis of New York's prosperity and that his was the city's only newspaper sounding the alarm about abolitionism.[19] As sectionalism fed on economic turmoil, Van Evrie leaned further to the South. Unlike Southern secessionists, he hoped to drag Northerners along with him. But he had joined the effort to bully King Cotton's Northern courtiers into submission. He remained a nationalist, but his case for slavery borrowed from fire-eaters who were prepared to dissolve a Union they could not dominate. No wonder Southern subscribers were impressed.

Van Evrie redoubled his efforts for Union on enslavers' terms following John Brown's raid on Harpers Ferry. Captured on October 18, 1859, and hanged on December 2, Brown blended the moral zeal of William Lloyd Garrison with the subversiveness of Hinton Helper and the martyrdom of Charles Sumner. Van Evrie's editorial response was predictable. Smugly observing that enslaved people had rebuffed them, he blasted Brown's "foolish fanatics" for scheming to unleash "anarchy and bloodshed . . . over the entire South." Abolitionists and Republicans who had incited Brown were culpable, as were tepid Northern Democrats who shrank from endorsing slavery. Brown himself was a "traitor to his country, to his race, to the principles of republican liberty, and a blasphemer of God Almighty" who rebelled against a racial order that Van Evrie claimed was decreed by Heaven and ratified by the Founding Fathers.[20] But Van Evrie did more than fulminate. The outpouring of Northern sympathy for Brown was as politically salient as the raid itself.[21] In response, Southern fire-eaters preached secession, while ostensible moderates, including majorities in several Southern state legislatures, demanded direct trade with Europe and boycotts against the North.[22] Once again, Van Evrie had to reassure proslavery Southerners that neither commercial retaliation nor political separation were necessary. To placate Southern fears, he organized Northern backlash.

Van Evrie and Horton used the *Day Book* to orchestrate a ringing proslavery statement from New York's commercial community. Three days before Brown's execution, Van Evrie called for a "Sympathy with the South" meeting, where New Yorkers would deplore "the motives and acts of Old Brown and his followers." By providing a counterweight to the mass meetings of Northerners who lionized Brown, Van Evrie hoped to stigmatize them as a fanatical minority and assure proslavery Southerners that most Northerners were friendly. He asked like-minded readers to send him their names.[23] The project quickly gained momentum, and Van Evrie began printing letters of support on December 3.[24] He claimed to have received five hundred names in just two days and more than three thousand by December 6, boasting that they came from among "the very best [mercantile] houses and leading men of the city."[25] Simultaneously, he teased a *Day Book* special issue that would celebrate New York's Southern trade, showcase antipathy for Brown, and publicize the upcoming sympathy meeting. He would send free copies to Southern "Merchants and Business Men," and offer Northern advertisers discounted rates and the promise of extensive Southern circulation.[26] To spread the word, he dispatched Horton's brother on an advertising tour in the South.[27] Once more, sectional strife provided a golden opportunity for the strident nationalist. Alert to both the dangers of Southern retaliation and the opportunities for self-promotion, Van Evrie's sympathy campaign was an elite initiative rooted in New York's business community. The *Day Book*'s class orientation, ideology, and business model aligned neatly, erasing the line between newspaper marketing and political activism.

Released on December 15, 1859, the special issue amplified a chorus of antiabolitionism. Van Evrie included an editorial denouncing Frederick Douglass and a letter to the editor penned by Edmund Ruffin.[28] But the highlight was the proclamation entitled "The North and the South. Justice and Fraternity." It opened by condemning "the crimes of John Brown and his confederates," defending the Constitution as construed in the *Dred Scott* decision, and denying that any "irrepressible conflict" divided North and South. Rather, there was "a natural and necessary affinity between them," and their "different forms of industry" strengthened the bond "by enabling them to supply each other's wants." Here was a proslavery message tailored for the *Day Book*'s audience. The article closed by announcing that the Southern sympathy meeting would convene at the Academy of Music on Monday, December 19, at 7 p.m., with New York Mayor Daniel F. Tiemann presiding. Some twenty thousand people had endorsed it, and Van Evrie printed all their names. The first installment filled more than three and a half columns; the second appeared the following day. The densely packed signatures sent two messages: New York's business community was politically sound, and the *Day Book* was its mouthpiece.[29]

The sympathy campaign sprang from a different source than the city's 1863 draft riots. The explosion in 1863, fueled by racism, class hatred, and wartime suffering, remains notorious as the epitome of working-class backlash against emancipation.[30] But the New Yorkers mobilized in Van Evrie's 1859 crusade were an affluent bunch, mostly native-born business owners who feared disruption of interregional trade. The organizing committee included James W. Beekman, a rentier with a $200,000 real estate portfolio; Joshua J. Henry, a dry goods importer who specialized in Southern commerce; B. M. Whitlock, an importer of luxury goods; John Jacob Astor Jr., son of the famous fur trader and real estate tycoon; James Brooks, a former Whig destined for infamy as a Copperhead Democrat; and A. T. Stewart, a dry goods merchant who pioneered the department store.[31] For them, elite Southerners were clients and colleagues; Irish immigrants were servants.

The signers represented a cross-section of the business community. Elites included railroad magnate Erastus J. Corning (recipient of Abraham Lincoln's 1863 public letter on civil liberties), lawyer and future presidential candidate Samuel J. Tilden, and Democratic financier August Belmont. But even the humbler cosigners were generally well-off. A sample of a hundred signers clarifies the social base of Van Evrie's Southern sympathy campaign. With an average age of thirty-eight, mean real estate holdings of nearly $13,000, and mean personal property of some $6,300, they embodied Victorian respectability. At a time when only 5 percent of New Yorkers boasted over $10,000 in assets, more than a third of the sample did. A small majority employed at least one servant, and more than three-quarters were native-born, with the immigrants hailing mainly from Germany or England. Twenty (a plurality) were merchants; another eighteen were retailers, eighteen were manufacturers, fifteen worked as clerks, eight as professionals, five as bankers, and four worked in editing or publishing. Only one was a laborer. This profile probably resembled Van Evrie's antebellum local readership.[32]

Several thousand New Yorkers packed the Academy of Music, an opera house on East Fourteenth Street, on the evening of December 19 to express their sympathy with the South, while thousands more thronged the streets outside. The theater was festooned with patriotic regalia and quotations from George Washington, Andrew Jackson, and naturally, Daniel Webster. Attendees passed resolutions praising the Union and the Constitution, decrying the Harpers Ferry raid as treason, and lamenting that slavery had become "mingled with party politics." Van Evrie later grumbled that these airy abstractions failed to meet the occasion.[33] But he savored the showcase speech delivered by lawyer and Democratic star Charles O'Conor, entitled "Negro Slavery Not Unjust." O'Conor echoed most Northern conservatives by arguing that slavery was protected by the Constitution. Had he stopped there, Van Evrie would have derided him as another spineless Northern Democrat. But O'Conor rushed onward, proclaiming: "*I insist that negro slavery is not unjust. . . . It is not unjust; it is just, wise, and beneficent.*" Slavery, he insisted, "is benign in its influences upon the white man, and upon the black. . . . I maintain that it is ordained by nature; that it is a necessity of both races; that, in climates where the black race can live and prosper, nature herself enjoins correlative duties on the black man and on the white, which cannot be performed, except by the preservation, and . . . the perpetuation of negro slavery." Like Van Evrie, he praised Chief Justice Roger Taney's opinion in *Dred Scott* and damned Hinton Helper and John Brown in the same breath. Like Van Evrie, he urged Northerners to reject politicians who tolerated slavery as a necessary evil and instead support those who endorsed it as "just, benign, lawful, and proper." Only on this ground could patriotic Northerners protect the Union; national cohesion required proslavery consensus.[34] To broadcast O'Conor's "bold, manly and truly philosophical speech," Van Evrie and Horton published it in the *Day Book* and sold pamphlet copies for six cents each.[35]

Basking in his self-image as the paladin of proslavery Unionism, Van Evrie made no distinction between political crusading and newspaper marketing. Mailing sample issues to Southern merchants, promoting the sympathy meeting, and plastering *Day Book* advertisements on the pamphlet edition of O'Conor's speech served two interlocking aims: disseminating proslavery nationalism and promoting the newspaper. Whether his late 1859 campaign changed Northern minds and soothed Southern nerves is not clear, but it did boost subscriptions. As usual, it was sectional conflict, not harmony, that juiced sales.

The Harpers Ferry crisis proved so profitable that Van Evrie began printing regular updates on the influx of new readers. Between December 5 and 23, 1859, he published sixteen tables tallying new subscribers from each post office. The total was 3,422, with a lopsided regional distribution that reflected the *Day Book*'s soaring appeal in the South. Nearly 85 percent of new subscribers lived in slave states, probably a larger proportion than his readership overall, meaning that his audience was becoming more predominantly Southern over time. New readers were concentrated in the Deep South, with over half hailing from the seven cotton states stretching from South Carolina to Texas. Alabama was home to the largest number of new subscribers, with Mississippi second on the list. Indiana was the only free state to crack the top ten. Proportionately, the regional discrepancy was even starker. Since white Southerners represented only 30 percent of the nation's white population, they were vastly overrepresented among new readers. In the South, Van Evrie snagged 3.6 new subscribers per 10,000 white residents, while in the North, he gained only 0.3 subscribers. Mississippi led the pack with nearly 10 new subscribers per 10,000 whites; Alabama was close behind, followed by South Carolina and Florida. Among the free states, only Vermont (1.21), Indiana (1.15), and New Hampshire (1.01) topped one new subscriber per 10,000 whites.[36]

Records from the Henderson, North Carolina, post office illuminate Van Evrie's late antebellum Southern subscribers. Then part of Granville County and close to Warren and Franklin Counties, Henderson was the hub of a rich cotton- and tobacco-growing region. Over half the local population was enslaved, and area plantations were among the most lucrative in the state. In 1860, Warren, Granville, and Franklin ranked first, second, and sixth, respectively, among North Carolina counties for tobacco output, and Franklin was also a major cotton producer.[37] Not surprisingly, local whites eagerly supported a proslavery commercial newspaper. A few Henderson post office customers took the *Day Book* before 1858, including James H. Wiggins, who became the area's first subscriber in April 1850 when he owned $8,000 in real property and enslaved two children. By 1857, five more subscribers had signed up, including a physician, a minister, a merchant's clerk, and two grocers. Prosperous, educated, and commercially oriented, they fit the *Day Book* subscriber profile.[38]

A smattering of new readers subscribed in 1858 and 1859, but it was in the first quarter of 1860 that the *Day Book* boom reached Henderson. Between January 1 and April 1, fifteen subscribers began taking the paper. A wealthy bunch, they owned, on average, $24,170 in property and seventeen enslaved people, with median values of $8,500 and four persons. Another twenty new subscribers signed up before July 1, nine more before year's end, and seven more in the first quarter of 1861. Typical subscribers included Isham Cheatham, a sixty-five-year-old planter who enslaved twenty-six people and was described as "one of the most influential citizens of the county"; planter E. A. Cheek, an enslaver of seventy-three persons who was an ardent Democratic partisan and temperance activist; and Lewis H. Kittle, a merchant and former postmaster who owned a farm and nine enslaved workers and served as trustee for a private academy.[39] Subscribers living in Henderson itself held, on average, 1.9 times more real property than the average household and 3.6 times more personal property. Fifty-four percent of Henderson's 131 households included enslaved people; by comparison, 77 percent of *Day Book* subscribers lived in slaveholding households.[40]

The Henderson subscribers read widely but selectively. Because postal records arranged subscription information by both periodical and subscriber name, one can reconstruct the reading habits of *Day Book* subscribers, who received forty-two other periodicals in the 1850s. Three trends emerge. First, very few Henderson subscribers read other New York City newspapers. Fifty-nine locals subscribed to the *Day Book* between 1850 and 1861, and only three of them simultaneously received another New York paper; two read the *Herald* and one the *Ledger*. At least in north-central North Carolina, planters' favorite Manhattan periodical was the one run by Van Evrie. Of course, the playing field was tilted in his favor. The suppression of antislavery publications meant that, in Henderson and across the South, Van Evrie faced no competition from periodicals such as the *National Anti-Slavery Standard*. Second, *Day Book* readers were staunch Democrats. Ten of them also subscribed to the Warrenton *News*, a local Democratic organ. Readers of the Raleigh *Democratic Press* (later the *Weekly State Journal*) and the Raleigh *North Carolina Standard* were also well represented among Van Evrie's fans. Finally, *Day Book* readers were, at least on paper, a pious group. Thirteen of them—more than for any other single periodical—also took the *North Carolina Christian Advocate*, a Methodist publication produced in Raleigh. Other religious periodicals popular among *Day Book* readers included the *Biblical Recorder*, a Baptist journal from Raleigh; the *Methodist Protestant*, published in Baltimore; and the *Richmond Christian Advocate* (Methodist). Van Evrie's popularity among Protestants suggests that his effort to reconcile polygenism with Scripture was successful. Some scholars argue that polygenism failed in the South because of its heretical implications.[41] But Henderson readers clearly did not regard Van Evrie's polygenism as a deal-breaker. Less original but much cagier than anticlerical polemicists like Josiah Nott, Van Evrie made inroads among Southern Christians.

Late antebellum readership trends followed the *Day Book*'s editorial tilt. Van Evrie touted his circulation statistics as proof of vibrant growth, but they reflected a dangerous irony: The *Day Book* was most popular in the South, where secession fever was hottest. Disunion would wrest the mantle of proslavery nationalism away from the United States. It would thrill the British aristocracy. And it might place thousands of loyal readers beyond reach. Thus, for Van Evrie, preserving the Union was not merely a matter of ideology; it was essential for business. He had made a proslavery commercial journal pay. But as he anticipated another divisive presidential contest, a new question taunted him: If his political project failed and the Union collapsed, could the *Day Book* survive?

Van Evrie's experience organizing the Southern sympathy campaign informed his presidential politicking in 1860. Confident that he had the visibility and connections to make a difference, he and Rushmore Horton worked with local business and political elites to elevate a proslavery nationalist Democrat to the presidency.

To manage their campaign for the White House, Van Evrie and his cronies gathered at Lafarge House. Constructed in 1853 "in a style of unsurpassed excellence," Lafarge House towered over Broadway between Bleecker and Amity Streets and was touted as one of Manhattan's most luxurious hotels—and then immediately went up in flames.[42] Rebuilt at a cost of $300,000, including $20,000 for its signature white marble facade, the elegant hotel reopened in 1856.[43] It was especially popular among the Southern planters and merchants who visited New York each year. Perhaps because of its advertisements in Southern newspapers, proprietor Henry Wheeler's Democratic loyalties, or his policy of employing "colored" servants ("numbering upward of eighty"), stylish Southerners found Lafarge House a congenial home away from home.[44] Tellingly, Van Evrie established his permanent residence there in 1859.[45]

Van Evrie and Horton, joined by a cabal of politicians, editors, and merchants, made the luxury hotel—which boasted its own telegraph office and was a quick omnibus ride away from Printing House Square—their headquarters.[46]

They first formed a shadowy group called the Radical Democratic Association (RDA). Alarmed by the "progress of Abolition sentiments at the North," as evinced in the response to John Brown, the RDA organized at Lafarge House on December 1, 1859. Horton, always more sociable than Van Evrie, was secretary. Members hoped to sway Northern Democratic opinion ahead of the party's upcoming national convention. Characteristically, Van Evrie and Horton believed the surest strategy was to circulate the *Day Book* and their other publications. So, the RDA contacted Democratic editors and operatives to request lists of local party loyalists categorized according to their views on Stephen Douglas. The plan was to launch a direct-mail campaign and target Democratic voters with "Anti-Abolition documents."[47] Infuriated by Douglas's rejection of key proslavery policies—admission of Kansas as a slave state, repeal of the ban on Atlantic slave trading, and enactment of a federal slave code for the territories—Van Evrie and Horton sought to forestall his nomination by persuading Northern Democrats to demand a proslavery candidate in 1860.[48]

Soon after, the RDA began soliciting new members, inviting those who agreed with Charles O'Conor that "Negro slavery is not unjust" to join.[49] But many of its members also adopted more overt modes of activism. On December 7, around a hundred New Yorkers convened at Lafarge House to publicize and plan Van Evrie's "Sympathy with the South" meeting. A *Charleston Mercury* correspondent saluted these "friends of the South," who included "leading merchants and business men, with a fair representation of legal ability," and predicted that their "grand mass-meeting" at the Academy of Music would surpass the city's 1850 Union rally.[50] As always, business mixed with politics. After the sympathy meeting, Van Evrie printed a full-page advertisement for Lafarge House in the pamphlet version of O'Conor's infamous speech. Lafarge House was thus both the birthplace and a beneficiary of the Southern sympathy meeting organized by its well-connected resident.[51]

As the 1860 campaign opened, Van Evrie and the Lafarge House crowd navigated the fragmentation of the Democratic Party. After proslavery delegates bolted from the party's Charleston convention in May, dueling factions nominated rival candidates. Most Northern Democrats supported Stephen Douglas and popular sovereignty. Most Southern Democrats—and a vocal minority of Northerners, including President James Buchanan—backed John C. Breckinridge of Kentucky, running mate Joseph Lane of Oregon, and a proslavery territorial policy. Disgusted by Douglas's apostasy, Van Evrie fired off angry editorials. As delegates sparred in Charleston, he blasted Douglasites as "bullies, strikers, and political gamblers."[52] Thereafter, he framed the intraparty conflict as a clash between principled patriots and office-hungry hacks. Douglas's popular sovereignty doctrine was a cowardly dodge. Real leaders preached the pure proslavery line. "The time for compromise, and contrivance, and non-committalism has gone by," Van Evrie proclaimed, and Democrats peddling popular sovereignty were "vastly more dangerous" and "a thousand times over more contemptible" than avowed antislavery activists.[53] He distinguished between Democratic ideals—particularly slavery as the basis of white men's liberty and prosperity within the Union—and the Democratic Party, an organization that *should* defend those ideals but was corrupted by Douglas and his ilk. As in 1856, and as he would, with one flagrant exception, thereafter, Van Evrie labored to pull the party toward his own inflexible dogma. If Democrats followed, so much the better; if not, he would buck party discipline. Always, he argued, it was "vastly more important to stand by the vital principles of Democracy than strive to preserve a mere party organism labeled the 'Democratic Party.'"[54]

Van Evrie floated several Democratic tickets, including one featuring his patron Jefferson Davis alongside Charles O'Conor.[55] But when proslavery Democrats nominated Breckinridge and Lane, he cheerfully endorsed them. His admiration for Lane dated back to the Mexican-American War, when Lane's rowdy recruits rescued him at Puebla. Soon after the nomination, he privately congratulated Lane and predicted success. To prevail, he argued—using his trademark scare quotes—that Northerners must "be enlightened on the subject of 'slavery.'" Nudge New York and Pennsylvania out of the Republican column, and Breckinridge would win. Secure New York alone, and the election would go to the House of Representatives, where Breckinridge could prevail. Van Evrie was prepared to convince Northerners to vote for a proslavery ticket. "I *can* make the Day Book the most effective agency in this campaign," he promised, "and desire to do so of course."[56] He was equally enthusiastic in public. He called Breckinridge and Lane "gallant" leaders of a Democratic army who marshaled under a banner proclaiming "White men must rule America" and were ready to "wage unceasing, never-ending, unrelenting war with Abolitionism in all its Protean shapes, forms and colors." Van Evrie knew no politics but proslavery politics. He urged "every friend of the Union and the Constitution" to "rally to the support of Breckinridge and Lane."[57]

Van Evrie fought hard throughout the campaign. His strategy hinged on New York, and because he regarded New York City as the key to the state, he focused on persuading local Democrats to abandon Douglas. Thus, he spent as much time denouncing the Douglasites as rebuking the Republicans. He blasted Douglas as an "audacious pretender" who hawked popular sovereignty like a patent medicine instead of curing sectionalism with a bracing dose of positive-good proslavery nationalism.[58] By obscuring the grotesque connection between antislavery and monarchy, Douglas's duplicitous campaign was "doing mighty mischief in the North without even a possibility of doing any good in the South."[59] His only honorable option was to withdraw and thus avoid throwing the election to Lincoln.[60] Disgusted by calls for the fusion of New York's anti-Republican elements, Van Evrie urged Democrats to close ranks behind the Simon-pure Breckinridge and Lane.[61]

As in 1856, the *Day Book* presses cranked out campaign materials. Van Evrie, Horton & Co. released another edition of *Negroes and Negro "Slavery,"* priced at six cents per copy or four dollars per hundred. They also printed a pamphlet featuring Roger Taney's *Dred Scott* ruling, a polygenist essay by Samuel Cartwright, and an exuberant introduction by Van Evrie. O'Conor's "Negro Slavery Not Unjust" completed the arsenal of documents that "should be in the hands of every person who expects to refute the arguments of the Republicans."[62] The three tracts signaled Van Evrie's equation of proslavery propagandizing with partisan electioneering. He rejected hedging, trimming, and tacking toward the center; ideological purity was the key to electing Democrats and preserving the Union. Hereafter, even when pragmatic Democrats denounced him for dragging them down, he refused to moderate, obfuscate, or temporize. Convinced that slavery was scientifically sound, biblically sanctioned, and politically vital, Van Evrie was determined to convert enough white Northerners to prevail on these terms.

Van Evrie and Horton also plunged into local activism. Since they regarded New York City as a decisive battleground and could activate the network behind the Southern sympathy meeting and the Radical Democratic Association, they quickly took the lead in the Manhattan movement for Breckinridge. They signaled their intentions at a June meeting of the "Constitutional Democratic Association" held—where else?—at Lafarge House. As recorded by secretary Rushmore Horton, the association endorsed the *Dred Scott* decision and protection for slavery in every territory, aligning themselves with the Democratic Party's proslavery wing.[63] Shortly afterward, Van Evrie and a familiar cohort of elite allies formalized their leadership of the city's Breckinridge campaign. They followed the Southern sympathy meeting template: Hold a small gathering to plan and then advertise a later mass rally in a major Manhattan venue. The preliminary meeting took place on July 6 at the Irving Building, just up Broadway from Lafarge House. There, Van Evrie, O'Conor, and "other prominent politicians, editors and merchants" organized Manhattan's Breckinridge operation. They crowned the Kentuckian as the true Democratic candidate and appointed two committees: one to manage the general campaign and another to plan a ratification meeting, where New York Democrats would endorse Breckinridge's nomination. The ratification meeting committee included Joshua J. Henry (fresh from the Southern sympathy meeting's organizing committee), Stephen P. Russell (president pro tem of the

Constitutional Democratic Association), and the tireless Horton. The general campaign committee was run by John A. Dix (a vice president of the Southern sympathy meeting), New York customs collector Augustus Schell, and John R. Dickinson, brother of the New York senator who endorsed Van Evrie's *Negroes and Negro Slavery*.[64]

Public meetings to ratify party nominations were common in antebellum politics, but in 1860 they assumed extra significance for the divided Democrats. When Van Evrie and his comrades gathered on July 18 to endorse Breckinridge and Lane, they were asserting legitimacy as well as rallying the faithful. Festivities began at seven o'clock with a canon salute. An hour later, the doors of Cooper Union—which had hosted Abraham Lincoln that February—opened to the excited crowd. Van Evrie claimed an attendance of ten thousand; even Greeley admitted that the venue "was in a few minutes packed in every part." As he jostled his way inside, Van Evrie saw that the organizing committee had done well. While waiting for the proceedings to begin, attendees listened to patriotic music and read the banners that bedecked the hall. One targeted Lincoln: "The Rail-Splitter shall not Split the Union." Another yoked Douglas's popular sovereignty to abolitionism: "John Brown was a Squatter-Sovereign." A third hailed Breckinridge and Lane as "the standard-bearers of the Union and the Constitution."[65]

John T. Henry, a member of New York's City Council, called the meeting to order and yielded the floor to the chair, John H. Brower. A cotton merchant who ran the New York and Texas Packet Line and had been the Texas Republic's consul in New York, Brower epitomized the *Day Book*'s local audience. In his fiery speech, Brower denounced Douglasites as traitors, deemed Breckinridge the genuine Democratic nominee, and urged listeners to gird for battle. Afterward, the names of the meeting officers were read aloud and applauded. Van Evrie was among the vice presidents, as were Charles O'Conor, Augustus Schell, Alexander Stewart, Stephen P. Russell, and John A. Dix. Secretaries included George W. Olney Jr. and the ubiquitous Horton. Honorifics duly bestowed, it was time to pass the resolutions. One endorsed Breckinridge and Lane. Another rehashed Van Evrie's Mexican lessons by denouncing Republican plans to stymie slavery's expansion, liberate enslaved people, and promote a "mixture of races and consequent social equality, by which they would reduce our glorious country to the condition of Mexico and Central America." A third resolution blasted opposition to slavery as a scheme to "engraft upon this country the forms and errors of monarchical institutions," thus making Van Evrie's conspiracy theory official doctrine. A fourth urged patriots of all parties to support Breckinridge and Lane. After a long speech from former New York Senator Daniel S. Dickinson and the reading of letters from James Buchanan and Charles O'Conor, the meeting adjourned.[66]

Van Evrie celebrated the meeting as "a triumphant success." In breathless prose, he relished attendees' "unbounded enthusiasm" and the "thunder tones" with which "the PEOPLE of New York City" had "rebuked" the Douglasites.[67] But he did not coast through the campaign's home stretch. Along with penning editorials, he worked to harness *Day Book* readers to the campaign, monetize electoral enthusiasm, and create synergy between political campaigning and newspaper marketing. The key was the subscriber club.

Ten days after the ratification meeting, Van Evrie printed a call for "Clubs! Clubs!! Clubs!!!" "Now is the time," he declared, "to get up clubs for the WEEKLY DAY-BOOK everywhere." Breckinridge's stock was soaring "and it only needs that the people should understand the real issue, to give us the most glorious Democratic victory since the days of Andrew Jackson." Of course, the path to enlightenment ran through the *Day Book*. To maximize its reach, clubs could buy the newspaper at special campaign-season rates: ten dollars for twenty copies, twenty dollars for fifty copies, and thirty-five dollars for one hundred. Intriguingly, Van Evrie offered bulk discounts to "Town Committees" and "Clubs" of all sorts, not just *Day Book* clubs.[68] The implication was that local Breckinridge and Lane committees—like the one he helped establish in New York—would enroll their members. *Day Book* readers should all be Breckinridge voters; Breckinridge voters should all be *Day Book* readers. Material and ideological support would flow both ways between the newspaper and the campaign. The paper churned out partisan appeals; the campaign boosted subscriptions by marketing the newspaper through local political networks. Was Van Evrie dedicating his publishing company to the Breckinridge campaign? Or was he turning the Breckinridge campaign into a massive *Day Book* promotion? In practice, the answer was both.

Van Evrie campaigned tirelessly, but by November he sensed that Lincoln would win. Just before Election Day, he printed an editorial entitled "Disunion." Like his editorials on the Southern direct-trade movement, it writhed and twisted from point to point. Van Evrie first expressed reluctance about discussing disunion at all. But his hesitation was not rooted in fear; indeed, it would be better to shatter the Union "into a thousand fragments" than allow Republicans to execute "their traitorous and infamous policy of free negroism." Bravado aside, Van Evrie regretted that the Republican Party "casts its portentous shadows over this great and glorious land." The slaveholding Union, with its "twenty-five millions of citizens, untainted with royalty or negroism," and its "four millions of negroes," had escaped the "corrupt influences of the old world" and created a flourishing republic. But it was in grave danger. Proslavery Southerners, of course, were not at fault. If secession and war destroyed the Union, the "dupes and tools of England" in the North would be responsible. But unlike fire-eaters who prayed for Lincoln's victory so they could launch a Southern Confederacy, Van Evrie lamented the prospect of secession. The torch of proslavery nationalism might soon pass to a Southern republic. He would never condemn his Southern friends and patrons for rupturing the Union he loved, for he shared their dedication to slavery. But he mustered no enthusiasm for Southern separatism. All he could do was hope for a Breckinridge victory.[69]

The miracle never came. Lincoln won nearly every Northern state on his way to an Electoral College triumph. True, he ran poorly in New York City, where he lost every ward to the fusion ticket that Van Evrie despised. But he carried the state by fifty thousand ballots and snagged nearly 54 percent of the free-state popular vote.[70] Van Evrie had boasted that appeals to patriotism, racism, and self-interest would prevail. Perhaps this was mere posturing. Or maybe he needed to leave his Manhattan bubble. Probably he overestimated the *Day Book*'s persuasive power. But certainly, Van Evrie had failed.

Weeks later, Van Evrie published a letter from Jefferson Davis written on the eve of the election. Its tone was friendly, but it foreshadowed the political and professional crises facing Van Evrie as the slave states hurtled toward secession. Davis, as always, valued his efforts. He rejoiced that the book-length edition of *Negroes and Negro "Slavery"* was in press, exulted over the *Day Book*'s fifty thousand weekly subscribers, and saluted it as a "valuable auxiliary." But he also resolved to secede if Lincoln won: "The independence and equality of the States, and the safety of their domestic institutions must be preserved." Nevertheless, Van Evrie printed the letter under the title "How the Union Can Be Saved," and in his commentary, he urged Northern whites to save the country by safeguarding slavery.[71] Yet secession was propelled by the conviction that last-minute reconciliation was impossible. And even if white Northerners experienced the mass conversion that Van Evrie envisioned, what exactly could they *do* to halt disunion? Long on exhortation and short on strategy, he had no answer. By the time he printed Davis's letter, the machinery of disunion was grinding away as white Southerners—his patrons, ideological allies, and a majority of his subscribers—transferred proslavery nationalism to a new republic. Van Evrie had sustained his proslavery Northern newspaper amid sectional conflict. But could it survive secession? And what would become of his slaveholding Union after the slave states departed?

Chapter 11

Crisis

Abraham Lincoln's February 1860 visit to New York helped make him president, but his triumphant return portended crisis. When Lincoln passed through on February 19, 1861, en route to his inauguration, seven slave states had seceded; the other eight teetered on a knife's edge. Yet New Yorkers still gave him an exuberant welcome. After he detrained and boarded a carriage bound for Astor House, a quarter of a million people saluted him with "continuous cheering from the depot to the hotel." Patriotic bunting and banners hung everywhere, from ships in the harbor to downtown hotels. In Printing House Square, all the newspaper offices displayed the Stars and Stripes. All, that is, but the *New York Day Book*.[1]

It was an ominous moment for John Van Evrie. As the Union crumbled, he grew increasingly isolated from his Southern patrons and Northern allies. True, there was still Southern sympathy in New York; one irate sea captain greeted Lincoln by hanging his effigy from a yardarm.[2] But Northerners' hostility to secession and swift mobilization for war caught Van Evrie off guard. The political landscape shifted abruptly, and he struggled for balance. Formerly, he drew rhetorical power from ruthless consistency. Whatever the situation, he repeated his mantras about polygenism, whites' shared interest in Black subordination, and slavery's vital contributions to national welfare. However persuasive he was in the 1850s, his crusade foundered in 1861. The war came. And as the conflict thrust new questions to the forefront, Van Evrie had few answers. What if Unionism now meant fighting enslavers instead of idolizing them? What if the mantle of proslavery nationalism had passed to a new polity? What if shared racism could not keep white men from butchering each other?

Disunion exposed Van Evrie's ideological rigidity and presented him with a triple conundrum. Politically, it shattered his proslavery nationalist project. Unionists were not united behind emancipation, but secessionists loudly resolved to safeguard slavery within a new and improved republic. Financially, it severed his ties to Southern subscribers and forced him to recalibrate his readership. Legally, it pushed him onto thin ice as he clashed with federal officials over the limits of dissent. By August 1861, starved of revenue and tainted with treason, Van Evrie faced ruin.

Van Evrie had long predicted that white Northerners would regain their senses and avert secession by quelling the abolitionists. In striving to enlighten them, he had focused on New Yorkers, particularly the merchants whose dependence on the South and affinity for planter-politicians, he calculated, would put them in the vanguard of a proslavery Unionist reaction. These forecasts were not unrealistic. In 1850, New York merchants celebrated the Union-saving compromise and condemned antislavery activists who defied it. In 1859, Van Evrie coordinated merchants' indignant response to John Brown. And in 1860, Lincoln lost every Manhattan ward. Surely, merchants would ride to the rescue again in 1861.

Events seemed to follow this script when Lincoln's victory touched off twin panics in New York. One was economic. As storm clouds gathered, Southern buyers canceled orders and halted debt payments. Commodity prices plunged, credit contracted, unemployment spiked, and the city lurched into a recession worse than the one in 1857 because there was no thriving Southern trade to offset other losses.[3] Van Evrie claimed vindication, crowing that New York business leaders, the "*hired hands*" of Southern planters, were "positively subservient" to King Cotton. They must make amends soon or be destroyed.[4] Simultaneously, he printed a long exposé on the city's white underclass. Unlike Nathaniel Stimson, he did not claim that white paupers would be better off as slaves, but he did accuse Republicans of concealing their misery. Anticipating a shift in the *Day Book*'s class orientation, Van Evrie asserted that poor whites, devastated by the recession, were paying the price for Republican heresy.[5]

The other postelection panic was political. While Congress haggled over Union-saving bargains, New York merchants organized to promote peace at nearly any price. On December 15, two thousand merchants gathered on Pine Street (one block north of Wall Street) to reproach the Republicans, implore Southerners not to secede, and advocate proslavery legislation, including a federal slave code for the territories and the repeal of Northern states' personal liberty laws. Chaired by Charles O'Conor and attended by a familiar roster of politically active merchants, this meeting was precisely the response Van Evrie had anticipated, and he heartily endorsed it.[6] Thereafter, merchants kept pushing compromise, even after South Carolina seceded in late December and other cotton states followed in January. They sent delegations to Washington, DC, to urge conciliation and in March organized the American Society for Promoting National Unity as a counterweight to the antislavery fanaticism and hasty Southern reaction they blamed for the crisis.[7] Some even suggested municipal secession to make New York an independent city-state. The idea surfaced during the 1860 campaign and gained notoriety when Mayor Fernando Wood publicly supported it in early January. Powerful business and political leaders, including Augustus Schell and James Brooks, countenanced the idea, and Van Evrie gave it a respectful hearing. But he hoped to forestall secession altogether.[8] Shortly after Wood's secessionist appeal, Van Evrie exhorted voters to "hold monster meetings all over the North, and denounce the traitors to their blood as well as to their country, who would negroize this glorious Republic. . . . If this is done promptly, all will be well."[9] It was an imprecise plan, but proslavery Unionism, not peevish separatism, remained his watchword.

Amid the cascading crisis, Van Evrie again resolved to rescue the republic by transforming Northern opinion. When asked whether he would relocate the *Day Book* to the South, Van Evrie insisted that disunion was temporary and pledged that his paper would stand firm in Manhattan, "right in the face of its bitterest enemies," and continue its "battle . . . for the northern mind."[10] He deployed his heaviest artillery in January 1861 by publishing the full-length version of *Negroes and Negro "Slavery."* As the Union disintegrated, he advertised the book as a definitive refutation of "anti-slaveryism" and predicted it would "create a greater impression upon the public mind than any work published for years."[11] It was a bold pledge, but Van Evrie never soft-pedaled his heroic pretensions.

The original *Negroes and Negro Slavery* pamphlet from 1853 exuded the zeal of a nationalist battling foreign foes. That spirit infused the 1861 book, but it mingled with the weariness of an expert trying to save his fellow citizens from themselves by dispelling stubborn errors in popular understanding. The thrust of the preface was *I told you so.* "Since the first edition of this work was issued," Van Evrie began, "startling and deplorable events have occurred." The British-spawned "delusion" of racial equality "has culminated in disunion and civil war." Republicans who parroted "British writers and abolition societies" were poised to take power and shred the Constitution. To escape their "malignant fanaticism," white Southerners had seceded. Northerners had ignored Van Evrie's warnings for eight years and now confronted calamity.[12]

At this moment of maximum peril, Van Evrie posed the question that underpinned the sectional conflict: "Is the negro, except in color, a man like ourselves, and therefore naturally entitled to the same liberty?" Republicans, he argued, answered yes, and if they were right, slavery was indeed an abomination. But he rejected their premise and reached the opposite conclusion: "The negro is a different and subordinate being, and in his normal condition at the South." His book would prove it. Bearing the torch of polygenesis, the author-hero would illuminate the foundations of American society. He would explicate "grand and momentous truths" in a manner "clearly comprehended by the masses," charging only one dollar for the 339-page volume. And he would inspire action. Readers would see that "their own liberty, welfare, and prosperity" were menaced by the antislavery crusaders propelling them toward "the greatest calamity ever inflicted on a civilized people." They would terminate the "causeless and senseless, but frightful sectional conflict now raging" and produce a "universal uprising of the northern masses in favor of a government of WHITE MEN, and UNION with the South." This was Van Evrie's final bid to transmute scientific racism into the cement of Union.[13]

After the breathless preface, the 1861 edition of *Negroes and Negro "Slavery"* offered little that Van Evrie had not written in the 1853 pamphlet or the *Day Book*. He reiterated his conspiracy theory of antislavery's origins. He used his book learning and Mexican adventures to explain polygenism, which he presented as consistent with biblical teachings and the lessons white Americans drew from daily interactions with Black people. Hardly a heresy, polygenism revealed God's design for humanity, which conveniently matched the existing hierarchies of American society. Next came a series of chapters, previously published in the *Day Book*, detailing physiological differences between the races, perceptible in everything from skin and hair to droplets of blood. Proving the *distinctiveness* of human species and *separateness* of their creations, however, was of secondary importance. Van Evrie's main objective was to deduce social status from comparative anatomy. Always impatient with academicians who quibbled over human origins, Van Evrie promoted polygenism because it told white Americans what they already knew: God had designed Black people for servitude.

The book's second half covered equally familiar ground. Citing Mexico, Van Evrie warned that racial intermixture caused social degeneration. Addressing a controversy that had divided the proslavery faithful, he endorsed the Atlantic slave trade. Returning to his core message, he praised Southern society for equalizing whites while making Black people uniquely happy, civilized, and productive. And, extending a key theme from the pamphlet, he extolled Southern enslavers as guardians of democracy. Rebutting Republicans' "Slave Power" thesis, Van Evrie proclaimed that mastery made Southern elites appreciate white men's natural equality. Their alliance with the Northern working class was the bedrock of American democracy. Black slavery, therefore, was of "measureless benefit . . . to the freedom, progress, and prosperity of the laboring and producing classes of the North, and, indeed, to all mankind."[14] Van Evrie again nudged the *Day Book* away from business interests and toward the broader appeals, prevalent in his earliest writings, about the stake common whites had in slavery. Strategically, this made sense because Van Evrie sought to transform mass opinion. He might also have worried that humbler Northern whites had swallowed Republicans' class-conscious

Slave Power rhetoric. Certainly, it betokened a growing disillusionment with New York merchants that soon triggered a major rupture.

Thousands of Americans shared Van Evrie's desire to preserve both slavery and the Union, especially in the border slave states, where proslavery Unionism persisted long after the secession crisis.[15] But in the free states and the Deep South, events had already outpaced him. His hectoring offered little to the majority of Northern voters who had voted Republican or to the even larger majority who resented Southern fire-eaters' resolve to rule the Union or ruin it. And while his social ideals resonated with Confederates, they had already plunged into separatism. Their proslavery zeal eclipsed their American nationalism, and indeed some denounced the Union for not being what Van Evrie insisted it was: proslavery by design. Secession signaled their rejection of Van Evrie's faith that the United States was and always would be a bastion of Black subordination.

Consider the notorious speech delivered in Savannah by Alexander H. Stephens, the vice president of the Confederate States. On March 21, the cadaverous Georgian announced that the Confederacy's "corner stone rests upon the great truth, that the negro is not equal to the white man; *that slavery—subordination to the superior race—is his natural and moral condition*." This language so closely resembled Van Evrie's sloganeering that Stephens might have been inspired by the New Yorker. But while their social premises aligned perfectly, Stephens's nationalist conclusions directly contradicted Van Evrie's. Stephens acclaimed the Confederate government as the "first in the history of the world based upon this great physical, philosophical and moral truth." The Confederacy repudiated the founding principle of the United States, which, Stephens groused, was equality, including "equality of races," as expressed in the Declaration of Independence. Embedded in the country at its birth, this "error" was ineradicable.[16] Stephens cast the Confederacy not as a replica of the United States but an improvement on a fatally flawed prototype. In blaming Thomas Jefferson for this blunder, he joined a long line of Southern reactionaries who denounced the Virginian as a hopeless dreamer and branded his doctrine inimical to slavery. For them, creating the Confederacy was not an attempt to restore the spirit of 1776 but a bid to build a better republic on the rock of inequality.[17]

The cornerstone speech unwittingly exposed the chasm between Van Evrie and Confederate nationalists. Throughout his public career, Van Evrie praised the United States in the same terms that Stephens hailed the Confederacy: as a proslavery republic rooted in racial hierarchy. It was on this basis that he asserted the superiority of American society, which secured white men's equality, over Britain's unnatural class system, which created disparities among biological equals.[18] Ever since the *Dred Scott* decision, he had located in the Constitution the nation's "fundamental doctrine": "*Inferiority of social and political position for the negro race, and superiority for the white race, is the natural order of American society.*"[19] For years, he had revered Jefferson as the original planter-democrat and quoted him on the title page of *Negroes and Negro "Slavery"* as the progenitor of polygenesis. But now, a leading Confederate rationalized secession by arguing that the Union's fundamental faults, inflicted by Jefferson, made it unsafe for slavery. Stephens rejected Van Evrie's vision of the Union's past in order to glorify the Confederacy's future. Van Evrie was as committed to slavery as any Confederate. But unlike Confederates, who supported secession either as a necessary evil or a positive good, Van Evrie bewailed it as the fruit of British antislavery agitation. His disagreement with Confederates, like his departure from kinfolk in Upper Canada, turned not on racism or slavery but on national loyalty. And when Stephens cheered the Union's demise, he celebrated the ruin of Van Evrie's political project.

Van Evrie awkwardly applauded Stephens's oration. As in his fumbling responses to Southern direct-traders, he studiously ignored conflicts with an ideological ally. In early April, he asked Stephens for a copy of the speech, which had "excited great comment in the North."[20] Shortly after, he tried to reconcile Stephens's appeal with his own nationalist vision. The natural subordination of Blacks to whites, he editorialized, was the "principle . . . at the base of American civilization as well as the 'corner stone' of Democratic institutions in the Confederate States." He hoped that white Northerners would realize this in time to dethrone the Republicans and restore the Union. But he glossed over the divide between what Stephens thought the United States could be and what Van Evrie insisted it always was.[21] Four days later, Confederate artillerists opened fire on the flag of a republic that Stephens had deemed inhospitable to slavery. Van Evrie was stuck praising the Confederacy's social order while bewailing secession.

Ironically, he also unwittingly incited Southern separatism. As secessionists shattered his adopted country, Van Evrie echoed their claims about the Republican Party and thus undermined the Southerners whose help he desperately needed: white Unionists. In his effort to stir racist Northern backlash, Van Evrie stoked Southern secession by casting Republicans as abolitionist radicals. Beleaguered white Southern Unionists mourned his blunder.

Throughout the secession crisis, Van Evrie attacked Lincoln and his ilk as fanatics hell-bent on freeing slaves and imposing racial equality. They cloaked themselves in moderation to deceive voters, he claimed, but they aimed to block slavery's expansion, withdraw federal support from enslavers, and unleash emancipation. Republicans differed from avowed abolitionists only in the insidious means they applied toward the same end: "the final abolition of the supremacy of the white man over the negro." And because they had deluded so many people, Republicans were "a million times over more dangerous" than abolitionists.[22] These were the same arguments that immediate secessionists deployed against Southern Unionists who insisted that Republicans posed no urgent threat.[23] And while historians continue to debate the nature of the antebellum Republican Party, what mattered most in 1861 was that the fire-eaters convinced Southern whites to secede.[24]

Van Evrie did not intend to promote secession. He sought to rouse Northern backlash by shifting the conversation away from the Slave Power and onto his favored terrain of racist nationalism. But, as in the angry aftermath of the Panic of 1857, he leaned so close to Southern extremism that he amplified secessionist logic. And given his large Southern readership, he risked inflaming the movement to destroy the nation he sought to preserve. Southern Unionists saw the danger. Consider Andrew Denny, the Alabama physician who joined a *Day Book* subscriber club in 1858. In spring 1861, he was a proslavery Unionist—the kind of Southerner whose outlook best matched Van Evrie's—who feared that secession was a "suicidal" measure (indeed, "the *strongest possible abolition* movement") that would destroy slavery. For this reason, he explained to a friend, he deplored Van Evrie's recent editorials:

> I have taken the New York Day Book, and *have been* pleased with its style and spirit, until lately; *but lately* I have become disgusted with its exhibition of *rancorous party spirit*: and so, when just on the point of ordering Dr Van Evrie's book, I have concluded that I could expend the same amount more satisfactorily.
>
> His paper *has been* useful for him, but *now* I think that is calculated to aggravate the evils of dissension &c which are agitating the whole country—*if northern* people *would* read his Day Book, & his work on Negroes, it would probably do *them* some good; *but not the* already-too-much-excited Southern people.[25]

Anti-Republican diatribes might boost proslavery Unionism in the North. But in the South, the *Day Book* emboldened the fire-eaters who were shredding Van Evrie's slaveholding republic in order to build a better one.

By April 1861, Van Evrie's crusade was collapsing. To white Northerners, he issued a strident demand to repudiate the Republican Party they had just elevated to power. To white Southerners, he presented himself as a steadfast ally while lamenting disunion, bolstering arguments for secession, and ignoring the contradictions between Confederate nationalism and proslavery Unionism. He hoped that racist outrage would save the country. Yet even before the shooting started, masses of Northerners began rallying against secession; after Fort Sumter, their militancy reached new heights. Dismayed and disoriented, Van Evrie continued his flailing attempt to stop white men from warring over slavery.

If disunion left Van Evrie feeling abandoned by Southern friends, the free-state response left him feeling betrayed by Northern allies. In January, he skewered Northern Democrats as "worn-out political hacks" who had dithered for ten years and only now bestirred themselves to save the Union. The noble Northern masses, not corrupt Democratic officeholders, would salvage the proslavery Constitution.[26] Even worse, in Van Evrie's view, was the response of New York's business community to the outbreak of war in April. Support for proslavery reconciliation evaporated, dividing most Manhattan merchants from the editor who for years had posed as their spokesman and tutor.

New Yorkers had turned out in droves to support compromise, but after Fort Sumter fell, they gathered in record crowds to support war. On April 20, a quarter of a million people (then the largest demonstration in the city's history) converged at Union Square to express their readiness to fight the rebels. They represented all classes and parties: Democrats and Republicans, merchants and manufactures, plebians and elites. Even Moses Taylor and Alexander T. Stewart, veterans of the Southern sympathy and Breckinridge campaigns, came and vowed to crush the rebellion.[27] New Yorkers were closing ranks. "We begin to look like a United North," wrote lawyer George Templeton Strong on April 15, the day Lincoln called for 75,000 volunteers. That was bad news for Van Evrie. The "little *Day Book*" and other proslavery papers, Strong gloated, "show no signs of reformation yet, but . . . the growing excitement against their treasonable talk will soon make them more cautious in its utterance."[28]

The reckoning came quickly. Two days later, Strong was working in his downtown office when he heard a commotion outside. Through the window he spied a column of "mostly decently-dressed people, but with a sprinkling of laboring men." The throng halted before the office of the *Journal of Commerce*, shouted at the occupants, and cheered when they hoisted the Stars and Stripes.[29] Now numbering in the thousands, they approached the *Day Book* building, filling Printing House Square so completely that vehicles could not pass. The multitude "set up a storm of terrible hissing and howling" and threatened to pelt the building with stones. Cowering behind a squad of police officers, Van Evrie relented. Lacking both a flag and flagpole, he borrowed a banner and hung it out the window. This placated the "mob," which then moved on to the *Express*.[30]

The response of merchants to Fort Sumter was less physically intimidating but more politically portentous. Van Evrie had counted on their opposition to the war; now he was bitterly disappointed. Two days after the mobbing of the *Day Book* office, New York City's Chamber of Commerce declared its support for the Lincoln administration. Business owners pledged individual loyalty, including many who had backed Van Evrie's efforts in 1859 and 1860: John Jacob Astor Jr., Hiram Ketchum, August Belmont, Alexander T. Stewart, Moses Grinnell, and Moses Taylor, among others. Soon, many of them—including Taylor, Stewart, and Astor—joined the Union Defense Committee to coordinate local mobilization efforts. They lent their influence, skills, and resources to the war effort, helping to raise and equip sixty-six volunteer regiments by year's end. (Many of these regiments assembled at barracks erected near the *Day Book* office in City Hall Park.) Manhattan business leaders also subscribed enormous war loans, with New York State contributing 80 percent of the first $260 million raised for the war. Mobilization lifted New York out of its secession-induced slump: Shipyards increased output, manufacturers signed lucrative contracts, and merchants hoped that a swift victory would revive commerce.[31] Manhattan's western traders and industrialists relished the boom, which "has forever released us from the bondage to cotton, which for a generation has hung over us like a spell, destroying all freedom of commercial or political action, and rendering us slaves to the most absurd delusions."[32] Even Southern traders fell into line. Royal Phelps, a merchant who had helped organize the Pine Street peace meeting, vowed to "support my Government . . . without reservation."[33] Draped in a US flag, erstwhile secessionist Fernando Wood urged his neighbors to unite and "conquer a peace." "I am with you in this contest," he proclaimed. "We know no party now."[34]

Imprisoned in his obstinate ideology, Van Evrie struggled to respond. Cotton, he insisted, was the crux of New York's prosperity; now, New Yorkers were rallying against the cotton kingdom. Slavery, he insisted, buttressed white liberty; now, white men were arming against enslavers. Racism, he insisted, was the bond of Union; now, his closest allies had seceded and his nearest neighbors were preparing to kill them. His world upended and confidence shaken, Van Evrie brooded. The day after Confederates began shelling Fort Sumter, he lined the *Day Book*'s columns with mourning stripes and announced the outbreak of "Civil War! Civil War!" He could only "beg and beseech that this most unnatural and bloody strife be stopped."[35] Fantasies of white men smiting Black Republicans gave way to supplication. A week later, while Confederates celebrated Sumter's capitulation, Van Evrie moaned that "this is the most bitter, the most sorrowful day of our life."[36]

As Unionists girded for combat, Van Evrie lashed out against enemies and former allies alike. After militant Manhattanites forced him to display the flag, he sulkily recalled his service against the "mongrels of Mexico" and blasted Republicans for "seeking to pervert the instinctive patriotism of the people to the base uses of Abolitionism."[37] Buried in this outburst was an important insight—it was difficult to peddle proslavery patriotism while rebels built a republic on the cornerstone of Black servitude. But this awareness gave Van Evrie little comfort. And as merchant capital poured into the war effort, Van Evrie assailed the business community that had nurtured the *Day Book* since 1848. Merchants thought they could "*preserve the Union by force*," he wrote in early May, and thus regain the lucrative Southern trade. In this, "they are destined to be terribly mistaken." Only conciliation could restore the Union; "fratricidal civil war" would wreck it beyond repair.[38] Two weeks later, he denounced the "'money power' of the North" for aligning with "the 'anti-slavery' government at Washington" in the mad effort to "crush the South into submission" and "restore the southern trade to this city." "As a class," he seethed, "the capitalists and men of large wealth among us are the most ignorant . . . and certainly the most selfish of any portion of our people."[39] After years of courting Manhattan's elites as customers, enlisting them as allies, and admiring them as avatars of proslavery nationalism, Van Evrie now reviled them as cat's-paws for abolition.

As a newspaper proprietor, he needed subscribers; as a political crusader, he needed disciples. But as Southern planters seceded and Northern merchants mobilized against them, where could one turn? Van Evrie reflexively resorted to his oldest patrons. In mid-March, he appealed to Jefferson Davis, who was now president of the Confederacy. Van Evrie flaunted his "great Pro-slavery publishing concern" and boasted that, in the North, the *Day Book* alone vindicated the "*Southern Cause*." But the paper needed steady income, so he solicited George W. Olney Jr.'s appointment as Confederate commercial agent in New York City. Convinced that cotton exports would continue flowing through Manhattan, Van Evrie urged Davis to establish official representation there and, "when things are more settled," promote Olney to consul.[40] Davis never replied. But the request reflected Van Evrie's ideological affinities and naive faith that Manhattan would become the emporium of the Confederacy.

More portentous was his search for support from white Northern workers. Signs of the *Day Book*'s lurch from commercial journal to labor advocate appeared early in the secession crisis. In January, Rushmore Horton organized a meeting of "working-men" at Brookes Hall to denounce Republicans for provoking war, assailing slavery, and plotting to install a military dictatorship. Departing from his habitual claims that merchants had the most to lose from disunion, Van Evrie endorsed the meeting by arguing that the rich could weather a civil war and perhaps even profit from it, but poorer folk faced "starvation and death."[41] Thereafter, themes of class conflict and white workers' interest in preserving peace and slavery proliferated in his writings. His reportage on Manhattan's white underclass cast them as victims of Republican agitation.[42] In *Negroes and Negro "Slavery,"* he concluded that defending slavery was essential to white workers' prosperity and equality.[43] And he escalated these arguments after the war began. In his response to the crowd that besieged his office, Van Evrie alleged that the "laboring classes" would, in the event of emancipation, suffer most from "monstrous affiliation" with free Black people.[44] By summer, he described soldiers' wives starving while "speculators" and "partizan hacks" reaped windfall profits. In a vitriolic August 8 editorial, he argued that Republicans and business leaders were reducing "the laboring classes" to "inevitable slavery." They would divide American society into "artificial classes" of "capitalists and paupers," fostering "all those terrible crimes, the offspring of want and suffering, which degrade and disfigure European society."[45]

These appeals foreshadowed four years of antiwar, anti-emancipation, and anti-administration rhetoric. But gazing back to the 1850s, it was striking how far the *Day Book* had traveled. Stimson contemplated white workers' enslavement, battled the printers' union, and denounced strikes by arguing that laborers shared their employers' interests.[46] Upon assuming proprietorship, Van Evrie continued the *Day Book* as a commercial paper that catered to New York's business community.[47] Throughout the late 1850s, his dire predictions about disunion emphasized collapsing commercial profits, bank failures, and business closures—not the anguish of the urban poor.[48] Now, he abruptly aligned himself with the masses. Why? Maybe he was goaded by class resentment rooted in his adolescent business failure or his quarrels with affluent in-laws. More likely, he responded to opportunism, pique, and necessity: eager to denounce Republican elitism, disillusioned with merchants' prowar activities, and desperate to recruit new readers, he crowned himself the tribune of the white working class.

But these demagogic appeals also evoked Van Evrie's earliest independent writings, reviving themes he had muted since joining the *Day Book*. Like many proslavery writers, he had weaponized white poverty to condemn Black emancipation.[49] In 1853, he defined antislavery as a foreign plot to splinter the Union, impose artificial class hierarchies on the New World, and plunder white laborers through banks, bonds, and tariffs.[50] Now, in his August 8, 1861, editorial, Van Evrie claimed vindication. The Union *was* divided; hence his somber response to secession. Class divisions *were* hardening; hence his exposés of urban want. Businesses *were* reaping windfalls; hence the outcry against corrupt politicians and the "shoddy aristocrats" who made fat profits by selling trashy goods to the army.[51] Republicans *were* assailing slavery; hence the passage, just two days before, of the Confiscation Act, which authorized Union soldiers to seize enslaved people involved in the Confederate war effort.[52] On August 8, Van Evrie described the consummation of a plot he had identified eight years before, using rhetoric that signaled his break with the merchant capitalists who had nurtured the *Day Book* and inspired its name. Behind the scenes, Van Evrie and Horton continued collaborating with antiwar business leaders. But their public pronouncements turned demagogic. In time, they would foster some of the worst violence ever seen in New York.

In the summer of 1861, however, popular backlash targeted the *Day Book* and its allies. "New York is in a perfect ferment," Rushmore Horton complained privately, "and our enemies here are trying to excite . . . mob violence against us."[53] Indeed, suspect newspapers were attacked across the free states. No one masterminded this outburst among citizens, soldiers, and officials from every level of government. No Lincolnian Leviathan sought to outlaw dissent.[54] But the campaign culminated in a crackdown that threatened the *Day Book*'s existence.

Van Evrie did not endorse permanent Confederate independence. He wanted the Union restored under Chief Justice Roger Taney's proslavery constitution. But most Northerners defined treason far more expansively than levying war against the United States or giving aid and comfort to its enemies.[55] Van Evrie's editorials certainly met this looser standard. He castigated Lincoln as a race-mixing abolitionist and the war as the "final degradation and ruin of American freedom."[56] He mocked the "absurd" notion that "a people so brave, so free, with such principles and such resources" as the Confederates could be conquered.[57] He encouraged the "virtuous and patriotic masses of the people" to protest.[58] With Horton and other antiwar editors, he promoted a peace petition.[59] After Fort Sumter's fall, and especially as rumors of rebel plots multiplied after the July 21 debacle at Bull Run, these sentiments sounded disloyal. Unionists deemed the *Day Book* an enemy of the republic.[60] A Pennsylvanian castigated the *Day Book* and other "secession papers" for "crying against the war, against the administration, against every means used to put down this rebellion, and prefacing all their treasonable acts with a cry for *peace, peace*. . . . Do these men want us to make peace with rebels, highwaymen, and cut-throats? . . . Would they have us go on bended knees to Jeff. Davis & Co. and implore them to give us peace?"[61]

The *Day Book* quickly became associated with treasonous speech, treacherous deeds, and traitorous people. It was widely regarded as both a marker and an instigator of disloyalty. An alleged spy arrested in New York was identified as a regular contributor to the paper, a fact cited as proof of his guilt.[62] From Ohio came reports of rebel sympathizers who had "laid aside the Constitution and the Bible," "taken up the New York *Day-Book*," and plotted subversion.[63] A British visitor to Baltimore gauged the citizenry's rebellious mood by the number of newsboys hawking the *Day Book* every evening.[64] Startled by disloyalty festering across the Hudson, Horace Greeley blamed the *Day Book*, "the text-book of New-Jersey Secessionists."[65] Some Democrats agreed: A county Democratic convention in Pennsylvania condemned the *Day Book* as a "vile sheet" that was "poisoning the minds of too many to feelings of disloyalty," while a Maine Democrat disavowed it as an "ultra proslavery paper" that was not a party organ at all.[66] Especially alarming were rumors that fifth columnists circulated the paper as part of a seditious plot. Speculation peaked in August, when almost anything seemed possible. An Ohioan described the "Great Conspiracy" of Breckinridge Democrats to undermine the free states. Directed by a "secret conclave" in Washington, agents incited anti-administration fervor, and to spread the word, "the New York Day Book, the vilest secession sheet on the continent, is scattered by the thousand through every county of the North."[67] Some observers accused wealthy turncoats of subsidizing the paper's free distribution, a charge that was plausible since this was the strategy used to broadcast the *Negroes and Negro "Slavery"* pamphlet.[68] Others tied Van Evrie's paper to disloyal organizations, including the Knights of the Golden Circle and Connecticut's shadowy "D. B. Society," which, if it existed, took its name from the *Day Book*.[69]

Having ascribed enormous power to the *Day Book* and its sinister sponsors, Unionists retaliated. Some demanded federal surveillance of its readers; one urged that the paper's 120 Chicago subscribers were "sympathizers with treason" and must be watched.[70] Others were more proactive. Residents of Scranton, Pennsylvania, drove William Halsey, a *Day Book* subscription agent from Ithaca, New York, out of town for having "uttered the rankest treason."[71] On board a Brooklyn ferry, *Day Book* assistant editor C. Chauncey Burr provoked a squad of soldiers with "obnoxious" comments; upon landing, they grabbed Burr and forced him to buy a round of champagne and toast the Union.[72] Several Northern editors tried to exclude Van Evrie from the news network by refusing to continue the customary exchange of their papers for *Day Book* issues.[73] Unionists never sacked the *Day Book* office, but the paper turned up in wreckage elsewhere. When irate citizens raided the Concord *Democratic Standard*'s premises in mid-August, they found a letter from Van Evrie seeking information about the sentiments of New Hampshire's

Democratic editors, a discovery that fueled conjecture about treasonable plotting.[74]

As editors, soldiers, and citizens besieged the *Day Book* from below, government officials closed in from above. The first target was patronage. Days after Manhattanites forced Van Evrie to hoist the national flag, Democrat Francis I. A. Boole exhorted the Common Council to drop the *Day Book* as an official paper of the Corporation of the City of New York and thus deprive it of $30,000 in annual advertising fees. Branding the *Day Book* a "secession paper," Boole's resolution declared it the council's duty "to rebuke treason wherever it can."[75] The Board of Councilmen voted 17–4 to strike the *Day Book* from the roster of Corporation papers. After Van Evrie refused to raise the flag in honor of Elmer Ellsworth, the dashing New York colonel who became the first Union officer killed in action in late May 1861, the Board of Aldermen followed suit in assailing the paper.[76] Believing that the "pestilent" *Day Book* subsisted on patronage, a San Francisco correspondent anticipated its "speedy death."[77] That Democrats struck this blow underscored Van Evrie's isolation.

Republicans delivered the next wallop, one calculated to finish the job. In late August, the Lincoln administration banned the paper from the mail. Even if Van Evrie, Horton & Co. survived the loss of patronage, it could not maintain mass circulation beyond New York without postal delivery. The process began on August 16 when a grand jury for the US District Court for the Southern District of New York presented the *Day Book* and four other newspapers for "encouraging rebels now in arms against the Federal government" and "expressing sympathy and agreement with them . . . and dissatisfaction with the employment of force to overcome them."[78] Six days later, the district attorney ordered federal marshals to seize all copies of the five papers and prohibited postal employees from forwarding any future issues through the mail.[79] By this time, *Day Book* circulation had rebounded to 25,000 subscribers, far fewer than the 40,000 reached in 1860, but the number was growing despite the loss of the Southern market.[80] Now, Van Evrie would lose all sales beyond New York newsstands and suffer a corresponding decline in advertising revenue. The *Day Book* teetered on the brink of destruction.

Federal suppression ignited controversy. Van Evrie likened it to King Herod's Massacre of the Innocents and deemed it an "unconstitutional usurpation" by a party that, since "getting into power under the pretence of regard for the negro, has riveted the chains of slavery upon millions of white men."[81] Confederate editors concurred, citing it as proof of Republican tyranny. The *Richmond Enquirer* mourned Van Evrie's "fearless journal," while a Tennessean wondered whether "even the people of the North" would "submit to such a despotism!"[82] Yet vitriol did not change reality, and on September 28, Van Evrie printed the *Day Book*'s final issue, closing with a valedictory boast about "teaching the same doctrines and proclaiming the same principles" from his first issue to the last.[83] He flaunted inflexibility as a badge of heroism.

Rival editors relished the *Day Book*'s ruin. One scoffed at the "wretched concern, owned and edited by a South Carolinian and two renegade Yankees."[84] The *New York Times* gloated over "the demise of a sheet which has often made us laugh at, if it has never made us laugh with it." To "the ethnologic Van Evrie," the *Times* extended mock sympathy: "his occupation gone, and an unbelieving world not yet converted to his doctrine" of polygenism.[85] *Vanity Fair* offered a poem: "The *Day-Book* has gone dead, breathed its last sigh / To rank rebellion—its last lies were solemn; / Struggling its former ones to qualify: / Raise it a monument—a broken Column."[86] The *Chicago Tribune* simply observed that, with the *Day Book*'s demise, "treason has lost one of its most sycophantic and sneaking supporters."[87]

Whether they stressed the *Day Book*'s force or its frailty, its racism or its disloyalty, most Northern critics believed that the public sphere was finally cleansed of its toxic presence. But a few demurred. The *New York Times* warned that its neighbor was "not dead—it but sleepeth."[88] Perhaps the editorialist knew Van Evrie personally or better judged the popular demand for his product. Whatever the reason, the prediction was apt. Van Evrie had been muzzled, but the silence only lasted a few days.

Chapter 12

War

It was May 1862, and Confederates were reeling. In Virginia, George B. McClellan's legions neared Richmond. Out west, federal troops held New Orleans and prepared to overrun the entire Mississippi Valley. John Van Evrie watched anxiously from Manhattan as the Republican war machine rumbled toward what he was sure was an abolitionist objective. Brooding as he recovered from a serious illness, Van Evrie scribbled a note to W. Stump Forwood, a proslavery Marylander and confidant, that revealed his understanding of the war. Van Evrie doubted the "capacity of a Southern Confederacy" to maintain its independence. Certainly, resistance to Republican "lunatics" was imperative; for Southern whites, "total extinction" was better than abolition. But in a world that was hostile to slavery, permanent separation would lead to "the social ruin and destruction" of a Southern republic. Only when all civilized people accepted "the simple but stupendous truth which I have sought to inculcate"—that Black people's "normal condition" was subordination to whites—would Southern society be safe. And in that scenario, disunion would be unnecessary. Slavery, he suggested, was too important to be left to the Confederacy. The United States needed slavery, and slavery needed the United States. Van Evrie cheered rebel victories but never sought disunion. Proslavery American nationalism, not Southern separatism, was his polestar; reunion under Roger Taney's constitution was his goal.[1]

Implicit in the letter was Van Evrie's unshakable self-image as a national savior. If Northern voters repented, the old Union could be restored. Since repentance required swallowing his "simple but stupendous truth," Van Evrie's success was imperative. Previous failures to smother Republicanism, prevent Lincoln's election, and forestall secession had not dampened his determination. The self-styled editor-hero was undaunted.

Yet over the previous year, plummeting revenues and the postal ban had made it difficult just to stay in business. Van Evrie's most urgent task throughout the Civil War was survival. Keeping the presses running and maximizing circulation were preconditions for realizing grander dreams. But his struggle was not purely defensive; the war was a period of evolution as well as endurance. Working with Rushmore Horton, he launched a spate of innovations, many of which became permanent features of their business.

Van Evrie's influence peaked during Reconstruction, and it was amid wartime travails that he laid the foundation for postwar success.

The most obvious novelties were the *Day Book*'s increasingly shrill overtures to white working-class men, which upended the paper's elite prewar class affiliation, aligned its content with Van Evrie's early writings, and anticipated its broad postwar readership. The paper also echoed Peace Democratic and Copperhead periodicals, which braided racism and anti-abolitionism with critiques of wartime finance and defenses of civil liberties.[2] Some historians link Van Evrie's propaganda directly to the racist violence unleashed during New York's 1863 draft riots.[3]

But demagogic appeals to white workers were part of a larger effort to bring Van Evrie's "simple and stupendous truth" to a diverse audience. His aim was not to incite class war but to unify whites around proslavery reunion. With Southern trade disrupted and many merchants backing the war, Van Evrie and Horton could not rely on old business models. Nor were they content to preach to the converted—not when they believed that saving American democracy depended on transforming mass opinion. Thus, out of necessity and conviction, Van Evrie and Horton diversified their catalog of publications, broadened their readership, and collaborated with elite-led organizations to restore the Union of 1860. They churned out a cornucopia of print matter, from cheap pamphlets and broadsides to middlebrow literary magazines, calibrating distinct appeals for specific constituencies to forge a reactionary coalition of white Northerners awakened to their racial interests. They nurtured a network of merchants and professionals who pooled their resources to sway the masses. They maintained a love-hate relationship with a rudderless Democratic Party that never quite satisfied them. And they dabbled in rebel schemes that culminated in a terrorist attack on Manhattan. Given Van Evrie's belief in his heroic destiny, nothing less than convincing white Northerners of all classes would suffice.

Throughout the Civil War, Van Evrie, Horton & Co.'s weekly newspaper remained their centerpiece publication. In its columns, Van Evrie condemned the war, incited backlash, and organized elite activism. To resume publication after the *Day Book* was barred from the mail, he quickly introduced a replacement. Just one week after terminating the *Day Book*, Van Evrie launched the *New York Weekly Caucasian*.[4]

The paper's name continued Van Evrie's weaponization of science to buttress his politics and burnish his brand. Use of "Caucasian" as a racial classifier was roughly as old as the United States. And just as citizens of the young republic used racism to reconcile ideals of liberty with acts of domination,

Enlightenment authors used "Caucasian" to naturalize hierarchies in an era of soaring idealism and brutal imperialism. In 1785, Christoph Meiners divided humanity into two branches: Caucasian and Mongolian. Like generations of previous theorists, Meiners believed that humans originated in the Caucasus Mountains; like generations of future scribblers, his placement of "Caucasian" people at humanity's birthplace made fair skin the norm, casting all other groups as degenerations from a white archetype. Ten years later, another German-speaking naturalist, Johann Friedrich Blumenbach, incorporated Meiners's terminology into a five-part classification scheme with Caucasian, Mongolian, Ethiopian, American, and Malay branches. A monogenist who rejected racist rationalizations for slavery, Blumenbach nevertheless charted a fateful course. Never mind that categorizers quarreled over counting the races—or that Blumenbach himself moved from a four- to a five-race framework between editions of his *On the Natural Varieties of Mankind*. Never mind that the "Caucasian" skull that inspired him belonged to a woman who had been enslaved by Russian invaders. Blinded by aesthetic preferences and certain that his own ancestors were the original human type, Blumenbach fabricated the classificatory framework later adopted by proslavery polygenists like Samuel Cartwright, Josiah Nott, and John Van Evrie.[5]

Eager to exhibit his erudition, Van Evrie often used "Caucasian" for "white." Indeed, his very first article touted the natural law "which forever places the Negro in subordination to the Caucasian," sketching the thesis he would repeat ad nauseam.[6] Now he emblazoned it on the masthead of his paper. And, in a sign of his influence, the name caught on. Copycat *Caucasian* newspapers appeared in Lexington, Missouri, and Carlisle, Pennsylvania, in 1866; Chico, California, in 1868; Alexandria, Louisiana, in 1874; and thereafter in Shreveport, Raleigh, and Clinton in North Carolina.[7] Van Evrie was the first to use the moniker. But long after he reinstated the *Day Book* name in October 1863, *Caucasian* endured among his imitators.

A Van Evrie paper by any other name reeked of racism. Just as his arguments remained stable amid antebellum strife, they persisted across wartime revolution. From 1861 to 1865, he insisted that reunion must be peaceful and that the sole basis for peace was the proslavery constitution enshrined in Taney's *Dred Scott* opinion. As soon as Northerners "abandon their monstrous delusion" of antislavery "and stand by the Constitution as interpreted by the Supreme Court," he wrote in 1863, "all conflict will cease, and Union, peace and harmony will again be universal among us."[8] Van Evrie repeated this mantra in his "Anti-Abolition Union Paper" throughout the conflict while denouncing the federal pivot toward emancipation and lamenting the Confederate rejection of reunion on any terms.[9] (He chided Southern separatism, but it was abolitionism that he hated, as summarized in the title of an 1864 editorial:

"Death to Abolitionists."[10]) To make his case, Van Evrie rehashed old themes. He condemned abolitionism as a conspiracy against white men's freedom, citing wartime infringement of civil liberties as fresh proof of a pet theory.[11] He proclaimed that Southern slavery was not slavery at all but the natural status of Black people in American society; he argued that science had settled this issue and that Republican policies were monstrous aberrations.[12] Occasionally, he still mentioned New York's dependence on the cotton trade, though the urban economy's refusal to collapse weakened his scaremongering.[13] Of course, he promoted his personal brand, advertising the *Caucasian* as edited by "a scientific student of the question of races."[14] On basic issues, he was immovable.

Continuity of content aside, Van Evrie and Horton innovated throughout the war. They tested novel appeals, launched new publications, and cultivated contacts at home and abroad. Through this restless activity, they pursued the conjoined goals of boosting circulation, raising revenue, and shaping Northern politics. Saviors of the republic had to stay in business.

Soon after introducing the *Caucasian*, Van Evrie and Horton milked their brief suppression by posturing as victims of tyranny. In the winter of 1861–62, they waged a multipronged campaign against Lincolnian despotism. They printed broadsides protesting their treatment.[15] They published editorials defending press freedom and urging fellow editors to join the outcry, themes that Van Evrie hammered for the rest of the war.[16] When the *Caucasian* was briefly barred from the mail in late 1861, they composed a widely reprinted public rejoinder. Insisting that they aimed neither to hobble the war effort nor sponsor secession but to defend "*the subordination of the negro to the white* man as the normal order of American society," they denounced the "injustice" and "cruelty" of their persecution.[17] In late winter, they circulated petitions insisting on equal mail access for Democratic papers.[18] And they wrote directly to President Abraham Lincoln to pledge fealty to the Union, as they understood it, and to demand postal service.[19] Vindicating the First Amendment gave Van Evrie a valuable talking point. It dovetailed with his antiabolitionism, which he always framed as a defense of white freedom, but could also appeal to readers who were genuinely concerned about civil liberties.

Despite the postal disruptions, Van Evrie's circulation quickly rebounded. Shortly before its suppression, the *Day Book* boasted 25,000 weekly subscribers.[20] Van Evrie reported healthy growth in the summer of 1862 and launched a club formation campaign in late 1863, seeking to capitalize on the backlash against emancipation and conscription. Using the catchphrase "White Men

Must Rule America," which anticipated a more influential future slogan, he extended the club crusade well into 1864.[21] That August, subscriptions topped 47,000, and by year's end, Van Evrie claimed more subscribers than any other Democratic weekly.[22] Timely content, memorable marketing, and the venerable club strategy enabled Van Evrie and Horton to rebuild their subscriber list after the lean summer of 1861.

New subscribers hailed exclusively from Union states, but scattered *Day Book* and *Caucasian* issues did reach Confederate territory when agents smuggled copies through the lines, passing them from hand to eager hand. Confederate journalists celebrated their arrival, proclaiming that Van Evrie alone uttered the truth about conditions in the North. Some reprinted *Day Book* and *Caucasian* issues almost in their entirety.[23] Yet while this serendipitous circulation kept Van Evrie's name before Southern readers, it yielded no revenue. Cut off from most of their prewar subscribers and politically alienated from much of Manhattan's commercial community, Van Evrie and Horton needed new ways to peddle their products to diverse Northern readers.

One highly visible strategy was to speak to, and ostensibly for, white working-class men. Before secession, the *Day Book* rarely addressed labor issues and harped on abolition's danger to Northern merchants, not wage earners. When it noticed white workers, it was at least as likely to criticize (or crush) their activism as to cheer it. But during the secession crisis, Van Evrie and Horton began paying attention to political gatherings of white workers and framing their anti-Republican, anti-abolition, and pro-peace appeals in class-conscious terms. Van Evrie continued this throughout the war. In a typical editorial addressed "To Workingmen," he insisted that laboring whites had the most to lose from emancipation. Sheltered by wealth from degrading interracial competition or fraternization, affluent whites would suffer little. But common whites, he argued, had only their God-given superiority—their "unmixed blood," "vigorous intellect," and "untiring energies"—to sustain them. If federal officials promoted abolition and what Van Evrie called "mongrelization," those advantages would vanish. Why ostensibly superior whites would fail in competition against Black people or deign to have children with them, he did not say. But he warned that abolition would lead to intermixing (as in Mexico), Black-on-white violence (as in Haiti), and the dominion of a British-style aristocracy.[24] Less frequently, Van Evrie criticized inflation, taxation, and wartime finance for grinding the poor to fatten the rich.[25] But these issues were neither close to his heart nor strategically helpful. Indeed, vocal class protest unsettled Van Evrie, who scolded labor leaders' "shortsighted" propensity to "ascribe all their troubles to capitalists."[26] Rather than battle their employers, they should vote out the Republicans. For Van Evrie, class strife was useful only insofar as he could channel it into partisan politics—and monetize it through sales.

Van Evrie's appeals resonated with many disgruntled white workingmen, including the draft rioters who paused their bloody rampage to cheer outside the *Caucasian* office in July 1863.[27] But working-class Northern whites formed a large, diverse, and internally divided group whose support both parties sought throughout the war.[28] Republicans warned that Democrats would betray white workers to the Slave Power. Inadvertently echoing Van Evrie's claim that "working people" had the most at stake in the conflict, Lincoln accepted an honorary membership in the New York Workingmen's Democratic Republican Association by asserting that rebel aristocrats were waging "a war upon the rights of all working people."[29] Democratic advocates retorted that Republicans were conscripting workingmen for a war that would enrich financiers and industrialists and inundate Northern markets with cheap Black labor. Van Evrie's overtures to workingmen continued a battle for their loyalties that he had begun in his antebellum attacks on the Slave Power theory. Now isolated from Southern subscribers, he ratcheted up these appeals in hopes of swelling his readership and winning over a key constituency. The internal tensions of this strategy emerged during Reconstruction, when Van Evrie, rigidly focused on Black subordination, clashed with Democratic Party rivals who wanted to campaign on currency and public finance.

Van Evrie and Horton also lured less-affluent readers with a growing catalog of cheap materials. Before the war, they had produced little besides the newspaper. Aside from Van Evrie's own *Negroes and Negro "Slavery,"* their presses issued only three pamphlets through 1860.[30] Even Horton's biography of James Buchanan was published by another Nassau Street firm, Derby & Jackson. During the war, however, they cranked out broadsides, pamphlets, and speeches, all at bargain prices. These included the Anti-Abolition Tracts, a series of pamphlets sold at "the lowest possible rate" of six cents per copy, one dollar for twenty, or four dollars for one hundred. Mostly written by Van Evrie, they contended that races were separate species, abolition was a foreign plot, and the *Dred Scott* decision was the basis for reunion.[31] In 1863, Van Evrie republished his book-length *Negroes and Negro "Slavery"* and the *Dred Scott* pamphlet.[32] The pamphlet cost only twenty cents and the book a dollar, with free copies available to anyone who formed a *Day Book* subscriber club of twenty members.[33]

Another discount publishing campaign involved collaboration with professional politicians: printing speeches. Before the war, Van Evrie, Horton & Co. had published only two speeches, one by Charles O'Conor and the other by presidential candidate John C. Breckinridge. But between 1861 and 1865, they published nine orations by a roster of prominent Peace Democrats, including congressional representatives John McKeon, James Brooks, and Benjamin Wood of New York; Governor Horatio Seymour; former New York attorney general John Van Buren; Ohio representative Samuel Sullivan Cox; and Indiana representative Daniel W. Voorhees. A medley of congressional orations, addresses to grassroots organizations, and convention speeches, the published editions were inexpensive (single copies cost a nickel) and intended for mass distribution (bulk rates were two dollars per hundred copies or fifteen dollars per thousand).[34] Van Evrie and Horton worked with authors to ensure textual accuracy, while the firm handled distribution through individual and organizational contacts across the North.[35] For Peace Democrats eager to broadcast their diatribes against war, emancipation, invasion of civil liberties, and anything resembling racial equality, Van Evrie's printing press and distribution network were vital.

But the hunt for new readers involved more than hawking cheap wares. To maximize their market share, Van Evrie and Horton also targeted educated and prosperous Northerners, primarily with a monthly literary magazine named the *Old Guard*. With roots in the 1780s, literary magazines flourished after 1830 as a middlebrow alternative to the penny press. Whereas penny papers, with their low prices and tawdry content, were marketed to urban workers, literary magazines boasted more exclusive pricing and sophisticated material. They included women's periodicals like the *Ladies' Repository*, political journals like the *United States Magazine and Democratic Review*, and general publications like the *North American Review*. All shared a middle- and upper-class orientation reflected in both content (poetry, short fiction, reviews, and essays on history, politics, and science) and self-consciously elevated style. They aimed for a large readership while "insisting on this audience's distinction from the untutored masses." By the Civil War, the country supported eighty-seven literary magazines but not one for Democrats: the *United States Magazine and Democratic Review* had folded in 1859.[36]

Charles Chauncey Burr targeted this niche when he unveiled the *Old Guard* in 1862. Born in Maine, Burr dabbled in everything from antislavery work to promotional efforts for Lola Montez, an Irish-born adventurer and revolutionary who toured the United States in 1857. Burr was on the *Day Book* payroll when his Confederate sympathies outraged Union recruits on a Brooklyn ferry in 1861. The following year, he went independent and produced three issues of the *Old Guard*, a title that likened Peace Democrats to a cadre of French counterrevolutionaries who opposed the Terror. When the threat of post office suppression abated in January 1863, Burr began the monthly publication of a periodical that soon became notorious for its anti-administration and anti-abolition invective delivered through a literary magazine.[37] The January 1863 issue set the tone. It featured a lithographic portrait of New York

Governor Horatio Seymour, a poetic paean to George Washington, and political essays, including a critique of the war debt, a theological attack on abolition, and a tribute to John C. Calhoun. The articles shared Van Evrie's politics but were longer and more polished, and the blend of prose, poetry, and portraiture was tailored for learned readers.[38] Subsequent issues emphasized politics with a sprinkling of other content, from translations of classic texts to a history of kissing in poetry.[39] The portraits featured a rogue's gallery of Democratic luminaries, including Clement Vallandigham, Samuel Sullivan Cox, and Roger Taney.

The *Old Guard*'s formal relationship with Van Evrie began with its second volume in 1864. Burr announced that he would retain editorial control and do most of the writing, while "those well-known and esteemed publishers" Van Evrie and Horton handled printing and marketing. Thereafter, the *Old Guard* bore the imprint of Van Evrie, Horton & Co.[40] Van Evrie in turn printed exuberant notices of every new issue in the *Day Book*.[41] He also used it as an outlet for his own writings, especially his more abstruse scientific racist work. His first *Old Guard* piece, "The American Races," appeared in March 1865; over the next four years, he contributed nineteen more essays, mostly adapted from *Negroes and Negro "Slavery."*[42] While Van Evrie introduced few new ideas in Burr's magazine, he used it to reach educated readers during the period of his peak popularity.

Van Evrie also began attracting international collaborators and audiences. Before the Civil War, he read many European racial theorists but forged few connections abroad. During the war, however, he entered a transatlantic proslavery polygenist network. The turning point was his January 1864 publication of a lecture by British polygenist James Hunt. Born in 1833, Hunt joined the Ethnological Society of London as a twentysomething maverick who scorned his elders' intellectual timidity and bleeding-heart politics. Unlike their Continental counterparts, who by the 1850s had given polygenism serious consideration, most British scientists clung to monogenism and sympathized with humanitarian causes, including antislavery. Not Hunt. Inspired by Scottish polygenist Robert Knox, Hunt relished polygenism and proslavery politics. When the Civil War began, he befriended Henry Hotze, the Swiss propagandist who promoted the Confederate cause through his London weekly, *The Index*. And, in his own act of secession, Hunt left the Ethnological Society to establish the Anthropological Society of London as a polygenist rival. It was before this group that, in November 1863, Hunt delivered his signature screed, *On the Negro's Place in Nature*. In sixty pages (in which he cited Van Evrie four times), Hunt defined the races as distinct species, proclaimed Black people's innate inferiority, and argued that they achieved their highest potential in the Confederacy, laboring in "natural subordination" to whites.[43] Hunt had grasped Van Evrie's "stupendous truth" and hurled it into the face of the British scientific establishment.

Van Evrie allied with Hunt against the haughty Britons he blamed for disunion. On January 2, 1864, he printed a long extract from Hunt's lecture in the *Day Book*. Weeks later, he released a fifteen-cent pamphlet edition as the fourth Anti-Abolition Tract, praising it as "the most compact and condensed epitome of scientific authorities" on race and slavery and urging its circulation among Republicans "and all others opposed to the Supremacy of the White Race."[44] He supported Hunt until the latter's death in 1869. Van Evrie's posthumous tribute to "The Best Man in England," first published in the *Day Book*, was widely reprinted, including in the *Old Guard* and the Anthropological Society's *Anthropological Review*.[45] The polygenist circuit of reciprocal praise and citation remained unbroken.

By joining Hunt's crusade, Van Evrie courted controversy and increased his visibility. American critics condemned him for printing Hunt's blasphemy and treason. The *Christian Ambassador*, a New York Universalist weekly, dismissed Hunt's essay as "a tissue of twaddle in the interest of southern slavery and consequently of secession."[46] More novel were the international responses to his edition of Hunt's lecture. It was no coincidence that Van Evrie's name began appearing in publications throughout Europe in 1864. In Britain, conflict over Hunt's oration heightened awareness of Van Evrie's work. Admirers praised him as a sage who had studied Black people firsthand.[47] Detractors denounced him and Hunt as "tools of the Southern confederacy."[48] But they all noticed the American agitator who appeared on the British intellectual battlefield. His notoriety also spread to the Continent. In works on "Wild Africa," "The Natural Position of the Negro," and "The Black Race," French, German, and Italian authors evaluated not only the American edition of Hunt's lecture but also Van Evrie's own writings.[49] The New York scribbler had piggybacked on Hunt's infamy to enhance his reputation in Europe.

By diversifying their catalog, Van Evrie and Horton managed to survive the Civil War. But who supported them? The petition campaign during the spring of 1862 provided clues. Buried in the National Archives are fifteen petitions demanding that "THE NEW YORK CAUCASIAN, and all other Democratic papers now excluded from the mails," enjoy "the same privileges" as "Republican and Abolition papers."[50] Van Evrie might have printed the petition forms, which all feature the same statement, with blank spaces for the town, county, and state where it circulated, followed by scores of signatures. Ironically, most of the petitions were brought to the US Senate floor by Republicans (including Ira Harris of New York, whose daughter Clara sat near Lincoln the night he was assassinated) and then referred to the Committee on Post Offices and Post Roads.[51] Gathered in Ohio, New York, Vermont, Iowa, Pennsylvania, and New Jersey, the petitions provide 922 names, not necessarily of *Caucasian* subscribers but of Northerners willing to support it. In the absence of subscriber lists, these petitions provide more information about Van Evrie's wartime fans in the North than any other source.

Analysis of a randomly selected sample of 199 individuals (20 percent of the signers from each petition) offers an intriguing portrait. Nine of the fifteen petitions came from counties that Lincoln carried in 1860, suggesting that, politically, most signers felt embattled rather than ascendant. With one exception, all of the signers were male, a striking contrast to the antislavery petitions signed by thousands of women.[52] Northern women certainly read Van Evrie's work, but few petitioned on his behalf. While the preponderance of men seems predictable, other trends offer more surprises. Some scholars have assumed that Van Evrie's Northern support came primarily from the white proletariat, particularly Irish immigrants.[53] The New York City petition does contain many Irish names, most of them recorded with the same pen and in the same handwriting, suggesting either that one person recorded the names of illiterates—unlikely to be newspaper readers—or that the names were invented. Either way, this petition is an outlier.

The other fourteen petitions show that support for Van Evrie was far more widespread than a focus on the New York draft riots might suggest. Among the non–New York City signers, a majority were native-born household heads who lived in their birth state. Most owned real and personal property and, in most cases, at least a plurality were farmers. To sharpen this analysis, each petitioner sample was compared with a random census sample drawn from the same community. The comparison, explained more fully in appendix 1, indicates just how deeply rooted and affluent the petitioners were compared to their neighbors. In half of the non–New York City comparisons, the signers were more likely to be born in-state. In nine communities, the random individuals were more likely to be foreign born; in only one case (Monroe, New York), the signers were more likely to be immigrants. In ten cases, signers held, on average, more real property than the random sample; they held more personal property, on average, in eight cases. In eleven of fourteen communities, signers were either equally or more likely to be farmers; in twelve communities, they were equally or more likely to be merchants—a finding that reflects the *Day Book*'s commercial focus. In ten cases, the random individuals were more likely to be laborers or unskilled workers; in the other four, they were equally likely.

Historians' emphasis on the immigrant urban white working class as a bastion of Northern racism, anti-abolitionism, and anti-administration sentiment is not wrong, but it is incomplete. The pro-*Caucasian* petitions reveal deep reactionary currents among native-born, rural, and wealthy white Northerners. Like subscriber club organizers, petitioners tended to be locally prominent and politically engaged. They included Lewis S. Partridge, a forty-two-year-old native-born resident of Norwich, Vermont, who owned $5,000 in real estate, served as postmaster during the Pierce years, and was later a delegate to the 1864 Democratic national convention.[54] Westfield, New Jersey, petitioner Edwin Downer Jr. was a Princeton-educated Presbyterian clergy member whose household included Betsey Canton, an elderly Black servant who was likely formerly enslaved.[55] Robert Thompson Wallace of Muscatine, Iowa, lived in a hotel when he signed the petition, but he was an ambitious young merchant who converted commercial success into political power; by 1882, this "uncompromising Democrat" had become mayor.[56] Van Evrie's message resonated with Northern whites who had flush pockets, deep roots, and vested interests in preserving the status quo.

With new publications, a diversified readership, and growing international stature, Van Evrie and his firm were thriving. For those who abhorred his ideas, the stakes in the struggle seemed enormous. Previous reports of Van Evrie's professional death were greatly exaggerated. How could he be stopped?

Van Evrie's foes were a varied lot: Some loathed his heresy, others his bigotry, and still others his sympathy for rebels. War sharpened their dislike, but his opponents never converged on a single counterstrategy. Some simply denounced his newspaper as "malignant," "virulent," and packed with "hashed up treason."[57] Others deflated his pretensions with sarcasm. In a review of the Anti-Abolition Tracts, Elizur Wright, a founding member of the American Anti-Slavery Society, jeered their publisher as "Dr. Van Evrie, M. D." and facetiously likened him to Isaac Newton.[58] A Republican critic diagnosed him with "negrophobia," characterized by an obsession with race and a compulsion to kick the downtrodden.[59] Meanwhile, a few rebutted his arguments by dissecting his methods and citing contrary scriptural and scientific authorities.[60] But in a fractured media marketplace, these rejoinders risked preaching to the converted; abolitionist and Republican readers needed little convincing. Desperate to stanch the flow of Van Evrie's venom at the source, many critics urged military authorities to prohibit the circulation of his newspaper. They echoed the San Francisco writer who marveled that Van Evrie had avoided arrest, deemed polygenism "absurd," and called for banning the *Caucasian*.[61]

Union officers sporadically outlawed sales of Van Evrie's paper in the areas under their command. These interventions confirm that martial rule was most severe in the border states, Union-occupied rebel regions, and the trans-Mississippi West.[62] In 1863, Union generals barred circulation of the *Caucasian* in St. Louis, the Department of the Pacific, Missouri's Sainte Genevieve County, and the Department of Kansas.[63] (In Baltimore, authorities prohibited all newspapers from printing extracts from the *Caucasian*.[64]) The following year, officers in Louisville and Memphis imposed similar bans, authorizing soldiers to arrest vendors who sold the paper.[65] Variously praised as vital for national security and denounced as oppressive, most military bans proved short-lived. The May 1863 California ban, for instance, was rescinded after one year.[66] Where higher authorities failed, Van Evrie's most zealous foes sometimes took matters into their own hands. From the bloody borderland of Missouri to the rocky hills of Vermont, Union soldiers and irate citizens seized bundles of his paper, shredded individual copies, and threatened distributors. These local, intensely personal campaigns reflected the home-front determination to silence Van Evrie's discordant voice.[67]

Patchwork restrictions and interdictions, however, did not throttle Van Evrie's business. Indeed, he proudly cited them in wartime advertisements, suggesting that he viewed the backlash as a marketable badge of honor.[68] Perhaps for this reason, rivals sought other ways to damage his business. One strategy was to cease exchanging with Van Evrie. Some editors refused to send him copies of their papers or to receive or reprint material from his publications in return. Editors' free exchange of issues, a venerable practice subsidized by the post office, facilitated the flow of information and promotion of a newspaper's name. To shun Van Evrie's paper was to block his access to valuable advertising venues and sources of content, and only a few editors went this far.[69] Another option was to reject *Day Book* advertisements, a policy adopted by the *American Agriculturist*, a New York monthly whose proprietors refused to print ads for a newspaper "which greatly aided to stir up bitterness and rebellion at the South."[70] Yet despite the efforts of opponents who marshaled patriotism and piety against Van Evrie, they never managed to muzzle him.

Efforts to suppress Van Evrie's publications peaked in 1863 and 1864, likely in part because of his ties to the New York draft riots. Incensed by emancipation, inflation, and conscription, thousands of white New Yorkers erupted into violence on July 13, 1863. Mobs spent four days killing and burning, targeting bastions of Republican authority and the Black people they blamed for the war. When the smoke cleared, dozens of buildings, including the Colored Orphan Asylum, were destroyed and some 119 people were dead, including Black men lynched on Manhattan lampposts.[71] Contemporaries and historians alike implicated the Peace Democratic press in these atrocities, but while recent studies have focused on Van Evrie, nineteenth-century observers pointed more often to *Old Guard* editor Chauncey Burr.[72] Some eyewitnesses accused Burr of igniting racist resentment in his "inflammatory harangue to the lowest order of Irish laborers" on the eve of the mayhem.[73] Burr denied responsibility and bizarrely blamed "negro-equality revolutionists" for the carnage.[74] For his part, Van Evrie denounced the "terrible riot" but pinned it on a Republican administration he deemed more "lawless" than the rioters. Emancipation, conscription, and the war itself, he argued, were revolutionary crimes that had provoked the counterrevolution in Manhattan.[75] As usual, Van Evrie saw class conflict as a partisan opportunity. He chided rioters' excesses, ignored their victims, and tried to channel public outrage into partisan opposition.

While the riots inevitably captivated attention, Van Evrie's critics would have been even more alarmed had they known what he was doing behind the scenes. Van Evrie and Horton sought to wield political power as elite operators working the levers of public opinion and Democratic Party machinery. Continuing the modes of top-down activism they had used before the war, Van Evrie and Horton mobilized affluent Manhattan Democrats to sway the multitudes and pilot the party to victory in 1864.

The wartime Democratic Party retained sizable voter support but lacked cohesive leadership and was riven by factionalism. Broadly split between War Democrats who cooperated with Republicans and Peace Democrats who sought immediate reconciliation with the rebels, deeper party divisions were even more kaleidoscopic. Democrats defied easy categorization. Thousands served in uniform; a few tried to liberate Confederate prisoners of war. Some celebrated Black enlistment; others incited racist violence. Most wanted the Union restored but argued incessantly over the means. Many worried that the party would never recover from what one called "the most disastrous epoch" in its history.[76] Exacerbating the challenges of running a wartime opposition party and containing the centrifugal forces of factionalism was the death of Stephen Douglas, the "acknowledged leader" of Northern Democrats, in June 1861. In an icy obituary, Van Evrie damned him with faint praise and summoned a new captain to rally the faithful.[77]

Although he never sought political office, Van Evrie anointed himself the oracle of the ideals that would unify Democrats and propel them to victory. The party's disarray tantalized him with the opportunity to propound the platform on which Democrats could coalesce. Van Evrie always believed that ideological purity and single-minded racism would ensure electoral triumph. Thus, he proclaimed that Douglas's successor must "be inspired with the new impulse of the white man's supremacy and the negro's subordination as the essential principles of Democracy," for this was the "great truth that now needs a leader to rally the people to its support."[78] Throughout the war, he presented his "great truth" as the antidote to abolitionism and disunion *and* the basis for a partisan renaissance. It was to unite Democrats behind his agenda that he and Horton toiled in the crucial period between the Emancipation Proclamation and the 1864 election.

They started by organizing an elite group to propagate Van Evrie's case for proslavery reunion. This was a job for the gregarious Horton. On February 9, 1863, he and five cronies met in a residence on West 28th Street to establish the Democratic Anti-Abolition State Rights Association of the City of New York (renamed the Anti-Abolition State Rights Society in April 1864). The founders resembled leaders of the Southern sympathy and Breckinridge campaigns.[79] Theodore Martine, who hosted the first meeting and served as treasurer, was a real estate tycoon and former commissioner of deeds worth nearly $80,000.[80] Jacob Harson Varian Cockroft was a merchant and regular Democratic candidate for city and state offices.[81] Samuel Minster was a German-born cloth merchant who employed three servants in his Ninth Ward home.[82] C. Godfrey Gunther, a wealthy fur merchant, soon prevailed in his second run for mayor, thereby bringing City Hall under the control of a charter member of Horton's Association.[83] The sixth founder was Thomas B. Chase, a *Caucasian* employee and former Custom House clerk.[84]

The founders ratified a constitution and declaration of principles previously drafted by Horton. Their mission was to mold public opinion "by means of organization, addresses, public meetings, tracts, pamphlets and lectures." They would "disseminate true Democratic Republican principles," "combat the false and baneful doctrines of Abolitionism which seeks to overthrow the Supremacy of the White Race," and "restore harmony of sentiment between the people of the northern and southern States," all to promote the "union and welfare" of what they called "our entire country," Confederate war aims notwithstanding. In language that echoed Van Evrie (and was likely written with his input), Association members promoted proslavery reunion as the basis for peace.[85] They organized in opposition to the Union League, which at that time was a network of posh clubs that supported the administration by subsidizing document distribution. Soon, they also battled against the Loyal Publication Society, another elite New York pro-administration initiative for distributing documents that commenced days later.[86] Horton and friends resented Republicans' appropriation of Unionism: "We warn the Northern masses against the danger of mistaking the expiring ravings of Abolitionism . . . for the sentiments of a patriotic love for a 'Union.'" Theirs was an elitist brand of activism, claiming that "we" the cognoscenti will enlighten the "masses" by leveraging personal fortunes to broadcast Van

Evrie's publications. Funded by ten-dollar initiation fees and annual dues, the Association held monthly operational meetings and an annual dinner on April 13 to honor the birthday of its claimed ideological ancestor, Thomas Jefferson.[87]

Horton's dream of opening Association branches in every New York City ward never materialized, but membership grew swiftly, with more than thirty initiates approved at the first meeting alone. Between 1863 and 1868, some eighty individuals became members. Many were old Van Evrie associates, including Benjamin Wood, Charles O'Conor, Gideon J. Tucker, and Samuel F. B. Morse. Some were high-profile rebel sympathizers, including lawyers Jeremiah Larocque and Algernon Sydney Sullivan, who defended Confederate sailors charged with piracy, and Francis Hopkins, a Brooklyn merchant who in 1861 fled to New Jersey to avoid arrest for his secessionist sentiments.[88] A few, like Gunther, had held high office. The Association's longtime president George W. Varian had served in the state legislature and on the Board of Aldermen, while John McKeon was a former member of Congress and US district attorney.[89] Others were eminent professionals. Dr. Lewis A. Sayre was a pioneering orthopedic surgeon and future president of the American Medical Association; Stephen P. Russell was a judge; and John Mullaly edited the Irish Catholic *Metropolitan Record*.[90] A plurality of the members were merchants, including Southern traders like John S. March.[91] Tellingly, while merchant capitalists dominated the roster, few industrial capitalists—who tended to support the Republicans—appeared there. An exception was Nathan A. Baldwin, a mass producer of straw hats sold for use by enslaved laborers in the South.[92]

Regardless of occupation, most Association members were rich. Six of them—Philip W. Engs, John H. Brower, Stephen W. Gaines, John Egerton, Loring Andrews, and Charles O'Conor—boasted fortunes exceeding $100,000.[93] Of the forty-three members whose wealth appears in the 1860 census, the mean value of their estates was $34,400 (median $12,000). The Association attracted elites who refused to rally around the flag. At one Jefferson birthday dinner, members toasted themselves as "The State Rights Merchants of New York—A small but gallant band, who never sold their principles for contracts, nor bartered their consciences for greenbacks."[94]

As in many organizations, most of the work was done by a few dedicated members. None were more active than Rushmore Horton. Before his death in 1867, Horton attended every meeting, drafted nearly every published statement, and served on most of the committees that planned events, solicited speakers, and recruited members. Beginning in April 1864, he also served as recording secretary, leaving his distinctive scrawl in the minute book. In turn, Horton—and, by extension, Van Evrie—used the Association to amplify his own message with support from powerful allies who cycled in and out of active membership. Many only attended the annual Jefferson dinners, which drew scores of celebrants. These swanky soirees convened at luxurious venues, including the St. James Hotel and Maison Dorée, which challenged Delmonico's for the title of Manhattan's most sumptuous restaurant. Attendees devoured oysters, turtle soup, mutton, beef tenderloin, quail, duck, Charlotte de Russe, meringue, and vanilla ice cream; sipped bourbon and fine wines; and savored cigars. The 1865 gathering cost over $350—more than enough to pay the commutation fee for a Union conscript.[95]

In later years, the Association lost momentum as members prioritized feasting as their primary public duty. But under Horton's influence in 1863 and 1864, they strove to sway public opinion. Many of their most ambitious efforts failed. They could not get Clement Vallandigham to speak at Cooper Union. A planned lecture series quickly fizzled out. No satellite clubs were ever established. But they succeeded in passing resolutions, making speeches, and offering toasts that were published in the *Day Book* and reprinted elsewhere. They also subsidized the printing of 250,000 pages of propaganda in their first year alone. For *Day Book* readers, it was all standard fare, but because these materials bore the Association's grandiose name, they gave the appearance of expressing widespread opinion. It was an astroturf movement, but it connected Van Evrie to a network of powerful Peace Democrats who promulgated his "great truth" throughout the second half of the war.[96]

Horton's club denounced recreant Democrats as well as abolitionists. At the 1864 Jefferson dinner, Chauncey Burr blasted the War Democrats and their "monstrous desertion of principle." Rebuking those who bought war bonds, backed prowar candidates, or joined the army, he insisted that "the man who supports this war is not only not a Democrat, but he is at war with the Democracy."[97] Van Evrie concurred. There were only two sides in politics, he insisted: the "'anti-slavery' . . . disunion war party," which included War Democrats, and the "pro-'slavery' Union peace Democracy."[98] And when Democrats underperformed at the polls, he invariably faulted their reticence in assailing the war, emancipation, and Black equality. Timid temporizing, he proclaimed, "chilled" Democratic fervor and cost decisive votes.[99] To Van Evrie the purist, all but the most strident Peace Democrats were betraying their nation, race, and party.

But War Democrats held powerful positions in party leadership and enjoyed tremendous popular support. Generals like George B. McClellan, Daniel Sickles, and John McClernand led Union soldiers into battle. In Congress, politicians like Reverdy Johnson and Francis Kernan voted for more resources to prosecute the war. And as chair of the Democratic National Committee, New York financier August Belmont searched for a prowar candidate who could recapture the White House. When Van Evrie preached that only a peace platform and candidate could rescue the Democrats and restore the Union, he collided with a mighty wing of his own party. Democrats brought three years of seething internal divisions into the 1864 election, with the fate of the party and the nation hanging in the balance.[100]

Adopting his savior pose, Van Evrie urged the nomination of a peace candidate and peddled his newspaper to organizers of Democratic campaign clubs.[101] Horton disseminated documents through the Anti-Abolition State Rights Society and coordinated with Peace Democrats like Connecticut's Thomas H. Seymour to send like-minded delegates to the national convention in Chicago.[102] But their efforts failed. While the convention tapped Peace Democrat George H. Pendleton for the vice presidency and wrote a peace plank into the platform, the nomination of Belmont-backed George B. McClellan over both Thomas Seymour and Horatio Seymour for president was a triumph for the prowar wing. And while some Peace Democrats initially embraced McClellan as their best option, his acceptance letter pledged to win the war before parleying with rebels.[103] Among the outraged Peace Democrats was Van Evrie's Maryland confidant W. Stump Forwood, who lamented that "a *war Democrat* has been nominated" and indeed "one of the most conspicuous military leaders of all," who has waged "this most iniquitous war upon Republican institutions and personal liberty." With striking understatement, he mused that Peace Democrats "are placed in a most unpleasant dilemma."[104]

Van Evrie responded with customary brashness. He mailed McClellan a copy of *Negroes and Negro "Slavery."* In his cover letter, he bragged about his racial expertise and the *Day Book*'s influence, framed the Union and abolition as mutually exclusive, and instructed McClellan to do his assigned reading and campaign accordingly. Van Evrie closed with an emphatic promise: "*If . . . you would pledge yourself to strong and eternal hostility to Abolitionism and for the restoration of 'the Union as it was' on the white basis all will be well.*"[105] McClellan's reaction to the presumptuous gift is unknown, though he did mark the letter "Answered." His reply did not placate its recipient. Van Evrie continued to peddle his paper as a Democratic campaign sheet but never endorsed McClellan, who snagged only twenty-one electoral votes en route to defeat. In his postmortem, Van Evrie drew the inevitable conclusion: Democrats lost because they abandoned their principles. To win, they must advocate for peace, reunion, Black slavery, and white equality. "When the Democratic party comes into power," he wrote, "it will come in as a Peace and not a War party." Now patriots must help him "lay the foundations of a *real* Democratic party."[106]

Soon after, fire bells pierced Manhattan's chilly evening air. At 8:43 p.m. on November 25, 1864, a guest at the St. James Hotel (site of the Anti-Abolition State Rights Society's Jefferson dinner the previous April), smelled smoke and raised the alarm. Minutes later and a mile and a half south, another fire broke out at the St. Nicholas Hotel. By ten o'clock, fires were reported at Lafarge House, the Metropolitan Hotel, Brandreth House, Belmont House, and other major hotels, as well as at P. T. Barnum's museum. Panicked hotel guests poured into the streets. Theatergoers next door to Lafarge House rushed for the exits. Anxious rumors swiftly outpaced sober facts. Yet the fires were extinguished almost as soon as they were discovered. They never caused a general conflagration, and the damage at each hotel was confined to a few rooms. New Yorkers had been nervous since Election Day, and the *New York Times* quickly blamed the flames on a "Rebel Plot."[107] But what had happened?

The truth emerged in January 1865 when a rebel agent was arrested and taken to New York for trial. Scion of a wealthy Louisiana family, Robert Cobb Kennedy was expelled from West Point and descended into dissipation until the Civil War. After being captured, he escaped to Canada and joined a network of secret agents who, funded by Confederate envoy Jacob Thompson, conspired to launch attacks south of the border. Thompson recruited Kennedy into a plan to seize New York on Election Day, November 8, 1864. Confederate agents would coordinate with local sympathizers, including *Freeman's Journal* editor James A. McMaster, to light diversionary fires and then capture government offices, liberate prisoners at Fort Lafayette, and overrun the city with an anticipated army of 20,000 Copperheads. By late October, Kennedy and seven comrades were in New York, finalizing preparations with McMaster, James Brooks, and Rushmore Horton. A habitual joiner, Horton added terrorism to his résumé.

Their plan was ruined by a vigilant War Democrat. General John A. Dix, who had helped suppress the draft riots, smelled trouble and asked General Benjamin F. Butler for additional soldiers to police the city through the election. Butler's 3,500 reinforcements made an intimidating show of force, and while Horton wanted to execute the plan, most of Kennedy's co-conspirators balked. By late November, McMaster and the Copperheads abandoned the effort, while Kennedy and the Confederates decided simply to burn as much of Manhattan as possible. Their incendiary activities on November 25 could have done much more damage if they had left windows open to fuel the flames with fresh oxygen.[108]

It was a dirty, desperate scheme that reflected the despondency of Van Evrie and Horton's subversive coterie. The war they bemoaned was approaching its fifth year. The president they loathed had won reelection. Conscription and emancipation proceeded apace. Northern whites showed little sign of rising en masse to restore the antebellum Union. Northern Democrats remained bitterly divided, and many were determined to win the war. That it was James A. Dix—a Manhattan businessman and Breckinridge supporter—who forestalled the Election Day plot underscored Van Evrie and Horton's political isolation. Anyone who dreamed of reviving the republic of 1860 would have to heal deep fissures between Unionists and Confederates, between Republicans and Democrats, and among Democrats themselves.

But Van Evrie resolved to do exactly that. As usual, he offered a venomous credo to inspire the faithful. Five weeks after Appomattox, he penned a long editorial outlining his vision of the future. American politics was a battle between "white men and mongrels," he wrote; between "those who desire to preserve a white, untainted, glorious America, as from 1789 to 1860, and those who desire to amalgamate four millions of negroes in our political system, and deform and transform the American people into vagabond hordes of mongrels as in Mexico." He resolved to unite the nation's reactionary forces for a new phase of the fight.[109]

During four years of war and revolutionary change, Van Evrie had learned nothing and forgotten nothing. He still reduced politics to a binary struggle between dastardly egalitarians and stalwart patriots. He still brandished Mexico as a cautionary tale. He still saw the antebellum republic as the model for the future. And he still saw himself as a leader of the virtuous host.

But neither his friends nor his foes, nor the terrain on which they fought, had passed through the war unchanged. His Northern and Southern readers had only recently stopped slaughtering one another on the battlefield. His relationship with the fragmented Democratic Party was strained. Slavery's enemies still held the high ground of patriotism. Black civil rights and suffrage were on the horizon. Van Evrie would have to forge a new coalition while surviving the bruising media marketplace. Alas, he was adapting. He now spoke of *mongrels* and *mongrelism*, not abolitionists and emancipation. He was crafting new language to define a fresh campaign: perhaps not to defend slavery, exactly, but to impose modes of racist domination that were more protean—and perhaps more widely popular than the property rights of a regional oligarchy. Already in 1865, he was commencing that political project and refining its idiom. And already he was finding it quite profitable.

Chapter 13

Memory

On a foggy fall day in 1864, James Franklin Fink and George Washington McMains collided on the battlefield. Their paths to Cedar Creek were soaked in blood. Fink had enlisted in the Fifth North Carolina Infantry Regiment as a nineteen-year-old private in June 1861. He fought in all the major eastern campaigns and watched his brother Jacob die. Now he and the rest of Jubal Early's Army of the Valley were trying to ease pressure on besieged Richmond by threatening Washington. On October 19, they surprised Phil Sheridan's Federals and drove them from their camps. Sheridan raced back from Washington to rally his troops, including McMains and his comrades in the Twenty-Second Iowa Infantry. The Iowans had entered service in 1862 and suffered badly at Vicksburg, where they briefly breached rebel defenses in a costly assault before transferring east in May 1864. Now they joined the Federal counterattack and put Early's men to flight. Among the scores of Confederates captured that day was James Fink.[1]

Both Fink and McMains survived the war and raised large families. Fink moved to South Carolina and married Mary Jane Smith, who bore eight children. The fourth arrived in 1874. Called "Uncle Van" by younger relations, his full name was Van Every Fink. McMains returned home to his wife Mary Ann; their third child, born in 1869, went by "Van," but his official moniker was Van Evrie McMains.[2]

These war stories illuminate the challenge confronting John Van Evrie in 1865. Keen to build a national subscriber base for the *Day Book* and a national constituency for the Democratic Party, he had to reunite readers who had spent four years locked in brutal combat. This meant appealing to veterans from both sides and marketing a New York newspaper across a fractured continent. It required healing the Democratic Party's sectional and factional fissures. And it challenged him to rally white Americans around a new polygenist political project in the wake of emancipation.

That Fink and McMains both named sons after Van Evrie reflects the editor's vile success in surmounting these obstacles and, indeed, in achieving his peak influence. As shown in this chapter and the next, between 1865 and 1868, Van Evrie recovered the financial ground lost during the war, cultivated a national readership, and nurtured the coziest relationship with the Democratic Party that he would ever enjoy. Before and during the war, he struggled to align his business, partisan, and ideological efforts. What sold papers had not always elected Democratic candidates or fostered sectional harmony. But in the early years of Reconstruction, Van Evrie rebranded the *Day Book*, revitalized the Democratic coalition, and redefined his political agenda. Tellingly, he also made his most notorious contribution to the racist lexicon.

But all his efforts were not equally successful. Consider Van Evrie and Rushmore Horton's ventures into Civil War commemoration. Their efforts are intriguing, not least because scholarship on postwar memory has focused on Republicans, abolitionists, and ex-Confederates rather than on Copperheads. Van Evrie and Horton sketched a fascinating memorial vision: a pro-Confederate account that explicitly celebrated slavery while urging reconciliation on a polygenist basis. This agenda overlapped with, but differed from, other variations of the Lost Cause. Nuanced histories of pro-Confederate memory show that the Lost Cause was neither monolithic nor static. Early contributions by diehards like Jubal Early acknowledged slavery's centrality in antebellum conflict and the Confederate project, but unrepentant sectionalism proved unpalatable to Northern audiences. By the 1880s, a romanticized version that elided slavery and celebrated states' rights and battlefield valor had gained predominance. Historians debate how thoroughly Northern and Southern whites had reconciled by the dawn of the twentieth century, but they generally concur that the sanitized and nostalgic version of the Lost Cause played better nationwide.[3]

Van Evrie and Horton blended the diehards' explicitly proslavery content with the whitewashers' nationally oriented reconciliatory goals. Echoing their defense of slavery as the basis of American democracy, not Southern separatism, they elevated Confederate history as an exemplar for whites nationwide and Confederate ideals as the foundation for reunion. For them, the Lost Cause was not a balm for coping with defeat but a new teaching tool in their long campaign to convert white Northerners to the political positions espoused by Southern fire-eaters. Thus, their efforts to harness Civil War memory to anti-Reconstruction politics were driven not only by a desire to navigate wartime ruptures but also to continue antebellum struggles. And their insistence on celebrating the Confederacy's proslavery war demonstrates that merely *remembering* slavery did not guarantee a commitment to egalitarian politics.[4] If whites ultimately reconciled by forgetting slavery, it was not for lack of effort on Van Evrie's part.

But while he and Horton made enduring contributions to the Lost Cause library, their short-term effects were unimpressive. The sharply sectionalized responses to their work suggest that collective memory was a flimsy foundation for white unity immediately after the war. More successful were their efforts to shape white Northerners' understandings of current events. Even if unprepared to honor the Confederacy, racist Northerners could sympathize with Southern whites once the Union was restored. Committed to a narrative of Reconstruction as an unmitigated disaster that threatened the purity and power of an ostensibly superior race, Van Evrie made headway by opening the *Day Book*'s columns to Southern authors seeking national audiences. By focusing on the troubled present and uncertain future, Van Evrie began to rebuild political ties between erstwhile enemies like James F. Fink and George W. McMains.

In spring 1865, Americans faced momentous questions left unanswered by the Confederacy's defeat. When and how would the seceded states return to the Union? Would the Thirteenth Amendment—passed by Congress but not yet ratified by three-quarters of the states—finally end slavery? How far would the nation go toward racial equality? During Reconstruction, Americans debated these issues through electoral politics and paramilitary violence.

Northern Democrats entered Reconstruction eager to rebuild their national organization but divided over how to handle a Republican Party buoyed by patriotic fervor and military triumph. Intraparty quarrels hinged on principle and pragmatism. Secession was defeated, to be sure, but how much revolutionary change should Democrats endorse? Some were ready to swallow a large dose. Nearly a quarter of congressional Democrats voted for the Thirteenth Amendment, hoping to remove slavery from politics, defang Republican criticism, and woo moderates who would vote Republican as long as the Slave Power endured. As Senator John B. Henderson of Missouri put it, the Democratic Party would prevail once it "shall cease to be the advocate of African slavery."[5] In mid-to-late 1865, Democratic pragmatists tacked toward the political center by praising Union soldiers, repudiating secession, acknowledging slavery's destruction, and applauding Andrew Johnson, a longtime Democrat who joined Abraham Lincoln atop the 1864 Union Party ticket and became president in April. Most New York Democrats followed suit at their September 1865 convention. They endorsed the Thirteenth Amendment and wrote a state ticket that included War Democrats, Union Party Democrats, and moderate Republicans—and excluded Peace Democrats.[6]

Northern Peace Democrats denounced this strategy. What would it profit the Democrats, if they should win elections and lose their souls? They lambasted Republican warmongers, rejected Black suffrage, and urged restoration of white Southerners to power.[7] Van Evrie was among the most clamorous of this camp. As always, he saw stridency as the basis for party unity and ideological purity as the key to electoral success. True Democrats, he announced in July 1865, were adamant on the "negro question." Repurposing polygenism, he proclaimed: "The negro is a different and subordinate being, and hence the *test* of Democracy . . . is equality for white men and subordination for negroes."[8] Upholding Black subordination meant resisting wartime innovations like emancipation and Black military service and opposing Republican Reconstruction, including the Thirteenth Amendment. Upholding white equality meant restoring the seceded states, under white rule, to the Union. Upon this program alone could Democrats reunite and prevail. Disdaining Democrats who meekly accepted the war's consequences, Van Evrie vowed: "We shall recognize no 'revolution as accomplished.' Never! Never! When the Abolitionists tell us they have triumphed, we tell *them* the fight has just begun."[9]

Van Evrie fought on multiple fronts. First, he had to stabilize the *Day Book*'s finances; editorial vitriol was useless if his business folded. He needed to expand his subscriber list, particularly among the white Southerners who before 1861 comprised a majority of his readers and presumably shared his postwar vision. Second, he had to convince readers to resist Republicans' Reconstruction program, assuring white Southerners that victory was possible and white Northerners that victory was vital. The two-pronged struggle paralleled Van Evrie's antebellum crusade; once again, he aimed to unify white Americans on Southern terms.

He launched a Southern marketing campaign shortly after the war ended. By September 1865, advertisements in Southern periodicals promoted the *Day Book* as "The White Man's Paper" and offered discounts to members of subscriber clubs: $2 per annual subscription, $17.50 for clubs of ten, and $30 for clubs of twenty. To gratify old fans, he offered back issues to Southerners whose prepaid subscriptions had been interrupted by the war.[10] Simultaneously, Van Evrie solicited advertisements from Northern merchants seeking Southern customers. Reminding prospective advertisers that he had reached 25,000 Southern subscribers before the war, he promised to reconnect with them "as fast as mail facilities will permit" and offered advertisers, for $0.40 per line, "the VERY BEST MEDIUM" for Southern marketing.[11] Van Evrie regained profitability by late 1866.[12]

White editors in the South cheered the *Day Book*'s return to their communities. Certain that the *Day Book* "is too well known in the South to require an introduction," a Mississippian redundantly praised it as "thoroughly Democratic in sentiment," politically "firm and unswerving," and "deserving the support of all well-thinking men."[13] A Georgian admired its defense of "constitutional rights" against "faction and radical theories" and encouraged its wide circulation in the South, "that section whose liberties are most immediately in peril."[14] Effusive endorsements of other Van Evrie, Horton & Co. publications also reminded longtime readers of their New York ally and introduced new readers to his wares.[15]

Van Evrie and Horton reciprocated by promulgating ex-Confederates' views of the recently ended war in two ways: serving as their advocates and providing them with a platform to address a national audience. During the war, they had lamented the prospect of permanent separation. Now they recognized that contests over memory would shape the politics of Reconstruction.[16] And with ex-Confederates back in the Union, Van Evrie and Horton eagerly enlisted them as allies and elevated them as exemplars. Northern whites' perceptions of their erstwhile enemies were crucial. If Confederates were traitors, perhaps they deserved what they got from Republicans who wanted to enfranchise Black men and penalize rebel leaders. But if Confederates had fought nobly for white civilization, perhaps their hostility to Reconstruction was noble, too. Van Evrie and Horton broadcast the latter view. Arguing that Confederates had been correct about everything but disunion, they championed the social and political vision of ex-rebels within the re-United States, hoping that the memory of a glorious defeat would rally white Americans against Reconstruction.[17]

Before Confederate apologists built monuments, they wrote books. Immediately after the war, white Southern authors began defining the articles of their commemorative faith: the legality of secession, the benevolence of slavery, the bravery of Confederate soldiers, and the tragedy of their defeat by a numerically superior foe. Richmond journalist Edward A. Pollard set the tone and bestowed a lasting appellation in his 1866 volume, *The Lost Cause: A New Southern History of the War of the Confederates.* Alongside eager endorsements from Confederate generals Robert E. Lee and Joseph E. Johnston, Pollard printed one from the *Day Book* that extolled the book's "excellent style" and predicted its "wide circulation."[18]

But crafting the Lost Cause was not solely a Southern project. Van Evrie and Horton were especially vociferous Northern promoters. Chauncey Burr's *Old Guard,* the middlebrow magazine published by Van Evrie, Horton & Co., made an early bid to market the Lost Cause nationwide. Nine months after the surrender at Appomattox, *Old Guard*'s monthly portraits began to showcase Confederates. Robert E. Lee appeared in the January 1866 issue, followed by Stonewall Jackson, Joseph E. Johnston, and others for the rest of the year. Paired with hagiographic life sketches, these likenesses thrust the Confederate pantheon into Northern parlors. Mixed responses reflected lingering rancor. Lee thanked Burr for his "advocacy of right and liberty" and hoped for reconciliation within the "Union, as established by our forefathers."[19] But Northern backlash was intense. Public denunciations of Burr's "secesh tone" and private death threats showed that many Northerners were not ready to venerate rebels.[20]

More important was Rushmore Horton's contribution to Lost Cause literature, *A Youth's History of the Great Civil War in the United States.* Published by Van Evrie, Horton & Co. in August 1866 after months of promotion, the book, though rarely cited in studies of Civil War memory, went through several printings, including a German edition, and sold over 95,000 copies by 1869. The 387-page volume was accessibly written, priced at $1.50, and calibrated to persuade white Northerners of the Confederacy's virtues and Reconstruction's vices. Ostensibly a chronicle of the past, *Youth's History* was a future-oriented exhortation to restore the Union as it was, not the Confederacy as it might have been.[21]

The book's coverage of the Civil War's causes, course, and consequences reflected Van Evrie's influence. Horton defined the war as a struggle between monarchy and democracy, rooted in the skirmishes between Alexander Hamilton's Federalists and Thomas Jefferson's Democrats. Following their defeat in 1800, Federalists, egged on by perfidious Britons, resolved to regain power by inciting hostility toward slavery. This partisan ploy evolved into a moral crusade during the 1820s and 1830s, when abolitionists spread the "popular delusion" of racial equality. By the 1850s, abolitionist fanatics and monarchical despots had formed the Republican Party; its triumph forced Southern whites to secede. Republicans waged the ensuing war on two fronts: against the South and against those Northerners—like Van Evrie and Horton—who had the "independence and courage" to defy them. Republicans were now ascendant, but Horton's readers could conquer a better future.[22]

Particularly in the book's detailed military narrative, Horton anticipated most Lost Cause precepts. He reviled the usual villains: Benjamin Butler, for his heavy-handed occupation of New Orleans; Ulysses S. Grant, for his cold-blooded attrition strategy; William T. Sherman, for torching Columbia, South Carolina.[23] He honored Confederate icons like John Hunt Morgan.[24] He invented racist vignettes featuring faithful "old darkeys" who spoke in dialect and rejected freedom.[25] He exalted the "gallant and glorious struggles" of Confederates and insisted that only "overwhelming physical force" had compelled their surrender.[26]

But in two respects, *Youth's History* deviated from later Lost Cause norms. First, Horton dwelled on the treatment of Northern dissenters, including the suppression of Democratic newspapers (the *Day Book* is alluded to but not named) and the incarceration of Copperheads. Southern apologists sometimes cited these episodes as proof of Lincolnian tyranny. But the level of detail, including the circumstances of specific arrests and conditions of confinement, revealed how personal these sections were to Horton and the Peace Democrats

"Abolition Officers Driving Negroes from the Plantations," from R. G. Horton, *A Youth's History of the Great Civil War in the United States, from 1861 to 1865* (New York: Van Evrie, Horton & Co., 1867). This illustration reinforced one of the key arguments of Horton's history of the Civil War: that emancipation was a misguided measure, forced upon allegedly contented enslaved people by fanatical abolitionists and deluded Union soldiers. Courtesy of HathiTrust.

who provided him with the particulars.[27] Second, slavery and racial hierarchy dominated Horton's account of sectional conflict. Horton proudly proclaimed that Southern whites seceded to "save themselves from the horrible consequences of amalgamation and social death. . . . They knew that to equalize the races was simply to follow the fate of Mexico and Central America."[28] He praised the Confederate constitution for clarifying Black people's "inferior position," noting that "this was, after all, the turning point of the whole issue between the North, as represented by Lincoln and his party, and the South."[29] Echoing Van Evrie on the disaster of Latin American abolition, Horton hailed the Confederates' defense of slavery and civilization.

Given Horton's audience and purpose, the Confederates' proslavery war was precisely what made their history usable. He sought not to decontaminate the Confederacy for future readers in the twentieth and twenty-first centuries but to exhort nineteenth-century Americans to rebuild a white man's republic. He aimed not to stroke Southern egos but to stoke Northern outrage against Reconstruction. *Youth's History* was the sequel to Van Evrie's *Ne-*

groes and Negro "Slavery." Van Evrie tried to stem an onrushing revolution, while Horton hoped to reverse the tide, but their rationales were the same. Both defended slavery and racial hierarchy as national blessings. Both lauded white Southerners as paladins of democracy. Both urged white Northerners to recognize an ostensibly regional cause as their own. Crucially, both refrained from demonizing the North in toto. Van Evrie never joined Southern proslavery writers in denouncing Northern society. Similarly, the antagonists in Horton's tale are not the Damn Yankees but the Republicans. Northern soldiers are victims of Republican propaganda; heroes appear among Confederates and Peace Democrats alike.

Horton explained this in a prefatory note "To the Reader." He directed *Youth's History* first "to the Northern people," to expose the real "aims and objects" of the "Tory, Monarchical or Abolition party" and turn them against it. He added a special appeal to Northern soldiers "who were deluded by the Abolitionists into believing that they were fighting to preserve republican institutions." White Northerners had blundered, but Horton wanted to change their minds, not castigate their errors; the non-abolitionist majority was redeemable. Horton also offered the "Southern people" the book as encouragement. "Wrong can only be temporarily successful," he promised, and "it needs only faith in the power of the press to yet overthrow the Abolition revolutionists." Here were echoes of Van Evrie's infatuation with author-heroism, and when read alongside the eight pages of advertisements for Van Evrie, Horton & Co. publications appended to the volume, it was obvious which press he had in mind. Finally, Horton presented the book "to all classes, and especially to the young," in hopes that they would restore the "grand old Union." It was not the Confederacy that should rise again, but the Union of 1860.[30] Slavery's future was unclear, but Horton's reference to the "so-called Amendment to the Constitution" that Republicans had "forced on the country . . . against the free and unbiased action of the people" suggested that he did not accept the Thirteenth Amendment as final.[31] He closed the book with a call to undo all that the war had wrought except for reunion:

> Whether the Union of our fathers, the Government as *it was formed*, can ever again be restored, remains to be seen! Yet that ought to be the supreme object to which every American, old and young, should now devote his life. Let every young man, then, register a solemn vow in Heaven, that, if God spares his life, he will devote it to the sacred duty of rolling back this abolition monarchical revolution—to spreading the truth in relation to it, and thus educating a generation to hate it.[32]

Horton urged resistance, but not of South against North or the Confederacy against the Union. His appeal was partisan. He focused squarely on the struggle over Reconstruction and aimed to rebuild a national Democratic Party coalition. Advertisements for *Youth's History* made this plain by presenting it as a "candid and impartial History . . . from a Democratic standpoint. . . . It will be just such a book as every Democrat, North or South, will desire to place in the hands of his children."[33]

But the book's reception reflected persistent sectionalism. White editors in the South welcomed *Youth's History*, praising its publishers as "*Southern* in their sentiments" and urging "our schools, all over the South," to adopt the text for classroom use.[34] They loved that Horton's "partiality" was "all on the Southern side of the question."[35] These compliments missed the point, celebrating his tome as a regional vindication rather than a partisan attack. (They did, however, elevate Horton into the Lost Cause elect. Lauded in *Confederate Veteran* magazine, endorsed by the United Daughters of the Confederacy, quoted by twentieth-century apologists, and reprinted in 1925 by Southern Publishing Company and again by Confederate Reprint Company in 2015, *Youth's History* remains a staple of the genre.[36]) Meanwhile, in the North, critics conflated Horton's sectional and partisan allegiances, echoing Republicans' "bloody shirt" rhetoric that associated the Democratic Party with Southern treason. One reviewer facetiously commended *Youth's History* to "Democrats! Friends! Countrymen and Secessionists!" and mused that anyone could enjoy it, as long as they "believe that the South were victors in the late struggle, that Slavery is still an American institution, and that two and two make five."[37] Horton's foray into Civil War memory-making reflected the difficulty of rebuilding a Democratic national majority. As long as the book was praised as a *Southern* history and condemned a specimen of *Democratic* treason, Horton and Van Evrie had much work to do.

Youth's History was Van Evrie, Horton & Co.'s principal contribution to Civil War commemoration, but Van Evrie occasionally reiterated its themes when addressing Southern allies. Consider a striking *Day Book* editorial published in July 1873 in response to reports that Jefferson Davis was composing a memoir. Van Evrie applauded his old patron but devoted the column to lecturing ex-rebels on how to write their history. "It has been the fatal mistake of Southern leaders, and generally of Democrats," he opined, "to regard what was called the 'slavery question' as incidental." To Van Evrie, Lost Cause writers' habit of eliding slavery's centrality in Civil War history distorted the war's meaning and dimmed the Confederacy's glory. In fact, he argued, most white Northerners voted Republican because they hated slavery. During the war, they assailed slavery, not "State sovereignty," and Confederates fought to preserve a "white man's government." Because this struggle continued in Reconstruction, Confederate history remained instructive. Once white Northerners grasped polygenist truths about Black subordination and white democracy, they would expel Republicans from power and restore the Union of 1860. But they would never do so if pro-Confederate history "ignores the flesh and blood" of the war "and deals with it on the mere basis of State rights." Lost Cause writers must join Van Evrie in exposing "the real, stupendous question—a white man's government or a Mongrel concern." This argument resembled his message to Democrats who would accept Republicans' wartime revolution. Neither partisan advantage nor Confederate mythmaking should distract Reconstruction's foes from their duty. Still determined to unite white Americans around polygenism, Van Evrie urged Davis to tell "the real truth" so that the Southern cause could prevail nationwide.[38]

Van Evrie's experiments with commemoration paralleled his activities during the secession crisis: In both cases, he was out of step with prevailing trends in both the North and the South. On one hand, he asked Northerners to relinquish all they had won, save bare reunion. On the other hand, he ordered ex-Confederates to stop whitewashing their struggle. Perhaps sensing these contradictions, Van Evrie limited his engagement with Civil War memory to a handful of editorials. For a nationalist committed to polygenist politics, it was more prudent to look ahead than linger in the past.

Memory politics led Horton and Van Evrie into a minefield, but commentary on current events seemed likelier to bridge sectional divisions. The *Day Book* editors followed a playbook from the 1850s, when Van Evrie and his predecessor, Nathaniel Stimson, helped Southern correspondents from Bleeding Kansas reach Northern readers. During Reconstruction, reportage from the South was similarly politicized. Republican papers spotlighted racist atrocities committed by paramilitary groups like the Ku Klux Klan. Democrats countered with tales of Black savagery, white victimhood, and Republican corruption. Whose story would white Northerners believe? Their votes were necessary to sustain Reconstruction, so the stakes of the journalistic struggle were enormous.[39]

Van Evrie and Horton solicited Southern authors with promises of a Northern readership. In late 1865, they urged Alexander H. Stephens, the former Confederate vice president, to publish his in-progress book with their firm, emphasizing that the North was "now the place where public opinion must be reached to place things as they were, as *they ought to be*." Stephens placed his *Constitutional View of the Late War Between the States* with a Philadelphia publisher, but Horton invited him to contribute something to *Old Guard*.[40] Equally futile was Van Evrie's attempt to publish a compendium of Jefferson Davis's speeches. Although Davis's elder brother Joseph praised the idea, it never materialized.[41] Other prominent Lost Cause writers, however, including

Bernard J. Sage, William Henry Peck (who regarded Horton as his "best and dearest friend"), and John Esten Cooke, did publish books with Van Evrie, Horton & Co.[42] Cooke also wrote for *Old Guard*, as did William Gilmore Simms, George Fitzhugh, and Edward A. Pollard.[43] Their works honored the Confederacy and the Southern political and social order from which it sprang.

But the most urgent writings, addressing the present, appeared in the *Day Book*. Its most prolific and important Reconstruction-era correspondent was William F. Samford. Van Evrie first published the Alabamian in late 1866, and for the next decade, Samford, writing under the name "Warwick," penned a flood of letters denouncing Republican governance, racial equality, and the entire Reconstruction project. Through these widely reprinted "Warwick Letters," Samford and Van Evrie promulgated a vicious narrative that long outlived biracial democracy in the South. Their partnership was powerful because they were perfectly matched. Born in Georgia, Samford graduated from Randolph-Macon College in 1837 and practiced law for ten years. He retired to an Alabama plantation, briefly edited a newspaper, and earned a reputation for proslavery extremism through his extensive political writings. In 1860, Samford owned $15,000 in real and $39,000 in personal property, including sixty-five enslaved people. Ten years later, his real estate had declined in value by one-third and his personal property shriveled to $1,500. He seized the chance to retaliate through the *Day Book*.[44]

The Warwick Letters gained national notoriety and inspired anti-Reconstruction authors into the twentieth century.[45] In scores of lengthy dispatches, Samford contended that Reconstruction was a disaster because Black people were unfit for freedom. Initially, he cloaked this thesis in paternalism, lamenting the "stupendous wrong and folly" of "taking a poor, ignorant, childlike race from under the fostering care of a patriarchal government," though his brooding over Black workers' demands for wages betrayed more self-interested motives.[46] After the onset of Radical Reconstruction, which brought Black suffrage and Republican ascendency to Alabama, Samford abandoned noblesse oblige. He shrieked that four million "African barbarians" ruled the South.[47] He bemoaned the "reign of terror" imposed by "an infuriated, savage, negro soldiery!"[48] He caricatured Black politicians, describing one as having an "apish head and snaky eyes and bulbous lips" and "the facial expression . . . of a logger-head turtle."[49] Echoing Van Evrie, he defined the "great issue" as "whether the White or the Mon[g]rel races are to govern this great country?"[50] He urged Democrats to save the day. "There is, under God, but one salvation for this poor country of ours," he wrote, "and that is in the restoration of the *glorious Constitution* of our grand, old, inspired fathers. Nobody can restore that but *the people* of the Democratic party."[51]

And he joined Van Evrie in scourging moderate Democrats as "rotten at heart, Mongrel to the core."[52]

Newspapers from Maine to Idaho reprinted the Warwick Letters. Admirers praised Samford's courage to "speak the truth and clothe it in plain language," deeming his letters alone worth the price of a *Day Book* subscription.[53] Critics mocked him as a specimen of the South's "sham aristocracy," reared in a plantation society that "bred conceit as naturally as putrefaction breeds maggots," and rejected his likening of Southern whites to Prometheus. "There was a Prometheus in the South, chained to the mount of suffering," retorted a New Englander, "but his skin was dark and the vulture which tormented him was the 'Southern gentleman.'"[54] But Samford's message gained traction among the Confederacy's former foes. A Union veteran from Iowa wrote to Samford expressing his "earnest sympathy" with Southern whites "in this hour of affliction."[55] Northern editors reprinted the Warwick Letters, widening their reach beyond the *Day Book*'s subscriber base.[56] And while their influence defies exact calculation, Samford's dispatches joined a torrent of racist prose that eroded white support in the North for Reconstruction. Directly anticipating James S. Pike's reportage from South Carolina and Zebulon L. White's from Alabama, Samford's writings fueled a Northern backlash by vilifying Reconstruction as an orgy of fraud and depravity.[57] Publishing the Warwick Letters was one of Van Evrie's most important maneuvers in the war against Reconstruction.

Without subscription lists, Van Evrie's success in recruiting former Unionists and Confederates is difficult to measure directly, but other sources can help. One is the census, which reveals that James F. Fink and George W. McMains were not alone in naming sons for the *Day Book* editor. Thirty-eight boys, born between 1859 and 1881, received the first or middle name "Van Evrie" (or an alternate spelling). None received the moniker before 1859, suggesting that the New Yorker's notoriety sparked the trend, and none received it after 1881, except for six sons born to fathers named Van Evrie. Names reflect parents' values; in the case of children named for public figures, names can reveal political commitments.[58] Analysis of the first generation of honorific namings, which closely paralleled the rise and fall of Van Evrie's fame, shows that enthusiasm for the propagandist peaked during Reconstruction and transcended sectional lines. Sons of Union and Confederate veterans bore his name far into the twentieth century.

Half of Van Evrie's thirty-eight first-generation namesakes came from families that regularly bestowed notable names. Many of their fathers bore illustrious monikers, including three named for George Washington, one for John Marshall, and one for Samuel Houston. Names given to the siblings of the young Van Evries are even more revealing because they indicate that the christeners considered the professional racist part of the American pantheon. Two Van Evries had brothers named for George Washington, two for Benjamin Franklin, three for Thomas Jefferson, and one each for Lafayette, James Monroe, Aaron Burr, Walter Scott, Grover Cleveland, and Horace Mann. Couples who named one son after Van Evrie and another after Washington made a loud statement about race and patriotism.

Tracing namings across time and space illuminates the contours of Van Evrie's appeal. Appendix 2 charts the number of namesakes born each year and suggests that his renown peaked well into Reconstruction, with a plurality of namings occurring in 1872. Van Evrie is best remembered today for his antebellum and wartime writings, but three-quarters of his namesakes were born between 1865 and 1881, suggesting that his personal popularity soared amid the backlash against Reconstruction. The persistence of honorific naming into the late 1870s—which, we will see, was the downslope of Van Evrie's popularity—also indicates that committed supporters venerated him to the end.

His fame was national. A small majority of Van Evrie's namesakes were born in the North: seventeen were born in current or former slave states, while twenty-one hailed from free states (see appendix 2). Because of Van Evrie's renown in the Border South, moreover, nearly two-thirds of his namesakes came from Union states. Closer analysis of state origins reveals patterns consistent with other clues about the geography of Van Evrie's support. None of the namesakes came from New England; five came from the Mid-Atlantic region, seven from the Old Northwest, and eight from Iowa and Kansas. Iowa stands out with the most namesakes, followed by New York. One namesake came from the Pacific Coast. Southern Van Evries included four from the border states, four from the Upper South, and nine from the Deep South.[59] These findings suggest that Van Evrie's most fervent followers lived in the South and the West rather than the Northeast. Coupled with the occupational data analyzed below, they also reaffirm Van Evrie's strong support in rural areas. Van Evrie does not appear in V. Jacque Voegeli's study of racism in the Civil War–era Midwest, but naming patterns suggest that he accurately identified the "Middle West"—Ohio, Indiana, Illinois, Iowa, Michigan, Wisconsin, and Minnesota—as the region, outside the South, that was "most firmly committed to white supremacy."[60]

Nineteenth-century mobility meant that many young Van Evries were born in different states than their parents. But the small free-state majority reappears in parental birthplace data. Birth states for all but four of the 76 fathers and mothers could be positively identified, and slightly over half of both groups hailed from free states. Southerners were, however, more prevalent among the namesakes' grandparents. Birthplaces for 133 of the 152 grandparents of young Van Evries could be identified. Among them, 74 (56 percent) were born in slave states, and a large majority (71 percent) of namesakes had at least one Southern-born grandparent, including 10 of the 21 Van Evries born in free states. These findings affirm the political importance of migration: Many white Southerners carried vehement anti-abolitionist opinions into Western free states.[61] Yankee migrants did not have to learn racism from transplanted Southerners, but Van Evrie's popularity in the Northwest had roots in slave soil.

Like the readers who organized clubs or signed petitions, the vast majority of the namers and their parents were native-born. None of the namesakes' parents were born abroad, and only two of the grandparents came from foreign countries: one from Germany and one from France. These are striking figures, given that nearly 15 percent of the US population in 1870 was foreign-born. Namers were not European immigrants seeking the prerogatives of whiteness; they were homegrown bigots eager to define their native land as a white man's country.[62]

Similarly revealing are the occupations of the namesakes' fathers, which reflect Van Evrie's popularity among rural dwellers of moderate means. Occupational information was available for thirty-seven of the fathers: Twenty-three were farmers, two were farm laborers, and ten had multiple occupations, combining farming with carpentry, blacksmithing, milling, or other work. Thus, all but two of the namesakes' fathers were farmers for at least part of their working lives; the outliers were an Iowa blacksmith and a Texas judge. None of the fathers were dockworkers, miners, factory hands, or railroad workers. Van Evrie's most dedicated fans were not cogs in the industrial machine.

Most of the fathers were farmers or artisans of middling means. Thirty-one of them could be identified in the 1870 census: Their mean real property was worth $2,015; their mean personal property was valued at $1,177. Wealth is not static, and ardent support for Van Evrie was associated with both upward and downward mobility. William Barnhill, for instance, named his son Van Evrie in 1874 after losing considerable property during the Civil War. In 1860, Barnhill, a resident of Noxubee County, Mississippi, owned $1,200 in real estate and two enslaved people. Ten years later, he was left with $360 in real estate, $390 in personal property, and no enslaved labor. In Lexington County, South Carolina, John Pickens Jones plunged deeper into desperation during the 1860s. A nonslaveholding farmer, Jones owned $400 in real estate in 1860, but his real property in 1870 was worth only $150, even as his household had expanded from three children to six. Born in 1878, Willis Van Evrie Jones was another mouth to feed.

Others had prospered during the war. Samuel Houston Smith was a merchant in DeKalb County, Tennessee, in 1860, where he owned $6,000 in personal property. He subsequently expanded his wealth and diversified his pursuits; by 1870, was a farmer and merchant with $2,500 in real estate and $16,780 in personal property. Naming his son Vanevrie N. Smith reflected defiance rather than despondency. Samuel liked grandiose names: Vanevrie's brothers included Napoleon Bonaparte Smith and Stephen A. Douglas Smith. (Their sister had to settle for Elizabeth—though perhaps she was named for the English queen.) Some Northern namers were similarly successful. Iowa farmer Curtis Hatfield prospered in the 1860s, increasing his real property value from $3,500 to $11,000 and his personal property from $688 to $1,200. Naming his son Curtis Van Evrie Hatfield in 1875 reflected political commitment, as Hatfield favored Copperhead monikers. His daughter Laura, born in 1865, bore the middle name Vallandigham as a tribute to the infamous Clement Vallandigham who ran for governor of Ohio in 1863 from his exile in Canada.

Few namers were enslavers. Of thirty-seven households identified in the 1860 census, only two held human chattels that year. Thus, of the sixteen slave-state households for which data are available, 12.5 percent included enslaved people in 1860, roughly half the regional average. On one hand, this underestimates familial ties to slavery, since two Van Evries had a grandparent who enslaved people in 1860, and a third had a grandfather who was an enslaver in 1850. Thus, five of the sixteen namesakes born in slave states entered families with direct interests in slavery. On the other hand, most namesakes were born after emancipation. Only nine arrived before 1865, and six of them were born in free states. Of the three born in slave states, only one namesake entered a slaveholding household, having been born in Texas in 1859 to a father who was a lawyer and judge and who enslaved three people in 1860. The prevalence of nonslaveholders reflects Van Evrie's post-emancipation popularity and his appeal to whites of all classes and sections.

This is confirmed by the fact that namers fought on both sides of the Civil War. The fathers' mean birth year was 1836, placing them squarely in the generation that matured during intense sectional conflict and bore the brunt of combat.[63] Their rates of military participation are revealing. Among the twenty fathers born in free states, four definitely served in the Union army, one probably did, and eleven definitely did not; the service records of the others are unknown. Three of the nonparticipants were too young. If they are removed from consideration, along with the four unknowns, thirteen possible soldiers remain; four (31 percent) or five (39 percent) of them wore Union blue, a rate of service slightly lower than the 41 percent for Northern white men born between 1822 and 1845.[64] This discrepancy is unsurprising, given Van Evrie's vehement opposition to the war. At least one namer evidently shared that disdain: James Wellington Baker enlisted in the 134th New York Infantry but deserted soon after collecting his $50 bounty.[65]

More fathers born in slave states served in the Civil War. Of the sixteen, six definitely served in the Confederate army, three probably did, five did not, and one is unknown; another, John Marshall Cox of West Virginia, fought for the Union. Two of the five nonparticipants were too young for service. Among the nine fathers of military age who were born in the eleven states that seceded, six definitely served in the Confederate army and three possibly did, thus approaching a 100 percent rate of service, which is consistent with the 75 percent rate for the Confederacy as a whole.[66] Not all saw extensive combat. Archibald R. Ellis was a laborer in a North Carolina Local Defense battalion. Everett Lewis, a judge and the only active enslaver among the namers, served in the Texas coastal artillery. But slave-state namers were at least as enthusiastic about the Confederate cause as their neighbors were.

The partisan loyalties of most namers are unknown, though most undoubtedly were Democrats. Scattered evidence reflects the intensity of their party fealty, with references to Democratic devotion in even the briefest biographical sketches. James Wellington Baker, the New York bounty jumper, was, according to a local historian, "a very successful business man" who was "active in town affairs" as an officeholder and "a Democrat in politics."[67] Similarly, a Michigan chronicler noted that William Ford of Kalamazoo County "was a staunch Democrat in politics, in which he always manifested a good degree of interest."[68]

Regardless of region, Van Evrie's keenest admirers tended to be deeply rooted rural dwellers reared amid the sectional strife of the 1840s and 1850s. Democratic in politics and mostly farmers by occupation, they idolized Van Evrie, but not because they sought acceptance in a new country or solace in the urban labor market. Whether rising or falling in prosperity, they cheered him as a guardian of privileges they currently enjoyed or hoped to regain, and as a powerful opponent of the abolitionists and Republicans who menaced the racist hierarchy that they equated with liberty. They ranked Van Evrie alongside the Founders as a figure worthy of veneration and made their sons living monuments to his message.

Van Evrie, Horton & Co. assailed Reconstruction on multiple fronts. Dabbling in the struggle over Civil War memory, they praised the Confederacy for defending slavery and urged Southern Lost Cause propagandists to follow suit. But in the war's immediate aftermath, they made greater inroads by publishing work that focused on the present. White Northerners who choked on Confederate hagiography might relish racist reportage on Reconstruction, especially since Van Evrie no longer had to convince them to love slavery or the Slave Power. Abolition had uncoupled racist domination from a system of property rights that bolstered a rebellious aristocracy, and while Van Evrie never accepted slavery's demise, he now had a wider platform upon which to unite a national audience.

An early test came with the first postwar presidential election in 1868. To empower the cross-sectional coalition he struggled to build and give electoral weight to the budding alliance between James F. Fink and George W. McMains, Van Evrie needed to align his crusade with the Democratic Party. His next challenge was to show Democratic insiders that his plan could work.

Chapter 14

Supremacy

John Van Evrie and William F. Samford agreed that only an ideologically purified Democratic Party could restore the old Union. Braiding polygenism with partisan strategy, Van Evrie wrote Samford that "God has made white men and negroes *different* and *therefore* they *must* be governed by different rules as the founders of American liberty provided for in 1787 and the stupid and benighted Democrats who assent to the 'situation' are simply assenting to national death and disintegration."[1] As in the antebellum and war years, Van Evrie spent Reconstruction trying to influence the Democratic Party by prescribing the platform on which its discordant factions could unite and prevail. He achieved maximum success in 1868 and indelibly stamped the vocabulary of American racism.

Major gains in the 1867 elections, including capturing the New York State Assembly, raised Democratic hopes for the 1868 presidential race. But they also sharpened debates over strategy. Van Evrie's plan stemmed from his hatred of what pragmatists eventually called the "New Departure": an effort to shed Democrats' proslavery and secessionist image by modulating hostility to Reconstruction and embracing fresh issues. Proponents warned that spouting racism and decrying abolition empowered Republicans to tar Democrats as unabashed traitors. New York's leading Democratic organ, the *World*, made this case, even advising white Southerners to undercut the Republicans by accepting Black suffrage and soliciting Black votes.[2]

Van Evrie blasted the New Departure as ideologically abhorrent and strategically flawed. Uncompromising defense of the old Union, he insisted, was essential to restoring Democratic power and saving American civilization. He developed this argument in a December 1865 public letter to President Andrew Johnson. Van Evrie opened by reviewing his Mexican journey, scientific studies, and polygenist perspective, claiming that "I understand the subject of 'slavery' better than any other living man." He rehashed his theory about abolitionism's foreign origins. And he warned that the country was hurtling toward disaster because of "Abolition—a mad and impious effort . . . to abolish the natural distinctions of race fashioned by the hand of God." Van Evrie's views had not budged since 1853. But promoting them *then* meant preserving the status quo; now it meant reversing revolutionary change. He urged Johnson, as "a Southern man, a democrat," to ride to the rescue. Johnson must "remove the foreign pressure from the subjugated States, and leave them to govern themselves and to provide for the subordinate race that Providence has entrusted to their care and guidance, just as they have always done." Whether this meant reimposing slavery was not clear; the Thirteenth Amendment had been ratified seventeen days before. Certainly, it meant accepting the Black Codes recently enacted by state legislatures in Mississippi and South Carolina to subjugate Black laborers and circumscribe Black citizenship. Grounded in proslavery polygenism, Van Evrie's postwar vision was as reactionary as any entertained in the South.[3]

Over the next three years, Van Evrie pounded this theme in column after vitriolic column. Democratic defeats in the 1866 midterms prompted editorials on polygenism, abolition's antidemocratic origins, and Democrats' duty to crush "Mongrelism" and "restore the 'Union as it was.'"[4] In 1867, the onset of Radical Reconstruction and progress toward ratification of the Fourteenth Amendment elicited similar exhortations. Decrying "compromise, and dodgery, and abstractions," Van Evrie told Democrats:

> We must restore the White Republic of Washington, or collapse into the rottenness, social disintegration and death of Mexico. Freedom, Democracy, civilization, society itself, cannot live an hour with Mongrelism. God has made the white man superior and the negro subordinate, therefore human society is forever impossible save "as it was" in the South, and there will never be peace or prosperity until Mongrelism be beaten down and the Union restored as it came from the hands of Washington.[5]

This was all that mattered. Alarmed by Western Democrats' efforts to campaign on debt and currency questions, he deemed it "folly" to risk "national safety" by discussing economics before defeating the "Abolition lunacy."[6] During the war, Van Evrie occasionally berated Republicans for running up debt and allowing investors to fatten on federal bonds. But now he saw economic topics as dangerous distractions. They might further fragment the Democratic Party, pitting the supporters of inflation and paper currency (greenbacks) against East Coast business elites and other gold standard stalwarts. Racism seemed the only basis for Democratic unity, so Van Evrie sought to shelve economic issues and unite white Democrats across class and regional lines. After toppling Reconstruction, they could quibble over currency. Until then, they must focus on race.[7]

As always, Van Evrie's noxious talent lay not in generating new ideas but in marketing old ones. His postwar editorials recycled familiar content: The polygenism and conspiracy mongering he used to defend slavery in the 1850s and oppose emancipation during the war now infused his crusade against Reconstruction. He also indulged his penchant for sloganeering. In the 1850s, Van Evrie adorned his prose with catchphrases. Denials that *the negro is a black white man*, denunciations of *free negroism*, and the scare quotes around *slavery* embellished his brand. Now, while his core political position was unchanged, he adapted his vocabulary. His use of novel terminology was hardly unique; terms like "carpetbagger" and "Klansman," coined in the early postwar years, proliferated as writers sought new terms for debating revolutionary change.[8] For Van Evrie, this meant devising new slogans to denounce foes and rally friends. Republicans preached "mongrelism," a term that condemned emancipation and Black suffrage by locating them on the slippery slope toward interracial sex and national ruin.[9] Democrats must defend the *white republic* (often rendered in all capitals), a phrase Van Evrie used interchangeably with *the Union as it was* for what he believed was established in 1787 and affirmed in the *Dred Scott* decision.[10] Accordingly, he advertised the *Day Book* as both a Democratic organ and the "White Man's Paper," or "A Paper for White Men."[11] This fusion of racial identity, racist policy, and partisanship structured his anti-Reconstruction crusade. Van Evrie expected to prevail by sharpening the color line, framing politics as a battle between Democratic "white men" and Republican "mongrels."

One of his slogans proved especially effective in aligning his efforts to market the *Day Book*, demonize Reconstruction, and unite fractious Democrats. It also caught on with other writers and long outlived its popularizer. This was *white supremacy.*

Historian Barbara Fields notes that "white supremacy is a slogan, not a belief." This distinction clarifies rather than diminishes the phrase's historical significance. "A slogan," Fields observes, "has the purpose of summarizing different beliefs in such a way as to provide a basis for common political action among those holding these beliefs, in spite of their differences."[12] In the postwar South, *white supremacy* for a wealthy landowner might mean keeping close control over Black sharecroppers, while for poor whites it might mean keeping Black people at a distance, in separate train cars and ramshackle schools. Van Evrie's decisive role in popularizing the term sustains both Fields's general interpretation and specific word choice. Before *white supremacy* featured in Democratic electioneering, and before it became a staple of reactionary political rhetoric, Van Evrie deployed the phrase in advertising. While it quickly facilitated his campaign to unify and purify the Democratic Party, it emerged from efforts to boost *Day Book* readership. It first caught on as a slogan for selling newspapers.

Van Evrie was not the first to combine "white" with "supremacy," but the phrase was rarely used before he popularized it. Ironically, it first appeared in an 1824 pamphlet by a British abolitionist. In a lengthy footnote on the Haitian Revolution, T. S. Winn argued that the 1791 slave insurrection was not sparked by an emancipation decree but by white resistance to change. The lesson: Britons must enact emancipation on their own terms before enslaved people "forcibly acquire it for themselves." Managed abolition was compatible with colonial rule; revolutionary overthrow was not. If Black people rebelled, "it may be too late by any means . . . to reduce them to order and obedience under White supremacy."[13] The term reappeared in the 1830s as slavery was being abolished in the British Caribbean. Observers pondered whether whites or Blacks would dominate the post-emancipation colonies, with the possible outcomes described as *white supremacy* and *negro supremacy*.[14] Another flurry of uses occurred in the early 1850s amid rumors of abolition in Spanish Cuba, again surfacing in speculations about an ostensibly zero-sum balance of power.[15] Van Evrie's knowledge of the phrase's origins is unclear, but the parallels with the 1860s are striking. "White supremacy" was not yet a slogan, but it materialized at moments when challenges to property rights in persons destabilized broader political systems.

Amid escalating sectional conflict in the 1850s, scattered American uses of the phrase presaged the major shift of the 1860s in two ways. First, they were prescriptive rather than descriptive, offering proslavery exhortations instead of labels for future scenarios. Second, Van Evrie figured prominently in the story. An early omen came in May 1851, when George W. Williams of Abbeville, Alabama, twice invoked "white supremacy" while announcing his candidacy for the state legislature. His hard-fought campaign, waged amid an ultimately abortive Deep South secession movement, turned on protecting slavery. Williams, an ex-Whig running as a hardline Southern Rights candidate against a Unionist rival, framed the issue as the survival of civilization, stating, "It is not a question of property, it is a question of white supremacy, of State Rights, of freedom from impertinent interference of liberty to manage our own affairs; and of duty to retain the trusts that God has given us." He proclaimed that Southern whites must gird themselves for secession while dictating their terms for staying in the Union.[16] Henry County voters evidently agreed, because Williams prevailed despite the general success of Unionist candidates statewide.[17]

More portentous was Van Evrie's first use of the phrase in a *Day Book* editorial printed on May 5, 1856. Amid a tirade about slavery as the basis of democracy, calculated to convince Northerners to shun the Republicans and welcome slavery into Kansas, he urged that political institutions must honor the "natural law of white supremacy and negro subordination."[18] This formulation foreshadowed several trends in his work. The pairing of "white supremacy" with "negro subordination" regularly reappeared as a shorthand for aligning social relations with polygenist doctrine. Moreover, prior to emancipation, Van Evrie used the phrase "white supremacy" to mean slavery. He clarified this in a pair of 1861 editorials that accused Republicans of seeking "the abolition of white supremacy over the negro, or slavery, as they term it."[19] It was a logical move for a writer who denied that American slavery was *slavery* at all. If "white supremacy and negro subordination" signified the institutionalization of natural roles, then Van Evrie's sporadic pre-1865 references to "white supremacy" served the same purpose as placing *slavery* in scare quotes—namely, to vindicate slavery by renaming it.

Eleven weeks after the May 1856 column appeared, Jefferson Buford of Alabama admonished advocates of "white supremacy in the South" to join his proslavery expedition to Kansas.[20] Buford, a *Day Book* reader and occasional correspondent, almost certainly borrowed the slogan from Van Evrie. When he marched into Bleeding Kansas under a banner inscribed "The Supremacy of the White Race," he blared Van Evrie's nascent slogan as a battle cry for paramilitary fighters mobilized to safeguard slavery's western flank. And the fact that Buford, like Williams, was a longtime Whig, showed the slogan's potential to transcend not only factional and sectional divisions but party lines as well.[21]

Yet while Van Evrie occasionally referred to white supremacy in the late 1850s and early 1860s, it was not part of the *Day Book*'s brand. Nor had the phrase caught on widely. As shown in appendix 3, it was seldom used before 1865, and most uses were reprints of Buford's 1856 address or of Van Evrie's writings. Notwithstanding war and emancipation, the draft riots, and the roiling debates about a post-emancipation United States, most of the scattered appeals to "white supremacy" came from Van Evrie and a few imitators.

That changed in 1865, when a *Day Book* advertising campaign made *white supremacy* central to Van Evrie's public image and etched the phrase into the American political vocabulary. Deployed to brand Van Evrie's product and promote his cause, the phrase appeared in *Day Book* advertisements throughout the country, first in Northern papers in the spring and then in Southern papers by late summer. At precisely the moment when Van Evrie set out to rebuild his national readership, reunite a splintered Democratic Party, and rally white Americans against Reconstruction, he made *white supremacy* his mantra. Initially, it was part of a recital of the *Day Book*'s creed, a summation of the "Union as it was" that Democrats must restore. In a typical prospectus, printed in an Ohio newspaper in March 1865, Van Evrie described the *Day Book* as "the organ of Democratic principles—the genuine, old-fashioned principles upon which our Government was founded. It is for white supremacy, State sovereignty and a Federal Union as the cardinal landmarks of American Government and Civilization. It goes for white men being superior and negroes inferior, just as God made them."[22] He apparently liked the results because in June, he printed the tripartite slogan in all capitals.[23] By August, he had replaced the prospectus with streamlined ads that listed subscription rates beneath the *Day Book*'s motto: "Devoted to the Great Principles of White Supremacy, State Sovereignty and Federal Union."[24] In early 1866, he began printing the slogan in the *Day Book* itself, including in a subscriber club call that hailed the "great fundamental principles of white supremacy, state sovereignty, and federation as the rocks upon which the Constitution and the Union were built."[25]

The slogan was both sweeping and usefully vague. It certainly encapsulated Van Evrie's vision of Confederate social and political ideals ascendant within a restored Union. Black people must be subservient; state governments must enforce that subordination; and the centralization of federal power must be reversed. This was the essence of his appeal to Andrew Johnson, of Rushmore Horton's *Youth's History*, and of the Warwick Letters. But endorsing *white supremacy* did not commit him on every postwar issue. Obviously, it signaled antipathy to Republicans and New Departure Democrats. Undoubtedly, it meant opposition to abolition, but he repeated the slogan long after ratification of the Thirteenth Amendment. It also repudiated Black suffrage and officeholding, Black landownership and occupational mobility, the Freedmen's Bureau, and other facets of Republican Reconstruction. But emancipation raised complex questions that the slogan left unanswered. Upon what terms would Black agricultural workers labor for white landowners? How much geographic mobility should freedpeople enjoy—and what if they sought better prospects in the West or North? How would abolition reallocate political power within the Southern states, where the demise of the three-fifths rule bolstered representation for counties with large Black populations? These issues threatened to inflame class and regional divisions among whites, including among *Day Book* readers. But odes to white supremacy masked these divisions, invoking shared prejudice without advocating specific policies. Readers could project their views onto the term and feel that Van Evrie spoke for them. This was a powerful slogan.

Other Democratic editors promptly borrowed the phrase to peddle their own wares. In December 1865, nine months after Van Evrie's white supremacy ad campaign commenced, Peace Democrat and veteran editor William H. Munnell released the prospectus for his new Cincinnati weekly, the *West and South*. Seeking to unify Southern and Western Democrats, Munnell preached state sovereignty and free trade. He also deemed "white supremacy and negro subordination to be the true relation of the two races" and championed "the social and political supremacy of the white race over the negro."[26] A month later, the editors of the Cambridge City, Indiana, *Western Mirror* smugly reprinted a *Day Book* endorsement: "The *Mirror* comes out distinctly on the DAY-BOOK platform of white supremacy and negro subordination, holding that the latter is the true position of the negro race." Van Evrie was proud of his slogan but also eager to see others adopt it, adding: "This is beginning to be a popular platform for the Democratic press just now."[27]

This was no idle boast. As shown in appendix 3, between 1866 and 1868, *white supremacy* metastasized in Democratic journalism. Editorialists invoked it regularly in the 1867 state elections. They proclaimed, "Our party is contending for white supremacy, and it has no concessions or compromises to make on that subject."[28] Copying Van Evrie's couplet, they urged Democrats to "let the watchword be '*white supremacy and Negro subordination.*'"[29] Sometimes they combined it with other slogans; an Ohio editor advised: "Let your rallying cry be, 'Equal Taxation and White Supremacy.'"[30] And they wielded it to impose the color line, arguing that white voters must oppose the Republicans. From Wilmington came a typical refrain: "The great and solemn duty of every white man in North Carolina . . . is to vote. . . . The happiness and prosperity of the white masses—white supremacy—the welfare of North Carolina—hang in the balance."[31] Van Evrie's fingerprints remained on the slogan, particularly when attached to *Negro subordination*, but it had become the common property of his party.

The slogan spread far beyond editorials. Authors of public letters employed it in 1867, often placing it in quotation marks to accentuate its novelty. In October 1867, an Ohio opponent of Black suffrage urged a rival to "identify yourself, with the one who holds that this is a white man's government . . . and who have just born aloft to victory, the glorious banner of 'white supremacy.'"[32] Grassroots groups adopted it as well. In April, Cincinnati Democrats resolved that "white supremacy and negro subordination is the best condition of the races."[33] And as they anticipated the 1868 presidential contest, some Democrats tied the slogan to specific candidates. In late 1867, the Illinois *Statesman* endorsed Clement L. Vallandigham, placing his name over a litany of slogans: "*Redemption of Government Bonds in Greenbacks, or Repudiation. White Supremacy, State Sovereignty and Federation, are the Foundation Pillars of the American Republic.*"[34] Van Evrie likely winced at the intermixture of the currency question. But this usage showed how far his influence over the Democratic Party had spread and how swiftly his ad campaign had infused a partisan crusade.

Van Evrie encouraged partisan adaptation of the slogan, particularly in his second book, which went through two editions in 1868. Not coincidentally, it was also the first book ever to bear his infamous phrase in its title: *White Supremacy and Negro Subordination; or, Negroes a Subordinate Race, and (So-Called) Slavery Its Normal Condition.* Released early in the year, *White Supremacy and Negro Subordination* was a minimally revised version of *Negroes and Negro "Slavery."* In a new preface, he lamented that the 1861 book had failed to forestall disunion. Now, Republicans ruled the South "by military force," had "torn four millions of negroes from their normal condition," and were "striving to 'reconstruct' American society on a Mongrel basis, as in Mexico, Central America, etc." In the other new section, a sixty-page appendix, Van Evrie expanded his analysis of Latin American history and warned that the whole hemisphere would slide into barbarism if Reconstruction continued. Likening Republican policy to the misrule that created Latin America's "Mongrel Republics," he claimed that political equality would promote interracial sex, biological degeneracy, and civilizational collapse. He urged a "social restoration" that would undo Reconstruction and "return to the Constitution and the Union 'as it was.'" To effect this, "every man, and woman too, in this broad land *must* accept the simple but stupendous truth of white supremacy and negro subordination" or else suffer "years of social anarchy, horror, and misery!"[35] Van Evrie had little fresh material but still believed that the doctrine he had preached for fifteen years was the most vital lesson white Americans could learn. He had failed in 1861. Now, flaunting a new title that was permeating the public sphere, he tried again.

With Democrats already weaving the language of white supremacy into presidential politics, it was natural for Van Evrie to deploy *White Supremacy and Negro Subordination* as a campaign text. He did this explicitly in the second edition, issued soon after the first. It was identical except for a note "To the Reader" inserted near the table of contents. In simple prose, accessible to what Van Evrie called "the commonest reader," it summarized the book's assertions about racial difference, the naturalness of the "so-called slavery of the South," and the dangers of allowing "the whole gang of Abolition mongrels"—Republicans in Congress—to steer the country toward Latin American ruin. Van Evrie closed with a partisan appeal, adding that the book would "teach you, finally, how you should act and vote in the great Presidential contest now inaugurated, and to be decided next November."[36] Van Evrie again vaulted into partisan campaigning, repackaging old ideas in time for Democrats' first bid to defeat Reconstruction in a national election. In two short years, his newspaper's slogan had become the catchphrase of a political movement. His partisan influence was soaring.

Democratic leaders mimicked Van Evrie's messaging because it promised solutions to their own problems. Van Evrie used white supremacy to reunite readers on a single-issue platform of racist reaction. Democrats faced similar internal dissensions, and many folded his slogan and strategy into their efforts to recapture the White House. Thus, in 1868, the party's interests and Van Evrie's aligned snugly. Never before or after would Democrats run a campaign that so closely followed Van Evrie's playbook.

Democrats divided along several axes: Union veterans versus unrepentant rebels, Western inflationists versus Eastern hard-money advocates, reactionary ideologues versus New Departure pragmatists. Leading contenders for the presidential nomination included Ohio inflationist George H. Pendleton, Union general Winfield Scott Hancock, and New York's former Copperhead governor Horatio Seymour, who condemned the Fourteenth Amendment and insisted that the states must govern Black citizenship and suffrage. Shortly before the party's July national convention in New York City, Van Evrie, anticipating Seymour's selection, sent him a copy of the *Day Book* and some unsolicited advice. Warning that "our Republican Institutions are in the utmost danger," Van Evrie deprecated the "ignorance and moral cowardice" of Democrats who, by swallowing Republicans' radicalism, blinded the masses to the "audacious impositions of the Mongrel Faction." Seymour should promise voters one thing: "*Restoration of that very Union they went to war for, and nothing else*," meaning white supremacy, state sovereignty, and federal Union. On this platform Democrats would "sweep over the land like a whirlwind" and save the country.[37] But other Democrats, including Manton Marble of the *World*, demurred. Worried that a reactionary campaign would play into Republicans' hands, they backed Salmon P. Chase, a Supreme Court justice and moderate Republican with sterling state-rights credentials whose candidacy, as part of a New Departure strategy, would inspire Republican defections and foster realignment that favored the Democrats.[38]

Packed into Tammany Hall, Democratic delegates cast twenty-one indecisive ballots before the Ohioans threw their support to Seymour, expecting him to decline and make way for Chase. Seymour baffled their plans by accepting the nomination. Thus, a maneuver meant to promote moderation saddled Democrats with a Copperhead whose name evoked the draft riots. Privately, many Democrats lamented Seymour's selection, predicting that he would lure few Republicans away from their war hero nominee, Ulysses S. Grant. Indeed, Seymour's nomination left Democrats little to campaign on besides racism. Although a Unionist, Seymour had no record of military glory. His hard-money principles precluded economic appeals to Western inflationists. And when his running mate, Missouri's Francis P. Blair Jr., loudly damned Reconstruction and demanded white rule in the South, the die was cast: Democrats would run on white supremacy.[39]

By campaigning on their lowest common denominator, Democrats embraced what Van Evrie deemed their highest calling. He called the nomination a "providential" choice.[40] He plastered the candidates on the *Day Book* masthead, with an extra flourish: "SEYMOUR, BLAIR, AND WHITE SUPREMACY."[41] He flooded the country with cheap "Tracts for the Times," marketed to Democratic clubs, state and local party committees, and individual buyers. Mostly warmed-over antebellum and wartime pamphlets, they included James Hunt's polygenist "The Negro's Place in Nature."[42] Van Evrie printed editorials and Warwick Letters that framed the election as a choice between the white republic and savagery.[43] He urged readers to support their paper and party by organizing subscriber clubs, whose members enjoyed rock-bottom rates during the campaign.[44]

Democrats raised a racist groundswell for Seymour. One editor celebrated their unity, proclaiming, "There is but one sentiment, one feeling and one impulse that animates that body, and it is *white supremacy*."[45] In California, Democratic orators urged voters to "Rally!" for "Seymour and Civil Law! Blair and White Supremacy!"[46] Pennsylvania Democrats told voters to choose between "Seymour and white supremacy—Grant and black domination."[47] Racist caricatures, demagogic oratory, and paramilitary violence were mainstays of Democratic campaigning.[48] Van Evrie loved it. He applauded the "extraordinary outbreak of patriotic sentiments" that would propel the "great and invincible Democratic legion" to victory.[49]

Some Democrats, however, believed their party was following Van Evrie into defeat. During the 1867 state races and the 1868 campaign, they shuddered when Republican editors cited *Day Book* editorials as proof that Democrats still had abhorrent ideas and traitorous hearts. One Iowa Republican ridiculed Van Evrie and other "newspaper kings of their national party" and quoted liberally from their "startling advocacy" of "treason."[50] Nervous Democrats winced when Van Evrie and Chauncey Burr let loose, arguing that they simply provided "a constant supply of ammunition for the enemies of the Democratic party."[51] Worried about their image, New Departure Democrats denied that Van Evrie spoke for them.[52] Theirs was not a majority view, but the debate over Van Evrie's representativeness reflected his outsized public influence as both reactionary oracle and target for Republican counterattacks. The undercurrent of intraparty criticism, moreover, kept the dispute over the Democratic Party's future simmering throughout the 1868 contest.

Van Evrie's critics were right: Seymour's campaign inflamed hatred but failed at the polls. Grant won nearly 53 percent of the popular vote and an imposing Electoral College victory, 214 to 80. Seymour became the first Democratic nominee to win New York since 1852, but he took only seven other states and was shut out of New England and the Midwest. Comparing Democratic vote share in 1864 and 1868 suggests that the white supremacy campaign gained traction on the Pacific Coast (Democrats gained eight points in California and four in Oregon) and in the Border South (with large Democratic gains in Kentucky, Maryland, Missouri, and West Virginia). But it alienated voters in New England (where Democratic vote share fell everywhere outside Massachusetts), most of the old Northwest, and Pennsylvania. In other races, Democrats made small gains in the House of Representatives but lost two Senate seats and won only three out of twenty gubernatorial elections. Their bitter defeat, according to one historian, "marked the bankruptcy of their strategy pursued since the end of the war." Many Democrats, desperate for fresh leadership and ideas, turned toward the New Departure.[53]

Van Evrie did not. In his postmortems, he ranted about Republican schemes to "transform the homogeneous Republic of Washington into a Mongrel nation, like Mexico and South America."[54] But he also criticized Democrats, claiming that a more aggressive campaign would have swept every state outside New England. With self-serving logic, he exhorted Democratic editors to whip party leaders into shape, as if winning votes was solely a matter of willpower.[55] The tension between hero-editor and practical politicians had returned. Having learned nothing from the defeat of a campaign conducted in his own grotesque image, Van Evrie maintained the course he had followed for fifteen years. He would brook no New Departure. But what would he do the next time his principles conflicted with party loyalty? And how far would he go to restore the "white republic"?[56]

Chapter 15

Blood

Captain Elihu G. Barker relaxed in his Marion, Arkansas, home on a hot summer evening in 1868. A Union veteran, Freedmen's Bureau agent, and Republican legislator, Barker personified the Reconstruction regime that Democrats despised. He was a marked man. An attempted assassination two years before had taken his left arm. Now another lurking foe tried to finish the job. As Barker leaned his head on his hand, someone fired a load of buckshot through the window. Two pellets shattered Barker's right wrist and forearm; three others tore apart his face. He lay unconscious until courageous friends carried him to a doctor, an ex-Confederate who risked reprisal to treat him. Weeks later, Barker passed through Memphis on his way to recuperate in the North. A newspaper correspondent detailed his "shocking" condition: Barker's one arm hung mangled in a sling, "while his face was literally a mass of raw flesh held together by strips of adhesive plaster."[1]

Press coverage of the shooting was predictably divided. Democrats alternately denied the attack's political motivation and insisted that Barker deserved it.[2] Republicans blamed "rebel Ku-Klux" or "a Seymour and Blair man" for the crime.[3] But "Hernande," the Memphis reporter haunted by Barker's injuries, dug deeper. Why were ex-rebels still so militant? Hernande blamed media consumption. Most white Southerners, Hernande claimed, read little and were goaded to violence by their social superiors, those "counsellors and advisers of the great masses throughout the rural districts." They in turn only read material that "panders to their most bitter prejudices and hatreds." Vicious media incited vile misdeeds. One of the worst offenders, Hernande believed, was "the *New York Day Book*."[4]

It was no coincidence that John Van Evrie began to face accusations of fomenting violence during Reconstruction. After 1867, he unleashed apocalyptic and bloodthirsty prose that surpassed even his earlier diatribes against John Brown and emancipation. His marketing efforts followed suit, and by 1870, he was directly peddling his wares to members of Southern paramilitary groups committed to overthrowing Reconstruction by any means necessary. Newspaper advertising, partisan mobilization, and political terrorism melded in the crucible of Radical Reconstruction. Van Evrie made the *Day Book* a mouthpiece for the ferocious campaign to topple Reconstruction and vanquish the Republicans nationwide.

This escalation was principally a response to Black suffrage, a concept that had alarmed Van Evrie ever since he contacted John C. Calhoun in 1846. Now the drumbeat of Black enfranchisement resounded everywhere: another New York constitutional convention in 1867; the advent of Black voting in the South in 1868; Congressional passage of the Fifteenth Amendment in February 1869 and its ratification in 1870. In hindsight, Van Evrie's frantic response might seem excessive. After all, Jim Crow regimes would crush biracial democracy in the South by the end of the nineteenth century. White Northerners rejected Black suffrage in several state referenda, revealing that hostility to political equality ran deep throughout the country. Even the Fifteenth Amendment was weaker than it might have been. Because it prohibited discrimination instead of affirming a right to vote or hold office, it provided a fragile foundation for democracy that crumbled under literacy tests, whites-only primaries, and other racist stratagems that received Supreme Court sanction in *Williams v. Mississippi* (1898).[5]

Peering into an opaque future, however, Van Evrie could only pine for counterrevolution. Presently, he confronted Black men's incorporation into the body politic, which he termed "Mongrelism." The word evoked interracial sex and prophesized that political equality would lead to social intimacy, racial pollution, and the barbarism that Van Evrie associated with Mexico. But it also reflected fears that suffrage itself was a point of no return, a radically inclusive act that, according to polygenists, would make equal what God had created unequal. Van Evrie hated emancipation but could imagine alternative forms of racist exploitation, including the segregated labor market that barred most Black workers from skilled occupations in the North. But suffrage meant citizenship. It incentivized white politicians to consider Black men's demands, collaborate with them in coalitions, and recognize them as peers. More than antislavery activism or even abolition, Black suffrage threatened what Van Evrie called democracy: equality among biological equals and the subordination of inferiors. Identifying the "so-called Fifteenth Amendment" as "the final consummation of the Mongrel revolution" that began with Lincoln's election, Van Evrie urged resistance at all costs.[6]

Thus, while there was consistency in Van Evrie's course through Reconstruction—hatred for the New Departure, devotion to polygenism, and determination to peddle the *Day Book* nationwide—his content and marketing became increasingly bloodthirsty. Tracing his ugly prose through the networks that fueled political and paramilitary backlash reveals an important dimension of Reconstruction's history. Van Evrie did not singlehandedly orchestrate the onslaught that called itself Redemption. But he understood the symbiosis between journalism and partisanship, between mass marketing and grassroots activism, and he simultaneously incited armed resistance while monetizing the backlash against biracial democracy.[7]

Black suffrage alarmed Van Evrie, not least because it stoked smoldering struggles within the Democratic Party. Manhood suffrage, which arrived in the former Confederacy in 1868 and went national in 1870, forced Democrats to choose between assailing Black voters and wooing them. After Horatio Seymour's defeat in the 1868 presidential election, many pragmatists preferred the New Departure over conceding a vital constituency to the Republicans. Neither ex-Confederates nor Copperheads were immune to this logic. In Alabama, New Departure Democrats mocked hardliners for crying over spilled milk and argued that Black suffrage was a "fixed fact," that snagging even a few thousand Black votes could be decisive, and that refusal to try was the "height of folly."[8] Similar reasoning convinced Ohio's Samuel Sullivan Cox, who admitted that "the inevitable Colored Cuss" was already "here! in Senate and as a voter, and he will soon be everywhere whether we like it or not."[9] This was indeed a striking departure for a Copperhead whose 1863 anti-emancipation screed was published by Van Evrie, Horton & Co.[10] In New York, prominent Democrats—from *World* editor Manton Marble to Fernando Wood, municipal secessionist and venomous Freedmen's Bureau critic—jumped on the New Departure bandwagon. Democratic principles of decentralized and thrifty government, they insisted, were too precious to sacrifice on the altar of racism. By 1872, Democrats had even engaged a Black orator, Isaac L. Hunter, to deliver a July 4 address at Tammany Hall.[11]

Van Evrie assailed the New Departure at every opportunity. Democratic politicians who courted Black voters were "corrupt or benighted," and editors who backed them were "negroized." The party was not worth saving if it needed Black votes.[12] The Democrat who "assents to a Mongrel citizenship" was "a traitor to Democracy and a fool to boot."[13] Marble's *World* was a "political prostitute."[14] Wood was a gutless blowhard who did not represent "the real Democracy of the country."[15] In a rare signed article, which tacitly admitted the New Departure's practical appeal, Van Evrie beseeched Southerners not to accept it out of desperation, promising that a lily-white Democratic Party would rescue them from Republican rule.[16] Throughout the late 1860s and early 1870s, Van Evrie begged Democrats to stand firm. He deployed the *white supremacy* slogan in this intraparty struggle, proclaiming "White Supremacy the Sole Test of Democracy" and urging stalwarts to hoist the "White Banner of Liberty" and protect the "White Republic of Washington" against anyone, of any party, who would erect a monstrous mixed polity upon its ruins.[17]

These diatribes heightened the tension between Van Evrie, the ideologue who considered the Democratic Party a means to an end, and party devotees willing to stretch their principles to win votes. This conflict ebbed in 1868. But as the New Departure gained momentum, Van Evrie resumed his habitual role of holding party leaders' feet to the fire. In a typical outburst, he used sarcastic scare quotes and militant metaphors to warn partisan hacks against selling out for electoral advantage:

> If the "Democratic party" cannot come up to this level [opposing Black suffrage], or if the policy-mongering cowards that have so long paralyzed the body and enfeebled the soul of American Democracy attempt some half-way "policy" . . . they will be trampled under the mighty tread of the millions, and scattered to the winds of heaven in this glorious march of the people for the recovery of their freedom. And all who are not with us *are against us*—all who fail to stand by White Supremacy are Mongrels, of course—all who refuse to march under the banner of the White Republic of Washington are traitors or fools of necessity, and will be trampled under the mighty tread of the White Republican party.[18]

Van Evrie pledged allegiance to the "White Republic," not to any party organization. Charmed by the catchphrase, he crafted another slogan: "The White Republic Against the World." He unveiled this saying in an 1868 editorial but made far more sustained use of it beginning in 1870, when Van Evrie inscribed the slogan under a portrait of himself marketed to subscriber club members. Later, he used it as the title of a March 1871 political cartoon. "The White Republic Against the World" contained a winking double entendre—Van Evrie and friends against *everyone*, and specifically against *Marble's hated newspaper*—and scorned "Mongrels" of all partisan complexions.[19]

Consistent with his critique of the New Departure, Van Evrie demanded that Democrats remain a one-issue party until the White Republic was safe. Early in 1869, he admitted receiving piles of mail from readers interested in debt and currency questions. But he cautioned against wasting time on greenbacks or other "absurd" schemes and urged Democrats to focus on ousting the Republicans who piled up debt during their wicked war.[20] Two years later, he repeated this injunction, adding that other Democratic causes—"State rights, tariffs, revenue reform, the rights of labor or repudiation"—all depended on "Restoration of the White Republic." He titled the editorial "White Supremacy—The Only Issue."[21]

For Van Evrie, restoring the "White Republic" meant rescuing democracy from Black suffrage. He defined democracy as the alignment of political and social relations with polygenist tenets that prescribed equality among white

Portrait of John H. Van Evrie, ca. 1870, by W. G. Jackman. Van Evrie offered thirteen-by-sixteen-inch copies of this portrait, which featured his signature and the slogan "The White Republic Against the World," at discounted prices to readers who organized *Day Book* subscriber clubs. Used with permission of the American Antiquarian Society.

men and subordination of everyone else. In his ostensibly scientific analysis, the health of the body politic depended on its racial purity. Black suffrage, he argued, would be "absolutely fatal to liberty," for "to equalize and amalgamate with negroes . . . must necessarily debauch and ruin" American society "beyond the hand of resurrection to restore it."[22] Before 1861, he assailed abolition as a plot to destroy American democracy by fomenting sectional strife. After 1865, he attacked Black enfranchisement as a scheme to poison American democracy by integrating the polity. "The negro cannot be amalgamated in our nationality," Van Evrie wrote. "He is a foreign substance—a different species—a subordinate creature . . . and therefore, all that is done, all the blood shed and money wasted to include him in American citizenship, and all that may be done hereafter by the powers of hell and the father of lies, are in vain."[23] Echoing his efforts to reconcile polygenism with Christianity, Van Evrie blasted Black suffrage as a crime against God and nature.

Editorial incantations could not dispel the specter of Black suffrage. Van Evrie resisted it on multiple fronts, shifting between state and national venues and using familiar organizations and strategies to marshal armies of reaction. He remained on the defensive, however, and as biracial democracy neared victory, he grew increasingly violent.

New York State became a key battleground over the franchise in 1867. Referenda to equalize suffrage rights by removing the racist property requirement had failed in 1846 and 1860, but Union victory and slavery's abolition energized another attempt at the 1867 state constitutional convention. Black suffrage faced serious opposition in the North, as evidenced by recent defeats in Connecticut, Wisconsin, and Minnesota. But New York Republicans, emboldened by grassroots support and buoyed by winning a majority of convention seats in April's special elections, resolved to insert an equal suffrage provision in the new constitution. Some Democrats, including Manton Marble, preached acquiescence, but most were eager to tar Republicans as wild-eyed radicals.[24] Van Evrie predictably warned that the "Abolition-Monarchy party" meant to force "negro suffrage" on New York.[25]

Meanwhile, Rushmore Horton reactivated the dormant State Rights Society to campaign against the amendment. Originally founded as the Democratic Anti-Abolition State Rights Association to oppose emancipation and the Republican war effort, the group had not met since its Jefferson birthday dinner in April 1865. Two years later, and just ten days before the special election for state convention delegates, it reformed at the New York Hotel. Horton served as recording secretary and sat on the executive committee; the president was Democratic politico George W. Varian. Thereafter, the Society welcomed Jefferson Davis (en route to Canada after his release from incarceration at Fort Monroe) to Manhattan, lobbied the Broadway Railroad Company to resegregate its cars, and sponsored lectures by *Old Guard* editor Chauncey Burr.[26]

But its top priority was resisting Black suffrage. At the June 14 meeting, Horton suggested appointing a committee to write a memorial to the constitutional convention that was then gathered in Albany. Colleagues concurred and named Horton to the committee alongside John Mullaly, editor of the *Metropolitan Record*, an Irish Catholic and Copperhead organ, and Martin H. Duckworth, a wealthy Manhattan merchant.[27] Their memorial, dated July 8, parroted Van Evrie's polygenist case against equal suffrage, which rested on his maxim about political institutions harmonizing with God's handiwork: Government "cannot justly create distinctions where the Creator has made none, nor can it justly ignore those which the Creator has made." Just as God created two unequal sexes, only one of which was enfranchised, so, too, were there multiple unequal races. "The negro," they pronounced, "is by nature unequal to the white man, and therefore cannot have a right to the white man's equality." Violating natural law risked disaster. Cribbing from Van Evrie, Horton and his colleagues insisted that Black suffrage would foster "social equality" and "social amalgamation, the mixture of blood," and ultimately "social death" and "annihilation." Like the "Mongrel Republics south of us," the United States would succumb to "degradation, disease and filth." Speaking for the Society, the memorialists "beseech[ed] the Constitutional Convention . . . to confine the suffrage solely to persons of pure white blood." Published in the *Day Book* and as a pamphlet, and reprinted in newspapers nationwide, the memorial amplified Van Evrie's polygenist campaign against Reconstruction.[28]

The New York reactionaries initially prevailed. Their ethnological claptrap gained traction within the convention thanks to Democratic delegate Henry C. Murphy, founding editor of the *Brooklyn Daily Eagle*, who cited skull measurements as proof of Black inferiority.[29] And while the convention's Republican majority adopted an equal suffrage provision, Democratic gains in the fall state elections frightened them. As a result, when the convention reassembled in 1868, Republicans detached the equal suffrage amendment from the proposed constitution and submitted it separately in the November 1869 referendum. Equal suffrage ultimately failed by a vote of 282,403 to 249,802. Van Evrie's neighbors were especially adamant: seven out of ten Manhattan voters opposed the amendment.[30]

Yet the New York phase of the anti-Black suffrage crusade also marked the end of Horton's career and the State Rights Society's serious involvement in politics. Two months after publishing the memorial, the forty-year-old

Horton died suddenly of a lung ailment. Van Evrie lined the *Day Book*'s columns in black and eulogized his partner as an "earnest Democrat, of the State Rights school, and profoundly convinced that the doctrines of a White Republic and homogeneous citizenship, as upheld by THE DAY-BOOK, was absolutely vital to American liberty."[31] Grief did not keep Van Evrie from repeating his mantra or hawking his wares; only bitter experience would reveal his reliance on Horton's business acumen. Admirers praised Horton as "an able journalist" and "an industrious, energetic Democrat," and compilers of the *American Annual Cyclopaedia and Register of Important Events* noted his passing.[32] A State Rights Society committee escorted Horton's remains to his hometown of Fishkill.[33]

The Society barely outlived its most zealous member. After publishing the suffrage memorial, the group suspended operations before gathering in March 1868 to plan the annual Jefferson birthday dinner in April. Evidently convinced that festive consumption was smart politics, members hosted the gala as their final collective act. They followed Van Evrie's lead to the end, toasting "White Supremacy—the doctrines of the framers of our Constitution and the keystone of the arch of our civilization."[34] But although Horton and the State Rights Society won a posthumous victory over New York's equal suffrage amendment, the organization—Van Evrie's closest link to grassroots politics—perished with the activist. Thereafter, Van Evrie relied on subscriber clubs and other, more murderous networks to disseminate his ideas.

Van Evrie's triumph proved hollow because by 1869, the struggle over Black suffrage had shifted to the national stage. Congressional passage of the Fifteenth Amendment early that year betokened a transformation of American politics, and its looming ratification forced opponents of Black suffrage to mobilize nationwide. Infuriated, Van Evrie unleashed his most violent prose and tapped directly into paramilitary organizations to promulgate his message.

Van Evrie anxiously traced the Fifteenth Amendment's progress. Shortly after Congress approved it, he castigated creeping "Mongrelism": the incorporation of "four millions of a widely different and subordinate species of human kind" into "American citizenship." This had ruined Mexico and would doom the United States to "hideous anarchy" or "military despotism."[35] By September 1869, seventeen states had accepted the amendment, but Van Evrie insisted that the "iniquitous measure" could still be blocked. Resistance must not end with ratification, he added, for in that event "every patriot" must "set himself resolutely to the task of undoing the State-annihilating and civilization-destroying act."[36] Early in 1870, shortly before Congress certified ratification, Van Evrie escalated his attack by denouncing the amendment as a "fraud." State legislatures from New York to Missouri had approved it against the public will as expressed in referenda on Black suffrage. "The people," he thundered, "are cheated." The Fifteenth Amendment was an "act of despotism, which the people ought to resist in any and every way which should secure them their rights." Coupled with Van Evrie's apocalyptic warnings about the downfall of civilization, this call clearly countenanced bloodshed.[37]

He persisted even after the Fifteenth Amendment took effect. Never gracious in defeat, he urged coordinated nationwide opposition, with his readers, now christened the "Day Book Army," in the vanguard.[38] In a typical editorial entitled "Shall Democracy Perish on This Continent?" he warned that European aristocrats anticipated American democracy's "degrading, devilish and beastly social death" through "Mongrelism" and "amalgamation." He exhorted Democrats to prepare for a "fearful struggle" and, braiding polygenism with Christianity and constitutionalism, to "*organize as rapidly as possible, on the simple, vital, everlasting foundations fixed by the hand of God Almighty, and embodied in the written Constitution of their fathers.*" They must rout Republicans and "policy-mongering Democrats" and restore the Union of 1860.[39] Later that summer, Van Evrie predicted that the "gallant and glorious White Democracy will sweep like a whirlwind over the land and restore the Republic of Washington, even if they have to slaughter millions of negroes and coolies that obstruct their path to liberty and safety."[40] Chillingly, he envisioned what an indignant white majority would do if the Fifteenth Amendment endured: "The masses will then rise up and slaughter the traitorous villains that have torn down the republic of their fathers and sought to build up a Mongrel concern on its ruins." Van Evrie hoped to elect a president in 1872 who would simply "ignore" the Reconstruction amendments. Ominously, his alternative to Democratic victory—toppling the government and massacring the incumbents—paralleled the insurgency in the South.[41]

Indeed, Van Evrie both encouraged that insurgency and used it to push his products in the media marketplace. During Radical Reconstruction, it was not only his prose that grew more bloodthirsty but also the networks through which he advertised his publications. He still nurtured subscriber clubs. But by 1870, he had tapped into other organizations as well, melding his marketing apparatus with the Southern paramilitary campaign against Reconstruction.

Throughout Reconstruction, Van Evrie regularly pressed readers to extend his reach and bolster his finances by forming subscriber clubs. In a standard appeal, he requested the names of prospective readers who should receive sample copies. He also reminded subscribers "How to Help The Day-Book," urging them to "show the paper, or talk to your friends about it," "get up a club," or encourage the local postmaster "or some influential friend" to organize one.[42] Club members received discounted subscriptions, but Van Evrie added other incentives. In late 1870, he commenced a club campaign to boost circulation to a hundred thousand before the next presidential election. If victory were not inducement enough, he added a "Splendidly Executed Thirteen by Sixteen Inch Library-sized Steel Plate Likeness" of himself, bearing his signature and the "White Republic Against the World" slogan. Only subscribers could purchase the portrait, which was not sold in stores; single subscribers could have it for $2.50, while club members could buy the portraits in bulk for $2 apiece.[43] Later club campaigns operated in a similar fashion. In spring 1873, Van Evrie offered gold diamond-pointed pens at discounted rates to club organizers, while "Ladies" could choose a Singer sewing machine.[44] More than ninety club agents claimed their rewards, and Van Evrie ran another gold-pen campaign in 1874.[45]

But he also pursued new marketing channels that emerged in the fight against the Fifteenth Amendment. This was not the first time he linked his advertising apparatus to adjacent political networks. During the 1860 presidential election, he integrated Democratic Party machinery into a subscription drive by promoting the *Day Book* to Breckinridge and Lane clubs. Comparable efforts during Reconstruction, however, differed in two ways: The clubs lasted beyond one election cycle, and many were explicitly violent. Electoral politics blended into terrorism across the Reconstruction South, and Van Evrie harnessed this militant mobilization to sell his publications. The key organizations were White Men's Clubs.

The earliest self-styled White Men's Clubs formed in the South, independently of Van Evrie's influence, in late 1867 and 1868. Their founders sought to smother biracial democracy in its cradle by defeating new state constitutions that mandated equal suffrage. As indicated by their names, the clubs were also designed to draw the color line in Southern politics. Complexion must dictate partisanship; white men must not vote Republican. Historian Hannah Rosen notes that planters and professionals in Arkansas organized White Men's Clubs before the 1868 state elections to unite white voters—some of whom, especially former Unionists in the Ozark region, seemed likely to back the Republicans. Club members pledged to prevent "negro rule" by supporting the "White Man's Party." Not coincidentally, this meant fidelity to the old elite. Much like the "white supremacy" slogan, organizers used White Men's Clubs to stifle conflicts over class, geography, and wartime loyalty at a moment when Black suffrage made divisions among whites particularly threatening to elite power.[46] Other White Men's Clubs appeared in 1868 in North Carolina, Louisiana, South Carolina, and Maryland. All sought to array white voters against Republicans, enfranchised Black men, and the new state constitutions. Unlike the Ku Klux Klan, the clubs operated openly, holding parades, barbecues, and courthouse meetings. But they also practiced intimidation by coordinating efforts to deny jobs and credit to Black voters.[47] Thus, they paralleled Van Evrie's campaign against the New Departure.

Van Evrie resuscitated the White Men's Club movement shortly after ratification of the Fifteenth Amendment. In a spate of articles in the spring of 1870, he exhorted readers to organize clubs as the basis of national resistance to Republicans' revolution. On May 7, he published a letter from "Japheth" (whose pseudonym evoked the Curse of Ham, racists' favorite story from the Book of Genesis) urging opposition to "Mongrelism." Bemoaning Democrats' cowardice and the white majority's disarray, Japheth pressed foes of Black suffrage to combine for the "overthrow of Mongrelism and the restoration of the Constitution" and to act quickly, as the "deadly coils of the huge black serpent are drawn closer and closer." But how? By establishing "WHITE MEN'S Associations" across the land. Van Evrie's readers would lead the way: "Let the movement begin with the subscribers to THE DAY-BOOK. Let each one of these immediately set about forming a White Man's Association in his ward, town, or neighborhood." Members would cooperate with kindred clubs to "driv[e] the Mongrel party from power" and "restor[e] the constitutional White Man's Government we inherited from our fathers." They would sponsor speakers, circulate documents, and report to the *Day Book*, whose columns would trace their progress and inspire emulation. With Van Evrie's office as their hub, the Associations would form a "grand federal organization" that would crush "Mongrelism" forever.[48]

Van Evrie seconded Japheth's appeal in an editorial commanding "brave and faithful Democrats" to form "white associations every where, sending out tracts, pamphlets, &c." They would "expose the hideous lunacies of the hour" and thus help "overthrow the hideous power at Washington."[49] One week later, he stressed that deliverance depended on reader-led grassroots action. "There is but one method by which to obtain the political and social salvation of the country," he argued—namely, through "the organization of 'White Men's Clubs,' and the circulation of those publications only which labor for 'White Supremacy.'"[50] Effective activism meant local networking and information warfare. Van Evrie long saw himself as the author-hero who could convert mass sentiment. Now he nurtured White Men's Clubs as a grassroots movement that would spread his message into every nook and cranny of the country.

It was both highly logical and deeply self-interested for Van Evrie to identify print media circulation as the key to victory. His faith in the power of words informed his decision, two decades before, to devote his pen to what he—and, because of his influence, myriad others—called white supremacy.

Naturally, he believed Democrats could demolish Reconstruction by flooding the public sphere with texts. But his promotion of White Men's Clubs sounded like a marketing campaign because it was that, too. His May 14 summons made this clear: "Your first step in the work will be to obtain each one more reader for THE DAY-BOOK. . . . Send on your list of subscribers; two, ten, twenty, or a hundred. Commence the work now."[51] Undoubtedly aware of the clubs' earlier appearance in the South, Van Evrie revived them as the core of a national reaction against Black suffrage and Republican political power—and a new *Day Book* marketing network. White Men's Clubs had an urgent political purpose, but from the start of Van Evrie's initiative, they also resembled subscriber clubs.

Like-minded readers, editors, and politicians echoed Van Evrie's appeals. Subscribers encouraged one another in letters to the *Day Book*. A Texan urged fellow readers to support "the White Man's Party" against "all so-called amendments, acts and laws" that conflicted with "our white system of government." Everyone could help. Readers were urged to "circulate Democratic books, newspapers and tracts all over the land—place THE DAY-BOOK in every voter's hands," because "in 1872 DEMOCRACY MUST TRIUMPH and the *White Republic of Washington* be restored."[52] Democratic editors from Pennsylvania and Ohio to Wisconsin and Alabama reprinted Van Evrie's exhortations to start White Men's Clubs and disseminate documents.[53] Sensing partisan advantage, Democratic insiders echoed his call. In June 1870, the Democrats of Fayette County, Pennsylvania, resolved that "white men's clubs should be organized in every locality where white men are esteemed to be better than negroes, for the purpose of restoring the power of this government to the keeping of white men."[54]

As the club movement gained momentum, Van Evrie ensured that it advanced both his promotional and political aims. In February 1871, he launched an advertising campaign that fully integrated grassroots mobilization with product marketing by directly targeting club members. In advertisements entitled "The White Man's Club Library," he offered sets of a dozen Van Evrie, Horton & Co. books and pamphlets for just five dollars. These texts comprised "the political library needed by white men" and illuminated "the great American question of this century—WHITE SUPREMACY AND NEGRO SUBORDINATION." None of the texts were new; instead, the library drew from Van Evrie's existing inventory. Titles included *White Supremacy and Negro Subordination*, which he had rereleased in 1870, along with the old Anti-Abolition Tracts, Horton's *Youth's History*, James Hunt's *The Negro's Place in Nature*, and Chief Justice Roger Taney's *Dred Scott* opinion.[55] Van Evrie thus spurred club members on to the grotesque task remaining before them: overthrowing Reconstruction. As the chief supplier of cheap print media, he would furnish their ammunition for the propaganda war against the Republicans. And by hawking his wares through the expanding network of White Men's Clubs, he monetized the grassroots campaign for what he had branded "white supremacy."

Van Evrie's message resonated with whites who brooked no compromise with Reconstruction. Indeed, *Day Book* issues joined cockades and buttons as instantly legible badges of political loyalty.[56] Take the confrontation between New Departure and hardline Democrats at an 1870 meeting in Arkansas. When a party boss introduced resolutions that endorsed Black suffrage, one "old man, with the New York *Day Book* in his pocket, said he had come up to 'jine' a White Man's Party," and refused to yield when rebuked for quoting Van Evrie's inflammatory prose.[57] A year later, a *Tribune* correspondent visited a South Carolina farmhouse that afforded few luxuries beyond "an old copy of the *New-York Day Book*" lying on the table. The farmer prayed for Democratic victory and deliverance from Black suffrage; his wife said she would rather die than see another Republican president. Their visitor mused that his host "obviously got his political ideas from *The Day-Book*, and did not believe in the New-Departure!"[58] *Day Book* readers were numerous as well as visible in the early 1870s, which marked the peak of Van Evrie's influence. More parents named newborns for him in 1872 than any other single year. Subscriptions rose from 35,000 in 1869 to 45,000 in early 1872, when *Day Book* advertisements appeared in 1,500 newspapers.[59] Van Evrie loathed Republicans but relied on the backlash against them to grow his brand and court customers. By inciting and piggybacking on the campaign against Black suffrage, Van Evrie expanded his market share. Just as he had profited from sectional conflict in the 1850s, he now capitalized on the clash over Reconstruction.

The relationship between publisher and movement was reciprocal. Van Evrie's subscriber list swelled as he energized the club campaign, and his "Day Book Army" furnished foot soldiers for the assault on Reconstruction. White Men's Clubs certainly mobilized Democratic voters. But they also spawned terrorist squads that helped drive the Republicans from power.

The partisan paramilitary organizations that "redeemed" Southern states by toppling their Reconstruction governments bore many names, some of which signaled their racist commitments: White Line, White League, Knights of the White Camelia. Contemporaries and historians have traced many of them to the White Men's Clubs of the early 1870s.[60] Take Mississippi, where numerous White Men's Clubs formed shortly after Van Evrie's 1870 appeal. Founders announced their intentions in local Democratic newspapers, which coordinated their activities and spread their message. Black men must never vote, hold office, or serve on juries, proclaimed one club promoter. "White men shall govern."[61] By 1874, the clubs had bred White Man's Party organizations and the infamous White Lines or White Leagues. During 1874's midterm elections and state contests the following year, White Leaguers assassinated Republican officeholders, attacked Republican political rallies, and intimidated Republican voters. Protracted violence around Vicksburg killed hundreds of Black Mississippians between December 1874 and January 1875 alone. Self-styled White Men's Clubs continued their terrorist campaign even after Mississippi's "redemption" in 1875, particularly in Black-majority counties like Wilkinson, where a fresh wave of White Men's Clubs organized to purge Republicans from local offices. Club members abducted Alfred Black, a farmer and labor organizer, and hanged him by the neck until he pledged never to vote Republican. Others threatened to murder the county supervisor, Alexander Branch, if he did not resign.[62]

White Men's Clubs and Van Evrie's malign influence fomented violence in Louisiana as well. The Knights of the White Camelia, which terrorized Republicans in 1868, grew from a White Man's Club formed in 1867.[63] Seven years later, the White League movement commenced with the establishment in March 1874 of the Alexandria *Caucasian*—one of the newspapers that copied the *Day Book*'s old moniker. Like Van Evrie, the *Caucasian*'s editors urged white unity against enfranchised Black men. White Louisianans must organize a "white man's party" and make the next election a "fair, square fight, Caucasian versus African." The White League movement caught fire in the spring and summer of 1874. Some White Leaguers called their associations "white men's clubs," including the eight formed in Claiborne Parish by dry goods merchant Robert P. Webb. In Coushatta that August, White Leaguers murdered six white and some twenty Black Republicans, including Levin Allen, who was burned alive. The following month, thousands of Leaguers attempted a coup d'état in New Orleans that left more than thirty people dead.[64] This was what "resist[ing] in any and every way" looked like.[65]

Not every White Man's Club formed in response to Van Evrie's exhortations, but the symbiosis between newspaper promotion, partisan mobilization, and paramilitary atrocities invigorated the campaign against Reconstruction. Van Evrie goaded readers to armed resistance while marketing his wares through organizations that coordinated efforts to impose Democratic rule and white supremacy at all costs. He instructed subscribers in methods of activism that would expel Republicans from power, restore the White Republic, and not coincidentally, recruit additional subscribers; he meant to profit from insurgency. Counterrevolution was the work of many hands. But Van Evrie provided an idiom ("Mongrels," "white supremacy"), an apocalyptic rationale for violence, and an actionable program for readers to follow. In the early 1870s, they pursued "Redemption" through a mass movement that blended subscriber networking with voter mobilization and terrorism. And while his disgust for the New Departure heightened tensions with top Democrats, Van Evrie's cooperation with the White Men's Club movement harmonized his business interests with his ideological commitments in ways that increased popular pressure on wavering party leaders.

His efforts anticipated the presidential election of 1872. Like the Texan who urged club promotion and the South Carolina couple who hated Black suffrage, Van Evrie awaited the "great political crisis of 1872" with excitement and anxiety.[66] As a physician who inhabited a classics-steeped culture, he understood *crisis* as a turning point, a moment of decisive change for weal or woe, and he expected to shape the outcome. His subscription drives were calculated to maximize revenue and readership before the campaign season. His assaults on the New Departure sought to push Democrats into the uncompromising stance he deemed essential for victory. His appeals to racist solidarity attempted to peel white voters away from the Republicans.

Indeed, Van Evrie could hardly wait for the election that he hoped would terminate Radical Reconstruction. But he did not anticipate how it would inflame the struggle between party loyalty and ideological purity that long plagued his relationship with Democratic insiders. He did not expect that, when forced to choose between adamant activism and cold calculation, he would fail his own test. He did not foresee that the crisis of 1872 would mark the beginning of the end of his career.

Chapter 16

Decline

Like a hunter tracking a wounded but dangerous beast, William Penn Nixon kept a wary eye on the *New York Day Book*. In early 1879, the seasoned Republican journalist reminded readers that John Van Evrie was still active. "It may surprise many persons to hear that the New York Day Book, an old slave-drivers' organ . . . still lives, and makes its sickly appearance occasionally in New York." He cited "Grant," a poem published in the *Day Book*, which denounced the ex-president as an aspiring Caesar and culminated in a call to "Kill!" Nixon mocked the overwrought verses but kept monitoring Van Evrie's output.[1]

That summer, George Warner of Kansas complained to a local newspaper about his experience as a *Day Book* subscriber. He and four friends paid their dues, but after receiving a few back numbers and two new issues, they had heard nothing from the publishers since May. Either the post office had blundered, or the paper was a "swindle."[2]

Four years later, the Louisville *Courier-Journal* printed a reader's inquiry: "What has become of the New York Day Book?" The editor wearily replied: "We answer this regularly every four months. It is dead."[3]

These vignettes depict the *Day Book*'s end as a slow demise rather than a stunning denouement. After years of grabbing attention with catchy slogans and noisy feuds, Van Evrie's career seemed destined for an explosive finale. Instead, he and his newspaper faded away. Indeed, Van Evrie departed so quietly that some Americans forgot that he was still in business in 1879, while others wondered about his fate four years after he printed his final issue. What explains this protracted decline? Why did the *Day Book* go out with a whimper?

Van Evrie's downfall began in 1872 when he endorsed a bitter rival for president. His business lingered for seven more years, but the misstep irreparably damaged his personal brand and his company's finances. Van Evrie maximized his influence in the late 1860s and early 1870s by aligning his financial, partisan, and ideological objectives, as enshrined in his *white supremacy* slogan and monetized in his White Men's Club initiative. Subsequent blunders shattered this alignment. White Americans were no less bigoted in 1879 than in 1870, but Van Evrie no longer commanded enough of their attention or money to remain solvent. His career as a professional racist foundered when he seemed to place expediency ahead of principle. A gadfly who flaunted his political purity while scourging Democratic "traitors" could not afford to flinch.

Van Evrie projected confidence as 1872 dawned, but his company was already faltering. Although still called Van Evrie, Horton & Co., the firm had lost business manager Rushmore Horton in 1867. Contemporaries knew nothing of Van Evrie's youthful failures in Canada or his Ohio bankruptcy, but they recognized that Horton's death was a disaster. One journalist later recalled that "Dr. Van Evrie, with all his ability as a writer, was not qualified as a manager of the establishment."[4] Ill omens appeared by the early 1870s. One involved the *Old Guard*. In December 1869, Van Evrie bought out Chauncey Burr and put Thomas Dunn English in charge of the periodical. A University of Pennsylvania School of Medicine graduate and poet, playwright, and novelist, English was also a prominent New Jersey Democrat and former state legislator. He tried to enhance the *Old Guard*'s literary reputation, but the periodical survived only one more year before printing its final issue in January 1871.[5] This was part of a broader retrenching at Van Evrie, Horton & Co. Total employees fell from forty in 1860 to twenty-four in 1870, invested capital decreased by 50 percent to $10,000, and the value of output dropped 14 percent to $78,000.[6] Early in 1871, the firm departed Printing House Square for shabbier quarters on Beekman Street.[7] Van Evrie's own productivity was slackening. He authored no books or pamphlets after 1868 and, following the rerelease of *White Supremacy and Negro Subordination* in 1870, produced nothing new beyond the *Day Book* editorial page. After printing a torrent of texts during the Civil War and early Reconstruction years, his firm likewise published no new works after 1870. The company continued selling older titles, including those in the "White Men's Club Library," but it generated no fresh content.

Van Evrie's growing dependence on the *Day Book* for revenue created a dilemma. As a propagandist and would-be party kingmaker, he wanted to maximize circulation by minimizing subscription fees. But as a business owner, he could cut prices only so far. Lacking Horton's guidance, he rolled the dice in July 1871 by announcing a new *Day Book* club price of just $1 per year ($1.50 for single subscribers).[8] Advertising his product as the "Dollar Day Book" and "The Cheapest Paper in the World," Van Evrie sustained the promotion through 1872 as a bid to boost his influence during the presidential canvass. But he was selling the *Day Book* below the cost of production. Always a sharper polemicist than strategist, Van Evrie risked his firm's solvency in his crusade against Reconstruction. As he admitted in appeals to club organizers, he hoped that wider circulation would attract enough new advertisers to offset his losses on subscriber fees. His finances remained shaky, even as subscriptions peaked at 45,000 in 1872.[9]

But Van Evrie, like many contemporaries, was fixated on the presidential election and an apparently imminent partisan reshuffling. US political parties were always fluid coalitions rather than static monoliths, and as slavery, secession, and civil war receded into history, both the Republican and Democratic organizations seemed vulnerable.[10] "Political parties are not immortal," proclaimed Indiana's George Julian, whose own path through the Whig, Free Soil, and Republican parties proved his point. "They grow up out of certain political exigencies, and when the exigency passes away, the party itself is compelled to get out of sight."[11] The Republican Party was born in opposition to slavery's expansion and grew mighty enough to abolish slavery and crush rebellion. But as those issues died, some observers believed the party would follow. Others made similar predictions about the Democratic Party; by 1872, some pundits opined that its "final hour seems to have come."[12] Future party alignments were still hazy, but novel alliances based on fresh issues seemed in the offing.

Unlike those who welcomed new topics, Van Evrie clung to his old agenda. But he accepted partisan reordering because he was more loyal to what he thought the Democratic Party should be than to any existing institution. Independence was vital to his brand. He had advertised the *Day Book* as "an independent Democratic journal" or an "independent Democratic paper" since 1858.[13] He denied that it was a mere party "organ" and mouthpiece for organizational interests, boasting that he would "feel degraded" in that role.[14] Thereafter, he praised or condemned the Democratic Party as he saw fit. He campaigned ferociously when it met his standards but scorned Democrats who traded their principles for votes. He believed that American politics inevitably pitted aristocratic mongrelizers against lily-white Democrats, but the latter were not always synonymous with the Democratic Party. Indeed, while assailing the New Departure in 1870, Van Evrie envisioned a "White Republican" party triumphing over "Black Republicans" and Democratic apostates alike.[15] While not explicitly calling for a new organization, Van Evrie prioritized creed over nomenclature. Devoted to Reconstruction's demise and Black people's subordination, he lambasted anyone who sacrificed these goals for partisan advantage. As a self-appointed political oracle, he wanted Democrats to follow him to victory, but his fealty to them depended on their commitment to his cause.

Van Evrie continued criticizing Democratic leaders in early 1872. In a February editorial entitled "Are the Democratic Statesmen Demented?" he wondered if top Democrats had "sold their political birthright, and their honesty, integrity and manhood, to the corrupt and dominant power" of President

Ulysses S. Grant. This would explain their acquiescence to the postwar constitutional amendments and their reluctance to confront the "unmistakabl[y] evil" Republicans. The "seductive voices of the Delilahs of Mongrelism" had shorn the "political Samsons" who once boldly defended the right. Democrats must rally behind a steadfast leader, follow the *Day Book*'s hardline stance, and vanquish the Republicans for good.[16] This was essentially the same advice he had given for the past fifteen years. He hoped for a repeat of 1868, when Democrats coalesced around the white supremacy slogan. Instead, they would fragment, forcing Van Evrie to make agonizing decisions about his endorsements and confounding his habit of framing every election as a struggle between monarchical mongrelism and white men's democracy. Ironically, it was conflict among Democrats, not attacks from Republicans, that knocked Van Evrie onto the downward slope of his career.

In a double irony, it was Republican dissidents who sowed the Democratic discord. Since 1870, self-styled "liberal republicans" had criticized the Republican Party from within. Although they had battled the Confederacy and cautiously supported Reconstruction, liberal republicans feared that centralization and militarization were corrupting the government. They supported free trade, denounced railroad subsidies, urged amnesty for ex-Confederates, and sought to end the military occupation of the South. After triumphing in Missouri's 1870 state elections, they went national. A Liberal Republican Party coalesced in 1872, combining members of the original movement with new adherents, including erstwhile Radical Republicans like Charles Sumner and George Julian, who detested Grant's scandal-ridden administration. Their national convention would meet in Cincinnati in early May.[17]

Liberal Republicanism presented Democrats with both opportunity and peril. If Democrats stayed united and insurgents diverted votes from Grant, the Democratic candidate might prevail in a three-sided race. But because the Liberal Republicans counted former Democrats among their leaders and offered a plausible alternative to Grant's reelection, they might poach votes from the Democratic column. Indeed, they were banking on considerable Democratic support.[18] Not surprisingly, Van Evrie derided Democrats' flirtation with Liberal Republicanism for the same reason he disdained the New Departure: Both meant scrounging for votes by forsaking principle. "Certain policy-mongering Democrats have great hopes from the 'liberal republicans,'" he complained in February 1872, and would support their nominee "to beat Grant and get into power." Although he dismissed their pragmatism as "nonsense," he also knew that Democrats were desperate for a win.[19] Shortly before the Cincinnati convention, he called the meeting an "outrage upon white men" organized by "Black Republican" bigwigs eager to ditch Grant and "recover possession of the Mongrel machine" for themselves. If Democrats cooperated, the Liberal Republicans would exploit and then desert them, leaving the Democratic Party "demoralized, disintegrated, indeed, disheartened."[20] To save their party and country, Democrats must find a candidate who would "frankly and manfully" support the Union of 1860, one based on state sovereignty, "white citizenship," and the knowledge that "Negroes are a different and subordinate *species* of men, and cannot be amalgamated or incorporated into our nationality."[21] Van Evrie had not budged.

The Liberal Republicans clarified matters by nominating Horace Greeley for president. Born in New Hampshire, he became famous for editing the New York *Tribune* and promoting reforms, including Fourierism, homestead legislation, and antislavery.[22] The *Tribune* and *Day Book* were neighbors for over a decade, but their proximity was solely geographic. A Whig turned Republican, Greeley had spent his career condemning Democrats, particularly those of Van Evrie's stripe. He eviscerated the "sweeping and audacious assertions" in Horton's 1867 anti-Black suffrage memorial, marked Horton's death by recalling his "unflinching and unscrupulous support to the course of treason during the Rebellion," and called the *Day Book* "the most malignant and implacable Copperhead journal issued on earth."[23] Van Evrie responded to his nomination with the harshest words he knew. Greeley had a "monarchical idea of government" and had done more than anyone to propagate the "false and fatal theories" that slavery was wrong and that Black people were equal to whites.[24] According to Van Evrie, the only silver lining was that Democrats would never support such an obnoxious candidate.[25]

In fact, Greeley's nomination fractured the party. As their national convention in Baltimore on July 9 approached, Democrats clashed over choosing their own candidate or backing Greeley. Van Evrie's position was unequivocal. He condemned the Liberal Republican nominee as the "embodiment of the monstrous 'idea' of amalgamation of races, the most sinful, damnable and indeed impracticable idea that has ever debauched reason or defaced humanity since the world began."[26] He dredged up partisan *Tribune* editorials and asked how Democrats could vote for the author.[27] He printed letters urging Baltimore delegates to "spit" upon the Cincinnati nominee.[28] He mocked the "weakness and stupidity" of Democrats who favored Greeley over Grant as the lesser evil, likening them to soldiers who defected to an invading army.[29] He threatened to publish a list of pro-Greeley Democratic papers, evoking Nathaniel Stimson's strategy of shaming alleged turncoats.[30] Shortly before the Baltimore convention, he printed a note, penned at a meeting held at the *Day Book* office, asking anti-Greeley Democrats to prepare a decisive response to Greeley's nomination.[31] Van

Evrie believed his own supremely damning headline: "White Men Will Not Support Greeley."[32]

But other Democrats insisted it was prudent to support the Liberal Republicans. Still tainted by treason, many saw in Greeley's candidacy an opportunity to realize the renaissance promised by the New Departure. Party leaders like August Belmont collaborated with top Liberal Republicans and pressured Democratic editors to promote Greeley. Patronage-seekers also considered Greeley the lesser evil. Even some Southern Democrats, raring to end Reconstruction, reckoned that backing Greeley was worth it. The debate tore the Democratic Party along multiple axes: Northern hardliners against Southern pragmatists, rank-and-file purists against wily elites, Van Evrie's intransigents against New Departure moderates.[33]

Greeley enjoyed enough support among Democratic insiders, including Belmont, who opened the Baltimore convention with an eloquent endorsement, that the party nominated him on the first ballot.[34] Many Democrats fell in line, but dissidents organized a rival convention to meet in Louisville on September 3 and select a "Straight-Out" Democratic ticket. Their likeliest nominee was Charles O'Conor, the New York lawyer who deemed slavery "not unjust" and later headed Jefferson Davis's legal defense team. O'Conor loathed Greeley as the "tender-hearted Moloch whose life-long mission of hate has filled the land with fratricidal slaughter of the white race."[35] Straight-Out zeal burned hottest among Southern partisans like Alexander Stephens and old Copperheads like Chauncey Burr and Marcus M. "Brick" Pomeroy, editor of *Pomeroy's Democrat*, who had moved from Wisconsin to New York in 1869.[36]

Van Evrie joined the Straight-Out insurgency. Appalled by the Baltimore convention's "treason," he skewered its "preposterous and abominable proceedings," deemed its nomination a "revolting betrayal of the people," and vowed to uphold the "immutable and everlasting" dogma of white supremacy.[37] This was his natural response. He had worked closely with O'Conor in the 1859 Southern sympathy campaign, printing the lawyer's proslavery address, and in the final effort to forestall secession. Nor would this have been the first time Van Evrie endorsed him for high office. In April 1860, he had floated a Democratic ticket featuring O'Conor as Jefferson Davis's running mate.[38]

Greeley, meanwhile, was an implacable enemy. Since taking over the *Day Book*, Van Evrie had assailed the *Tribune* and its editor without mercy. Before the Civil War, he lambasted Greeley for jeopardizing New York's prosperity with protectionist and antislavery schemes.[39] He also blamed Greeley for the *Day Book*'s wartime suppression.[40] Perhaps for this reason, his postwar invective was even sharper. Greeley was a "veteran political humbug" who praised tariffs while printing the *Tribune* on imported paper.[41] He loved to "plunder laboring men for the benefit of capitalists" while posing as labor's champion.[42] He would "mongrelize this country" with the Fifteenth Amendment.[43] He was, in short, "An Evil Man."[44]

Personalities aside, Van Evrie was always ready to buck the party majority and support splinter movements he deemed more ideologically pure. Most recently, he opposed the New Departure. In 1864, he had refused to endorse George B. McClellan. And he had championed the Breckinridge and Lane movement in 1860, joining the proslavery bolters who rejected Stephen Douglas. Back then, he bragged that the *Day Book* "does not assume to be a mere party organ, trimming its sails and measuring its words, to suit party politicians or to conform to party exigencies, but on the contrary desires to discuss all questions, and most particularly the great specialty to which it is devoted, in the light of truth and on a basis of entire independence."[45] Devotion to his racist "truth" was the polestar of Van Evrie's politics and the basis of his brand. In 1872, his path clearly pointed toward Louisville.

Everything changed on August 10. *Day Book* readers who flipped to page four of that day's issue saw a new announcement on the masthead: "For President, HORACE GREELEY of New York. For Vice-President, B. GRATZ BROWN, of Missouri."

Van Evrie packed his columns with verbiage justifying his endorsement. Below the masthead was an editorial that he never expected to write: "Dr. Greeley on the White Supremacy Platform!" Torturing logic, he insisted that because Black voters remained "enslaved" to Grant's Republicans, Greeley had been forced onto the "White Man's Platform." His reasoning was cagey but confident: "The logic of events may yet place Dr. Greeley at the head of the White Supremacy party."[46] Another editorial lamented the Louisville convention's poor prospects and argued that Grant would win a three-way race. Parroting the lesser-evil logic that he previously mocked, Van Evrie concluded that Greeley "is immeasurably the superior of U. S. Grant, morally and politically, and he has promised to relieve the distracted South."[47] Here was the cornerstone of his case: Reconstruction was so terrible that it was worth electing Greeley to end it. Ironically, his portrayal of Reconstruction as a carnival of horrors now rationalized his endorsement of an antislavery activist for president. To bolster his argument, he ventriloquized white Southerners. In "'Anything to Beat Grant,'" Van Evrie attributed the title quotation to the white Southern masses, claiming that he was "overwhelmed by this cry from the South." Rejecting Greeley meant abandoning Southern whites to Republican rule.[48] Van Evrie reiterated this point in subscriber letters. Previous issues featured notes from Southerners who deprecated Greeley as an unelectable degenerate. Now the Southern-authored letters exalted him as a savior.[49]

Couched in Van Evrie's insufferable style, these explanations stank of special pleading. What really prompted his leap onto Greeley's bandwagon? Had cold calculation trumped ideological rigor? Perhaps. But electability never preoccupied him before, and for good reason: Van Evrie thrived on conflict, not victory. Hence his contempt for party operatives he derided as sellouts. They needed to win races and collect patronage, but Van Evrie's incentives were different. As an independent editor who had received no federal largesse since the 1850s, he could afford to prefer losing with the right candidate over winning with the wrong one. Indeed, defeat meant he could continue to rail against Reconstruction and ride the backlash. Democratic losses in 1860, 1864, and 1868 had not injured him, and his readership grew as Republicans' victories stacked up. Unlike the party hacks he hated, Van Evrie could prosper under a Republican presidency. Electoral logic made his course more, not less, perplexing.

The best explanation is that Van Evrie needed money. Although it must be used with care because it was written by a rival who profited from his disgrace, the fullest account of Van Evrie's decision was written by Brick Pomeroy in 1877. A fellow Copperhead who moved in similar circles, Pomeroy was well positioned to peer behind the scenes at the *Day Book*. In Pomeroy's telling, Van Evrie opposed Greeley for as long as possible, but the Dollar Day Book campaign had drained his funds. By August 1872, he either had to cease publication or "accept money that is always to be had by editors if they will endorse the actions of those who use money oftentimes to direct public opinion." It was "a question of life in dishonor or an honorable death." Van Evrie preferred dishonorable life and received $4,000 from Greeley's backers who were seeking to woo Democratic holdouts.[50] Given Van Evrie's financial struggles and the abruptness of his endorsement, this account rings true.

Pomeroy's narrative illuminates the collapse of Van Evrie's business model. For years Van Evrie had aligned his financial, partisan, and ideological interests through "white supremacy" and White Men's Club campaigns. In 1872, material exigency ripped them apart. Forced to choose between penurious purity and spineless salvation, Van Evrie chose the latter, sacrificing the independence that defined his brand. According to Pomeroy, the politicos who purchased Van Evrie's conversion anticipated this outcome: Their ultimate goal was not to win the *Day Book*'s support but "to kill it in the future." They reckoned that if the paper "could be made to endorse that which its editor had denounced, its subscribers, or the majority of them, would be so disgusted with it that they would abandon it, when it must go to the wall."[51] Van Evrie fell into their trap.

Backlash was swift and furious, egged on by Van Evrie's numerous rivals—including Pomeroy. The day after Van Evrie endorsed Greeley, Pomeroy blasted him for reducing politics to a "question of dollars and cents."[52] Republican editors mocked the *Day Book*'s erratic course and cited its endorsement as another reason why Republicans should reject Greeley.[53] Straight-Out leaders blamed the "defection" on frustrated ambition and financial necessity.[54] But it was the Democratic rank and file, including formerly staunch supporters, who reacted most fiercely. In Idaho, a new subscriber club gathered to peruse their first issue; alas, it was the one dated August 10. "How is this?" one member shouted at the organizer. "I am cheated all around—your *Day-Book* is the dirtiest Greeley sheet of all."[55] A Connecticut physician and veteran club member accused the paper of selling "its soul and principles to our greatest enemy" and refused to renew.[56] Pomeroy, who attended the Louisville convention, printed letters from livid readers who renounced the paper and, conveniently, praised *Pomeroy's Democrat* for standing firm. One Iowan, who had established a twenty-six member *Day Book* club, had taken the paper for twelve years and peddled it during the war, at the "risk of having my teeth knocked down my throat." Now he applauded Pomeroy. By broadcasting the anti–*Day Book* outcry and pushing his own paper as an alternative, Pomeroy beat Van Evrie at his own game. When the *Day Book* editor stumbled, a more stalwart reactionary hurried to supplant him.[57]

Van Evrie scrambled to survive, first by hedging his endorsement. Initially, he kept Greeley on the masthead while hoping that the Louisville convention would pick O'Conor. Greeley was the best choice in a two-way race, he maintained, but O'Conor might win a three-sided contest.[58] Two weeks later, he reflected on the doings at Louisville, where delegates offered O'Conor a nomination he promptly declined. Van Evrie claimed vindication and reiterated his support for Greeley.[59] But the following week, he removed Greeley's name and asked readers to support O'Conor by forming clubs, promoting the *Day Book*, and buying campaign texts.[60] Finally, on September 28, he affixed O'Conor's name to the masthead, resumed denigrating Greeley as an advocate of racial equality and interracial sex, and contended that O'Conor could win if readers disseminated Van Evrie, Horton & Co.'s wares.[61] Lest they fret that O'Conor was not actually a candidate, he publicized the lawyer's pledge, evidently given in a conversation between them, that he would run.[62]

In less than eight weeks, Van Evrie had lurched from attacking Greeley as a race-mixing monarchist, to promoting him as the paladin of white supremacy, to condemning him again. Critics mocked his equivocation; a Kentucky editor dryly taunted the *Day Book*'s "very singular instance of vacillation . . . on the Presidential question."[63] Nor did Van Evrie's damage control appease many Democrats. Rather, by straddling the intraparty debate, he drew fire from both sides. Pomeroy scourged him for backing Greeley, and Straight-Out readers terminated their subscriptions. But switching to O'Conor prompted indignant cancellations and outcry from pragmatists who argued that a third entrant would ensure Grant's reelection.[64] Some speculated that Grant partisans had bribed Van Evrie to endorse O'Conor, a charge the beleaguered editor strenuously denied.[65] He looked weak, desperate, and corrupt.

Grant's victory ensured that he remained a prime target for Van Evrie's editorial attacks. But the 1872 contest had marred the editor's brand, alienated readers, and hurt his bottom line. In his election postmortems, he grumbled that if Democrats had followed his advice and selected a sound candidate at Baltimore, they would have won.[66] He berated Southern Democrats for swallowing the Liberal Republicans' bait and promised that the *Day Book*, "the organ of White Supremacy and Straight-Out Democracy," would "never lead them astray."[67] He attempted to monetize Democrats' anxiety by urging them to join his 1873 promotion campaign.[68] This was how he always handled Democratic defeats. But Van Evrie was in trouble. When the compiler of a popular newspaper directory requested his 1873 circulation figures, he refused to reply.[69] Previously, Van Evrie always provided this data, and his numbers had held steady at 35,000 for years before spiking to 45,000 in 1872. Worried that critics would jeer 1873's dismal figure, Van Evrie clammed up. Postelection bravado notwithstanding, this silence spoke loudest.

Van Evrie flailed for balance after the 1872 disaster. With a shrinking subscriber list, dwindling cash flow, and a tarnished image, he searched for new friends. He remained committed to polygenist politics, but his career was sinking.

Desperation prompted his shocking overture to Senator Charles Sumner of Massachusetts. A leading Radical Republican, Sumner was an unlikely ally; indeed, Van Evrie had praised his infamous assailant, Preston Brooks, back in 1856. But Sumner had rebuked Grant and campaigned for Greeley, and Van Evrie was intrigued.[70] On Christmas Eve 1872, he wrote Sumner a bizarre letter that opened with backhanded compliments and ended with an invitation to champion white supremacy. Van Evrie conceded that Sumner's positions were "*logically Honestly* and *faithfully*" held but lamented that the senator had "devoted your magnificent talents and statesmanship" to racial equality. In fact, he countered, "The Negro . . . is a different and subordinate *species of* Human kind and *therefore* designed by the Almighty Creator for a different and subordinate social condition." Once Sumner grasped this, he could "lead this whole mighty people out of the awful ruin they are plunging into and not only become their next President but the greatest and most sublime benefactor of Mankind the World ever saw." In a postscript, Van Evrie self-identified as a "Naturalist who has given many years to the Study of Races" and wagered that in an hour, he could convince Sumner that "Amalgamation" was "a Sin against God and a crime against civilization."[71] Sumner never responded. Van Evrie, still convinced of his own infallibility, wrongly presumed he could convert an abolitionist. But his quest for comrades among Radical Republicans betrayed growing isolation.

Even more frantic was Van Evrie's hunt for new readers. His first editorial of 1873 admitted his "deep solicitation for the preservation of the life of the old DAY-BOOK," which had been "deserted" by Greeley Democrats "who left us in battalions." Ignoring his own gymnastics, Van Evrie boasted that he espoused the same principles as ever and thanked steadfast subscribers who, he hoped, would bring "thousands of the Greeley Democrats" back to him. Victory in 1874 depended on it; his business did, too.[72]

Van Evrie spent the year trying to boost revenue by tinkering with prices. Shortly before Election Day in 1872, he had suspended the Dollar Day Book campaign and raised dues, offering clubs of twenty a rate of $1.30 per person.[73] But in May 1873, he renewed the dollar offer for clubs of eight or more members. In a long editorial, he characteristically linked *Day Book* promotion to the Democratic Party's electoral prospects and the fate of white supremacy.[74] In August, Van Evrie pledged to continue the dollar promotion until Reconstruction ended. He wanted to keep the *Day Book* affordable for working-class whites, he wrote, as they suffered most from racial equality.[75] But it was difficult. In a series of October pleas, he exhorted readers to find new subscribers—he wanted 100,000—to finance the *Day Book*'s crusade. He was selling it below cost and losing $100 to $400 every week. In a signed appeal, he begged "earnest and faithful friends" to organize clubs so that the *Day Book* would be "again able to enter on the glorious work" to "save our country and our Democratic institutions from ruin."[76] As in his White Men's Club campaign, Van Evrie added material inducements, offering a luxury pen and, later, cash prizes to the most prolific boosters.[77]

Club organizers in 1873 were slightly less affluent than their antebellum counterparts, but Van Evrie still relied on prominent and prosperous citizens to ferret out subscribers. Appeals to white working-class men notwithstanding, local notables spearheaded the promotion of the *Day Book*. In spring 1873, Van Evrie printed the names of 112 club founders who earned the gold pen premium, 89 of whom could be positively identified in the 1870 census.[78] Two-thirds lived in ex-Confederate states; if the Border South is included, all but 19 resided in former slave states. With an average age of forty-nine years, mean real property valued at $3,753, and mean personal property of $1,453, they were solid, if not extravagantly wealthy, local fixtures. Nearly three in five were farmers, with artisans and merchants trailing behind. Humbler readers did initiate clubs, as evidenced by a sprinkling of four farm laborers and one railroad hand. But propertied individuals with leadership experience predominated. John McCullough of Greene County, Pennsylvania, was a "prosperous farmer," an "active member of the Presbyterian church," and a staunch Democrat who had run the county schools.[79] Wisconsin's William R. Spencer was a habitual joiner who remained active in the Odd Fellows and Masons until his death.[80] As justices of the peace, postmasters, and state legislators, Reconstruction-era club founders wielded substantial political power, uniformly as Democrats.[81] At least one had forgiven Van Evrie's fleeting Greeley endorsement. Nebraska business owner William P. Larsh regularly served as a delegate to his Democratic county convention but protested against Greeley by refusing to attend in 1872.[82] Several women formed clubs, including Nancy Dean of Alabama, Maria McGraw of Illinois, and Mrs. E. A. H. of Stockton, California, who proudly furnished her three sons "a white man's paper."[83]

Club founders were undoubtedly pleased that Van Evrie's product remained unchanged in 1873. He still blasted Black suffrage as the "greatest sin against God, and outrage on nature, and crime against civilization ever committed by mortals," thundering that "Satan himself" could not concoct a better scheme to "blot out their civilization, their morality, decency, purity, and finally, their actual physical existence."[84] Ten years after the Emancipation Proclamation, he mourned the destruction of slavery, which he still insisted had been the sole basis of national prosperity.[85] He rationalized racist violence, blaming Grant for the deaths of Black Southerners murdered by white paramilitaries and arguing that peace would reign if not for Republican intermeddling.[86] He criticized Democratic Party leaders for failing to restore the antebellum Union.[87] He chided Southern commemorators for treating slavery as incidental to the Civil War, arguing that the glory of Confederate history was its fight for "a White Man's Government."[88] And he dusted off the "White Republic Against the World" mantra, affixing it to his conspiracy theory about antislavery's aristocratic origins.[89] Only a few post-1873 *Day Book* issues survive, but there is no sign that Van Evrie changed course during his final five years as editor.[90] In a June 1874 letter to Jefferson Davis, he still envisaged Reconstruction's downfall, with Northern whites lynching abolitionists on "*Lamp Posts*" and Southern state governments restoring "*the Constitutional Union of 1787 & 1860*," slavery and all.[91]

But efforts to revitalize the *Day Book* failed. Van Evrie's fortunes fell even as the campaign against Reconstruction gained momentum. Why? Certainly, he was dogged by the disaster of 1872. Neither the pro-Greeley Democrats nor those who opposed him welcomed Van Evrie's lectures on political doctrine or party loyalty. Van Evrie also may have suffered from his political program's success; the coincidence of the *Day Book*'s demise and the culmination of racist "Redemption" in the late 1870s suggests as much. But even before then, some readers were already tired of his product. Consider the letter to the editor penned by A. F. Smith of New York in May 1873. He canceled his subscription and rejected Van Evrie's breathless calls to promote the paper. "According to THE DAY BOOK, the salvation of the country depends upon a large circulation of the same," Smith wrote. "Notwithstanding your frantic appeals to that effect, I am of the opinion that the 'Ship of State' will continue to float though in the hands of pirates."[92] For years, Van Evrie capitalized on antipathy to Reconstruction by promising readers that hawking his paper would swing the next, inevitably momentous, election. But these appeals grew tedious in repetition. Not every election could be the pivot point of history. Not every reader believed that peddling a newspaper would reverse the wartime revolution. Smith, who called Republicans "pirates," was politically aligned with Van Evrie. But he would not be goaded into another subscriber campaign framed as a battle for the white republic. Even readers who had stuck with Van Evrie through the gyrations of 1872 found his wares stale.

Circulation statistics document the *Day Book*'s decline. After hiding his 1873 figures, Van Evrie admitted to having only 15,000 subscribers in 1874. He treaded water in 1875, then business improved in 1876 and 1877, when circulation topped 20,000, likely because of election excitement. But subscriptions plummeted to 5,000 in 1878 and fell to 3,000 in 1879.[93] Dwindling subscription revenues, compounded by decreasing advertiser interest, devastated Van Evrie's finances. An April 1873 Dun report noted his refusal to cooperate; he was not speaking to credit agencies, either. The agent gathered that the newspaper "at one time was very successful, but of late, has grown somewhat unpopular" and struggled to repay its debts. Until Van Evrie rebounded, "we can only recommend a limited credit" on a short-term basis.[94] Neither the electoral controversy in 1876 nor Reconstruction's symbolic downfall in 1877 restored Van Evrie's popularity. In September 1876, he could barely afford to buy paper and begged Horatio Seymour for $500 to carry him through the election.[95] The following January, a Dun agent valued the firm at $40,000 but noted Van Evrie's habitual tardiness in repaying loans.[96] The money ran out within the year. His firm collapsed and the sheriff auctioned off its assets in December.[97]

The *Day Book* was not quite gone. In February 1878, the New York Day Book Co. was incorporated with nominal capital of $30,000. Van Evrie was one of the trustees as well as the editor; the business manager was Connecticut printer William C. Hutchings. This attempt to revive the paper was widely publicized, along with promises to resume the Warwick Letters. But sharp-eyed investigators were skeptical. Hutchings's Hartford business "made a disastrous failure a few years ago," according to a March 1879 Dun report, and most of the capital had not actually been paid. The managers operated on a cash-only basis, and the agent suggested "it would be well to hold them to these terms as there is no money at present." This was sound advice. By year's end, the New York Day Book Co. had folded without paying its debts.[98] Uncertainty lingered, but a Louisville editor guessed correctly when he announced in December 1879 that "the New York Day Book is probably dead."[99]

John Van Evrie's personal decline dragged on another seventeen years. He stayed in the New York area but appeared only in city directories, which reveal the reversal of his career trajectory. He vanished after the *Day Book* folded but reemerged in 1883, living in a lower Broadway building called Stevens House and giving his occupation as "journalist." He stayed for three years before disappearing and then resurfacing in 1888 as an "author" living at Colonnade House in Hoboken, New Jersey. The following year, Van Evrie called himself a "physician," although there is no evidence that he practiced medicine.[100] He is absent from all subsequent New York directories.

Van Evrie might have been suffering neurological degeneration. The first inkling of poor health appeared in a May 1862 letter, in which he apologized for a delayed reply: "I have been quite ill and therefore incapable of attending to numerous other correspondents, as well as yourself."[101] He never mentioned the illness again, but the subsequent deterioration of his handwriting suggests that he might have experienced a stroke or early symptoms of a neurodegenerative condition like Parkinson's disease.[102] Five years later, an eyewitness likened him to an "animated Egyptian mummie" who hobbled around, hunched and peering upward, a possible sign of Parkinson's-related posture problems.[103] By the 1880s, physical and cognitive decline might have compelled his withdrawal from public life.

On April 1, 1896, Van Evrie entered Long Island College Hospital in Brooklyn. Still clinging to old falsehoods, he or an associate gave his birthplace as "U.S." and occupation as "Physician." He lingered for six weeks before succumbing to "Senility" and "Haematoma"—probably a subdural hematoma—at 7 p.m. on May 17.[104]

Hours later, the Supreme Court ruled against Homer Plessy and upheld the constitutionality of Louisiana's segregated train cars.

Epilogue

Catherine Van Evrie brought her father's body from Brooklyn to Rochester and buried him next to Sophia in the Rochester family plot at Mt. Hope Cemetery.[1] Neither John nor his in-laws would have relished the prospect of eternity together, but once again the propagandist raised his profile through powerful patrons. At some point, John and Sophia's headstone cracked and fell. Ironically, it was repaired amid a larger refurbishing program during the summer of 2020. Precisely when many proslavery memorials came down, the modest monument to the popularizer of *white supremacy* was restored.[2]

John Van Evrie's passing elicited little comment and zero public reflection. The *New York Times* ran a brief death notice, but few other papers reprinted it.[3] His most notorious legacy—the "white supremacy" slogan—endured, most visibly as a rallying cry for perpetrators of the 1898 Wilmington Massacre and more insidiously for participants in countless other acts of racist violence in the Jim Crow era and beyond.[4] But Van Evrie, who had already faded from view after the *Day Book*'s downfall in 1879, descended deeper into obscurity.

Van Evrie's intellectual influence persisted in scattered footnotes and references. His writings remained a resource for a handful of writers who, well into the 1930s, cited him as an authority on race and slavery.[5] Most notable was the author of the "Negro" entry in the ninth edition of the *Encyclopædia Britannica* who, undeterred by Van Evrie's seething Anglophobia, listed *Negroes and Negro Slavery* in the topical bibliography.[6] But he was conspicuously absent from the early twentieth century's leading scientific racist works: Houston Stewart Chamberlain, Madison Grant, and Lothrop Stoddard all produced ponderous tomes without ever mentioning Van Evrie's name.[7] This can be attributed to polygenism's supersession by Darwinism and to theorists' penchant for parsing multiple races of Europe, an exercise Van Evrie anticipated and loathed.[8] Yet if academicians considered Van Evrie passé, he retained a smattering of popular support. Racists occasionally invoked him to condemn interracial marriage, including the Indianan who anachronistically credited Van Evrie for "extensive research in genetics" and rehashed the declining fertility thesis in 1977.[9] Equally enthusiastic was the Amazon.com customer who gave *Negroes and Negro "Slavery"* a glowing review in 2012.[10] Van Evrie's poison continues to circulate.

Yet his name and words are now at least as likely to appear in antiracist writings as in the scribblings of his ostensible intellectual heirs. Consider the repurposing of his work in two briefs filed on behalf of the plaintiffs in *Brown v. Board of Education* (1954). In one, *Negroes and Negro "Slavery"* appears alongside texts by Samuel Cartwright, James D. B. De Bow, and Josiah Nott to illustrate the "passionate defense of slavery, premised on the Negro's unfitness for freedom and equality," that informed efforts to subvert the Reconstruction amendments and "organize the community upon the basis of a superior white and an inferior Negro caste."[11] In the second brief, Van Evrie, Cartwright, and Nott appear as members of an "increasingly effective group" of the "South's most respected scientists" who argued for Black people's permanent inferiority.[12] Van Evrie's regional misidentification detracted little from the historical argument arrayed against the specious claim that separate was ever supposed to be equal. More recently, antiracists have transformed "white supremacy" from a reactionary battle cry into a target of activism. Critics have objected to the term's protean meanings.[13] But the phrase has always functioned as a slogan, building coalitions out of disparate individuals who disagreed on shades of meaning. If it now helps demolish racism, so much the better; Van Evrie would not appreciate the irony.

Van Evrie's legacy is bifurcated because what he bequeathed to the future was conflict, not consensus. This was not his aim, of course. He dreamed of a nation whose all-white citizenry marched in lockstep, forever submerging differences of class and region beneath a supposedly universal racial interest. He dreamed of a white republic, indivisible, dedicated to racist domination and governed by Democrats devoted to *Day Book* doctrine. Yet less than threescore years and ten after his death, a white Southern Democrat called for equal suffrage, promising to "overcome the crippling legacy of bigotry and injustice."[14] John Van Evrie contributed mightily to that legacy, but his dearest dreams went unfulfilled—not because progress is inevitable, but because the struggle never slackened. His ideas endure; so do those of his critics. From newspaper editors who dropped the *Day Book* from their exchange networks to theologians who skewered polygenism, and from the crowds who mobbed his office to the soldiers who defeated his Confederate friends, Van Evrie encountered untiring resistance even as he built a fearsome following. Neither story is complete without the other.[15]

Even in death, Van Evrie cannot dodge his detractors. When Catherine brought his body to Mt. Hope Cemetery, she laid him to rest near another journalist who died the previous year: Frederick Douglass. There they remain, a few hundred yards apart. Douglass kept a wary eye on Van Evrie because he understood the seductive power of telling people what they already believe and love to hear again. Douglass mocked Van Evrie's pompous posturing but neither wrote him off as insignificant nor despaired that he was unbeatable. Rather, he invited his allies to join the battle and vanquish Van Evrie by telling the truth.[16]

Appendix 1

Pro–Van Evrie Petitioners

For each of the fourteen communities (excluding New York City) that produced petitions supporting Van Evrie's postal access in 1862, I compared a random sample of the petitioners ("signers") with a random sample of individuals from the same county ("sample"), using 1860 census data to determine birthplace, property ownership, and occupation. I then compared the signers to the sample within each community. These tables summarize the key findings. The first table, for instance, indicates that in seven communities, signers were more likely to be living in their birth state, while in three communities, members of the sample were more likely to reside in their birth state, and in four communities, they were equally likely. Because census-takers overlooked many impoverished people, reliance on census data can skew results upward in terms of affluence. But because *both* samples draw from the census, comparisons between them reveal important patterns.

Living in birth state in 1860	
Signers more likely	***7/14***
Sample more likely	3/14
Equally likely	4/14

Farmers	
Signers more likely	***7/14***
Sample more likely	3/14
Equally likely	4/14

Foreign born	
Signers more likely	1/14
Sample more likely	***9/14***
Equally likely	4/14

Unskilled laborers	
Signers more likely	0/14
Sample more likely	***10/14***
Equally likely	4/14

Mean value of real property	
Signers' mean value higher	***10/14***
Sample mean value higher	4/14
Equal mean value	0/14

Merchants/entrepreneurs	
Signers more likely	***7/14***
Sample more likely	2/14
Equally likely	5/14

Mean value of personal property	
Signers' mean value higher	***8/14***
Sample mean value higher	6/14
Equal mean value	0/14

Appendix 2

The Namers

Namings by year: number of children born

Year	*Children named for Van Evrie*
1859	1
1860	2
1861	3
1862	1
1863	0
1864	0
1865	2
1866	2
1867	2
1868	1
1869	0
1870	2
1871	1
1872	6
1873	1
1874	4
1875	2
1876	1
1877	3
1878	2
1879	0
1880	0
1881	2

Namings by state: number of children from each state

State	*Children named for Van Evrie*
Alabama	1
Florida	1
Indiana	3
Iowa	7
Kansas	1
Michigan	1
Mississippi	2
Missouri	1
New York	4
North Carolina	1
Ohio	3
Oregon	1
Pennsylvania	1
South Carolina	3
Tennessee	3
Texas	2
West Virginia	3

Appendix 3
"White Supremacy" Usage

This graph shows the relative frequency with which "white supremacy" appears in newspapers from three digital databases: Chronicling America, Newspapers.com, and Newspaper Archive. The term was seldom used before the 1865 *New York Day Book* advertising campaign. The small uptick in 1856 reflects reprintings of Van Evrie's May *Day Book* editorial and Jefferson Buford's August call for volunteers to fight in Kansas.

To control for the growth of the publishing industry—there were more total words printed each year—I took the number of uses of "white supremacy," divided it by the number of uses of a neutral word ("one") whose usage grew proportionately with the total output of text, and then multiplied the result by 100,000. The resulting ratio is reflected on the y-axis. Usage in Newspapers.com, for instance, peaked in 1874 at 247.4 uses of "white supremacy" per 100,000 uses of the word "one." By controlling for the increase in total newspaper output, the graph shows how the term "white supremacy" became relatively more prevalent over time.

The table shows Van Evrie and the *Day Book*'s decisive influence in popularizing the use of "white supremacy" in the 1860s. The numbers in each column indicate the frequency of usage within that database in a given year, calculated as in the previous graph. Each cell is shaded according to the proportion of "Van Evrie related" uses of the phrase. These uses include references printed in Van Evrie's own writings, his advertisements, or his articles that were reprinted in other papers. For each year, I totaled the number of uses and calculated the percentage for which Van Evrie was responsible. He dominated usage during the crucial years around 1865. His proportion declined by 1867, not because the term was dying out, but because other ideologues had adopted it. Later upticks in Van Evrie–related usage coincide with *Day Book* advertising campaigns that used "white supremacy" as a slogan. None of these databases include the *Day Book* itself, so Van Evrie's dominance in usage reflects the pervasiveness of his advertisements and reprinted writings. Thousands of people who never read the *Day Book* were exposed to Van Evrie's words and ideas through other newspapers.

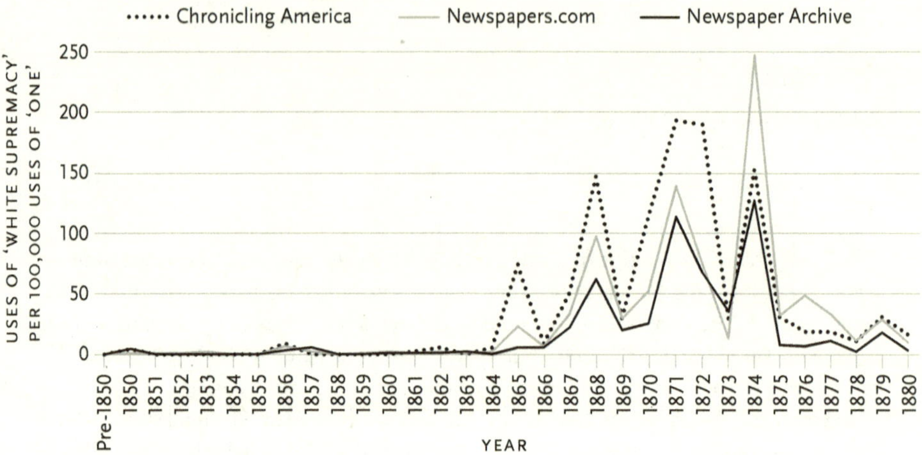

Usage of term "white supremacy"

Van Evrie's influence on "white supremacy" usage

	Chronicling America	*Newspapers.com*	*Newspaper Archive*
Pre-1850	0	0.23	0.16
1850	4.39	0.9	4.03
1851	0	0.86	0
1852	0	0.82	0
1853	0	2.29	0
1854	0	0	0
1855	0	0	0
1856	9.24	6.04	3.78
1857	0	2.59	6.01
1858	0	0	0
1859	0	1.1	0
1860	0	2.17	1.59
1861	1.76	1.06	1.09
1862	5.93	2.22	0.58
1863	0	0.57	2.14
1864	5.86	2.16	0.49
1865	73.77	23.58	5.82
1866	8.76	6.24	5.41
1867	50.65	33.01	21.98
1868	146.49	97.52	61.88
1869	30.14	30.27	19.78
1870	113.56	52.08	25.84
1871	193.54	139.26	113.69
1872	189.5	74.94	67.1
1873	29.43	12.73	35.07
1874	152.31	247.43	126.38
1875	31.09	31.61	7.2
1876	18.45	48.49	6.34
1877	18.74	33.29	11.17
1878	10.5	11.11	2.24
1879	30.31	28.9	17.73
1880	16.16	9.88	3.18

25–49% Van Evrie related

50–74% Van Evrie related

75–100% Van Evrie related

Notes

Abbreviations

BPL	County of Brant (ON) Public Library
DAASRAM	Democratic Anti-Abolition State Rights Association of the City of New York Minutes, 1863–68, Mss Collection 768, New York Public Library
DU	Rubenstein Library, Duke University
HBS	Baker Library, Harvard Business School
HWS	Warren Hunting Smith Library, Hobart and William Smith Colleges
LAC	Library and Archives Canada
LC	Manuscript Division, Library of Congress
LOA	Letters of Application and Recommendation During the Administrations of James Polk, Zachary Taylor, and Millard Fillmore, 1845–53, RG 59, microfilm M873, roll 89, National Archives (Washington, DC)
NARA	National Archives (Washington, DC)
NARAKC	National Archives Kansas City
NYDB	*New York Day Book*
NYPL	Manuscripts and Archives Division, New York Public Library
NYWC	*New York Weekly Caucasian*
PPMOP	Van Every, J. H. A.A.S., U.S.A., 1847–48, box 602, Series: Personal Papers of Medical Officers and Physicians, ca. 1861–1912, Records of the Adjutant General's Office, 1762–1984, RG 94, National Archives (Washington, DC)
SU	Department of Special Collections and University Archives, Stanford University Libraries
UNC	Wilson Library, University of North Carolina
UR	Rare Books, Special Collections, and Preservation, River Campus Libraries, University of Rochester
YU	Beinecke Rare Book and Manuscript Library, Yale University

Introduction

1. "The Newspaper Press of New York—The Day-Book," *Plantation* 2 (December 1860): 129 (quotation); Huff, "Joseph Addison Turner."

2. "Newspaper Press of New York," 136.

3. Historian George M. Fredrickson defines *racism* as "a rationalized pseudoscientific theory positing the innate and permanent inferiority of nonwhites" (Fredrickson, *Black Image*, xi). The term was not used in Van Evrie's day, but this definition captures his worldview.

4. "Newspaper Press of New York," 138.

5. "Research Projects in Progress, December 1941," in *Annual Report of the American Historical Association*, 43; Howard C. Perkins, "Description of the Subject," enclosed in Perkins to David Potter, May 20, 1944, box 6, folder 1, David Morris Potter Papers, SU.

6. For regional misidentification, see Sale, "Critiques from Within," 697–99; Osofsky, *Burden of Race*, 104, 109. For the "successful doctor" claim, see Wells, "Inventing *White Supremacy*," 49.

7. Perkins, "Description of the Subject."

8. S. J. Gould, *Mismeasure of Man*; Lurie, *Louis Agassiz*; Wish, *George Fitzhugh*; Faust, *James Henry Hammond*.

9. For Van Evrie's influence on American nationalism and education, see Yacovone, *Teaching White Supremacy*, 40–81.

10. Jacobson, *Whiteness of a Different Color*, 36.

11. Mendelberg, *Race Card*, 35.

12. Fredrickson, *Black Image*, 92.

13. J. H. Van Evrie to Jefferson Davis, March 12, 1861, reel 23, Confederate States of America Records, LC.

14. On the importance of studies that transcend the period, see Shelden, "Politics of Continuity and Change," 340.

15. Kraditor, *Means and Ends*; Sewell, *Ballots for Freedom*; Oakes, *Radical and the Republican*.

16. Alexander, "Revival of the Old Organization"; Furniss, *Between Extremes*; Gallman, *Cacophony of Politics*; Neely, *Lincoln and the Democrats*; Woods, *Arguing Until Doomsday*.

17. Recent studies that emphasize complicity include Farrow, Lang, and Frank, *Complicity*; Wells, *Kidnapping Club*; Schermerhorn, *Business of Slavery*; and Baptist, *Half Has Never Been Told*. These are powerful contributions, but critics note that shared culpability did not prevent disunion. See Oakes, "Capitalism and Slavery and the Civil War." See also Stephanie McCurry, "Plunder of Black Life: The Problem of Connecting the History of Slavery to the Economics of the Present," *Times Literary Supplement*, May 19, 2017.

18. Gordon, *Communications Revolution*; John, *Spreading the News*; Starr, *Creation of the Media*; Howe, *What Hath God Wrought*.

19. Fowler, *Unmailable*, 21–41; John, *Spreading the News*, 257–80; Leonard, *News for All*, 67–75; Nye, *Fettered Freedom*.

20. On journalism and segregation, see Forde and Bedingfield, *Journalism and Jim Crow*.

21. On editorial aspirations versus realities, see Lundberg, *Horace Greeley*.

22. Escott, *What Shall We Do with the Negro?*; Escott, *Worst Passions*.

23. Andrews, *North Reports*; Schiller, *Objectivity and the News*; Blondheim, *News over the Wires*; Risley, *Civil War Journalism*.

24. Neely, *Boundaries of American Political Culture*, 5; Huntzicker, *Popular Press*.

25. On the business of American journalism, see Daly, *Covering America*.

26. An excellent social history of print media is Leonard, *News for All*.

27. "Letter to Editors *Day Book*," *NYDB*, June 6, 1859.

28. Maxwell, *General Alumni Catalogue*, 661; *Blue Hen's Chicken and Commonwealth*, March 12, 1859.

29. Anderson, *Imagined Communities.*

30. Saxton, *Rise and Fall*; Roediger, *Wages of Whiteness*; Lott, *Love and Theft*; Ignatiev, *How the Irish Became White.*

31. Nicoletti, *Secession on Trial*, viii.

32. "Unfinished revolution" borrows from E. Foner, *Reconstruction.*

Chapter 1

1. Potter-MacKinnon, *While the Women Only Wept*, 63–93; Talman, *Loyalist Narratives*, 109–48; W. Brown, *Good Americans*, 195–96; "Extracts from Niagara Papers," in *Notes on Niagara*, 4.

2. Drew, *Refugee*, 17.

3. John M. Macrae, "A Van Every Family Story," unpublished manuscript in Van Every Family Fonds, reference no. R8018-0-7-E, LAC, 1–18; Piersol, *Records*, 1–29, 37.

4. Piersol, *Records*, 37–48; Coldham, *American Loyalist Claims*, 503; Smy, *Annotated Nominal Roll*, 187–89; "The New York Line of the Continental Army," in Fernow, *Documents*, 206; Land Petitions of Upper Canada, 1763–1865, David Van Every, Flamborough West, 1811, Volume 515, Bundle V 11, Petition 26, RG 1 L3, microfilm C-2947, LAC.

5. Cruikshank, *Story of Butler's Rangers*; Watt, *Burning of the Valleys*; Riddell, *Slave in Canada*, 20–21; Kelly, "Race and Segregation"; Winks, *Blacks in Canada*, 29–30, 150.

6. Quoted in Potter-MacKinnon, *While the Women Only Wept*, 114.

7. "Return of Families of Loyalists Receiving Provisions out of the Different Magazines or Depots in the District of Montreal from the 25th of October to the 24th of November 1780, Inclusive"; "General Return of Unincorporated Royalists and Families who Receive their Provisions gratis from Government from the 25th of March to the 24th of April 1781 Inclusive"; and "General Return of Unincorporated Royalists and Families who Received their Provisions gratis from Government from the 25th of August to the 24th of Sept[embe]r 1781 Inclusive," Loyalist Volumes, vol. 166, 57, 69, 94, Haldimand Papers, Manuscript Group 21, microform C-1475, LAC. The baptismal record of David Van Every is listed in Protestant Baptisms at Trois-Rivières, 1768–92, Quebec, Vital and Church Records (Drouin Collection), 1621–1968, Ancestry.com; Potter-MacKinnon, *While the Women Only Wept*, 109–22, 114 (quotation); Hansen, *Mingling*, 48–49; Siebert, "Temporary Settlement of Loyalists."

8. W. Brown, *Good Americans*, 175–76; Fryer, *King's Men*, 177.

9. Quoted in Brown and Senior, *Victorious in Defeat*, 29.

10. Craig, *Upper Canada*, 5–6; Fryer, *King's Men*, 326; "Return of Persons under the Description of Loyalists, Specifying the Number, Ages, and Sexes of Each Family in Capt John McDonell's Corps of Rangers at Niagara 30 November 1783," Loyalist Volumes, vol. 105, 394, Haldimand Papers, Manuscript Group 21, microform C-1475, LAC.

11. Caniff, *History of the Settlement of Upper Canada*, 185 (quotation).

12. Hansen, *Mingling*, ix (quotation); Craig, *Upper Canada*; A. Taylor, *Civil War*; Hatter, *Citizens of Convenience*; Broyld, *Borderland Blacks.*

13. Brown and Senior, *Victorious in Defeat*, 67; McCalla, *Planting the Province*, 15–16; Hansen, *Mingling*, 66–114.

14. Piersol, *Records*, 40.

15. "The Reminiscences of the Hon. Henry Ruttan," in Talman, *Loyalist Narratives*, 300–301; Durand, *Reminiscences*, 10; Wigmore, "Before the Railroad," 440; Elgersman, *Unyielding Spirits.*

16. Riddell, "Slave in Upper Canada," 377–79 (emphasis in original).

17. In 1792, David petitioned unsuccessfully to prevent his mother from selling land to Adam Vrooman. Notwithstanding this dispute, they had served together in Butler's Rangers and lived near each other in 1793. See Robert Collins McBride, "Sgt. Adam Vrooman UE (1753–8 January 1810) Acquires Land First Given to McGregory Van Every UE (27 April 1723–15 September 1786)," *Loyalist Gazette*, March 22, 2011.

18. Stouffer, *Light of Nature*, 13–14.

19. Winks, *Blacks in Canada*, 48.

20. Riddell, "Notes on Slavery," 396–97; Wigmore, "Before the Railroad."

21. Houston and Prentice, *Schooling and Scholars*, 37; Riddell, "Documents"; J. W. Grant, *Profusion of Spires*, 110–11; J. Roberts, "Mixed Assemblage"; Silverman, *Unwelcome Guests*; Frost, *I've Got a Home*; Hepburn, *Crossing the Border.*

22. A. Taylor, *Civil War.*

23. Land Petitions of Upper Canada, 1763–1865, Andrew Van Every, Flamborough, 1794, Volume 514, Bundle U-V 1, Petition 2, RG 1 L3, microfilm C-2842, LAC; Land Petitions of Upper Canada, 1763–1865: Peter Van Every, Flamborough, 1794, Volume 400, Bundle P 1, Petition 20, RG 1 L3, microfilm C-2488, LAC.

24. Land Petitions of Upper Canada, 1763–1865: David Van Every, Flamborough East and West, 1806, Volume 514A, Bundle V 8, Petition 2, RG 1 L3, microfilm C-2947, LAC; Green et al., *From West Flamborough's Storied Past*, 8.

25. Land Petitions of Upper Canada, 1763–1865: David Van Every, Flamborough West, 1802, Volume 514, Bundle U-V 5, Petition 25, RG 1 L3, microfilm C-2947, LAC. David Sr. wrote well, but David Jr. signed petitions with an X. Observers noted the decline of literacy among children, like David Jr., who were born during the early years of Loyalist settlement. See Caniff, *History*, 364.

26. "Early Records of St. Mark's and St. Andrew's Churches," 56.

27. Hickey, *War of 1812*, 66–68, 85–87; Hitsman, *Incredible War of 1812*, 77–93; A. Taylor, *Civil War*, 140–45, 187–99; Latimer, *1812*, 2–3, 60–83.

28. Land Petitions of Upper Canada, 1763–1865: David Van Every, Dumfries, 1824, Volume 516, Bundle V 14, Petition 8, RG 1 L3, microfilm C-2948, LAC.

29. A. Taylor, *Civil War*, 150; Turner, *Astonishing General*, 170.

30. Latimer, *1812*, 2–3. For Isaac Brock Van Every's birth year, see 1850 Manuscript Census, Rochester, Ward 3, Monroe County, NY, US Federal Census Collection, Ancestry.com.

31. A. Taylor, *Civil War*, 217–61, 382–407; Hitsman, *Incredible War*, 122–39, 188–205; Barbuto, *Niagara 1814*.

32. War of 1812: Upper Canada Returns, Nominal Rolls and Paylists, RG 9 1B7, vol. 16, 34–35, microform T-10384, LAC.

33. "Muster Roll of a Detachment of the 2d Regiment of York Militia, under Command of Col. Richard Beasley (attached to the right Division of the army) Stationed at Hutts House near St. David's from 25th June to 24th July 1814, Both days inclusive," War of 1812: Upper Canada Returns, Nominal Rolls and Paylists, RG 9 1B7, vol. 16, 36–38, microform T-10384, LAC; A. Taylor, *Civil War*, 300–304, 390–91; Latimer, *1812*, 287.

34. Quoted in A. Taylor, *Civil War*, 443.

35. Quoted in A. Taylor, *Civil War*, 443.

36. W. W. Smith, *William Wye Smith*, 56.

37. Based on the exact age listed on his death certificate, Van Every's birthday was October 11, 1814. John Henry Van Evrie Certificate of Death, May 17, 1896, Department of Health of the City of Brooklyn, no. 8637, New York City Municipal Archives.

38. J. Donald Wilson, "The Teacher in Early Ontario," in Armstrong, Stevenson, and Wilson, *Aspects of Nineteenth-Century Ontario*, 218–36, 222 (quotation); Houston and Prentice, *Schooling and Scholars.*

39. Carroll, *My Boy Life*, 77, 99; Durand, *Reminiscences*, 33; Caniff, *History*, 333–34.

40. Wilton, *Popular Politics*, 1–167; Craig, *Upper Canada*, 99–141, 188–206; White, *Ontario*, 87–100.

41. Wilton, *Popular Politics*, 27–36.

42. Gourlay, *Statistical Account*, 1:374.

43. Jasanoff, *Liberty's Exiles*, 12–13.

44. Grant, *Profusion of Spires*, 72, 85–100; Wilton, *Popular Politics*, 18.

45. "Early Records of St. Mark's and St. Andrew's Churches," 56.

46. Carnochan, *Names Only*, 8.

47. Grant, *Profusion of Spires*, 45–71.

48. Robert Collins McBride, "Warner Cemetery: An Important Piece of Canada's Heritage Worth Preserving," *Loyalist Gazette*, March 22, 2000.

49. 1851 Census of Canada East, Canada West, New Brunswick, and Nova Scotia, Canadian Census Collection, Ancestry.com.

50. McNairn, "Towards Deliberative Democracy"; Wallace, "Periodical Literature."

51. Quoted in LeSueur, *William Lyon Mackenzie*, 116 (first quotation), 132 (second quotation), 142 (third and fourth quotations).

52. Flint, *William Lyon Mackenzie*; LeSueur, *William Lyon Mackenzie*; Mackenzie, *Sketches of Canada*, 21–25, 46–49, 273–74.

53. "Agents for the Casket," *Canadian Casket* 1 (November 12, 1831): 21; Thomas Brewer Vincent, Sandra Alston, and Eli Maclaren, "Magazines in English," in Fleming, Gallichan, and Lamonde, *History of the Book in Canada*, 246–47.

54. Hiram Capron to Horace Capron, January 3, 1830, Hiram Capron Collection, BPL; *History of the County of Brant*, 463–88.

55. Young, *Reminiscences*, 210; "Samuel Vanevery" entry, Hiram Capron Account Book, 1828–31, 79, BPL.

56. The debts are recorded in American dollars in Schedule A in Case File No. 1501, Bankruptcy Act of 1841 Case Files, 1841–43, RG 21, NARAKC.

57. York, *Christian Guardian*, October 15, 1831, in Reid, *Death Notices*, 68.

58. Schedule A in Case File No. 1501, Bankruptcy Act of 1841 Case Files, 1841–43, RG 21, NARAKC; Hiram Capron Day Book Letter H, Account Book, 1833–41, BPL.

59. For the deaths of Sarah Eliza (Jones) Van Every and Ann Van Every, see "Sarah Eliza (Jones) Van Every," WikiTree, accessed August 12, 2025, www.wikitree.com/wiki/Jones-3606, and "Ann Van Every," WikiTree, accessed August 11, 2025, www.wikitree.com/wiki/Van_Every-27. On influenza, see Heagerty, *Four Centuries*, 1:212.

60. Bilson, *Darkened House*, 4, 52–64.

61. Baehre, "*Medical Profession in Upper Canada*," 103.

62. Houston and Prentice, *Schooling and Scholars*, 23; Carroll, *My Boy Life*, 278–79.

63. Strachan, *Visit*, 131.

64. Gidney and Millar, *Professional Gentlemen*, 4.

65. On Isaac Brock Van Every, see "Married," *Rochester Gem and Ladies' Amulet*, October 20, 1838; 1840 Manuscript Census, Rochester, Ward 3, Monroe County, NY, US Federal Census Collection, Ancestry.com; *Democrat and Chronicle*, May 4, 1887.

66. *Charter and Directory*, 91.

67. McKelvey, *Rochester.*

68. Watson, *Liberty and Power*; Cheathem, *Coming of Democracy.*

69. Schudson, *Discovering the News*, 12–60; Lee, *Daily Newspaper*, 97–132.

70. Grund, *Americans*, 1:198–202.

71. Starr, *Creation of the Media*, 130; Huntzicker, *Popular Press*, 1–2, 35–51; Sheppard, *Partisan Press*, 71–139; C. G. Smith, *Press, Politics, and Patronage*; Pasley, *Tyranny of Printers*, 348–99.

72. Harris, *In the Shadow*; Berlin and Harris, *Slavery in New York*; Gellman, *Emancipating New York.*

73. "The Growth of the Slave Trade," *New York Evening Post*, February 14, 1860 (quotation); Albion, *Rise of New York Port*, 95–121; Beckert, *Monied Metropolis*, 17–97; Schermerhorn, *Business of Slavery.*

74. Richards, *Gentlemen of Property*; Rice, "Anti-Slavery Mission"; Harris, *In the Shadow*, 195–201.

75. Burrows and Wallace, *Gotham*, 549–52; Harris, *In the Shadow*, 134–262.

Chapter 2

1. Joseph H. Foster and J. H. Van Every to E. Cutbush, January 14, 1836, Van Evrie, John H. file, box 79, College History—Biographical Files, HWS.

2. Advertisement in *St. Mary's Beacon* (Leonard Town, MD), November 21, 1861.

3. "Dr. Anson Colman," undated biographical sketch, box 1, folder 1, Anson Colman Papers, A.C71, UR.

4. Anson Colman to Sophia Elizabeth Colman, January 20, 1832, box 1, folder 3; Anson Colman to Catherine K. Colman, October 3, 1833, box 1, folder 4; Anson Colman to Sophia Rochester, June 23, 1835, box 1, folder 5, Colman Papers.

5. Catherine K. Colman to Anson Colman, December 10, 1832, box 1, folder 3, Colman Papers.

6. Drake, *Practical Essays*, 45.

7. *Circular and Catalogue*, 6.

8. Corner, "Early Medical Education"; Bordley and Harvey, *Two Centuries*, 15–19, 34–35; Kaufman, *American Medical Education*, 36–56; Duffy, *From Humors to Medical Science*, 62–70, 130–50.

9. Nimura, *Doctors Blackwell*, 41–45.

10. John Stauffer, "Introduction," in Stauffer, *Works of James McCune Smith*, xxi.

11. Grover, *Make a Way Somehow*, 7.

12. For textbooks required during Van Every's stint at GMC, see *Circular and Catalogue*, 7. Many thanks to Roraig Finney for helping me review these texts.

13. Cloquet, *System of Human Anatomy*, 105–6.

14. Dunglison, *Human Physiology*, 2:465, 467–68.

15. Richerand, *Elements of Physiology*, 378.

16. Dunglison, *Human Physiology*, 2:455–56, 462, 472, 476; Richerand, *Elements of Physiology*, 22, 60–61, 220, 375–79; Jackson, *Principles of Medicine*, 184, 220–22; Dewees, *Treatise on the Diseases of Females*, 219, 251–52.

17. Dunglison, *Human Physiology*, 2:472 (quotation), 476.

18. Fredrickson, *Black Image*, 71–96; Horsman, *Josiah Nott*; Smedley, *Race in North America*, 231–54; Dain, *Hideous Monster*, 197–226; Baum, *Rise and Fall*, 95–117; Sussman, *Myth of Race*, 25–44; Stein, *Measuring Manhood*, 27–87.

19. Livingstone, *Adam's Ancestors*, 26–51.

20. Jefferson, *Notes*, 153.

21. Van Evrie, *Negroes and Negro "Slavery"* (1861 ed.), title page.

22. White, *Account of the Regular Gradation*, 125.

23. Caldwell, *Thoughts on the Original Unity*.

24. Morton, *Crania Americana*; Morton, *Crania Aegyptiaca*.

25. Nott, *Two Lectures, on the Natural History*; Nott, *Two Lectures on the Connection*; Nott, *Essay on the Natural History*.

26. Rothstein, *American Physicians*; Duffy, *From Humors to Medical Science*, 80–94, 130–50; Rutkow, *Seeking the Cure*, 31–60.

27. Willoughby, *Masters of Health*, 2 (quotation); Savitt, *Race and Medicine*; Fabian, *Skull Collectors*; A. S. Curran, *Anatomy of Blackness*; Hogarth, *Medicalizing Blackness*.

28. Haller, "Negro and the Southern Physician"; Savitt, *Medicine and Slavery*; Owens, *Medical Bondage*.

29. Quoted in Sussman, *Myth of Race*, 31.

30. Scholars disagree on the relationship between polygenism and Christianity. For compatibility, see Kidd, *Forging of Races*, and Livingstone, *Adam's Ancestors*. Contrary accounts include Haller, *Outcasts from Evolution*, and Stanton, *Leopard's Spots*. On the monogenism versus polygenism debate among proslavery writers, see Luse, "Slavery's Champions."

31. Van Every never appears in the Geneva Medical College Collection, Archives and Special Collections, Health Sciences Library, SUNY Upstate Medical University. For similar results from a previous effort to document his medical studies, see Howard C. Perkins to Irene G. Harer, May 26, 1942, and Irene G. Harer to Howard C. Perkins, July 15, 1942, in Van Evrie, John H. file, box 79, College History—Biographical Files, HWS.

32. Edward M. Moore to My Dear Parents, July 31, 1837, box 1, folder 4, Edward Mott Moore Papers, A.M82, UR; Clerk of the Surrogate Court, Monroe County, NY, Will Book No. 2, 189, accessed August 12, 2025, https://mcnygenealogy.com/vr/will-book-2.htm.

33. Edward M. Moore to Lindley M. Moore, March 6, 1837, and M. U. Hicks to Edward M. Moore, February 27, 1837, box 1, folder 4, Moore Papers.

34. "Matthews," *Roman Citizen*, April 9, 1847; *Hobart College General Catalogue*, 46.

35. Drake, *Systematic Treatise*, 1:363–66; Floyd, *Medicine on the Maumee*.

36. *Maumee (OH) Express*, June 9, 16, 1838.

37. *Maumee (OH) Express*, July 7, 28, August 11, 1838.

38. *Maumee (OH) Express*, April 18, 1840; J. A. Smith, *History of Maumee*, 21.

39. Drake, *Systematic Treatise*, 1:363, 790; Cassedy, *Medicine and American Growth*, 50–54.

40. *House Documents* 173, 26 Cong., 1 Sess., 110 (Serial 366); Stockwell, *Other Trail of Tears*; Bowes, *Land Too Good for Indians.*

41. Waggoner, *History of the City of Toledo*, 553.

42. St. Luke and St. Simon Cyrene Episcopal Church, *Parish Register, Volume 1 (1820–1847)*, 168, Rochester Genealogical Society, accessed August 12, 2025, https://nyrgs.org/LukeSimonCyrene/1820_47ParishRegisterV1.pdf.

43. John H. Van Every to James K. Polk, March 15, 1845, LOA.

44. "The Cause of Democracy in Ohio Goes Bravely On!" *Ohio Statesman*, July 24, 1840.

45. "Democratic County Convention," *Ohio Statesman*, December 17, 1841.

46. John H. Van Every to James K. Polk, May 24, 1845, LOA.

47. Entry for March 6, 1838, vol. 2, Diary of Nathaniel Thrift Rochester, box 10, Rochester Family Papers, D.236, UR; "Receipts and vouchers in possession of Thomas H. Rochester, Treasurer of the Whig Central Committee of Monroe County, New York, for Election of 1844," box 2, folder 4, Nathaniel Rochester Family Papers, A.R66, UR.

48. Catherine Rochester Van Every baptism, May 5, 1844, St. Luke and St. Simon Cyrene Episcopal Church, *Parish Register, Volume 1 (1820–1847)*, 57, Rochester Genealogical Society, accessed August 12, 2025, https://nyrgs.org/LukeSimonCyrene/1820_47ParishRegisterV1.pdf.

49. Case File No. 1501, Bankruptcy Act of 1841 Case Files, 1841–43, RG 21, NARAKC.

50. Balleisen, *Navigating Failure.*

51. Liabilities are listed in schedule A and assets in schedule B, Case File No. 1501, NARAKC.

52. "The Bankrupt Estate of J. H. Van Every in account with Thomas Clark, 2nd Assignee for first four months ending the 31 day of May 1843," and certificate of bankruptcy, both in Case File No. 1501, NARAKC.

53. "Report of Property set off by Assignee," April 15, 1843, in Case File No. 1501, NARAKC.

54. "Money Received for the Recorder," *Episcopal Recorder*, March 19, 1842; *Spirit of Missions* (Burlington, NJ), July 1, 1843.

55. John H. Van Every to James K. Polk, March 15, 1845, LOA.

56. Holt, *Rise and Fall*, 183 (quotation); Silbey, *Storm over Texas*; Cheathem, *Who Is James K. Polk?*

57. John H. Van Every to James K. Polk, March 15, 1845, LOA (first quotation); Andrew Jackson to Thomas Hart Benton, May 14, 1844 (second quotation), Andrew Jackson Papers, LC.

58. John H. Van Every to James K. Polk, March 15, May 24, 1845, LOA.

59. Ashley Sampson to James K. Polk, June 6, 1845, LOA (quotation); Snodgrass, *Underground Railroad*, 472.

60. John H. Van Every to James K. Polk, March 15, 1845, LOA.

61. Ashley Sampson to James K. Polk, June 6, 1845, LOA.

62. John H. Van Every to James K. Polk, May 24, 1845, LOA.

63. John H. Van Every to James K. Polk, May 24, 1845; Ashley Sampson to James K. Polk, June 6, 1845, LOA.

64. Bonner, *Becoming a Physician*, 178; Shryock, *Medicine and Society*, 123–27.

65. Mt. Hope & Riverside Cemetery Records, unnumbered page, UR.

66. Catherine appears in Thomas H. Rochester's household in the 1850, 1860, and 1870 censuses; thereafter, she lived with other relatives. When Rochester died in 1874, he left her forty shares of railroad stock. Last Will and Testament, Thomas R. Rochester, executed

October 10, 1874, Record of Wills, Book No. 17, Monroe County, NY (Monroe Wills, Vol. 018, 1874–79), 75. Catherine was listed as an adopted daughter in his obituary: "Another Old Pioneer Gone," *Democrat and Chronicle*, October 7, 1874. For Catherine's ties to her father's friends, note her condolence letter to Hannah Horton, November 24, 1865, Rushmore G. Horton Papers, NYPL. For Catherine's charity, see "Rochester Female Charitable Society," *Democrat and Chronicle*, March 16, 1877; "Generous Gifts to Church Home," *Democrat and Chronicle*, November 12, 1903. On her death, see "Miss Van Evrie Buried," *Democrat and Chronicle*, December 31, 1922.

Chapter 3

1. "To Andrew Johnson, President of the United States," *NYDB*, December 23, 1865. The letter was republished as J. H. Van Evrie, "Negro Emancipation in America," *Anthropological Review* 4 (October 1866): 136–40.

2. "The Evening Day Book," *New York Tribune*, February 8, 1859.

3. Downs, "Mexicanization of American Politics."

4. Johannsen, *To the Halls*; Foos, *Short, Offhand, Killing Affair*; Greenberg, *Wicked War*; Guardino, *Dead March*.

5. "Speech on the Reception of Abolition Petitions, Delivered in the Senate, February 6th, 1837," in Crallé, *Works of John C. Calhoun*, 2:631.

6. Field, *Politics of Race*, 37, 43–79.

7. J. H. Van Evrie to John C. Calhoun, March 4, 1846, in Meriwether, Hemphill, and Wilson, *Papers of John C. Calhoun*, 22:660–62.

8. Field, *Politics of Race*, 61.

9. James K. Polk, "To the Senate and House of Representatives," in Richardson, *Compilation*, 4:442.

10. Guardino, *Dead March*, 31–202; Greenberg, *Wicked War*, 3–176; Eisenhower, *So Far from God*, 3–265.

11. Winders, *Mr. Polk's Army*, 10; Eisenhower, *So Far from God*, 288–90; Lander, *Reluctant Imperialists*.

12. J. H. Van Every to H. L. Haskell, June 1, 1847, PPMOP.

13. Henderson, *Hints on the Medical Examination*, 8 (quotation); McCaffrey, *Army of Manifest Destiny*, 23–27.

14. Henderson, *Hints on the Medical Examination*, rev. ed., 31–33, 32 (quotation).

15. "Victory on the Rio Grande," *Morning Express*, May 27, 1846 (first quotation); Greenberg, *Wicked War*, 113 (second and third quotations).

16. "Invasion of Mexico," *Indiana State Sentinel*, October 22, 1846 (first quotation); "The Energy of the War," *Sun*, December 1, 1846 (second quotation); Horsman, *Race and Manifest Destiny*, 240 (third, fourth, and fifth quotations), 208–48; Gómez, *Manifest Destinies*, 15–46.

17. Quoted in Holley, "I Shall Never Be a White Man Again," 262–63. See also T. D. Johnson, *Gallant Little Army*, 4, 149; McCaffrey, *Army of Manifest Destiny*, 66–79; Winders, *Mr. Polk's Army*, 168–85.

18. Quoted in Johannsen, *To the Halls*, 22.

19. Foos, *Short, Offhand, Killing Affair*, 125–34; Guardino, *Dead March*, 126–27, 132, 294–300.

20. Quoted in Johannsen, *To the Halls*, 22.

21. Quoted in Horsman, *Race and Manifest Destiny*, 241.

22. Quoted in Horsman, *Race and Manifest Destiny*, 242. See also Burge, *Failed Vision*, 37–39.

23. The payment record is in PPMOP.

24. J. H. Van Every to H. L. Haskell, June 1, 1847; George W. Morgan to Thomas Lawson, July 31, 1847, PPMOP.

25. Duncan, "Medical History," 437–38; Winders, *Mr. Polk's Army*, 152.

26. McCaffrey, *Army of Manifest Destiny*, 52–64, 52 (quotation); Winders, *Mr. Polk's Army*, 139–66; Irey, "Soldiering, Suffering, and Dying."

27. George W. Morgan to Thomas Lawson, July 31, 1847, PPMOP.

28. "Contract: Dr. Thos. Lawson Surg. Genl. with Dr. J. H. Van Every," PPMOP.

29. McCaffrey, *Army of Manifest Destiny*, 56–57; Winders, *Mr. Polk's Army*, 19; Eisenhower, *So Far from God*, 298, 303–4.

30. Eisenhower, *So Far from God*, 303–4, 310.

31. Entry for August 8, 1847, "The Diary of Robert Hagan, Assistant Surgeon, United States Army with the 14th Infantry in the War with Mexico, 1847–1848," Special Collections, University of Arizona.

32. J. W. Leigh Letter: Puebla, Mexico, to Mrs. Benjamin Watkins Leigh, Richmond, Va., October 2, 1847, Bancroft Library, University of California, Berkeley.

33. Entries for August 4, 1847 (quotations), July 27, 1847, Madison Mills Diary, Filson Historical Society, Louisville, KY; Cullum, *Biographical Register*, 1:135–36.

34. Entry for August 10, 1847, Mills Diary (emphasis in original); Duncan, "Medical History," 461; T. D. Johnson, *Gallant Little Army*, 149.

35. Entry for August 12, 1847, Mills Diary.

36. Entry for August 14, 1847, Mills Diary.

37. On Army surgeons' dissatisfaction with civilian doctors, see McCaffrey, *Army of Manifest Destiny*, 56–57.

38. John W. Dodd to Eliza Dodd, May 6, 1848, John W. Dodd Papers, YU.

39. T. D. Johnson, *Gallant Little Army*, 151–226; entries for August 21, 25, 26, September 4, 9, 1847, Mills Diary.

40. Entry for August 22, 1847, Mills Diary.

41. Entry for August 23, 1847, Mills Diary.

42. Entries for August 28, 29, 31, 1847, Mills Diary; Oswandel, *Notes*, 244–83.

43. Oswandel, *Notes*, 248, 250.

44. Entry for August 30, 1847, Mills Diary; Oswandel, *Notes*, 252; T. D. Johnson, *Gallant Little Army*, 248.

45. Entries for September 12, 15–25, 1847, Mills Diary; T. D. Johnson, *Gallant Little Army*, 248–49.

46. Thomas Laidley to John Laidley, October 16, 1847, in McCaffrey, *Surrounded by Dangers*, 108–9.

47. Entries for October 12 and 13, 1847, Mills Diary; T. D. Johnson, *Gallant Little Army*, 249–50; Oswandel, *Notes*, 284–352; Winders, "Puebla's Forgotten Heroes."

48. "Orders," *Flag of Freedom*, October 20, 1847.

49. Oswandel, *Notes*, 346.

50. Bodson, "Description of the United States Occupation," 2, 14.

51. "Woman Killed," *Flag of Freedom*, December 15, 1847; see also "Outrage," *Flag of Freedom*, November 24, 1847.

52. "Theatre," *Flag of Freedom*, November 27, 1847; "A Darkey's Idea," *Flag of Freedom*, November 10, 1847.

53. "Married," *Flag of Freedom*, January 29, 1848; *Flag of Freedom*, February 12, 1848.

54. Gregory D. Smithers contrasts Australian settler colonial policies, informed by monogenists like James Prichard, which promoted "whitening" Indigenous populations through intermarriage, with American policies, informed by polygenism, which sought to protect whiteness from contamination (Smithers, *Science, Sexuality, and Race*). Notions of uplifting Mexico through intermarriage revealed a lingering Prichardian influence that Van Every challenged in his publications. On wartime "whitening" and "annexation" discourse, see Guardino, *Dead March*, 115; see also Greenberg, *Manifest Manhood*, 23–26, 88–90, 122–27.

55. Mayer, *Mexico*, 2:158 (quotations); Mayer, *Mexico as It Was*, 170–71, 333.

56. Farnham, *Life and Adventures*, 413.

57. Lemire, *Miscegenation*, esp. 111–13.

58. Nott, "Mulatto a Hybrid." On polygenists' obsession with the declining fertility thesis, see Stanton, *Leopard's Spots*, 113–21, 137–44; Smedley, *Race in North America*, 244–46. One sign of polygenism's ascendency was the addition of the "mulatto" category to the 1850 census. Nott supported its inclusion, hoping that government-collected data would demonstrate diminished fertility. See Hochschild and Powell, "Racial Reorganization," 67. On the denigration of mixed-race people in polygenist proslavery thought, see Toplin, "Between Black and White."

59. Jefferson Davis, "Speech at State Fair at Augusta, Me.," in *Speeches of the Hon. Jefferson Davis*, 28.

60. 1850 Manuscript Census and Slave Schedules, Jasper County, GA, US Federal Census Collection, Ancestry.com.

Chapter 4

1. Adams, *Eulogy*, 85. Many thanks to Amanda Deanda for sharing this source with me.

2. Dunlap, *American Historical Societies*; Henle, *Rescued from Oblivion*; Cheng, *Plain and Noble Garb*; Karsten, *Patriot-Heroes*.

3. Carlyle, *On Heroes*, 1–2, 51–52, 177 (1, quotations).

4. Carlyle, *On Heroes*, 177–84 (emphasis in original).

5. Lundberg, *Horace Greeley*, 7, 18, 187n3 (quotation).

6. Thomas, *Liberator*, 129, 131–32.

7. Parfait, *Publishing History*; Brooke, *There Is a North*; Jordan-Lake, *Whitewashing* Uncle Tom's Cabin.

8. *Daily Union* (Washington, DC), July 22, 1848.

9. Rapport, *1848*; Roberts, *Distant Revolutions*.

10. Quoted in McPherson, *Battle Cry of Freedom*, 51.

11. *Congressional Globe*, 29 Cong., 2 Sess., app. 317 (February 8, 1847).

12. C. Morrison, *Democratic Politics*; Berwanger, *Frontier Against Slavery*; M. A. Morrison, *Slavery and the American West*, 39–95; Earle, *Jacksonian Antislavery*, 123–43.

13. "The Barnburners' Platform," *Weekly National Intelligencer* (Washington, DC), August 19, 1848 (quotation); Gara, "Slavery and the Slave Power"; Richards, *Slave Power*.

14. Blue, *Free Soilers*; Mayfield, *Rehearsal for Republicanism*; Earle, *Jacksonian Antislavery*, 163–80.

15. "Speech at Jackson," *Mississippian* (Jackson), October 20, 1848.

16. Crallé, *Works of John C. Calhoun*, 6:290–313.

17. On the compromise, see Hamilton, *Prologue to Conflict*, and Maizlish, *Strife of Tongues*. On conflicts over rendition of fugitives, see Wells, *Blind No More*; Delbanco, *War Before the War*; Blackett, *Captive's Quest*; Harrold, *Border War*, 138–58. For Eliza's flight, see H. B. Stowe, *Uncle Tom's Cabin*, 1:93–94.

18. "Inside History of the Kansas-Nebraska Bill—Its Consequences—The Political Future," *NYDB*, November 10, 1858.

19. *Congressional Globe*, 31 Cong., 1 Sess., app. 265 (March 11, 1850) (first quotation); *Congressional Globe*, 31 Cong., 1 Sess., 28 (December 13, 1849) (second quotation; emphasis in original).

20. Sperber, *Karl Marx*, esp. 214–98.

21. de Gobineau, *Inequality of Human Races*; Biddiss, *Father of Racist Ideology*.

22. de Gobineau, *Moral and Intellectual Diversity*, vi (first quotation); Biddiss, *Father of Racist Ideology*, 146–47, 147 (second quotation); Burnett, *Henry Hotze*. On the "scavenger" theme, see Solomos and Back, *Racism and Society*, 213.

23. Nott, *Two Lectures, on the Natural History*; Nott, *Two Lectures on the Connection*.

24. Quoted in Gossett, *Race*, 64.

25. Lurie, *Louis Agassiz*, 1–121.

26. Lurie, *Louis Agassiz*, 123–257, 257 (quotation); M. Rogers, *Delia's Tears*; Wallis, "Black Bodies."

27. Lurie, *Louis Agassiz*, 257–66, 261 (quotation); Gossett, *Race*, 59–60; Stanton, *Leopard's Spots*, 100–112; Horsman, *Josiah Nott*, 104–5, 116–17; Kendi, *Stamped*, 188–89.

28. Campbell, *Negro-Mania*, 10 (first quotation), 6 (second and third quotations); Heath, "Producers on the One Side."

29. "The Evening Day Book," *New York Times*, February 8, 1859.

30. Van Every received $100 for medical work between Toledo and New Orleans in May 1847, and $100 per month for work at Puebla between August 1847 and April 1848. The War Department paid him another $286.65 in 1849 for unspecified reasons. See *House Documents* Ex. Doc. 38, 31 Cong., 1 Sess., 41, 42 (Serial 576); *House Documents* Ex. Doc. 3, 31 Cong., 1 Sess., 559 (Serial 576). A hotel room cost $50 to $80 per week in midcentury Washington, so many residents lived in boardinghouses, which cost around $14 per week ($728 per year) for single room and board. See Shelden, *Washington Brotherhood*, 104.

31. Charvat, *Profession of Authorship*, esp. 168; Dowling, *Capital Letters*.

32. Luskey, *On the Make*; *Register of All Officers and Agents, 1849*, 128–30; *Register of Officers and Agents, 1853*, 131–35.

33. *Congressional Globe*, 30 Cong., 1 Sess., 723 (May 4, 1848).

34. *House Misc. Documents* 2, 32 Cong., 1 Sess., 18, 61 (Serial 652); *House Misc. Documents* 5, 31 Cong., 2 Sess., 114 (Serial 605); *House Documents* Ex. Doc. 88, 33 Cong., 1 Sess., 69 (Serial 724).

35. Jefferson Davis to Robert McClelland, October 6, 1854, in Crist et al., *Papers of Jefferson Davis*, 5:85–86.

36. *House Documents* Ex. Doc. 140, 34 Cong., 1 Sess. (Serial 864); *House Documents* Ex. Doc. 29, 34 Cong., 3 Sess. (Serial 897).

Chapter 5

1. "Public Lecture," *Charleston Courier*, March 14, 1853; *Richmond Dispatch*, April 19, 1853; "The Unity of the Human Race," *New York Evening Post*, reprinted in the *Democrat*, May 12, 1853. On the salience of 1853, see Kendi, *Stamped*, 198.

2. Horsman, *Josiah Nott*, 170–79; "Types of Mankind, or Ethnological Researches," *Weekly National Intelligencer*, February 26, 1853.

3. Mélonio, *Tocqueville*, 129.

4. J. H. Van Evrie, "Negroes and Negro Slavery," *Monthly Democratic Review* 1 (June 1853): 28–39. This periodical should not be confused with the *United States Magazine and Democratic Review*, established in 1837 and edited by John L. O'Sullivan.

5. Dr. Van Evne [John H. Van Evrie], "Slavery Extension," *De Bow's Review* 15 (July 1853): 1–14.

6. Van Evne, "Slavery Extension," 1, 2, 6, 11, 9, 10 (quotations). On Van Evrie's genocidal forecast, see Lewis, *Curse upon the Nation*, 129–31. On race- and climate-based arguments generally, see Asaka, *Tropical Freedom*.

7. See South Carolina representative Isaac Holmes's argument for Texas annexation, in *Congressional Globe*, 28 Cong., 2 Sess., app. 108 (January 14, 1845). On the twin fears of encirclement and insurrection, see Paulus, *Slaveholding Crisis*. Similar arguments infused secessionist rhetoric; see Dew, *Apostles of Disunion*, 35.

8. J. H. Van Evrie to Jefferson Davis, November 2, 1855, in Rowland, *Jefferson Davis*, 2:546 (emphasis in original).

9. Van Evrie, *Negroes and Negro "Slavery"* (Day Book Office ed., 1853), 3.

10. Charvat, *Profession of Authorship*, 287–88.

11. Van Evrie, "Negroes and Negro Slavery," *Monthly Democratic Review*, 28.

12. Van Evrie, "Negroes and Negro Slavery," 30, 31, 32, 35, 39 (quotations).

13. "The Star-Spangled Banner," *Monthly Democratic Review* 1 (June 1853): 39.

14. "Death of the Best Man in England," *NYDB*, reprinted in *Anthropological Review* 8 (January 1870): 97.

15. Van Evrie, *Negroes and Negro Slavery* (J. D. Toy ed., 1853), 1–3.

16. Compare Van Evrie, *Negroes and Negro Slavery* (J. D. Toy ed., 1853), 29, and Van Evrie, *Negroes and Negro "Slavery"* (Day Book Office ed., 1853), 29.

17. Van Evrie, *Negroes and Negro Slavery* (J. D. Toy ed., 1853), 31–32.

18. On Anglophobia, see Haynes, *Unfinished Revolution*, 290 (quotation); Jay Sexton, "Anglophobia in Nineteenth-Century Elections, Politics, and Diplomacy," in Davies and Zelizer, *America at the Ballot Box*, 98–117. For proslavery Anglophobia, see Hammond, *Gov. Hammond's Letters*; John C. Calhoun to William R. King, August 12, 1844, in *House Documents* 1, 28 Cong., 2 Sess., vol. 1, 38–45 (Serial 463); Cunliffe, *Chattel Slavery*, 56–68; Rugemer, "Robert Monroe Harrison"; Matthew Mason, "A World Safe for Modernity: Antebellum Southern Proslavery Intellectuals Confront Great Britain," in Barnes, Schoen, and Towers, *Old South's Modern Worlds*, 47–65; Paulus, *Slaveholding Crisis*.

19. Van Evrie, *Negroes and Negro Slavery* (J. D. Toy ed., 1853), 3, 9, 10, 11, 22, 29, 30, 31.

20. See Grayson, *Hireling and the Slave*; Fitzhugh, *Sociology for the South*. See also James Henry Hammond's "mudsill" speech, in *Congressional Globe*, 35 Cong., 1 Sess., app. 68–71

(March 4, 1858). On Fitzhugh and the abstract defense of slavery, see Fox-Genovese and Genovese, *Slavery in White and Black*. On claims of the superiority of white Southerners over Northern whites, see R. D. Watson, *Normans and Saxons*.

21. Van Evrie, *Negroes and Negro Slavery* (J. D. Toy ed., 1853), 30–31.

22. Van Evrie, *Negroes and Negro "Slavery"* (Day Book Office ed., 1853).

23. On wages, see *History of Wages*, 154, 160, 253.

24. Pillicoddle, "Correspondence of the *Boston Post*," *Boston Post*, December 20, 1853.

25. John, *Spreading the News*, 58–59.

26. Jacob W. Elseffer to John A. Quitman, February 20, 1856, box 5a, folder 4a; F. R. Witter to John A. Quitman, March 5, 1856, box 5a, folder 5; Thomas S. Harney to John A. Quitman, March 7, 1856, box 5a, folder 5; Isaac R. Wade to John A. Quitman, March 9, 1856, box 5a, folder 5, Quitman (John A.) and Family Papers, Mississippi Department of Archives and History, Jackson, MS.

27. *Abbeville (SC) Press and Banner*, January 12, 1854; *Greenville Patriot*, reprinted in *Lancaster (SC) Ledger*, January 18, 1854.

28. "Negroes and Negro Slavery," *True Democrat*, June 20, 1854.

29. Lacy, "Dr. Van Evrie on Negro Slavery," *Times-Picayune*, October 26, 1856.

30. *Abbeville (SC) Press and Banner*, January 12, 1854.

31. "The Philosophy of Negro Slavery—An Important Work—The Duty of the South," *Semi-Weekly Mississippian*, October 31, 1854.

32. "Cuba. Dr. Van Evrie's 'Negroes and Negro Slavery,'" *Delta*, reprinted in *Daily Union*, April 28, 1854.

33. "New Publications," *Weekly National Intelligencer*, July 22, 1854.

34. "Negroes and Negro Slavery," *NYDB*, reprinted in *Tri-Weekly Messenger*, September 1, 1855. The review, which sometimes included a lengthy extract from the pamphlet, was reprinted widely. See "Pro-Slavery," *National Anti-Slavery Standard*, September 1, 1855; see also *Alton (IL) Weekly Telegraph*, September 6, 1855.

35. "Dr. Van Evrie's Pamphlet," *NYDB*, reprinted in *Daily Louisville Democrat*, October 30, 1855 (first quotation); "Is a Negro a White Man?" *NYDB*, reprinted in *Liberator*, August 31, 1855 (second quotation). The former article was also widely reprinted; see *Eaton (OH) Democrat*, November 15, 1855; *Memphis Daily Appeal*, November 17, 1855; *Weekly Standard*, November 28, 1855; *Cooper's Clarksburg (VA) Register*, January 2, 1856.

36. "Is the Negro a White Man?—Dr. Van Evrie and the New York Day-Book," *Frederick Douglass' Paper*, September 14, 1855.

37. *National Era*, July 7, 1853.

38. "Locofoco County Convention—Its Nominations," *Cannelton (IN) Reporter*, July 11, 1855.

39. W., "Notes by the Way," *Frederick Douglass' Paper*, April 28, 1854.

40. Samuel F. B. Morse to N. R. Stimson, October 6, 1855, Rushmore G. Horton Papers, NYPL (emphasis in original).

41. William O. Goode to Thomas Massie, February 25, 1855, Massie Family Papers, Virginia Museum of History and Culture (emphasis in original). A second installment on Roman slavery appeared in the *Daily Union*, July 22, 1854, but received scant attention.

42. J. L. O'Sullivan to Stephen A. Douglas, February 10, 1854, box 4, folder 5, Stephen A. Douglas Papers, Special Collections Research Center, University of Chicago (emphasis in original).

43. J. H. Van Evrie to Jefferson Davis, November 2, 1855, in Rowland, *Jefferson Davis*, 2:546–47 (emphasis in original).

Chapter 6

1. "A Note from John Van Buren on the Election," *New York Times*, November 20, 1855.

2. Dana, *Meyer's Universum*, 1:275–76.

3. *Register of All Officers and Agents, 1851*, 56–78.

4. Rao, *National Duties*, 191–95.

5. Rao, *National Duties*, 194; Julian, *Political Recollections*, 13–15.

6. *House Report* 648, 36 Cong., 1 Sess., 25 (quotation), 176–78, 596–97 (Serial 1071); Summers, *Plundering Generation*, 239–60.

7. "A Note from John Van Buren on the Election," *New York Times*, November 20, 1855.

8. "An Honest Buchanan Organ," *Bangor (ME) Daily Whig and Courier*, September 27, 1856.

9. Dowling, *Capital Letters*, 18.

10. Osterhammel, *Transformation of the World*, 36.

11. Spann, *New Metropolis*, 406.

12. Stott, *Workers in the Metropolis*, 48–55; Huntzicker, *Popular Press*, 53–91.

13. Blondheim, *News over the Wires*, 11–67; Kielbowicz, *News in the Mail*, 109; Pred, *Urban Growth*; Starr, *Creation of the Media*, 174; Burrows and Wallace, *Gotham*, 674–90.

14. Stott, *Workers in the Metropolis*, 49, 64–67; Ware, *Industrial Worker*, 55–61.

15. Elizabeth D. B. Stoddard to Manton Marble, September 19, [1857], box 1, Manton Marble Papers, LC.

16. G. R. Taylor, "Gaslight Foster"; George G. Foster to Rufus Wilmot Griswold, November 23, 1835, and May 12, 1841, Letters to Rufus Wilmot Griswold, Albert and Shirley Small Special Collections Library, University of Virginia; "Memorial of a Number of Citizens of Mobile, Alabama, Praying the Incorporation of a National Bank," *Senate Documents* 22, 25 Cong., 1 Sess., 2 (Serial 309); "Memorial of a Number of Citizens of St. Louis, Missouri, Praying a Grant of Land to Aid in the Construction of the Mount Carmel and New Albany Railroad," *Senate Documents* 147, 26 Cong., 2 Sess., 8 (Serial 377); "Death of G. G. Foster," *New York Times*, April 17, 1856.

17. *War of the Rebellion*, ser. 2, vol. 2, 602–20; Schott, *Alexander H. Stephens*, 282; Samuel Anderson to Alexander H. Stephens, December 11, 1868, box 45; February 2, box 46; and March 22, 1869, box 47, Alexander Hamilton Stephens Papers, LC. Entry of August 28, 1865, in Avary, *Recollections*, 489; "Attempted Suicide of a Former Bookkeeper in the Comptroller's Office," *Hartford Daily Courant*, December 9, 1871; "A Georgian," *Macon (GA) Weekly Telegraph*, December 19, 1871; "Singular Suicide," *New York Herald*, December 24, 1874.

18. Entries for April 8 and August 4, 15, 31, 1855; February 27, August 29, October 2, 12, 26, and November 18, 1856; September 8 and October 18, 1857; March 20, 1858; April 8, 1859; January 8, August 21, and December 14, 1860; March 8, 1861 (quotations); June 7, 1862, Thomas Butler Gunn Diary, Lehigh University. See also Banks, *Sharpe*.

19. H. Davis, *Leonard Bacon*, 1–7; [T. Bacon,] *Delia Bacon*, 4–11.

20. H. Davis, *Leonard Bacon*, 9–35, 60–63; L. Bacon, *Plea for Africa*; Burin, *Slavery and the Peculiar Solution*; Polgar, *Standard-Bearers of Equality*, 250–51, 307–12.

21. H. Davis, *Leonard Bacon*, 37–39, 44–45, 70.

22. D. Francis Bacon to R. R. Gurley, June 16, 1836, reel 25, American Colonization Society Records, LC.

23. D. Francis Bacon to Walter Lowrie, September 24, 1836; D. Francis Bacon to Walter Lowrie, October 14, 1836; D. Francis Bacon to R. R. Gurley, October 20, 1836, reel 26, American Colonization Society Records, LC.

24. For the appointment, see Ralph Randolph Gurley to D. Francis Bacon, December 2, 1836, Ralph Randolph Gurley Letters, New-York Historical Society.

25. "Liberian Colonization," *North Star*, September 8, 1848; "Liberia and the Slave-trade," *North Star*, September 28, 1848 (quotation). On disease, see Shick, *Behold the Promised Land*, 26–28, 50. On colonists' efforts to suppress slave trading, see Akingbade, "Liberian Settlers."

26. "Colonization," *National Anti-Slavery Standard*, July 27, 1848; "Colonization Frauds Unmasked," *Liberator*, September 1, 1848; "Great Anti-Colonization Meeting in New York," *North Star*, May 11, 1849.

27. David Francis Bacon to Leonard Bacon, May 6, 1842, part 2, box 1, folder 3, Bacon Family Papers, Ms 46, Manuscripts and Archives Repository, Yale University; John Quincy Adams to David Francis Bacon, March 31, 1845, published as "A Legacy from John Quincy Adams to the Whig Party," *Pennsylvania Freeman*, May 31, 1849; Willie Person Mangum to David Francis Bacon, January 2, 11, 1845, Gen Mss Misc., Group 655, folder F-1, YU; D. Francis Bacon to Hamilton Fish, February 20, 1845, David Francis Bacon Letters, New-York Historical Society.

28. Bacon, *Progressive Democracy*.

29. "A Frank Confession," *Buffalo Courier*, August 26, 1848 (first quotation); "Jefferson and Whigs," *Buffalo Daily Republic*, March 16, 1849 (second and third quotations).

30. David Francis Bacon to Leonard Bacon, November 22, 1847, part 2, box 1, folder 3, Bacon Family Papers.

31. Fox, *New York City Newspapers*, 34; *New York Mercantile Union Business Directory*, 289.

32. Colt, *Science of Double Entry Book-Keeping*, 14–15.

33. "Odd Fellowship," *Tarborough (NC) Southerner*, May 7, 1868.

34. Barth, "Synthetic Misanthrope," 677; *New York Herald*, October 1, 1849.

35. P. S. Foner, *Business & Slavery*, 37–38.

36. "Annexation of Mexico," *Boston Evening Transcript*, February 1, 1848; "A New Evening Daily," *Scientific Mechanic*, January 15, 1848.

37. *Miscellaneous Documents of the House of Representatives*, 72.

38. "Colonization Again—Its Objects, Subjects and Agents," *NYDB*, July 11, 12, 15, 20, 1848, reprinted in *National Anti-Slavery Standard*, July 27, 1848; "Liberian Colonization," *North Star*, September 8, 1848; "Liberia and the Slavetrade," *North Star*, September 28, 1848; "Colonization Frauds Unmasked," *Liberator*, September 1, 1848.

39. "Cholera About," *Independent*, March 8, 1849; "Cholera at New York," *Jeffersonian Republican*, May 24, 1849; "Progress of the Cholera," *Daily Union*, June 1, 1849; *Hartford Daily Courant*, July 8, 1849.

40. "Letter from General Taylor," *Niles' Weekly Register* 71 (January 30, 1847): 342–43.

41. Myra Clark Gaines to David Francis Bacon, March 3, 1844, and November 22, 1848, Gen Mss Misc., Group 1841, folder F-1, YU; David Francis Bacon to Leonard Bacon, November 26, 1846, part 2, box 1, folder 3, Bacon Family Papers; Edmund Pendleton Gaines to David Francis Bacon, February 26, 1849, Gen Mss Misc., Group 1840, folder F-1, YU.

42. *New York Express*, January 22, 1847; "Letter from General Taylor," *Niles' Weekly Register* 71 (January 30, 1847): 342–43; "Gen. Taylor's Letter," *Weekly Arkansas Gazette*, February 13, 1847. On Bacon's involvement, see "The Letter of General Taylor," *New York Evening Post*, February 12, 1847; see also "Explanation Concerning Gen. Taylor's Letter," *Knoxville Register*, March 10, 1847.

43. "The Taylor Letter to Gaines," *NYDB*, reprinted in *North American and United States Gazette*, February 11, 1848.

44. "Gen. Taylor's Gaines Letter—The Suppressed Passages," *Washington (AR) Telegraph*, March 1, 1848 (first quotation); "Prospects of the Whigs," *Detroit Free Press*, March 1, 1848 (second quotation).

45. David Francis Bacon to Leonard Bacon, November 7, 1848, part 2, box 1, folder 3, Bacon Family Papers.

46. David Francis Bacon to Leonard Bacon, November 10, 1848, part 2, box 1, folder 3, Bacon Family Papers.

47. David Francis Bacon to Leonard Bacon, August 15, 1849, part 2, box 1, folder 3, Bacon Family Papers.

48. W. E. Haskins to Leonard Bacon, October 4, 1849, part 2, box 1, folder 3, Bacon Family Papers.

49. David Francis Bacon to Leonard Bacon, October 6, 1849, part 2, box 1, folder 3, Bacon Family Papers.

50. David Francis Bacon to Leonard Bacon, November 10, 1848, part 2, box 1, folder 3, Bacon Family Papers.

51. On the Tappans, see Wyatt-Brown, *Lewis Tappan*.

52. "Letter from John Brown, the Ferryman, to the N.Y. Evening Post," *Liberator*, January 24, 1851.

53. "Obituary. Nathaniel R. Stimson," *NYDB*, December 4, 1857.

54. *New York Spectator*, May 18, 1840.

55. *New York Evening Post*, December 30, 1842.

56. *New York Evening Post*, March 21, 1845.

57. *Doggett's New York City Directory, 1848–1849*, 389.

58. "Correspondence of the Crescent," *New Orleans Crescent*, August 10, 1849; *Doggett's New York City Directory, for 1849–1850*, 402.

59. "Libel," *Sun*, August 27, 1849; "Counter Libels," *Sun*, October 29, 1849.

60. "The Day Book Closed," *Pittsburgh Daily Post*, October 29, 1849; David Francis Bacon to Leonard Bacon, April 22, 1850, part 2, box 1, folder 3, Bacon Family Papers.

61. See Stimson's 1851 prospectus, which uses *New York Day Book*, in "Programme for 1851," *Literary World*, December 28, 1850, 535.

62. 1850 Manuscript Census, Queens County, NY, US Federal Census Collection, Ancestry.com.

63. 1850 Manufacturing Manuscript Census, New York County, NY, US Federal Census Collection, Ancestry.com.

Chapter 7

1. Henry Clay to G. G. Foster, April 2, 1850, in Hay and Reardon, *Papers of Henry Clay*, 693–94; "Life's Compromise," *New York Merchant's Day Book*, reprinted in *Weekly Raleigh Register and North Carolina Gazette*, May 1, 1850.

2. "Whig Prospects," *Cincinnati Enquirer*, October 31, 1851; "Harmony of the Whig Party," *Buffalo Courier*, October 10, 1853; *Miscellaneous Documents of the House of Representatives*, 83.

3. Holt, *Rise and Fall*, 635–764; Warner, "Silver Grays."

4. *Congressional Globe*, 31 Cong., 1 Sess., app. 265 (March 11, 1850) (quotation); Warner, "Silver Grays," 77–103.

5. *NYDB*, January 19, 1852.

6. "To Advertisers," *NYDB*, March 3, 1856.

7. "To Business Men," *NYDB*, February 3, 1859.

8. *NYDB*, February 29, 1860, and November 12, 1857.

9. "The Evening Day-Book," *NYDB*, September 1, 1859.

10. *Minutes of the Proceedings of a Convention*, 8, 10, 17, 22, 28. See also *Proceedings of the Fourth Convention of Merchants*; "A Scheme for Rebuilding Southern Commerce," *Southern Literary Messenger* 5 (January 1839): 2–12; Russel, *Economic Aspects*, 15–32; R. V. Watson, *Grand Emporium*.

11. "Direct Trade of Southern States with Europe," *De Bow's Review* 3 (June 1847): 557–59; "Direct Trade of Southern States with Europe. No. II," *De Bow's Review* 4 (October 1847): 208–26; "Direct Trade of Southern States with Europe. No. III," *De Bow's Review* 4 (November 1847): 337–56; "Direct Trade of Southern States with Europe. No. IV," *De Bow's Review* 4 (December 1847): 493–502.

12. *Congressional Globe*, 31 Cong., 2 Sess., 396 (January 31, 1851) (quotation); Russel, *Economic Aspects*, 93–122; Gardner, "Winning the Lower South," 199, 263–64, 338–39.

13. "The Moral, Religious, Philosophical and Abolition Anniversaries for 1850," *New York Herald*, April 30, 1850.

14. P. S. Foner, *Business & Slavery*, 55–87; Beckert, *Monied Metropolis*, 20.

15. Beckert, *Monied Metropolis*, 23, 26, 46–97; Spann, *New Metropolis*, 281–83, 402–3.

16. "New York Merchants and the South—Their Relation to Each Other, and Their Duty to the Union," *New York Merchant's Day Book*, October 15, 1850.

17. "Meanness Unexampled," *National Era*, October 31, 1850; "Sneers Will Not Answer," *Daily Ohio State Journal*, April 15, 1851.

18. *National Era*, April 10, 1851.

19. "Southern Patronage," *National Anti-Slavery Standard*, August 9, 1856.

20. "Base Fraud," *New York Courier and Enquirer*, reprinted in *National Anti-Slavery Standard*, February 13, 1851 (emphasis in original).

21. "New York Day Book and the Silk Merchants," *Daily Missouri Republican*, November 25, 1850; "New York Abolition Merchants. A Card," *Vicksburg Tri-Weekly Sentinel*, December 21, 1850.

22. *Camden (AL) Phoenix*, January 28, 1851.

23. "The New York Southern Paper," *South Carolinian*, reprinted in *Camden (SC) Weekly Journal*, January 10, 1851; "New York Day Book," *Wilmington (NC) Journal*, January 3, 1851; *Eastern Carolina Republican*, January 29, 1851; "The Lowest Deep of Dough-Faceism," *Brandon (VT) Post*, February 20, 1851.

24. *Camden (AL) Phoenix*, February 4, 1851; *Southern Shield*, February 8, 1851; "A Lesson for Abolitionists," *Semi-Weekly Standard*, February 12, 1851; "Negro Slavery," *De Bow's Review* 10 (March 1851): 325–26.

25. "New York Day Book," *Savannah Republican*, January 16, 1851.

26. "New York Day Book," *Wilmington (NC) Journal*, January 3, 1851.

27. "New York," *Waverly Magazine*, September 27, 1851.

28. N. R. Stimson to Millard Fillmore, November 7, 1850, reel 22, Millard Fillmore Papers, Buffalo and Erie County Historical Society.

29. "A Touching Appeal," *New York Times*, October 15, 1851.

30. W. H. Grinnell et al. to Daniel Webster, September 24, 1852, in Van Tyne, *Letters of Daniel Webster*, 538 (quotation); Charles L. Vose and Others to Mr. Webster, March 28, 1850, in Webster, *Private Correspondence*, 2:361; William M. Richards and Others to Mr. Webster, February 14, 1851, in Webster, *Private Correspondence*, 2:419; Remini, *Daniel Webster*, 662–81, 683, 695, 707–8, 726–55.

31. "Daniel Webster," *NYDB*, January 19, 1852; "The New-York Unionist" and "Daniel Webster for President," *NYDB*, February 20, 1852; "Public Meeting," *New York Times*, March 5, 1852.

32. "Mr. Webster and the Union Men," *NYDB*, March 10, 1852.

33. "Doings of the National Convention," *NYDB*, June 18, 1852; "Union of the Whig Party," *NYDB*, June 21, 1852; "Great Abolition Victory," *NYDB*, June 29, 1852.

34. *NYDB*, July 14, 1852; "Presidential Candidates," *NYDB*, October 1, 1852; "Who Shall We Vote For?" *NYDB*, October 26, 1852.

35. "The Opinion of the Press on the Results of the Election," *National Era*, November 11, 1852 (quotation); Beckert, *Monied Metropolis*, 87; P. S. Foner, *Business & Slavery*, 81–87.

36. "Parties in the Future," *National Era*, December 2, 1852.

37. "Harmony of the Whig Party," *Buffalo Courier*, October 10, 1853; *Daily Alabama Journal*, August 31, 1853; Edward Everett to N. R. Stimson, March 2, 1853, Rushmore G. Horton Papers, NYPL.

38. "Announcements," *Norton's Literary Gazette and Publishers' Circular*, new series, vol. 1 (July 15, 1854): 365. On Horton's Whig background, see the entry for August 22, 1844, R. G. Horton Diary, Rushmore G. Horton Papers, NYPL; "Assembly Dist. No. 1 Whig Convention," *Poughkeepsie Journal*, October 25, 1851; "Public Meeting," *New York Times*, March 5, 1852; "Whig Convention," *Poughkeepsie Journal*, May 1, 1852.

39. "The American Party," *NYDB*, August 8, 1853.

40. Ware, *Industrial Worker*, 55–61, 56 (first quotation), 230 (second quotation); Stevens, *New York Typographical Union*, 201–45.

41. Stevens, *New York Typographical Union*, 246–47; *New York Tribune*, April 12, 1853.

42. Advertisement in *New York Herald*, April 13, 1853 (first quotation); "Type Setting," *Una* 1 (August 1, 1853): 14 (second quotation); Stevens, *New York Typographical Union*, 229, 245.

43. "Type Setting," *Una* 1 (August 1, 1853): 14.

44. *Una* 1 (August 20, 1853): 15.

45. "New Era in Type Setting," *New York Democrat and Star*, reprinted in *Staunton (VA) Spectator*, April 20, 1853.

46. "Type-Setting and Women's Rights," *Brooklyn Daily Eagle*, September 2, 1853.

47. *Ohio Observer*, May 11, 1853.

48. "Job Printing Done by Girls," *New York Herald*, September 14, 1853; "Printing School for Girls," *North American and United States Gazette*, November 16, 1853; "Women as Type-Setters," *Life Illustrated*, October 3, 1857.

49. "The Day Book—The Pathfinder—and Douglass," *North Star*, June 17, 1853.

50. Blight, *Frederick Douglass*, 253–54, 772n22; W., "Notes by the Way," *Frederick Douglass' Paper*, April 28, 1854.

51. Douglass, *Claims of the Negro*, 15.

52. "Negroes and Negro Slavery," *NYDB*, reprinted in *Tri-Weekly Messenger*, September 1, 1855.

53. "Is the Negro a White Man?—Dr. Van Evrie and the New York Day-Book," *Frederick Douglass' Paper*, September 14, 1855.

54. "The New York Day Book—Its Politics, and Its Bad Grammar," *Frederick Douglass' Paper*, September 21, 1855.

55. "A Pro-Slavery Groan," *Frederick Douglass' Paper*, October 5, 1855.

56. *Frederick Douglass' Paper*, November 30, 1855.

57. *Macon (GA) Weekly Telegraph*, August 5, 1856.

58. Frederick Douglas, "A Nation in the Midst of a Nation," in McKivigan, Husband, and Kaufman, *Speeches of Frederick Douglass*, 103.

59. George G. Foster to Thurlow Weed, August 27, 1852, drawer 4, file 37, Thurlow Weed Papers, UR.

60. "David A. Wright," in Tuttle, *Biographies*, 159; "The New York Day Book," *Daily Union*, January 15, 1854.

61. "John Van Buren, General Pierce, and the New York Press," *New York Herald*, March 20, 1854.

62. L. Ray Gunn, "Antebellum Society and Politics (1825–1860)," in Klein, *Empire State*, 401–2, 405.

63. Herman J. Redfield to William L. Marcy, February 27, 1854, box 48, William L. Marcy Papers, LC.

64. "The Day Book," *Daily South Carolinian*, July 31, 1854; "Telegraphic Despatches," *Atlas*, September 15, 1854; "Correspondence of the Baltimore Sun," *Sun*, September 15, 1854.

65. William L. Marcy to the Proprietors of the "Day Book," November 27, 1854, and January 11, 12, 1855, Domestic Letters of the Department of State, 1784–1906, RG 59, NARA (M40–41); William L. Marcy to the Proprietors of the "Day Book," April 24, November 16, 1855, and W. Hunter to the Proprietors of the "Day Book," July 5, 11, 1855, Domestic Letters of the Department of State, 1784–1906, RG 59 (M40–42); J. A. Thomas to the Proprietors of the "Day Book," December 31, 1855, and January 16, May 6, 13, June 12, July 15, 1856, Domestic Letters of the Department of State, 1784–1906, RG 59 (M40–43); A. J. Thomas to the Proprietors of the "Day Book," November 4, December 13, 1856, Domestic Letters of the Department of State, 1784–1906, RG 59 (M40–44).

66. A. H. Bowman to the Publishers of the "Day Book," September 14, 1855, Records of the Public Buildings Service, 1801–2000, Series: Letters Sent, 1/1858–1/1930, Vol. 1, 301–401, Letters 142–19, RG 121, NARA. The US Post Office may also have supported Stimson after a New York Custom House official introduced him to Postmaster General James Campbell. Joseph C. Broadhead to James Campbell, February 17, 1855, Rushmore G. Horton Papers, NYPL.

67. *Daily South Carolinian*, October 24, 1854.

68. Barrett, *Old Merchants*, 5:190–98; "'Merchants' Telegraph' Newspaper," *New York Evening Post*, January 15, 1828; *Long-Island Star*, September 15, 1830; "Great Meeting at Tammany Hall," *New York Evening Post*, February 1, 1832; *Vermont Patriot and State Gazette*, October 28, 1833; "Quick Work," *Tennessean*, April 7, 1838; *Hartford Daily Courant*, February 26, 1839; *New York Evening Post*, September 1, 1840; *Buffalo Daily Gazette*, December 20, 1843; *Times-Picayune*, March 25, 1850; "Great Democratic Gathering at Newburg, New York," *York (PA) Gazette*, August 10, 1852; "Democratic State Convention," *Buffalo Daily Republic*, October 3, 1853.

69. "Democratic Union Convention," *New York Tribune*, December 18, 1854.

70. "Onerous Official Duties," (Washington) *Daily Intelligencer*, December 14, 1854.

71. "A Note from John Van Buren on the Election," *New York Times*, November 20, 1855.

72. Rafuse, *McClellan's War*, 3, 5, 8–66, 72 (quotation).

73. "Negro Slavery the Basis of Democratic Institutions, or Negro Subordination Essential to White Equality," *NYDB*, May 5, 1856.

Chapter 8

1. "Obituary. Nathaniel R. Stimson," *NYDB*, December 4, 1857.

2. "A Negro Not a White Man," *NYDB*, August 25, 1855.

3. "To the Readers of the New York Day Book," *NYDB*, September 15, 1855.

4. "Light Breaking In," *NYDB*, September 29, 1855; "Is (Negro) Slavery a State or a National Institution?" *NYDB*, October 13, 1855.

5. "The Great Issue," *NYDB*, June 13, 1856.

6. "Negro Slavery a 'Disgrace to the Nation,'" *NYDB*, January 22, 1856; "Human Races," *NYDB*, March 3, 1856; "The Duty of the North," *NYDB*, March 12, 1856; "Fifty Years of Abolition," *NYDB*, April 9, 1856; "Inferiority Not Degradation," *NYDB*, May 7, 1856; "The Unity of Mankind," *NYDB*, October 8, 1856; "The Principle of Slavery," *NYDB*, October 20, 1856; "A Plan for Exploding Delusion," *NYDB*, November 19, 1856; "The Facts in Issue," *NYDB*, September 28, 1856; "Human Liberty," *NYDB*, January 7, 1857; "Can a Negro Be a Citizen?" *NYDB*, March 28, 1857; "Abolition Moonshine—'Free' Labor in Virginia," *NYDB*, April 4, 1857; "Negro Freedom," *NYDB*, June 3, 1857; "The Progress of Truth," *NYDB*, June 13, 1857; "Negro Subordination," *NYDB*, November 11, 1857.

7. "The Great Issue," *NYDB*, March 20, 1856; "The Warfare on Democracy," *NYDB*, March 28, 1856; "Garrison and Seward—Abolitionism and Freesoilism," NYDB, April 21, 1856; "Negro Slavery the Basis of Democratic Institutions, or Negro Subordination Essential to White Equality," *NYDB*, May 5, 1856; "The Real Danger of the 'Slavery' Question," *NYDB*, May 28, 1856; "A Common Ground," *NYDB*, June 5, 1856; "The 'Friends of Freedom,'" *NYDB*, June 7, 1856; "The Northern Democracy," *NYDB*, June 20, 1856; "Sham Democracy," *NYDB*, October 15, 1856; "Working Men and 'Slave' Labor," *NYDB*, October 29, 1856; "Friends of the South," *NYDB*, February 2, 1857; "Democracy and 'Slavery'—What Are Their Relations?" *NYDB*, June 20, 1857; "Democracy and 'Slavery,'" *NYDB*, October 7, 1857; "Southern Statesmanship," *NYDB*, October 10, 1857.

8. "The Warfare on Democracy," *NYDB*, March 28, 1856; "The Warfare on the 'African Slave Trade,'" *NYDB*, April 5, 1856; "The Origin of the British Anti-Slavery Policy," *NYDB*,

April 7, 1856; "Slavery Extension," *NYDB*, April 14, 1856; "'Slavery Extension' Again," *NYDB*, April 23, 1856; "Aristocracy and Democracy—British Policy," *NYDB*, January 3, 1857; "Abolitionism an Ally of Monarchism," *NYDB*, January 17, 1857; "Monarchy vs. Democracy," *NYDB*, February 11, 1857; "Hypocrisy and Inhumanity of Abolitionism," *NYDB*, April 25, 1857.

9. Howard C. Perkins, "Description of the Subject," enclosed in Perkins to David Potter, May 20, 1944, box 6, folder 1, David Morris Potter Papers, SU.

10. "The Cincinnati 'Slave' Case," *NYDB*, March 5, 1856.

11. *NYDB*, October 11, 1856.

12. "Dr. Van Evrie's Pamphlet," *NYDB*, January 24, 1856.

13. Kielbowicz, *News in the Mail*, 109; Pred, *Urban Growth*, 139–42.

14. Samuel A. Cartwright, "Natural History of the Prognathous Species of Mankind," *NYDB*, November 10, 11, 1857.

15. "Ethnology(!)," *Liberator*, July 9, 1858; "The Sphere of Woman," *Daily Gate City*, May 29, 1858.

16. "The 'Slavery' Question," *NYDB*, March 23, 1857; J. S. McFarlane, "Suggestive Thoughts of Negro Slavery, and Kindred Subjects," *NYDB*, November 17, 18, 1857.

17. Miner, *Seeding Civil War*; Lundberg, *Horace Greeley*, 79–112.

18. "Correspondence of the Day Book," *NYDB*, April 2, 1856.

19. "The Ravages of Lane's Marauders—The History of Their Outrages," *NYDB*, October 28, 1856.

20. "Letters from the People," *NYDB*, January 21, 1857; Buford, *Genealogy*, 335–39; Fleming, "Buford Expedition"; "Negro Slavery the Basis of Democratic Institutions, or Negro Subordination Essential to White Equality," *NYDB*, May 5, 1856; "To the People of the South," *Richmond Enquirer*, August 1, 1856.

21. Woods, "Indignation of Freedom-Loving People."

22. "The Outrage," *NYDB*, May 24, 1856.

23. "Cowardice at a Premium," *NYDB*, July 14, 1856; "An Unparalleled Outrage," *NYDB*, July 15, 1856.

24. P. S. Brooks to Editor of Day Book, June 2, [1856], Rushmore G. Horton Papers, NYPL.

25. McCardell, *Idea of a Southern Nation*; P. Quigley, *Shifting Grounds*, 53–56.

26. George Fitzhugh, "Southern Thought," *De Bow's Review* 23 (October 1857): 339, 347.

27. Fitzhugh, *Sociology for the South*.

28. "What Is Free Society?" *NYDB*, March 4, 1857.

29. "The Names," *NYDB*, October 2, 1856.

30. "Southern and Western Trade Convention," *NYDB*, December 21, 1852.

31. *NYDB*, August 28, 1856; "Abolition and Anti-Abolition Merchants," *NYDB*, April 11, 1857.

32. "Abolition Merchants and the Day Book," *NYDB*, March 2, 1857.

33. "Then and Now," *NYDB*, April 2, 1852. See also "The Abolitionists—Their Position, Triumphs, and Boasts," *NYDB*, August 14, 1852.

34. "New York Merchants and the 'Slavery' Question," *NYDB*, December 11, 1857.

35. "Direct Trade—The Future of New Orleans," *NYDB*, January 5, 1857.

36. "Direct Trade—Where Is the Natural Market of the South?" *NYDB*, September 25, 1858.

37. Stimson endorsed Pierce in "The Renomination of Franklin Pierce," *NYDB*, April 10, 1856. But he hoisted Buchanan's name to the *Day Book* masthead on June 7, the day after the Democratic convention ended.

38. "The Great Issue," *NYDB*, June 13, 1856.

39. Horton, *Life and Public Services*, 427–28.

40. R. G. Horton to John C. Breckinridge, October 6, 1856, box 188, Breckinridge Family Papers, LC; John C. Breckinridge to R. G. Horton, November 9, 1856, Rushmore G. Horton Papers, NYPL; Isaac Toucey to R. G. Horton, April 10, 1857, Horton Papers, NYPL.

41. "Campaign Documents," *NYDB*, September 10, 1856.

42. "The Reaction in Ohio," *NYDB*, October 11, 1856. See also Jacob W. Elseffer to John A. Quitman, February 20, 1856, box 5a, folder 4a; F. R. Witter to John A. Quitman, March 5, 1856; Thomas S. Harney to John A. Quitman, March 7, 1856; Isaac R. Wade to John A. Quitman, March 9, 1856, box 5a, folder 5, Quitman (John A.) and Family Papers, Mississippi Department of Archives and History, Jackson, MS.

43. "The Modern Democracy," *Chicago Tribune*, December 28, 1855; "Two Good Papers," *Chicago Tribune*, April 4, 1856; "Significant," *Poughkeepsie Journal*, April 12, 1856; "Democracy and Slavery," *Hartford Daily Courant*, April 24, 1856; "Endorsement," *Atlas*, June 7, 1856; "'Democratic' Principles," *National Era*, August 7, 1856; "The Democratic Idea of Free Discussion," *Anti-Slavery Bugle*, August 16, 1856; "An Honest Buchanan Organ," *Bangor (ME) Daily Whig and Courier*, September 27, 1856; "Buchanan Democracy," *Liberator*, October 17, 1856; "A Professedly Democratic Print," *Detroit Free Press*, December 25, 1856.

44. "White Men to Be Made Slaves," *Kennebec Journal*, August 8, 1856; "Will You Think of It, People of Wisconsin?" *Milwaukee Daily Sentinel*, September 17, 1856; "The New 'Democratic' Doctrine," *Wisconsin Tribune*, September 23, 1856; "Facts for the People," *Buffalo Daily Republic*, October 11, 1856; "Position of the Douglas-Buchanan Party," *Central Transcript*, October 17, 1856; "The New 'Democratic' Doctrine," *Wyandot Pioneer*, October 23, 1856; "Slavery Extension Avowed!" *Orleans Independent Standard*, October 24, 1856. The editorial reached the British press in "A Modest Proposal," *Manchester Weekly Times and Examiner*, November 1, 1856. Emphasis in original.

45. Young Men's Fremont and Dayton Central Union, *New "Democratic" Doctrine*, 3; "Report of the Committee on Kansas Affairs and Slavery [1857]," in *Resolves of the State of Maine*, 53; *Kansas Struggle of 1856*, 9; *Journal of the Senate of Indiana*, 475; *Proofs for Workingmen*, 6.

46. "Speech of Mr. Downs, of Louisiana," *Daily Union*, February 24, 1850.

47. "The Day Book's Platform—Extension of Slavery—What Is Meant," *NYDB*, September 6, 1856.

48. "Working Men and 'Slave' Labor," *NYDB*, October 29, 1856.

49. "A Plan for Exploding Delusion," *NYDB*, November 19, 1856.

50. "Democratic Newspapers and Our Position," *NYDB*, December 19, 1857.

51. "Census of 1855," *New York Herald*, July 7, 1855; "The Democratic Press in New York," *Memphis Daily Appeal*, August 2, 1856.

52. "The Dred Scott Case," *NYDB*, March 7, 1857; "Can a Negro Be a Citizen?" *NYDB*, March 28, 1857 (quotations); "Can a Negro Be a Citizen?" *NYDB*, May 28, 1857; "The Dred Scott Case," *NYDB*, June 12, 1857. Emphasis in original.

53. *Dred Scott Decision* (1860), iii.

54. "The South—Southern Trade and Southern Payments—Another Appeal," *NYDB*, October 3, 1857.

55. *NYDB*, August 1, 1857.

56. Sweeney, *Lottery Wars*, 22–47; Bolster, "Georgia Plays the Numbers," 95–96.

57. "How Easy an Editor Can Put Himself into a Scrape Without Knowing It," *NYDB*, October 12, 1857.

58. "More Lotteries," *NYDB*, October 19, 1857; "Our Efficient District Attorney and the Gamblers," *NYDB*, October 20, 1857; "Where Was Our Efficient District Attorney?" *NYDB*, November 16, 1857.

59. Rubbinaccio, *Abraham Oakey Hall*, 58–62.

Chapter 9

1. "Sudden Death of N. R. Stimson," *New York Express*, December 1, 1857.

2. "Obituary. Nathaniel R. Stimson," *NYDB*, December 4, 1857; *National Era*, December 10, 1857.

3. J. H. Van Evrie to Jefferson Davis, March 12, 1861, reel 23, Confederate States of America Records, LC.

4. *Sun*, December 19, 1857.

5. New York Wills and Probate Records, 1659–1999, Letters of Administration (Kings County, NY), vol. 9–10, 251, Ancestry.com.

6. Letter no. XIV, December 2, 1857, in [Fuller,] *Belle Brittan*, 266.

7. "Money Value of New York Journals," *Weekly Indiana State Sentinel*, September 20, 1855. The *Herald* was valued at $500,000.

8. *Cincinnati Enquirer*, January 31, 1858.

9. "The Day Book—Its Editors—The Past and the Future," *NYDB*, December 16, 1857.

10. A. C. S. to Messrs. Van Evrie, Horton & Co, December 17, 1857, printed in "Democratic Newspapers and Our Position," *NYDB*, December 19, 1857.

11. "Democratic Newspapers and Our Position," *NYDB*, December 19, 1857.

12. "Government Patronage—The New York Day Book," *NYDB*, December 21, 1857.

13. "Sectional Equilibrium an Absurdity and Sectional Compromising Immoral," *NYDB*, January 16, 1858; "The 'Southern Oligarchy,'" *NYDB*, January 16, 1858; "The Niobe of Nations," *NYDB*, February 13, 1858; "'Slavery' and 'Freedom,'" *NYDB*, March 20, 1858; "Revival of Britishism in America—The Atlantic Telegraph," *NYDB*, August 28, 1858; "Negro 'Slavery' the Corner Stone of Our Republican Edifice," *NYDB*, September 11, 1858; "British Influence in the United States," *NYDB*, February 7, 1859; "Would Democracy Be Possible Without 'Slavery'?" *NYDB*, August 31, 1859.

14. "Advertising and New York Merchants," *NYDB*, March 6, 1858; "The Merchants of New York and the Safety of the Union," *NYDB*, June 16, 1858; "The 'Tribune Mercantile Advertiser,'" *NYDB*, August 23, 1858; "Direct Trade—Where Is the Natural Market of the South?" *NYDB*, September 25, 1858; "The Express on Commerce," *NYDB*, March 4, 1859; "What Supports the North?" *NYDB*, March 16, 1859; "Is the North Interested in 'Slavery'?" *NYDB*, March 29, 1859.

15. "Color," *NYDB*, December 14, 1858; "Hair," *NYDB*, March 3, 1859; "External Form," *NYDB*, April 12, 1859; "Brain," *NYDB*, August 12, 1859.

16. Edmund Ruffin, "Slavery and Free Labor Defined and Compared," *NYDB*, August 16, 29, 30, and September 3, 5, 12, 20, 28, 1859.

17. "A Great Doctor," *NYDB*, April 5, 1858 (first quotation); "The Downfall of Squatter Sovereignty—Political Combinations for 1860," *NYDB*, April 24, 1858; "Political Fallacies—Is Mr. Douglas a Statesman or Only a Demagogue?" *NYDB*, July 7, 1858 (second quotation); "Judge Douglas and the President," *NYDB*, September 21, 1858; "Popular Sovereignty," *NYDB*, December 7, 1858; "The Debate on Squatter Sovereignty," *NYDB*, March 7, 1859; "Senator Douglas's Hobby-Horse," *NYDB*, March 15, 1859; "Squatter Sovereignty," *NYDB*, September 13, 1859; "Douglasism," *NYDB*, September 20, 1859.

18. J. H. Van Evrie to Jefferson Davis, June 7, 1858, in Rowland, *Jefferson Davis*, 3:263–64.

19. "Democracy and 'Slavery,'" *NYDB*, May 22, 1858.

20. "The Newspaper Press of New York—The Day-Book," *Plantation* 2 (December 1860): 135, 136.

21. "Business Announcement," *NYDB*, June 1, 1858.

22. "Newspaper Press of New York," 135.

23. Olney, *Genealogy*, 75–76; "George W. Olney," *Weekly Underwriter* 94 (June 24, 1916): 729–30; 1850 Manuscript Census; 1850 Slave Schedules, St. Michael's and St. Philip's Parish, SC, US Federal Census Collection, Ancestry.com; George W. Olney Jr. passport application in US Passport Applications, 1867–73, roll 179, Ancestry.com; "Passengers," *Atlas*, October 25, 1855; "Personal Intelligence," *New York Herald*, July 9, 1856.

24. "Newspaper Press of New York," 135.

25. "Removal of the Day Book Office," *NYDB*, April 22, 1858; "Removal of the Day Book—The Future—Enlargement of the Daily," *NYDB*, May 1, 1858; "The Anniversary of Our Enlargement," *NYDB*, June 1, 1859; Gideon J. Tucker to Van Evrie & Horton, February 10, 1858, Rushmore G. Horton Papers, NYPL.

26. "The Evening Day-Book," *NYDB*, September 2, 1859; "Removal—Progress," *NYDB*, May 14, 1860.

27. "Increase of Circulation and Business of the Evening Day-Book," *NYDB*, February 13, 1860.

28. "Removal—Progress," *NYDB*, May 14, 1860.

29. "Correspondence of the Courier," *Charleston Courier*, January 17, 1860.

30. "Removal of the Day Book—The Future—Enlargement of the Daily," *NYDB*, May 1, 1858.

31. "Enlargement of the Evening Day Book," *NYDB*, August 16, 1858.

32. "The Evening Day-Book," *NYDB*, September 2, 1859 (emphasis in original).

33. "Enlargement of the Evening Day Book," *NYDB*, August 16, 1858.

34. "The Anniversary of Our Enlargement," *NYDB*, June 1, 1859; "The Evening Day-Book," *NYDB*, September 2, 1859; "Subscriptions to Weekly Day-Book," *NYDB*, December 24, 1859.

35. "Removal—Progress," *NYDB*, May 14, 1860.

36. "Letters from the People," *NYDB*, August 11, 1858.

37. McGovern, *John Mitchel*; "Is John Mitchel an American?" *NYDB*, July 14, 1859; "Business Notice," *NYDB*, August 2, 1859; "The Southern Citizen," *NYDB*, August 9, 1859 (quotation).

38. Van Evrie, Horton & Olney to J. H. Hammond, May 5, 1859, box 26, James H. Hammond Papers, LC. See also J. H. Van Evrie to Jefferson Davis, June 7, 1858, in Rowland, *Jefferson Davis*, 3:264.

39. Kielbowicz, *News in the Mail*, 100–101; Leonard, *News for All*, 50–51.

40. "TO YOU," *NYDB*, May 12, 1855; "The Weekly Day Book," *NYDB*, June 9, 1855; "The Day Book in Texas," *NYDB*, July 14, 1855 (quotation); "To Democrats, and White Men in General," *NYDB*, September 15, 1855; "The Weekly Day Book," *NYDB*, November 3, 1855; "The Prize," *NYDB*, November 10, 1855; "To Non-Subscribers," *NYDB*, November 24, 1855.

41. "Census of 1855," *New York Herald*, July 7, 1855; "The Democratic Press in New York," *Memphis Daily Appeal*, August 2, 1856.

42. "A Liberal Offer," *NYDB*, January 9, 1858; "Prospectus of the Weekly Day Book for 1858," *NYDB*, January 23, 1858; "Enlargement of the Evening Day Book," *NYDB*, August 16, 1858.

43. "Removal—Progress," *NYDB*, May 14, 1860.

44. "Letters from the People," *NYDB*, November 2, 1859; C. W. Jacobs Diary, Ms 802, Maryland Center for History and Culture; Jacobs, *Speech*; 1860 Manuscript Census, Worcester County, MD, US Federal Census Collection, Ancestry.com.

45. "Letters from the People," *NYDB*, January 23, 1858; 1860 Slave Schedules, Spalding County, GA, US Federal Census Collection, Ancestry.com.

46. "Letter to Editors of New York Day Book," *NYDB*, January 26, 1859.

47. Etcheson, *Emerging Midwest*.

48. "The Right Spirit," *NYDB*, July 28, 1855; *Early History of Michigan*, 566; "Letters from the People," *NYDB*, January 12, 1860; Merrill, *History of Androscoggin County*, 304, 771.

49. "Letters from the People," *NYDB*, January 12, 1860.

50. "Fallacies of the Protectionists—The Home Market Argument," *NYDB*, October 14, 1859; "New York Merchants and the 'Slavery' Question," *NYDB*, December 11, 1857; Porter and Livesay, *Merchants and Manufacturers*, 2–3, 7–12, 13–36.

51. Porter and Livesay, *Merchants and Manufacturers*, 13–36; Freehling, *Road to Disunion, Volume 1*, 41–42; Henkin, *Postal Age*.

52. A. Denny to W. Stump Forwood, June 13, 1858, box 1, folder 15, W. Stump Forwood Papers, UNC.

53. Cockrell and Ballard, *Chickasaw*, 11–12.

54. "The Second Rebellion," *Daily Cleveland Herald*, August 19, 1861.

55. "Letters from the People," *NYDB*, May 26, 1858 (quotation); "Letters from the People," *NYDB*, October 6, 1858.

56. *Portrait and Biographical Record of Lafayette and Saline Counties*, 445–46; 1860 Manuscript Census; 1860 Slave Schedules, Saline County, MO, US Federal Census Collection, Ancestry.com.

57. Napton, *Past and Present*, 895; 1860 Manuscript Census; 1860 Slave Schedules, Saline County, MO, US Federal Census Collection, Ancestry.com.

Chapter 10

1. D. Brown, *Southern Outcast*.

2. D. Brown, *Southern Outcast*, 124–51.

3. [De Bow,] *Interest in Slavery*; "Speech of Jefferson Davis Before the Mississippi Legislature, November 16, 1858," in Rowland, *Jefferson Davis*, 3:357.

4. "The Libeler of His Country," *NYDB*, April 15, 1858.

5. "What the Abolitionists Are Doing," *NYDB*, June 7, 1859.

6. "Non-Slaveholders in the South," *NYDB*, March 3, 1860.

7. "Cheated out of a Row," *Liberator*, January 18, 1861 (quotations); "Helper Again Stopped," *NYDB*, January 15, 1861.

8. "Negroes and Negro Slavery," *Daily Picayune*, February 10, 1861.

9. "Light Shining out of Darkness. Letter from Hinton Rowan Helper," *National Anti-Slavery Standard*, September 10, 1859.

10. Huston, *Panic of 1857*, 111–260.

11. "Hon J. R. Giddings' Address to the People of the 20th Congressional District of Ohio," *Vermont Watchman and State Journal*, July 9, 1858.

12. *Congressional Globe*, 35 Cong., 1 Sess., app. 68–71 (March 4, 1858).

13. "The Ground Tier Moved!" *Lewisburg (PA) Chronicle*, August 20, 1858; *Bangor Whig*, reprinted in *Randolph County Journal*, August 19, 1858.

14. Quoted in G. R. Taylor, "Wholesale Commodity Prices," 866.

15. "Free Trade—Mistake of New York Merchants," *NYDB*, August 6, 1858; "Fallacies of the Protectionists—The Home Market Argument," *NYDB*, October 14, 1859.

16. "New York a Southern City," *NYDB*, September 1, 1859.

17. "Southern Products and Southern Commerce the Great Bases of Northern Prosperity," *NYDB*, September 26, 1859.

18. "The Express on Commerce," *NYDB*, March 4, 1859.

19. "The North and the South," *NYDB*, March 20, 1858; "Speech of Senator Hammond, of South Carolina," *NYDB*, March 20, 1858.

20. "The Abolition Rebellion," *NYDB*, October 19, 1859 (first and second quotations); "The Foray of N——r Thieves at Harper's Ferry," *NYDB*, October 20, 1859; "Insanity of Anti-Slaveryism," *NYDB*, October 22, 1859; "A Model Democratic Paper," *NYDB*, November 16, 1859; "Was Old Brown an Apostle of Liberty or a Traitor to His Race and a Blasphemer of the Almighty?" *NYDB*, December 3, 1859 (third quotation).

21. Stauffer and Trodd, *Tribunal*.

22. "Movement in Virginia Looking to Direct Trade," *De Bow's Review* 27 (December 1859): 713–15; "Direct Trade" and "Tennessee Legislature," *Mississippian*, February 1, 1860; "Protecting Direct Trade," *Weekly Columbus (GA) Enquirer*, March 6, 1860.

23. "Sympathy with the South," *NYDB*, November 29, 1859.

24. "Our Opposition to the Abolitionists," *NYDB*, December 3, 1859.

25. "Sympathy with the South," *NYDB*, December 5, 1859; "The Spirit in This City," *NYDB*, December 6, 1859; "The Non-Committal Call," *NYDB*, December 6, 1859 (quotation).

26. "The Weekly Day-Book. Special Edition," *NYDB*, December 7, 1859.

27. *NYDB*, December 12, 1859.

28. "'Injustice to Fred. Douglass,' Letter from Mr. Ruffin," *NYDB*, December 15, 1859.

29. "The North and the South. Justice and Fraternity," *NYDB*, December 15, 1859.

30. Bernstein, *New York City Draft Riots*.

31. "The North and the South. Justice and Fraternity," *NYDB*, December 15, 1859; 1860 Manuscript Census, US Federal Census Collection, Ancestry.com; *"Southern Trade": An Epitome of Commerce North and South*.

32. "The North and the South. Justice and Fraternity," *NYDB*, December 15, 1859; 1860 Manuscript Census, US Federal Census Collection, Ancestry.com; Beckert, *Monied Metropolis*, 19.

33. "The Great Union Meeting at the Academy of Music," *NYDB*, December 20, 1859; "The Great Meeting at the Academy of Music," *NYDB*, December 20, 1859.

34. O'Conor, *Negro Slavery Not Unjust*, 9, 10, 11 (quotations, emphasis in original). On O'Conor's background, see Nicoletti, *Secession on Trial*, 49–62.

35. "Negro 'Slavery' Not Unjust. Speech of Charles O'Conor at the Union Meeting," *NYDB*, December 21, 1859. Emphasis in original.

36. The data come from the 1860 Manuscript Census, US Federal Census Collection, Ancestry.com, and the lists printed in the *NYDB* on December 5–9, 12–17, 19–22, and 23, 1859.

37. G. G. Johnson, *Ante-Bellum North Carolina*, 469–70, 482–84.

38. The record books are in William W. Reavis Papers, DU. Unless otherwise indicated, subscriber information comes from the 1860 Manuscript Census and 1860 Slave Schedules, Granville, Warren, and Franklin Counties, NC, US Federal Census Collection, Ancestry.com.

39. *Cyclopedia of Eminent and Representative Men of the Carolinas*, 2:299 (first quotation); "Voice of Warren," *North Carolina Standard*, July 1, 1840; "Democratic Meeting in Warren," *Weekly North Carolina Standard*, March 8, 1854; "Democratic Meeting in Warren," *Semi-Weekly North Carolina Standard*, March 7, 1860; "Great Union Temperance Meeting," *Raleigh Star, and North Carolina Gazette*, September 21, 1842; advertisement for Lewis H. Kittle & Co., *Oxford (NC) Mercury*, September 27, 1844; *Spirit of the Age*, November 23, 1853; *Table of Post Offices, 1846*, 95.

40. *Day Book* subscribers were similarly affluent in other areas served by the Henderson post office. Compared to the 123 total households in Ragland, for instance, subscribers held 2.2 times more real estate and 3.1 times more personal property. Forty-six percent of all households included enslaved people, but 89 percent of *Day Book* subscribers lived in slaveholding households. In Epping Forest, subscribers held 2.5 times more real property and 2.4 times more personal property, and the slave ownership rate of 67 percent far exceeded the 25 percent neighborhood rate.

41. Stanton, *Leopard's Spots*, 112, 192–96.

42. "Lafarge House, New York," *Tri-Weekly Commercial*, December 31, 1853; "Review of the Week," *New England Farmer*, January 14, 1854; "Another Conflagration," *New York Times*, January 9, 1854.

43. *New England Farmer*, December 2, 1854; *Charleston Mercury*, June 12, 1856.

44. "The Presidential Campaign," *New York Times*, October 4, 1860; Gobright, *New-York Hand Book*, 81–82, 82 (quotations).

45. 1860 Manuscript Census, New York City, 15th Ward, District 1, US Federal Census Collection, Ancestry.com; H. Wilson, *Trow's New York City Directory, 1861*, 873.

46. *Reuben Vose's Guide*, 120.

47. "A Secret Circular Brought to Light," *New York Times*, February 10, 1860.

48. On Douglas's position, see Woods, *Arguing Until Doomsday*, 179–94.

49. *New York Tribune*, December 25, 1859.

50. *Charleston Mercury*, December 12, 1859; "North and South: Sympathy with the South," *New York Times*, December 8, 1859.

51. O'Conor, *Negro Slavery Not Unjust*, 15.

52. "The Charleston Convention," *NYDB*, April 25, 1860.

53. "The Living and the Dead at Charleston," *NYDB*, May 1, 1860 (quotations); "A Fire Eater," *NYDB*, May 25, 1860.

54. "Democracy vs. the Democratic Party," *NYDB*, June 2, 1860 (quotations); "Ultraism—The *Wilmington Journal*," *NYDB*, May 29, 1860.

55. "Bogus vs. True Democracy at Charleston," *NYDB*, April 28, 1860.

56. J. H. Van Evrie to Joseph Lane, July 3, 1860, box 3, Joseph Lane Mss, Lilly Library, Indiana University, Bloomington (emphasis in original).

57. *NYDB*, July 7, 1860.

58. "A National Disease—How Shall It Be Cured?" *NYDB*, August 18, 1860 (quotation); "Who Broke the Bargain?" *NYDB*, September 15, 1860; "Position of Mr. Douglas," *NYDB*, October 13, 1860.

59. "Will Mr. Douglas Withdraw?" *NYDB*, September 1, 1860 (quotation); "Coalition Between the Douglasites and Black Republicans in Oregon," *NYDB*, October 6, 1860; "Could Mr. Douglas Be Elected?" *NYDB*, October 27, 1860.

60. "The Maine Election—Will Mr. Douglas Withdraw?" *NYDB*, September 15, 1860; "How Can Lincoln Be Defeated?" *NYDB*, September 22, 1860; "The Douglas Men Give Up the Contest," *NYDB*, September 29, 1860; "Shall We Abandon the Democratic Party?" *NYDB*, October 13, 1860.

61. "Fusion—Is it Possible?" *NYDB*, September 8, 1860; "Fusion at an End—Close Up the Ranks," *NYDB*, September 15, 1860; "Fusion or Union?" *NYDB*, October 6, 1860; "The Last Call," *NYDB*, November 3, 1860.

62. "Campaign Documents," *NYDB*, July 14, 1860.

63. "Shame on Southern Men," *Weekly Advertiser*, June 27, 1860.

64. "New York Correspondence of the Advertiser," *Weekly Advertiser*, July 18, 1860 (quotation); "Response from the People," *Constitution*, July 7, 1860; "Organization of a New Breckinridge and Lane Organization," *New York Herald*, July 7, 1860; "Meeting of the Friends of Breckinridge and Lane," *New York Times*, July 7, 1860.

65. "Rally of the National Democracy," *New York Tribune*, July 19, 1860 (quotations); "Grand Democratic Mass Meeting," *NYDB*, July 21, 1860.

66. "Rally of the National Democracy," *New York Tribune*, July 19, 1860 (quotations); "Grand Democratic Mass Meeting," *NYDB*, July 21, 1860.

67. "The Great Democratic Mass Meeting," *NYDB*, July 21, 1860.

68. "Clubs! Clubs!! Clubs!!!" *NYDB*, July 28, 1860.

69. "Disunion," *NYDB*, November 3, 1860.

70. Spann, *Gotham at War*, 4–5; Holt, *Election of 1860*, 176.

71. "How the Union Can Be Saved," *NYDB*, December 1, 1860.

Chapter 11

1. "Mr. Lincoln's Journey to New York," *Sun*, February 20, 1861 (quotation); Spann, *Gotham at War*, 8–9.

2. Spann, *Gotham at War*, 8.

3. P. S. Foner, *Business & Slavery*, 208–12; Burrows and Wallace, *Gotham*, 866.

4. "A Financial Solon," *NYDB*, December 1, 1860 (emphasis in original).

5. "The Poor of New York," *NYDB*, January 15, 22, 25, February 9, 1861; "Suffering and Want in New York," *NYDB*, January 22, 1861.

6. "The Political Crisis in New York," *NYDB*, December 22, 1860; "Mr. O'Connor's Speech," *NYDB*, December 22, 1860.

7. P. S. Foner, *Business & Slavery*, 224–74.

8. P. S. Foner, *Business & Slavery*, 285–96; McKay, *Civil War*, 23, 36–37; Mushkat, *Fernando Wood*, 110–13.

9. "Do They Represent the North?" *NYDB*, January 19, 1861.

10. "The New Year—The Future," *NYDB*, December 29, 1860.

11. "Dr. Van Evrie's Work on 'Slavery,'" *NYDB*, December 1, 1860.

12. Van Evrie, *Negroes and Negro "Slavery"* (1861 ed.), v–vi.

13. Van Evrie, *Negroes and Negro "Slavery"* (1861 ed.), vi–vii.

14. Van Evrie, *Negroes and Negro "Slavery"* (1861 ed.), 336.

15. Robinson, *Union Indivisible.*

16. "Political Movements in the Confederate States," *New York Herald*, March 27, 1861 (emphasis in original).

17. Bean, "Anti-Jeffersonianism"; McCurry, *Confederate Reckoning*, 1–2; Hébert, *Cornerstone*, 39–46.

18. Van Evrie, *Negroes and Negro "Slavery"* (Day Book Office, 1853 ed.), 11–12, 17–18, 23–25.

19. "The Day-Book for 1861," *NYDB*, October 20, 1860 (emphasis in original).

20. Van Evrie, Horton & Co. to Alexander H. Stephens, April 3, 1861, box 16, Alexander Hamilton Stephens Papers, LC.

21. "Negro Subordination or Negro Equality—Which Shall It Be?" *NYDB*, April 8, 1861.

22. "Garrison and Seward—Which Is Most Dangerous?" *NYDB*, January 17, 1861 (quotations). See also "Is Mr. Lincoln Conservative?" *NYDB*, November 17, 1860; "What Can Lincoln Do?" *NYDB*, November 24, 1860; "What Will Mr. Lincoln Do?" *NYDB*, December 1, 1860; "A 'White N——r' in Lincoln's Cabinet," *NYDB*, January 15, 1861; "Who Will Fight for N——r Liberty or 'Impartial Freedom'?" *NYDB*, January 22, 1861; "A Free Negro Republic in the North," *NYDB*, January 26, 1861; "What Does the Republican Party Propose to Do?" *NYDB*, January 28, 1861; "The Designs of the 'Republican' Party," *NYDB*, February 16, 1861.

23. David Clopton to William Burton, January 1, 1861, in W. R. Smith, *History and Debates*, 437–43; "Thomas R. R. Cobb's Secessionist Speech, Monday Evening, November 12," in Freehling and Simpson, *Secession Debated*, 19–26; "What Should Georgia Do?" *Daily Constitutionalist*, November 16, 1860.

24. Contrast Crofts, *Lincoln and the Politics of Slavery*, with Oakes, *Scorpion's Sting.*

25. A. Denny to W. Stump Forwood, April 4, 1861, box 1, folder 20, W. Stump Forwood Papers, UNC (emphasis in original).

26. "Is There a Northern Democracy?" *NYDB*, January 23, 1861.

27. Beckert, *Monied Metropolis*, 111–15; Burrows and Wallace, *Gotham*, 868–72.

28. Entry for April 15, 1861, in Nevins and Thomas, *Diary of George Templeton Strong*, 120–21.

29. Entry for April 17, 1861, in Nevins and Thomas, *Diary of George Templeton Strong*, 123.

30. "Show Your Colors," *New York Herald*, April 18, 1861 (first quotation); "Mob Law in New York," *NYDB*, April 18, 1861 (second quotation); "The Excitement in New York—Lawless Proceedings," *Sun*, April 19, 1861; "Excitement in New York," *Philadelphia Enquirer*, April 18, 1861.

31. Beckert, *Monied Metropolis*, 112–20; Spann, *Gotham at War*, 14–42; P. S. Foner, *Business & Slavery*, 306–17; Burrows and Wallace, *Gotham*, 873–76.

32. "Commercial Results of the War," *American Railroad Journal*, October 5, 1861.

33. "The Chamber of Commerce," *New York Tribune*, April 20, 1861.

34. Quoted in Mushkat, *Fernando Wood*, 116.

35. "Civil War! Civil War!" *NYDB*, April 13, 1861.

36. "The Union Gone!" *NYDB*, April 20, 1861.

37. "Mob Law in New York," *NYDB*, April 18, 1861.

38. "Making Money out of the South," *NYDB*, May 7, 1861 (emphasis in original).

39. "Shall New York Be Ruined?" *NYDB*, May 22, 1861.

40. J. H. Van Evrie to Jefferson Davis, March 12, 1861, reel 23, Confederate States of America Records, LC (emphasis in original).

41. "Working-Men, Arouse!" *New York Times*, January 15, 1861 (first quotation); "Meeting To-Night," *NYDB*, January 15, 1861 (second quotation); "Anti-Coercion Meeting," *NYDB*, January 16, 1861.

42. "The Poor of New York," *NYDB*, January 15, 22, 25, February 9, 1861; "Suffering and Want in New York," *NYDB*, January 22, 1861.

43. Van Evrie, *Negroes and Negro "Slavery"* (1861 ed.), 336.

44. "Mob Law in New York," *NYDB*, April 18, 1861.

45. "Social Diseases," *NYDB*, August 8, 1861.

46. "The Philosophy of Strikes," *NYDB*, April 9, 1853; "Mutual Dependence of Employer and Employee," *NYDB*, May 7, 1853.

47. "Democratic Newspapers and Our Position," *NYDB*, December 19, 1857; "Removal of the Day Book—The Future—Enlargement of the Daily," *NYDB*, May 1, 1858; "Enlargement of the Evening Day Book," *NYDB*, August 16, 1858; "The Evening Day-Book," *NYDB*, September 2, 1859.

48. "The Merchants of New York and the Safety of the Union," *NYDB*, June 16, 1858; "The Express on Commerce," *NYDB*, March 4, 1859; "What Supports the North," *NYDB*, March 16, 1859; "Is the North Interested in 'Slavery'?" *NYDB*, March 29, 1859; "Southern Products and Southern Commerce the Great Bases of Northern Prosperity," *NYDB*, September 26, 1859; "Business Relations Between the North and the South," *NYDB*, January 10, 1860; "Our Shipping Trade," *NYDB*, August 4, 1860.

49. Van Evrie's professional background and powerful patrons fit Gunther Peck's account of the emergence of white victimhood rhetoric among elite ideologues, who developed an "explicitly proslavery . . . narrative articulated *about* working-class people but not *by* them." G. Peck, "Labor Abolition," 97.

50. Van Evrie, *Negroes and Negro Slavery* (J. D. Toy, 1853 ed.), 31–32.

51. M. T. Smith, *Enemy Within*, 15–36.

52. Siddali, *From Property to Person*, 55–94.

53. R. G. Horton to William Winter, August 27, 1861, Autograph Letters Signed from R. G. Horton, New York, to William Winter, 1861, Ms Add. 1161, Folger Shakespeare Library, Washington, DC.

54. Blair, *With Malice Toward Some.*

55. Blair, *With Malice Toward Some*, 1–2.

56. "What Does It Mean?" *NYDB*, August 3, 1861.

57. "Fighting for Their Own Subjugation," *NYDB*, May 25, 1861.

58. "Peace Meetings," *NYDB*, August 3, 1861.

59. "Convention of Democratic Editors," *Brooklyn Daily Eagle*, June 28, 1861; "Anti-War Editorial Convention," *New York Herald*, June 28, 1861.

60. Ruehlen, "Specter of Subversion," 27–68; Michael J. Connolly, "'Irresistible Outbreaks Against Tories and Traitors': The Suppression of New England Antiwar Sentiment in 1861," in Jewett, *Battlefield and Beyond*, 173–95; Holzer, *Lincoln and the Power*, 335–75.

61. "Great Cry for Peace," *Piston (PA) Gazette*, August 15, 1861 (emphasis in original).

62. "Details of Eastern News," *Evening Bulletin*, September 9, 1861.

63. "No Change as Yet," *Scioto Gazette*, August 20, 1861.

64. "The Civil War in America," *Morning Post*, June 27, 1861.

65. "Secession Sympathizers in New Jersey, and What Makes Them So," *New York Tribune*, August 26, 1861.

66. "Letter from Bloomsburg, PA," *Philadelphia Enquirer*, August 30, 1861 (first and second quotations); *Rockland Democrat*, reprinted in *Bangor (ME) Daily Whig and Courier*, August 10, 1861 (third quotation).

67. "The Great Conspiracy—Its Elements at Work in the North," *Scioto Gazette*, August 27, 1861.

68. "The Egg That Hatched the Treasonable Brood," *Daily Cleveland Herald*, August 15, 1861; "Secession Sympathizers in New Jersey, and What Makes Them So," *New York Tribune*, August 26, 1861; "Notices to Correspondents," *Philadelphia Enquirer*, August 28, 1861.

69. "From Kentucky," *Chicago Tribune*, August 24, 1861; "Treason in Connecticut," *New York Times*, August 28, 1861.

70. "The Measure of Treason," *Chicago Tribune*, August 28, 1861.

71. "Notice to Quit," *Sun*, August 28, 1861. Halsey was another wealthy *Day Book* promoter. He owned property worth $50,000 and employed an Irish servant. See the 1860 Manuscript Census, Ithaca, NY, US Federal Census Collection, Ancestry.com.

72. "War Items," *Boston Herald*, May 8, 1861.

73. *Wilmington State Journal*, reprinted in the *Methodist*, August 3, 1861; *Bangor (ME) Daily Whig and Courier*, August 16, 1861; "The New York Day Book in the Wrong Pew," *Philadelphia Enquirer*, August 24, 1861.

74. "Traitors at the North," *Hartford Daily Courant*, August 17, 1861. On attacks against newspapers in summer 1861, see Connolly, "Irresistible Outbreaks," in Jewett, *Battlefield and Beyond*; see also David W. Bulla, "The Suppression of the Mid-Atlantic Copperhead Press," in Sachsman, *Press Divided*, 231–51.

75. "The War Feeling in the Common Council," *New York Herald*, April 23, 1861.

76. *New York Tribune*, May 17, 1861; "Board of Councilmen," *New York Tribune*, May 31, 1861; "Board of Councilmen," *New York Times*, June 7, 1861; Neely, *Lincoln and the Democrats*, 103.

77. "Letter from New York," *Daily Evening Bulletin*, June 4, 1861.

78. "Presentment of Newspapers in New York," *Sun*, August 19, 1861. The other newspapers were the *Journal of Commerce*, the *News*, the *Freeman's Journal*, and the Brooklyn *Eagle*.

79. "Seizure of the New York Daily News," *Philadelphia Enquirer*, August 23, 1861; "Seizure of Secession Newspapers," *Saturday Evening Post*, August 31, 1861; Fowler, *Unmailable*, 42–54.

80. "How to Do It," *NYDB*, July 20, 1861. Private correspondence confirms the *Day Book*'s growth in the summer of 1861. Five days after the paper was banned from the mail, Horton vented: "We have been doing exceedingly well, never better than of late, and to be closed up at the very time when success seemed opening to us is hard, very hard." Horton to William Winter, August 27, 1861, Autograph Letters Signed from R. G. Horton, New York, to William Winter, 1861, Ms Add. 1161, Folger Shakespeare Library, Washington, DC.

81. "The Suppression of Newspapers," *NYDB*, August 26, 1861.

82. “The New York ‘Day Book,’” *Richmond Enquirer*, October 8, 1861 (first quotation); “Progress of Despotism,” *Fayetteville (TN) Observer*, September 19, 1861.

83. “To Our Readers,” *NYDB*, September 28, 1861.

84. “Letter from New York,” *Hartford Daily Courant*, September 2, 1861.

85. “The Last of His Line,” *New York Times*, September 25, 1861.

86. “In Memoriam,” *Vanity Fair*, September 12, 1861.

87. *Chicago Tribune*, September 9, 1861.

88. “The Last of His Line,” *New York Times*, September 25, 1861.

Chapter 12

1. J. H. Van Evrie to W. Stump Forwood, May 18, 1862, folder 1, W. Stump Forwood Papers, DU.

2. On Peace Democrats, see Hutter and Abrams, “Copperhead Newspapers”; Wood, *Black Scare*; Escott, *Worst Passions*; Skidmore, “Copperhead Press”; Weber, *Copperheads*; Byron Andreasen, “Copperhead Christians and the Press,” in Sachsman, *Press Divided*, 269–78; Neely, *Lincoln and the Democrats*; Gallman, *Cacophony of Politics*.

3. Wells, “Inventing *White Supremacy*.”

4. “The Weekly Caucasian” and “The New Paper,” *NYWC*, October 5, 1861.

5. Baum, *Rise and Fall*.

6. J. H. Van Evrie, “Negroes and Negro Slavery,” *Monthly Democratic Review* 1 (June 1853): 39. Van Evrie’s classification scheme borrowed from Blumenbach, but it was also inconsistent. In a series of *Old Guard* articles published between January and June 1868, he used a six-part model, which added an “Esquimaux” race to Blumenbach’s five.

7. Directory of US Newspapers in American Libraries, Chronicling America, Library of Congress, accessed August 12, 2025, www.loc.gov/collections/directory-of-us-newspapers-in-american-libraries/?ops=AND&qs=caucasian&searchType=advanced.

8. “The Dred Scott Decision the Only Basis of Settlement,” *NYWC*, May 9, 1863.

9. “The Constitution as It Is and the Union as It Was,” *NYWC*, June 7, 1862; “If the War Is Successful, the Union Is Lost: If It Fails, the Union May Be Restored,” *NYWC*, April 11, 1863; “The Constitutional Reunion of the States,” *NYDB*, January 2, 1864; “The North Must Abandon Amalgamation and the South Secession,” *NYDB*, February 11, 1865. On the *Caucasian* as an “Anti-Abolition Union Paper,” see “Prospectus,” *NYWC*, February 8, 1862. For a critique of Republican abolitionism and Confederate separatism, see “National Murder—How Shall It Be Stopped?” *NYDB*, January 30, 1864.

10. “Death to Abolitionists,” *NYDB*, August 13, 1864.

11. “The Abolition Conspiracy Against White Men’s Liberty,” *NYWC*, November 2, 1861; “Is an Anti-Slaveryite a Monarchist?” *NYWC*, November 9, 1861; “The Overthrow of Democratic Institutions,” *NYWC*, September 27, 1862; “Regeneration of Democracy,” *NYWC*, October 4, 1862; “Abolition of Slavery Is the Destruction of Democracy,” *NYDB*, February 18, 1865.

12. “What Is Slavery?” *NYWC*, November 30, 1861; “Abolition of White Supremacy over Negroes,” *NYWC*, December 28, 1861; “The Signs of the Times,” *NYWC*, June 7, 1862; “‘Education’ of Negroes,” *NYWC*, June 14, 1862; “Who Are the Friends of the Negro?” *NYWC*, August 9, 1862; “Equality of White Men and Subordination of Negroes—The Normal Order of American Society,” *NYWC*, January 3, 1863; “The Irrepressible Conflict—‘Slavery’

or Amalgamation," *NYWC*, January 31, 1863; "Fighting for an Impossible Idea," *NYWC*, April 25, 1863; "The Inhumanity of Abolitionism," *NYDB*, January 28, 1865.

13. "What New York Has Lost by the War," *NYDB*, February 18, 1865.

14. See the *Caucasian* notices in *St. Mary's Beacon*, November 21, 1861; *Grand Haven (MI) News*, November 27, 1861; and *Clearfield (PA) Republican*, December 4, 1861.

15. *Exclusion of Newspapers*; New York Weekly Caucasian, *The White Man's Paper*.

16. "To Our Readers," *NYWC*, December 7, 1861; "The Position of the *Caucasian*," *NYWC*, December 21, 1861; "Exclusion of Newspapers from the Mail," *NYWC*, December 28, 1861. Later examples include "Freedom of Speech and Freedom of the Press," *NYWC*, July 12, 1862; "Another Example of Post Office Despotism," *NYWC*, November 22, 1862; "Free Discussion," *NYWC*, January 24, 1863; "The Abolition Despotism," *NYWC*, August 8, 1863; "Circulation of Newspapers," *NYDB*, January 30, 1864; and "Freedom of the Press Overthrown," *NYDB*, October 22, 1864.

17. "Freedom of Press. To the Public," *Bedford (PA) Gazette*, January 3, 1862 (emphasis in original).

18. "The Freeman's Journal," *Crisis*, April 23, 1862; "The Privileges of the Mails," *Crisis*, April 30, 1862.

19. Van Evrie, Horton & Co. to Abraham Lincoln, January 23, 1862, Abraham Lincoln Papers, LC.

20. "How to Do It," *NYDB*, July 20, 1861.

21. "Increase in Circulation," *NYWC*, June 14, 1862; "White Men Must Rule America," *Ashland (OH) Union*, November 18, 1863; "Clubs of Five," *NYDB*, May 14, 1864.

22. "Onward!" *NYDB*, August 13, 1864; "1865," *NYDB*, December 3, 1864.

23. "All Cut to Pieces," *Montgomery Daily Mail*, October 20, 1862; "The Despotism in Lincolndom," *Weekly Advertiser*, October 22, 1862; "Where Does the Money Go?" *Confederate Union*, February 17, 1863; "Thanks," *Natchez Daily Courier*, June 2, 1863; "New York Journals," *Chattanooga Daily Rebel*, June 21, 1863; "To Peace and Submission Men," *Daily Intelligencer*, August 28, 1863; "Items from the *New York Day Book*," *Houston Tri-Weekly Telegraph*, January 22, 1864. For a Confederate officer who relished Van Evrie's reportage, see the entry for December 18, 1862, in F. J. Taylor, *Reluctant Rebel*, 67. Southern Unionists lamented Van Evrie's uplifting impact on rebels; see *Nashville Daily Union*, May 5, 1863.

24. "To Workingmen," *NYWC*, April 5, 1862. See also "What Is to Be the Condition of Our Laboring Classes?" *NYWC*, December 28, 1861; "Workingmen and Their Duties," *NYWC*, August 9, 1862; "The Strikes for Higher Wages," *NYWC*, November 22, 1862; "The Condition of the Laboring Classes," *NYDB*, January 7, 1865.

25. "The Strikes," *NYDB*, November 28, 1863.

26. "The Strikes," *NYDB*, November 28, 1863. Gunther Peck argues that reactionary narratives of white victimhood "emerged in response to the radicalism of labor abolition, their effort to eradicate both chattel slavery and the injustices of factory work and political disfranchisement simultaneously." Anxious "slaveholders and their political allies" promoted victimhood narratives to co-opt and redirect white labor politics. G. Peck, "Labor Abolition," 90.

27. Bernstein, *New York City Draft Riots*, 19.

28. Gallman, *Cacophony of Politics*, 260–69.

29. "Presentation to President Lincoln of a Letter from the Workingmen's Democratic Association of New York," *Evening Star*, March 21, 1864.

30. The three publications were O'Conor, *Negro Slavery Not Unjust*, which Van Evrie, Horton & Co. published in 1859, and *Speech of Hon. J. C. Breckinridge* and *Dred Scott Decision*, both published in 1860.

31. *Valuable Anti-Abolition Publications*, 1 (quotation). The Anti-Abolition Tracts included *Abolition and Secession* (1862); *Free Negroism* (1862); *Abolition Conspiracy* (1863); Hunt, *Negro's Place in Nature* (1864); and *Six Species of Men* (1866). The first two were reissued as *Free Negroism* (1863) and *Abolition Is National Death* (1866).

32. Van Evrie, *Negroes and Negro "Slavery"* (1863 ed.); *Dred Scott Decision* (1863 ed.).

33. "Negroes and Negro Slavery," *NYDB*, November 14, 1863.

34. The nine addresses were *Speech of Benjamin Wood* (1862); *Two Proclamations* (1862); *Administration Reviewed* (1862); *Speeches of Hon. Horatio Seymour, and Hon. John Van Buren* (1862); *Speech of Hon. Horatio Seymour* (1862); *Peace and Union, War and Disunion* (1863); *Puritanism in Politics* (1863); and *Rights of the Citizen* (1863).

35. R. G. Horton to Samuel Sullivan Cox, February 11, 17, 1863, box 3, folder 96, Samuel Sullivan Cox Papers, Hay Library, Brown University.

36. Heather A. Haveman, "The Business of Literary Magazines in Nineteenth-Century America," in Lanzendörfer, *Routledge Companion to the British and North American Literary Magazine*, 114–23; Tim Lanzendörfer, "Introduction: The Meaning of the Literary Magazine," in Lanzendörfer, *Routledge Companion to the British and North American Literary Magazine*, 3 (quotation); Bohde, "Magazines as a Powerful Element."

37. Rogers, "C. Chauncey Burr"; Hubbell, "Charles Chauncey Burr"; "War Items," *Boston Herald*, May 8, 1861; "The Old Guard and the Democracy," *Old Guard* 1 (August 1863): 213.

38. "The Cost of the War, and Who Must Pay It," "Abolition Preachers vs. Christ and the Apostles," "The Prophecy of Calhoun," and "Acrostic on George Washington," *Old Guard* 1 (January 1863): 1–6, 7–12, 20–21, 21.

39. "A New Translation of the XIth Ode of Anacreon," *Old Guard* 1 (April 1863): 83; "Poetical History of Kisses," *Old Guard* 3 (February 1865): 76–79.

40. C. Chauncey Burr, "To Our Subscribers," *Old Guard* 1 (December 1863): 288.

41. "The Old Guard for January," *NYDB*, December 31, 1864.

42. "The American Races," *Old Guard* 3 (March 1865): 128–38. Some of Van Evrie's *Old Guard* pieces were signed, while others can be attributed to him by analyzing content and style.

43. Hunt, *On the Negro's Place*, 55 (quotation); Stepan, *Idea of Race*, 1–5, 32–33, 44–46; Burnett, *Henry Hotze*, 20–26, 200–203.

44. "The Negro's Place in Nature," *NYDB*, January 2, 1864; "The Negro's Place in Nature," *NYDB*, January 30, 1864 (quotations); Hunt, *On the Negro's Place*.

45. "Death of the Best Man in England," *NYDB*, November 6, 1869; "Editor's Table," *Old Guard* 7 (December 1869): 959–60; "Death of the Best Man in England," *Anthropological Review* 8 (January 1870): 97.

46. "The Negro's Place in Nature," *Christian Ambassador*, March 19, 1864.

47. "Africa Laid Open," *New Monthly Magazine* 130 (1864): 150, 152.

48. "The Negro's Place in Nature," *Quarterly Journal of Science* 1 (April 1864): 376–77.

49. N. F., "L'Afrique Sauvage," *Revue Britannique* 6 (1864): 93; "Ueber die Natürliche Stellung des Negers," *Aus der Heimath* 36 (1864): 566; Manetta, *Razza Negra*, 37–38.

50. Records of the United States Senate (RG 46), box no. 71, Sen 37A-H13, Petitions and Memorials, Committee on Post Offices and Post Roads, folder F. O. P., March 28–May 8, 1862, NARA.

51. *Congressional Globe*, 37 Cong., 2 Sess., 1131, 1370, 1537, 1581, 1677, 1843, 1935, 1950.

52. Zaeske, *Signatures of Citizenship*.

53. Wells, "Inventing *White Supremacy*."

54. 1860 Manuscript Census, Windsor County, VT, US Federal Census Collection, Ancestry.com; Goddard and Partridge, *History of Norwich Vermont*, 125; *Official Proceedings of the Democratic National Convention*, 13.

55. 1860 Manuscript Census, Union County, NJ, US Federal Census Collection, Ancestry.com; "Enviable Dismissal; or, Sudden Death Sudden Glory," *Gospel Magazine* 32, new series (August 1868): 428–30.

56. 1860 Manuscript Census, Muscatine County, IA, US Federal Census Collection, Ancestry.com; *Portrait and Biographical Album of Muscatine County*, 287 (quotation).

57. "Gambling for Judgeship," *New York Tribune*, October 26, 1863 (first quotation); "The Caucasian," *Boston Daily Advertiser*, May 12, 1863 (second quotation); "Prolific of Treason," *Idaho Tri-Weekly Statesman*, July 26, 1864 (third quotation).

58. Elizur Wright, "Anti Abolition Tracts," *Commonwealth*, March 12, 1864.

59. "Negrophobia," *Indiana True Republican*, November 28, 1861. See also "Defunct Newspapers," *Hartford Daily Courant*, September 18, 1861; "First of August at Abington," *Liberator*, August 5, 1864; "Negrophobia and Insanity," *Bangor (ME) Daily Whig and Courier*, April 13, 1865.

60. "Slavery and the Bible," *British and Foreign Evangelical Review* 12 (October 1863): 801–23. On abolitionists' critiques of proslavery science, see Herschthal, *Science of Abolition*.

61. "A Deserved Suppression," *Daily Evening Bulletin*, May 27, 1863. See also "Chronicles of the War. Latest News in Brief," *National Anti-Slavery Standard*, March 14, 1863; "Good for Blunt," *Weekly Champion and Press*, June 20, 1863; "Incendiary Sheets," *Village Record*, January 15, 1864.

62. Neely, *Fate of Liberty*.

63. "The Caucasian," *Boston Daily Advertiser*, May 12, 1863; *War of the Rebellion*, ser. 1, vol. 50, part 2, 456–57; *New York Herald*, May 9, 1863; "Good for Blunt," *Weekly Champion and Press*, June 20, 1863.

64. "A Correction," *Boston Herald*, June 23, 1863.

65. "Interesting Kentucky Items," *Cincinnati Enquirer*, November 12, 1864; *Bangor (ME) Daily Whig and Courier*, September 12, 1864.

66. "The 'Day Book' in California," *NYDB*, June 25, 1864.

67. *War of the Rebellion*, ser. 1, vol. 34, part 1, 1028; "Suppressed," *Burlington (VT) Daily Times*, October 28, 1862.

68. "The New York Weekly Caucasian," in *Defiance (OH) Democrat*, January 10, 1863; *Delphi (IN) Weekly Times*, March 7, 1863; *California (MO) Weekly News*, March 7, 1863.

69. *Bangor (ME) Daily Whig and Courier*, August 16, 1861; "The New York Day Book in the Wrong Pew," *Columbia County Republican*, reprinted in the *Philadelphia Enquirer*, August 24, 1861.

70. "The N.Y. Tribune, Herald, and Day-Book," *American Agriculturist* 24 (May 1865): 26.

71. Bernstein, *New York City Draft Riots*.

72. Wells, "Inventing *White Supremacy*."

73. "Things at the East," *Daily Evening Bulletin*, August 15, 1863 (quotation); "Richardson Among the Rioters," *Chicago Tribune*, June 26, 1864.

74. "Letter from Mr. Chauncey C. Burr," *New York Herald*, July 14, 1863. See also Berstein, *New York City Draft Riots*, 47.

75. "A Counter-Revolution," *NYWC*, July 18, 1863 (quotations); "Is It a Riot, a Mob, or a Revolution?" *NYWC*, July 25, 1863.

76. Silbey, *Respectable Minority*, x (quotation); Gallman, *Cacophony of Politics*.

77. "Stephen A. Douglas," *NYDB*, June 8, 1861.

78. "Stephen A. Douglas," *NYDB*, June 8, 1861.

79. DAASRAM.

80. *Boyd's New York City Tax-Book*, 133; H. Wilson, *Trow's New York City Directory, 1859*, 541.

81. "Mr. Cockroft," *Brooklyn Daily Eagle*, November 2, 1859; *Brooklyn Daily Eagle*, March 13, 1858.

82. 1860 Manuscript Census, New York City, Ward 9, District 4, US Federal Census Collection, Ancestry.com.

83. McKay, *Civil War*, 232–33.

84. 1860 Manuscript Census, Brooklyn, Ward 8, US Federal Census Collection, Ancestry.com; "Appointments in the New York Custom House," *New York Herald*, August 3, 1858.

85. Three versions of the constitution appear in DAASRAM. Horton's draft is tucked inside the back cover, while handwritten and published final versions are included in the minutes of the first meeting.

86. Freidel, "Loyal Publication Society."

87. DAASRAM; P. Taylor, *Most Complete Political Machine*.

88. 1860 Manuscript Census, New York City, Ward 16, District 2, US Federal Census Collection, Ancestry.com; Weitz, *Confederacy on Trial*; Bangs, *Reminiscences*, 156; *Brooklyn Daily Times*, December 15, 1904.

89. Sheldon, *Story of the Volunteer Fire Department*, 441.

90. *Biographical Sketch of Dr. Lewis A. Sayre*; 1860 Manuscript Census, New York City, Ward 21, District 1, US Federal Census Collection, Ancestry.com; George, "Catholic Family Newspaper."

91. 1860 Manuscript Census, New York City, Ward 16, District 3; 1860 Manuscript Census, New York City, Ward 16, District 4, US Federal Census Collection, Ancestry.com; H. Wilson, *Trow's New York City Directory, 1859*, 535.

92. 1860 Manuscript Census, Milford, New Haven County, CT, US Federal Census Collection, Ancestry.com; N. Stowe, *Sixty Years' Recollections*, 53.

93. Engs: 1860 Manuscript Census, New York City, Ward 9, District 4; Brower: 1860 Manuscript Census, Flushing, Queens County, NY; Gaines: 1860 Manuscript Census, New York City, Ward 7, District 4; Egerton: 1860 Manuscript Census, Baltimore, Ward 11; Andrews: 1860 Manuscript Census, New York City, Ward 18, District 3; O'Conor: 1860 Manuscript Census, New York City, Ward 12, District 3, US Federal Census Collection, Ancestry.com.

94. "Jefferson's Birthday," unidentified newspaper clipping in DAASRAM.

95. The bill of fare for the 1864 dinner is in DAASRAM. The bill for the April 13, 1865, Maison Dorée event is in Miscellaneous Papers Folder, Rushmore G. Horton Papers, NYPL.

96. DAASRAM; "Jefferson's Birthday," *NYDB*, April 23, 1864.

97. "Jefferson's Birthday," *NYDB*, April 23, 1864.

98. *NYDB*, July 2, 1864 (quotation); "The War Democracy," *NYDB*, May 14, 1864; "'Peace' and 'War' Democracy," *NYDB*, July 23, 1864.

99. "The Lesson of the Election," *NYDB*, November 7, 1863 (quotation); "Mr. Richardson on Negro Equality," *NYWC*, June 14, 1862; "The Next Presidential Election," *NYWC*, September 5, 1863.

100. Silbey, *Respectable Minority*, 89–114; Gallman *Cacophony of Politics*, 232, 237.

101. "The Day-Book for the Campaign," *NYDB*, July 23, 1864.

102. DAASRAM; Thomas H. Seymour to R. G. Horton, March 31, June 23, August 6, 1864, Rushmore G. Horton Papers, NYPL; R. G. Horton to Thomas H. Seymour, March 2, April 8, May 19, 1864, Thomas Henry Seymour Papers, Ms Seymt1868, Connecticut Historical Society, Hartford, CT.

103. Silbey, *Respectable Minority*, 115–39; Gallman, *Cacophony of Politics*, 241–44.

104. W. Stump Forwood to J. H. Van Evrie, September 12, 1864, box 1, folder 24, W. Stump Forwood Papers, UNC.

105. J. H. Van Evrie to George B. McClellan, Series 2: Correspondence II, George B. McClellan Papers, LC (emphasis in original).

106. "The Lesson of the Election," *NYDB*, November 19, 1864. Embittered Peace Democrats, including Horton, John Mullaly, and Chauncey Burr, briefly considered backing a third candidate, most likely Charles O'Conor or Thomas H. Seymour. See *New Haven Palladium*, September 16, 1864; "The Peace Democracy," *Hartford Daily Courant*, September 16, 1864.

107. "The Rebel Plot," *New York Times*, November 26, 1864.

108. Headley, *Confederate Operations*, 264–83; Brandt, *Man Who Tried to Burn New York*.

109. "White Men and Mongrels," *NYDB*, May 20, 1865.

Chapter 13

1. Civil War Soldiers and Sailors System, National Park Service, accessed March 12, 2026; Moore, *Roster*, 1:194; McKenna, *From Vicksburg to Cedar Creek*; Wert, *From Winchester to Cedar Creek*.

2. 1880 Manuscript Census, Lexington County, SC, US Federal Census Collection, Ancestry.com; "Van Every Fink," Find a Grave, accessed August 11, 2025, www.findagrave.com/memorial/78016371/van_every_fink; 1870 Manuscript Census, Mahaska County, IA, US Federal Census Collection, Ancestry.com; "Van Evrie McMains," Find a Grave, accessed August 11, 2025, www.findagrave.com/memorial/107775279/van_evrie_mcmains.

3. C. R. Wilson, *Baptized in Blood*; Connelly and Bellows, *God and General Longstreet*; Foster, *Ghosts of the Confederacy*; Gallagher and Nolan, *Myth of the Lost Cause*; Blight, *Race and Reunion*; Janney, *Remembering the Civil War*. On the persistence of proslavery in Lost Cause rhetoric, see Towns, *Enduring Legacy*, 48–52, 121.

4. See also Gannon, *Won Cause*.

5. *Congressional Globe*, 38 Cong., 1 Sess., 1462 (April 7, 1864).

6. Silbey, *Respectable Minority*, 177–83; Gambill, *Conservative Ordeal*, 20–39; Mushkat, *Reconstruction*, 74–75.

7. Silbey, *Respectable Minority*, 185–87.

8. "What Is a Democratic Paper?" *NYDB*, July 8, 1865 (emphasis in original).

9. "The Past and the Future," *NYDB*, reprinted in *Weekly Vincennes (IN) Western Sun*, June 10, 1865 (emphasis in original).

10. *Charleston Daily News*, September 11, 1865; *Natchez Daily Courier*, October 28, 1865.

11. "To Advertisers," *New York Times*, October 21, 1865.

12. New York, Vol. 194, 757, R. G. Dun & Co. Credit Report Volumes, HBS.

13. "The New York Day Book," *Natchez Daily Courier*, October 24, 1865.

14. "New York Day Book," *Southern Cultivator* 24 (April 1866): 92.

15. "The Democratic Almanac," *American Citizen*, February 10, 1866 (quotation); "Editorial Notes and Miscellany," *De Bow's Review* 1 (new ser.) (January 1866): 107; "New Almanac," *Clarksville (TN) Weekly Chronicle*, January 26, 1866; "The Condition of the South," *Daily Sun*, March 23, 1866; *De Bow's Review* 1 (new ser.) (April 1866): 446–47.

16. Blight, *Race and Reunion*, 31–139.

17. On Northern publishers and consumers' shaping of images of the postbellum South, see Prince, *Stories of the South*, 3–4.

18. Pollard, *Lost Cause*, "Testimonials," n.p. See also Connelly and Bellows, *God and General Longstreet*; Gallagher and Nolan, *Myth of the Lost Cause*; Blight, *Race and Reunion*; Maddex, *Reconstruction*.

19. Robert E. Lee to Chauncey Burr, January 5, 1866, Lee Letterbook No. 3, folder 2, DeButts-Ely Collection of Lee Family Papers, LC.

20. *Boston Evening Transcript*, December 24, 1866 (quotation); W. W. Rogers, "C. Chauncey Burr," 179.

21. Horton, *Youth's History*. All subsequent citations are to this edition. The German edition is Horton, *Volks-Geschichte*. For advertising and pricing, see "In Press—To Be Issued as Soon as Possible," *Fayetteville (NC) News*, May 1, 1866; "The Youth's History," *NYDB*, August 18, 1866; "The Youth History," *Plymouth (IN) Weekly Democrat*, August 23, 1866. On sales, see *Galaxy Advertiser* 9 (January 1869): n.p.

22. Horton, *Youth's History*, iii (first quotation), 309 (second quotation).

23. Horton, *Youth's History*, 182–85, 333, 357–60.

24. Horton, *Youth's History*, 297–99.

25. Horton, *Youth's History*, x (quotation), 186, 198–99, 216–19, 273–75, 282–83.

26. Horton, *Youth's History*, 366.

27. Horton, *Youth's History*, 258–69, 309–20.

28. Horton, *Youth's History*, 77.

29. Horton, *Youth's History*, 92–93.

30. Horton, *Youth's History*, v.

31. Horton, *Youth's History*, iv.

32. Horton, *Youth's History*, 387 (emphasis in original).

33. "In Press," *Louisiana Democrat*, July 25, 1866.

34. "Literary Notices," *Daily Intelligencer*, September 4, 1866 (emphasis in original); Edward G. Higginbotham to R. G. Horton, April 3, 1867, Rushmore G. Horton Papers, NYPL.

35. "Late Publications," *Daily Clarion*, August 29, 1866.

36. J. W. Duffey, "A Twice-Born Book," *Confederate Veteran* 24 (March 1926): 118; "A Youth's History of the Great Civil War," *Confederate Veteran* 24 (June 1926): 238; Mrs. John L. Woodbury, "New Edition of Horton's History," *Confederate Veteran* 36 (October 1928): 393; *Minutes of the Thirty-Eighth Annual Convention*, 197; Rutherford, *Truths of History*, 28, 29; "The Tragic Era," *Greenville (SC) News*, January 26, 1930.

37. "Democrats, Ahoy!" *Daily Dramatic Chronicle*, July 6, 1866. These denunciations echoed into the twentieth century; see Bentley, *Under the Search-Light*, 13. On "bloody shirt"

rhetoric, see L. L. Gould, *Republicans*, 44–45. On the persistence of Unionist and emancipationist sentiment, see Gannon, *Won Cause*; Janney, *Remembering the Civil War*; and Blight, *Race and Reunion*, 47.

38. "They Fought for a White Man's Government," *NYDB*, July 12, 1873.

39. Summers, *Press Gang*, 191–234; Parsons, *Ku-Klux*, 144–214; Abbott, *For Free Press*; Prince, *Stories of the South*, 52–93; Blair, *Record of Murders*; Forde and Bedingfield, *Journalism and Jim Crow*.

40. Rushmore G. Horton to Alexander H. Stephens, November 20 and December 5, 1865, Alexander H. Stephens Collection, Stuart A. Rose Manuscript, Archives, and Rare Book Library, Emory University (quotation from November 20 letter; emphasis in original); C. B. Richardson to Alexander H. Stephens, November 27, 1865, Alexander H. Stephens Papers, DU; Stephens, *Constitutional View*.

41. Joseph E. Davis to J. H. Van Evrie, May 23, 1866, and undated fragment, Joseph E. Davis Papers, Dolph Briscoe Center for American History, University of Texas at Austin; Joseph E. Davis to Jefferson Davis, July 14, 1866, in Crist et al., *Papers of Jefferson Davis*, 12:153–54, 155n4.

42. William Henry Peck to Mrs. Horton, September 26, 1867, Rushmore G. Horton Papers, NYPL (quotation); Centz [Bernard J. Sage], *Davis and Lee*; Peck, *Confederate Flag*; Cooke, *Heir of Graymount*.

43. Cooke serialized "The Battles of Virginia," and Simms did likewise with "Joscelyn; A Tale of the Revolution," in *Old Guard* 5 (1867); [George Fitzhugh,] "Evacuation Night in Richmond," *Old Guard* 5 (April 1867): 267–72; Edward A. Pollard, "Political Literature of America," *Old Guard* 6 (March 1868): 204–15.

44. Petrie, *William F. Samford*; 1860 Manuscript Census, Macon County, AL; 1860 Slave Schedule, Macon County, AL; 1870 Manuscript Census, Macon County, AL, all in US Federal Census Collection, Ancestry.com.

45. "Death of Hon. W. F. Samford," *Columbus (GA) Daily Enquirer-Sun*, July 5, 1894; Owen, *History of Alabama*, 4:1492.

46. Quoted in Petrie, *William F. Samford*, 480.

47. "Letter from Warwick," *NYDB*, February 28, 1868.

48. "Letter from Warwick," *NYDB*, reprinted in *Stark County Democrat*, October 27, 1870.

49. Quoted in Petrie, *William F. Samford*, 483.

50. *NYDB*, reprinted in *Mobile Register*, May 19, 1870.

51. *NYDB*, reprinted as "Ex-President Pierce," *Edgefield (SC) Advertiser*, August 7, 1867 (emphasis in original).

52. "Letter from Warwick," *NYDB*, June 18, 1870.

53. "Letter from J. R. Skiles," *Dallas Daily Herald*, December 26, 1868.

54. "Prometheus Bound," *Portland (ME) Daily Press*, January 7, 1867.

55. Quoted in "Letter from Warwick," *NYDB*, April 23, 1870.

56. *Stark County Democrat*, June 23, 1869, and April 20, October 27, 1870.

57. Pike, *Prostrate State*; Z. L. W., "A Slandered State," *New York Tribune*, October 8, 12, 15, 1874; Summers, *Press Gang*, 191–206; González and Torres, *News for All the People*, 151–53; Richardson, *Death of Reconstruction*, 101–12.

58. Karsten, *Patriot-Heroes*, 6. Unless otherwise indicated, data in this section come from the 1860 and 1870 Manuscript Censuses, US Federal Census Collection, Ancestry.com.

59. The Mid-Atlantic is defined as New York, Pennsylvania, and New Jersey; the Old Northwest includes Ohio, Indiana, Illinois, Michigan, and Wisconsin; the Border South encompasses Delaware, Maryland, West Virginia, Kentucky, and Missouri; the Upper South covers Virginia, North Carolina, Tennessee, and Arkansas; and the Deep South is comprised of South Carolina, Georgia, Florida, Alabama, Mississippi, Louisiana, and Texas.

60. Voegeli, *Free but Not Equal*, 1. The Western tilt is especially striking when populations are considered. Iowa housed 3.1 percent of the 1870 US population but accounted for 18.4 percent of the namesakes; Indiana's figures were 4.4 percent and 7.9 percent. The same comparisons show that the Northeastern industrial giants were underrepresented: New York housed 11.4 percent of the 1870 population but only 10.5 percent of the namesakes. Pennsylvania's figures were 9 percent and 2.6 percent. Massachusetts, home to nearly 4 percent of US residents, had zero namesakes.

61. Etcheson, *Emerging Midwest*.

62. On European immigrants and racism, see Roediger, *Wages of Whiteness*; Jacobson, *Whiteness of a Different Color*; and Ignatiev, *How the Irish Became White*. Immigrants did use "patriot-hero" names. Patrick and Sarah Plunkitt immigrated from Ireland to Manhattan, where their son George Washington Plunkitt was born in 1842 and later became a Tammany Hall boss. Other examples include Thomas Jefferson Meagher, born in Mississippi to Irish parents in 1877, and George Washington Schmidt, born in Ohio to German parents in 1872.

63. On generational patterns, sectionalism, and the Civil War, see Carmichael, *Last Generation*.

64. Marten, *Sing Not War*, 4.

65. "Baker, James Wellington," entry in 134th Infantry, New York, Civil War Muster Roll Abstracts, Ancestry.com.

66. Marten, *Sing Not War*, 4.

67. *Biographical Review*, 704.

68. *Portrait and Biographical Record of Kalamazoo, Allegan, and Van Buren Counties*, 256.

Chapter 14

1. J. H. Van Evrie to [William F. Samford], October 12, 1869, Samford-Wise Papers, Auburn University Archives and Special Collections (emphases original).

2. Mushkat, *Reconstruction*, 109–25; Silbey, *Respectable Minority*, 199–202; Erik B. Alexander, "The Fate of Northern Democrats After the Civil War: Another Look at the Presidential Election of 1868," in Gallagher and Shelden, *Political Nation*, 188, 192–97.

3. "To Andrew Johnson, President of the United States," *NYDB*, December 23, 1865. James Hunt republished the letter as J. H. Van Evrie, "Negro Emancipation in America," *Anthropological Review* 4 (October 1866): 136–40. On the Black Codes, see E. Foner, *Reconstruction*, 199–200.

4. "Face to Face with the Monster," *NYDB*, November 24, 1866 (quotations); "Becoming Mongrels to Defeat the Mongrels," *NYDB*, December 1, 1866.

5. "Lunatics and Fools—Which Is the Greatest Danger?" *NYDB*, July 20, 1867.

6. "The Greenback Scheme," *NYDB*, March 28, 1868 (quotations); "The Debt," *NYDB*, June 6, 1868.

7. For context, see Barreyre, *Gold and Freedom*.

8. Prince, *Stories of the South*, 53–54, 257n1.

9. "White Men and Mongrels," *NYDB*, May 20, 1865.

10. "The Democratic Platform," *NYDB*, June 6, 1868.

11. *Bedford (PA) Gazette*, June 9, 1865; *Charleston Daily News*, September 11, 1865; *Central Missourian*, October 14, 1865; *Natchez Daily Courier*, October 28, 1865.

12. Barbara J. Fields, "Ideology and Race in American History," in Kousser and McPherson, *Region, Race, and Reconstruction*, 156, 172n29.

13. Winn, *Emancipation*, 56–57, unnumbered footnote.

14. "Another Crisis," *Bristol Mercury*, May 4, 1839; "Morning Newspapers," London *Times*, reprinted in the *Standard*, September 10, 1839. Two other early uses were sharply critical of racism. From Australia, see *Tasmanian*, June 25, 1831; from India, see Bevan, *Thirty Years in India*, 2:299. For early use by a British author envisioning emancipation in the United States, see *Boston Morning Post*, November 8, 1832.

15. "Letter of Cora Montgomery," *New Orleans Crescent*, August 20, 1850; "Don Porfirio Vallente," *Daily Delta*, November 21, 1852.

16. "To the Citizens of Henry County," *Abbeville (SC) Press and Banner*, reprinted in *Spirit of the South*, May 20, 1851 (quotations); Garrett, *Reminiscences*, 369–71.

17. "Alabama Legislature," *Spirit of the South*, August 19, 1851; "The Elections," *Spirit of the South*, August 19, 1851.

18. "Negro Slavery the Basis of Democratic Institutions, or Negro Subordination Essential to White Equality," *NYDB*, May 5, 1856. The editorial was not widely reprinted, but see *Richmond Enquirer*, May 9, 1856, and *Autauga Citizen*, May 22, 1856.

19. "Abolishing White Supremacy," *NYDB*, January 25, 1861 (quotation); "Abolition of White Supremacy over Negroes," *NYDB*, December 28, 1861.

20. "To the People of the South," *Richmond Enquirer*, August 1, 1856.

21. W. L. Fleming, "Buford Expedition"; Freehling, *Road to Disunion, Volume II*, 125; "Letters from the People," *NYDB*, January 21, 1857.

22. "The Best New York Weekly," *M'Arthur Democrat*, March 9, 1865.

23. "The Best New York Weekly," *Bedford (PA) Gazette*, June 9, 1865.

24. "The New York Day-Book," *Staunton (VA) Vindicator*, August 18, 1865.

25. "Make Up Your February Clubs," *NYDB*, February 3, 1866.

26. "Prospectus of the West and South," *Staunton (VA) Vindicator*, December 8, 1865 (quotations); Earnhart, "*West and South*"; *History of Hardin County*, 521–22.

27. "Notices of the Mirror's Prospectus," *Western Mirror*, January 8, 1866.

28. Louisville *Courier* reprinted in "The Path to Peace," *Wheeling Daily Register*, November 26, 1867.

29. "Organize! Organize!" *Allen County Democrat*, June 16, 1867 (emphasis in original).

30. "The Grand Rally on the 27th, at Hayesville!" *Ashland (OH) Union*, August 21, 1867.

31. "Our Duty," *Wilmington (NC) Journal*, November 22, 1867.

32. "Truth Nailed to Earth Will Rise Again!" *Allen County Democrat*, October 23, 1867.

33. Quoted in "A New Democratic Development," *Portland (ME) Daily Press*, April 24, 1867.

34. Quoted in *Delaware (OH) Gazette*, November 22, 1867 (emphasis in original).

35. Van Evrie, *White Supremacy* (1st ed., 1868), v–vii (emphasis in original). "Mongrel Republics" is the title of the third chapter of the appendix.

36. Van Evrie, *White Supremacy* (2nd ed., 1868), ix–x.

37. J. H. Van Evrie to Horatio Seymour, June 1868, Horatio Seymour Papers (SC7008), New York State Library, Albany, NY (emphasis in original). He sent a nearly identical letter to Andrew Johnson: see J. H. Van Evrie to Andrew Johnson, 1868, reel 35, Andrew Johnson Papers, LC.

38. Alexander, "Fate of Northern Democrats," in Gallagher and Shelden, *Political Nation*, 192–97; Mitchell, *Horatio Seymour*, 391–96; Mushkat, *Reconstruction*, 128–30; Silbey, *Respectable Minority*, 199–204.

39. Alexander, "Fate of Northern Democrats," in Gallagher and Shelden, *Political Nation*, 201–5; Grossman, *Democratic Party*, 1–14.

40. "The Nomination—It is Providential," *NYDB*, July 18, 1868.

41. *NYDB*, July 18, 1868.

42. "Tracts for the Times," *NYDB*, August 15, 1868.

43. "Seymour and Restoration—Or Grant and Chaos," *NYDB*, October 10, 1868; "Voudou. The Negroes of the South Relapsing into Barbarism," *NYDB*, October 31, 1868; "Letter from Warwick," *NYDB*, October 3, 1868.

44. "The Day-Book for the Campaign of 1868!" *NYDB*, August 15, 1868.

45. "The Convention," *Wilcox Vindicator*, reprinted in *Moulton (AL) Advertiser*, July 10, 1868 (emphasis in original).

46. *San Francisco Examiner*, July 14, 1868.

47. *Indiana (PA) Democrat*, July 23, 1868.

48. Emberton, *Beyond Redemption*, 154–61; E. Foner, *Reconstruction*, 340–43.

49. "The Democratic Demonstrations," *NYDB*, October 10, 1868.

50. "A Representative Sheet!" *Daily Iowa State Register*, May 23, 1868. See also "Undefiled Democracy," *Daily Cleveland Herald*, February 12, 1867; "The 'Dead Past,'" *New Hampshire Statesman*, March 29, 1867; "A 'National' Democratic Organ," *Bangor (ME) Daily Whig and Courier*, April 20, 1867; "Let It Speak," *Bangor (ME) Daily Whig and Courier*, May 1, 1867; *Boston Daily Advertiser*, April 30, 1868; "The Democratic Dilemma," *New York Tribune*, July 4, 1868.

51. "Brace of Blackguards," *Republican Banner*, April 25, 1868. See also the New York *World* reprinted in *Republican Banner*, December 11, 1867, and especially the widely reprinted letter to the *Old Guard*, along with Burr's indignant reply, in "Editor's Table," *Old Guard* 6 (April 1868): 317–18.

52. "Good for Us," *New Hampshire Patriot and State Gazette*, April 3, 1867.

53. Gambill, *Conservative Ordeal*, 154 (quotation); Alexander, "Fate of Northern Democrats," in Gallagher and Shelden, *Political Nation*, 206–8.

54. "The Election—the Issue—the Future," *NYDB*, November 11, 1868.

55. "Democracy vs. Mongrelism," *NYDB*, November 14, 1868; "When the Democracy Will Be Victorious," *NYDB*, November 14, 1868; "The Cause of Defeat," *NYDB*, November 21, 1868.

56. "The White Republic Against the World," *NYDB*, November 14, 1868.

Chapter 15

1. "Tennessee," *Daily Cleveland Herald*, September 7, 1868 (quotations); "Attempted Assassination," *Memphis Evening Post*, August 14, 1868; "Capt. Barker," *Memphis Evening Post*, August 31, 1868; Clayton, *Aftermath*, 135–37; Howard, *Autobiography*, 2:380.

2. “Outrages,” *Daily Arkansas Gazette*, September 5, 1868; “Insincerity,” *Daily Arkansas Gazette*, August 25, 1868; “Capt. Barker,” *Memphis Daily Appeal*, September 1, 1868.

3. “Attempted Assassination,” *Memphis Evening Post*, August 14, 1868 (first quotation); *Memphis Evening Post*, quoted in “Insincerity,” *Daily Arkansas Gazette*, August 25, 1868 (second quotation).

4. “Tennessee,” *Daily Cleveland Herald*, September 7, 1868.

5. Wang, *Trial of Democracy*; Perman, *Struggle for Mastery*; Keyssar, *Right to Vote*, 69–93.

6. “Shall the Democratic Party Disband?” *NYDB*, March 12, 1870.

7. On Reconstruction’s violent overthrow, see Rable, *But There Was No Peace*; Egerton, *Wars of Reconstruction*; and Williams, *I Saw Death Coming*.

8. Quotations from W. W. Rogers, *Reconstruction Politics*, 127–28.

9. Quoted in Summers, *Dangerous Stir*, 247.

10. *Puritanism in Politics*.

11. Summers, *Dangerous Stir*, 247–48; Mushkat, *Fernando Wood*, viii, 191; Grossman, *Democratic Party*, 15, 23–50, 60–64; Erik B. Alexander, “The New Departure: The Northern Democratic Press and Reconstruction, 1868–1876,” in Sachsman, *After the War*, 21–30.

12. “Black Republicans and Colored Democrats,” *NYDB*, September 11, 1869; “Negroized Democratic Papers,” *NYDB*, August 20, 1870.

13. “Who Are Democrats?” *NYDB*, February 12, 1870.

14. “That Political Prostitute, the New York World,” *NYDB*, June 4, 1870.

15. “A New Platform for the Democracy,” *NYDB*, April 1, 1871. Van Evrie used at least as much column space arguing against the New Departure as he did bashing Republicans. See “The Disgraceful Surrender,” *NYDB*, July 8, 1871, and the subsequent reiteration of its themes.

16. J. H. Van Evrie, “To the Southern Readers of the Day-Book,” *NYDB*, February 20, 1869.

17. “White Supremacy the Sole Test of Democracy,” *NYDB*, May 28, 1870; “Up with the White Banner!” *NYDB*, April 30, 1870.

18. “The Republic of Washington Against the ‘World,’ the Flesh and the Devil,” *NYDB*, June 18, 1870 (emphasis in original).

19. See “The White Republic Against the World,” *NYDB*, November 14, 1868; see also “The White Republic Against the World,” an advertisement that featured the three-part mantra “Devoted to White Supremacy, State Equality, and Federal Union,” in *NYDB*, March 26, 1870. The cartoon appeared on the front page of *NYDB*’s March 18, 1871, edition. The signed portrait was announced in the *Day Book* on November 19, 1870, and featured prominently in the paper’s advertisements in 1871.

20. “The Abolition Debt,” *NYDB*, January 9, 1869.

21. “White Supremacy—The Only Issue,” *NYDB*, December 17, 1870.

22. “Shall the Democratic Party Disband?” *NYDB*, March 12, 1870.

23. “The White Republic Against the World,” *NYDB*, November 14, 1868.

24. Field, *Politics of Race*; Mohr, *Radical Republicans*, 202–34; Quigley, *Second Founding*, 51–69.

25. “The Constitutional Convention,” *NYDB*, April 20, 1867 (quotations); “New York Constitutional Convention,” *NYDB*, April 6, 1867.

26. DAASRAM.

27. George, "Catholic Family Newspaper"; H. Wilson, *Trow's New York City Directory, 1864*, 246; 1860 Manuscript Census, New York City, Ward 22, District 1, US Federal Census Collection, Ancestry.com.

28. "Memorial of the States Rights Society of New York, Against Negro Suffrage," *NYDB*, July 20, 1867. A clipping is pasted into DAASRAM. A copy of the pamphlet, which bears the same title, is found in the Miscellaneous Papers Folder, Rushmore G. Horton Papers, NYPL. Newspapers reprinted the memorial as "The Distinctions God Has Made—Sexes—Colors." See *Leavenworth (KS) Daily Commercial*, August 2, 1867; *Cadiz (OH) Sentinel*, August 7, 1867; *Urbana (OH) Union*, August 28, 1867. Van Evrie contributed a spate of editorials: "The State Convention and Negro Suffrage," *NYDB*, July 20, 1867; "The Constitutional Convention and Negro Suffrage," *NYDB*, July 27, 1867; "Shall New York Become a Mongrel State?" *NYDB*, August 3, 1867.

29. *Proceedings and Debates of the Constitutional Convention*, 1:236–37, 254–57, 313–14.

30. Mohr, *Radical Republicans*, 235–70; Field, *Politics of Race*, 199; Quigley, *Second Founding*, 68.

31. "Death of Mr. R. G. Horton," *NYDB*, September 28, 1867.

32. *Brooklyn Daily Eagle*, September 24, 1867 (first quotation); "News Summary," *Charleston Daily News*, September 28, 1867 (second quotation); *American Annual Cyclopaedia*, 577.

33. "Dead," *Clearfield (PA) Republican*, October 3, 1867.

34. "Jefferson's Birthday. Banquet at the St. James Hotel," *NYDB*, n.d., clipping in DAASRAM.

35. "Mr. Bayard's Speech on the Structure of the Government," *NYDB*, March 6, 1869.

36. "The Fifteenth Amendment," *NYDB*, September 4, 1869.

37. "The Fifteenth Amendment Fraud," *NYDB*, March 12, 1870.

38. "White Supremacy!! What the Day-Book Army Thinks. Letters from the People!!" *NYDB*, July 16, 1870.

39. "Shall Democracy Perish on This Continent?" *NYDB*, April 16, 1870 (emphasis in original).

40. "The White Republic at Any Cost!" *NYDB*, July 2, 1870.

41. "Which Shall Rule—White or N——r?" *NYDB*, June 11, 1870.

42. "Names, Names," and "Remember!" *NYDB*, January 2, 1869.

43. "Special Notice," and "The White Republic Against the World," *NYDB*, November 19, 1870.

44. "Further Inducements to Get Up Day-Book Clubs!" *NYDB*, March 8, 1873.

45. "Gold Pen Premiums," *NYDB*, May 24, 1873; "Gold Pen and Pencil Premium for 1874," *NYDB*, November 29, 1873.

46. Rosen, *Terror in the Heart of Freedom*, 127–29, 315n215; *Weekly Arkansas Gazette*, December 31, 1867; "A White Man's Movement," *New York Freeman's Journal and Catholic Register*, January 4, 1868; "The 'Connecticut Yankee' at Home," *Van Buren (AR) Press*, February 21, 1868; "Grand Barbecue!" *Van Buren (AR) Press*, February 21, 1868; *Arkansas Campaign Gazette*, March 13, 1868; "Take Notice," *Van Buren (AR) Press*, March 27, 1868; "Be Vigilant," *Weekly Arkansas Gazette*, May 17, 1868.

47. Cecelski, *Fire of Freedom*, 202; Bradley, *Bluecoats*, 182–83; Horn, *Invisible Empire*, 345; Vernon Burton, "Race and Reconstruction: Edgefield County, South Carolina," in Magdol and Wakelyn, *Southern Common People*, 214–15; Baker, *Politics of Continuity*, 158–59, 181;

R. E. Curran, *American Catholics*, 360. For contemporary coverage, see "Let Us Organize," *Sugar Planter*, January 18, 1868; "Meeting of the White Men's Club," *North Carolinian*, March 14, 1868; "Ratification Meeting," *Daily Sentinel*, March 16, 1868.

48. Japheth, "White Men's Associations!" *NYDB*, May 7, 1870. Ham sees his father Noah lying naked and drunk and urges his brothers, Shem and Japheth, to look, but they avert their eyes and cover his body. Upon awakening, Noah blesses Shem and Japheth and curses Ham's son Canaan, ostensibly the progenitor of modern Africans, to be their slave (Genesis 9:21–27). On its uses, see H. S. Smith, *In His Image*, 129–65; and Wood, *Arrogance of Faith*, 84–111.

49. "White Associations Everywhere!" *NYDB*, May 7, 1870.

50. "Come to the Work," *NYDB*, May 14, 1870.

51. "Come to the Work," *NYDB*, May 14, 1870.

52. "Organize!—Organize!!" *NYDB*, June 11, 1870 (emphasis in original).

53. "How New York 'Accepts the Situation,'" *York (PA) Democratic Press*, May 27, 1870; "Down with the Fifteenth Amendment!" *NYDB*, reprinted in *Stark County Democrat*, April 20, 1870, and in *Allen County Democrat*, May 4, 1870; "No N——r Democracy in Delaware," *NYDB*, reprinted in *Racine County (WI) Argus*, May 5, 1870, and *Democratic Enquirer*, May 11, 1870; "Get Up Your White Men's Clubs!" *NYDB*, reprinted in *Mobile Register*, April 24, 1870; *Monroe Journal*, May 14, 1870; "The Indebtedness of the States," *NYDB*, reprinted in *Democratic Enquirer*, July 27, 1870, and *Shelby Guide*, July 12, 1870.

54. "Fayette Democratic Convention," *Washington (PA) Review and Examiner*, June 15, 1870.

55. "The White Man's Club Library," *NYDB*, February 4, 1871. The campaign persisted; see "Day-Book Publications," *NYDB*, February 25, 1871, and reprintings of "The White Man's Club Library" in *NYDB*, March 4, 1871, and thereafter.

56. Fischer, *Tippecanoe and Trinkets Too*.

57. "From Bradley County," *Morning Republican*, September 15, 1870.

58. "Through the South," *New York Tribune*, July 8, 1871.

59. *Geo. P. Rowell & Co's American Newspaper Directory* (1869), 72; *Geo. P. Rowell & Co's American Newspaper Directory* (1872), 120; "Advertising in the Rural New Yorker," *Moore's Rural New Yorker*, January 20, 1872.

60. For South Carolina, see Stampp, *Era of Reconstruction*, 197–98.

61. Quoted in Wharton, "Race Issue," 366.

62. Wharton, "Race Issue," 367–70; Vernon Lane Wharton, "The Revolution of 1875," in Stampp and Litwack, *Reconstruction*, 474; Mitchell Snay, "White Leagues," in Ownby, et al., *Mississippi Encyclopedia*, 1323–24; Behrend, *Reconstructing Democracy*, 217–18; *Mississippi in 1875*, 1:883, 2:1406, 1614, 1628, 1637–41, 1696.

63. Horn, *Invisible Empire*, 345.

64. On the White League, see Tunnell, *Crucible of Reconstruction*, 194 (*Caucasian* quotations); and J. G. Taylor, *Louisiana Reconstructed*, 281–84. For continued use of the "white men's clubs" designation, see "Letter from Claiborne," *Daily Shreveport Times*, August 14, 1874. For Webb, see 1870 Manuscript Census, Claiborne Parish, LA, US Federal Census Collection, Ancestry.com; and Harris and Hulse, *History of Claiborne Parish*, 254–55.

65. "The Fifteenth Amendment Fraud," *NYDB*, March 12, 1870.

66. "Special Notice," *NYDB*, November 19, 1870.

Chapter 16

1. *Inter Ocean*, March 14, 1879.

2. *Winfield (KS) Daily Telegram*, August 26, 1879.

3. *Courier-Journal*, March 18, 1883.

4. "The New York 'Day Book,'" *San Francisco Examiner*, May 17, 1878.

5. C. Chauncey Burr, "A Card from the Editor," *Old Guard* 7 (December 1869): 960; W. W. Rogers, "C. Chauncey Burr," 180; "The Old Guard," *NYDB*, January 14, 1871.

6. Compare the entries in 1870 Manufacturing Census, New York City, Ward 4, District 1, and 1860 Manufacturing Census, New York City, Ward 4, District 3, US Federal Census Collection, Ancestry.com.

7. "Removal of the Day-Book," *NYDB*, April 29, 1871.

8. "The Presidential Campaign Opened!" *NYDB*, July 15, 1871.

9. "To Our Club Men," *NYDB*, February 3, 1872; *Geo. P. Rowell & Co's American Newspaper Directory* (1872), 120.

10. Shelden and Alexander, "Dismantling the Party System."

11. Quoted in Slap, *Doom of Reconstruction*, 165.

12. Quoted in Slap, *Doom of Reconstruction*, 50.

13. *Charleston Courier*, June 9, 1858; *Star of the North*, September 7, 1864; *Democratic Advocate*, December 9, 1869.

14. "Government Patronage—The New York Day Book," *NYDB*, December 21, 1857.

15. "The Republic of Washington Against the 'World,' the Flesh and the Devil," *NYDB*, June 18, 1870.

16. "Are the Democratic Statesmen Demented?" *NYDB*, February 24, 1872.

17. Slap, *Doom of Reconstruction*, 1–155.

18. Slap, *Doom of Reconstruction*, 130–31, 137–38, 147–48.

19. "Ye Smart Politicians!" *NYDB*, February 17, 1872.

20. "The Cincinnati Convention," *NYDB*, April 27, 1872 (first quotation); "The Cincinnati Convention," *NYDB*, April 20, 1872 (second, third, and fourth quotations).

21. "Will There Be a Democratic Convention?" *NYDB*, April 13, 1872 (emphasis in original).

22. Lundberg, *Horace Greeley*.

23. "More Ethnology," *New York Tribune*, July 24, 1867 (first quotation); "Obituary," *New York Tribune*, September 24, 1867 (second quotation); "Gambling for a Judgeship," *New York Tribune*, October 26, 1863 (third quotation).

24. "Has Mr. Greeley Outlived His Illusions?" *NYDB*, May 4, 1872.

25. "Escape from a Great Danger," *NYDB*, May 11, 1872.

26. "White Supremacy vs. Amalgamation," *NYDB*, June 1, 1872.

27. "Mr. Greeley's Dose for the Democracy," *NYDB*, June 1, 1872.

28. "Let Us Spit upon Their Candidate as well as Platform," *NYDB*, June 1, 1872.

29. "The Greeley Democrats," *NYDB*, June 15, 1872.

30. "Under-the-Coat-Tail Democrats," *NYDB*, June 8, 1872.

31. "Important Notice," *NYDB*, June 29, 1872.

32. "White Men Will Not Support Greeley," *NYDB*, June 29, 1872.

33. Slap, *Doom of Reconstruction*, 170–71, 188–92.

34. *Official Proceedings of the National Democratic Convention*, 3–5, 57–67.

35. Charles O'Conor to Samuel J. Tilden, August 24, 1872, Charles O'Conor Letters and Documents, Mss Col 6409, NYPL (quotation); Nicoletti, *Secession on Trial*.

36. Slap, *Doom of Reconstruction*, 192–93; Ross, *Liberal Republican Movement*, 146–49; "The Old-Line Democracy Won't Support Greeley," *Buffalo Evening Post*, August 3, 1872; "The Strayed-Outs," *Courier-Journal*, September 2, 1872.

37. "The Treason Consummated!—Greeley Nominated!" *NYDB*, July 13, 1872.

38. "Bogus vs. True Democracy at Charleston," *NYDB*, April 28, 1860.

39. "The 'Tribune Mercantile Advertiser,'" *NYDB*, August 23, 1858.

40. "The Day-Book and Its Readers," *NYDB*, July 27, 1872.

41. "The Lying, Humbugging New York Tribune," *NYDB*, July 24, 1869.

42. "A Champion of Labor," *NYDB*, January 5, 1867.

43. "Mongrel and N——r Governments," *NYDB*, September 11, 1869.

44. "An Evil Man," *NYDB*, April 21, 1866.

45. "Ultraism—The Wilmington Journal," *NYDB*, May 29, 1860.

46. "Dr. Greeley on the White Supremacy Platform!" *NYDB*, August 10, 1872.

47. "The Louisville Convention," *NYDB*, August 10, 1872.

48. "'Anything to Beat Grant,'" *NYDB*, August 10, 1872.

49. "The Man for the Hour," *NYDB*, August 10, 1872.

50. "The New York Day-Book," *Pomeroy's Democrat*, December 15, 1877.

51. "The New York Day-Book," *Pomeroy's Democrat*, December 15, 1877.

52. *Pomeroy's Democrat*, August 11, 1872.

53. *Daily Constitution*, August 16, 1872; "The New York Day Book," *Milwaukee Daily Sentinel*, August 16, 1872.

54. "Light from Louisville," *New York Herald*, August 30, 1872.

55. "A Good Joke on the Democrats," *Idaho Tri-Weekly Statesman*, August 17, 1872.

56. "What the People Say," *Pomeroy's Democrat*, August 24, 1872. See also "Democratic Voices from All Parts of the Country," *Atlanta Daily Sun*, September 3, 1872.

57. "Hang the Day Book," *Pomeroy's Democrat*, September 7, 1872 (quotation); "Another Day Book Reader," *Pomeroy's Democrat*, August 25, 1872; "The Day Book No More," *Pomeroy's Democrat*, August 31, 1872.

58. "The Louisville Convention," *NYDB*, August 31, 1872.

59. "The Failure at Louisville," *NYDB*, September 14, 1872. On the deliberations, see "The Louisville Convention," *Sun*, September 5, 1872; "The Straight-Outs," *New York Tribune*, September 5, 6, 1872.

60. "The Failure of the Greeley and Brown Movement!" *NYDB*, September 21, 1872.

61. *NYDB*, September 28, 1872; "Work to Be Commenced at Once," *NYDB*, October 5, 1872; "Mr. Greeley Moving for Miscegenation!" *NYDB*, October 5, 1872.

62. Editors cited this statement as proof that O'Conor was in the running. See *Princeton (NJ) Clarion*, October 3, 1872.

63. *Tri-Weekly Kentucky Yeoman*, October 8, 1872.

64. "Swallowing Greeley and His Falsehoods," *NYDB*, October 12, 1872; *Spirit of the Age*, October 10, 1872; *Donaldsonville (LA) Chief*, October 12, 1872.

65. *Natchez Democrat*, September 26, 1872; "Swallowing Greeley and His Falsehoods," *NYDB*, October 12, 1872.

66. "The Election," *NYDB*, November 9, 1872.

67. "To Southern Readers," *NYDB*, November 16, 1872.

68. "To the Readers of the Day-Book," *NYDB*, November 30, 1872; "To the Southern Democracy," *NYDB*, December 14, 1872.

69. *Geo. P. Rowell & Co's American Newspaper Directory* (1873), 149.

70. *Greeley or Grant? Speech of Hon. Charles Sumner*; Donald, *Charles Sumner*, 539–55.

71. J. H. Van Evrie to Charles Sumner, December 24, 1872, reel 60, Papers of Charles Sumner, Houghton Library, Harvard University (emphasis in original).

72. "We Greet You with 'The Compliments of the Season,'" *NYDB*, January 3, 1873.

73. "Terms for 1873," *NYDB*, November 2, 1872.

74. "The Dollar Day-Book," *NYDB*, May 10, 1873.

75. "To 'The Old Guard,'" *NYDB*, August 16, 1873.

76. J. H. Van Evrie, "A Personal Appeal to True Democrats," *NYDB*, October 18, 1873 (quotations); "'Let Us Reason Together!'" *NYDB*, October 4, 1873; "Plain Talk to Patriots," *NYDB*, October 11, 1873.

77. "Further Inducements to Get Up Day-Book Clubs!" *NYDB*, March 8, 1873; "Big Thief-Proof Cash Premium Scheme," *NYDB*, September 13, 1873.

78. "Gold Pen Premiums," *NYDB*, May 24, June 21, 1873. Unless otherwise indicated, information about the 1873 club organizers comes from the 1870 Manuscript Census, US Federal Census Collection, Ancestry.com.

79. Jordan and Hadden, *Genealogical and Personal History*, 3:845–46.

80. Crawford and Crawford, *Memoirs of Iowa County Wisconsin*, 1:288.

81. For the justice of the peace, see Maryland club organizer Christopher W. Lansdale in *Journal of the Proceedings of the Senate of the State of Maryland*, 837; see also Kentucky's Charles Ware in Perrin, Battle, and Kniffin, *Kentucky*, 870. For postmasters, see North Carolinians Elisha Wade in *Register of Officers and Agents, 1859*, 272; and S. J. Buie in Bowen, *United States Post-Office Guide*, 127. For state legislators, see Jason C. Whitson of North Carolina in *Journals of the Senate and House of Commons*, 5; and Daniel Boone Morgan of Kentucky in Rothert, *History of Muhlenberg County*, 94.

82. *Portrait and Biographical Album of Lancaster County*, 251–53.

83. "A Noble Woman Working in a Noble Cause," *NYDB*, March 22, 1873.

84. "Down with Negro Voting and Military Despotism!" *NYDB*, February 1, 1873.

85. "The Destruction of Negro Labor in the South," *NYDB*, February 22, 1873.

86. "Another Signal," *NYDB*, April 19, 1873; "The Only Remedy," *NYDB*, May 17, 1873; "Through Blood or Through Reason, the Union Must Be Restored," *NYDB*, July 19, 1873.

87. "There Must Be a Democratic Party," *NYDB*, April 12, 1873; "Restoration—The Sole Test of Democracy," *NYDB*, August 23, 1873; "The Union of Democrats for the Sake of the Union," *NYDB*, September 6, 1873; "The Mission of the Straight Democracy," *NYDB*, September 13, 1873.

88. "They Fought for a White Man's Government," *NYDB*, July 12, 1873.

89. "The White Republic Against the World!" *NYDB*, April 19, 1873.

90. Surviving issues are May 2, 23, 30, July 4, 11, 1874; August 14, 1875; March 25, November 4, 1876.

91. J. H. Van Evrie to Jefferson Davis, June 16, 1874, Virginia Museum of History and Culture (emphasis in original).

92. "Let Us Reason Together," *NYDB*, May 31, 1873.

93. *Geo. P. Rowell & Co's American Newspaper Directory* (1874), 228; *Geo. P. Rowell & Co's American Newspaper Directory* (1875), 146; *Geo. P. Rowell & Co's American Newspaper*

Directory (1876), 254; *Geo. P. Rowell & Co's American Newspaper Directory* (1877), 214; *Geo. P. Rowell & Co's American Newspaper Directory* (1878), 209; *Geo. P. Rowell & Co's American Newspaper Directory* (1879), 237.

94. New York, Vol. 438, 468, R. G. Dun & Co. Credit Report Volumes, HBS.

95. J. H. Van Evrie to Horatio Seymour, September 15, 1876, Horatio Seymour Papers (SC7008), New York State Library, Albany, NY.

96. New York, Vol. 438, 468, R. G. Dun & Co. Credit Report Volumes, HBS.

97. *Pomeroy's Democrat*, December 15, 1877; New York, Vol. 438, 468, R. G. Dun & Co. Credit Report Volumes, HBS.

98. New York, Vol. 438, 468, R. G. Dun & Co. Credit Report Volumes, HBS (quotations); *Columbus(GA) Daily Enquirer*, May 16, 1878; "The New York 'Day Book,'" *San Francisco Examiner*, May 17, 1878.

99. "Answers to Correspondents," *Courier-Journal*, December 14, 1879.

100. *Trow's New York City Directory, 1884*, 1712; *Trow's New York City Directory, 1885*, 1792; *Trow's New York City Directory, 1886*, 1959; *Trow's New York City Directory, 1889*, 2029; *Trow's New York City Directory, 1890*, 2027.

101. J. H. Van Evrie to W. Stump Forwood, May 18, 1862, folder 1, W. Stump Forwood Papers, DU.

102. Caligiuri and Mohammed, *Neuroscience of Handwriting*, 131–64.

103. "The N. Y. Day Book Man," *Hillsdale (MI) Standard*, August 6, 1867.

104. John Henry Van Evrie Certificate of Death, May 17, 1896, Department of Health of the City of Brooklyn, no. 8637, New York City Municipal Archives.

Epilogue

1. Mt. Hope & Riverside Cemetery Records, 667, UR.

2. David Kramer, "On the Defacing of 'Reflecting' in Nathaniel Square and Restoring the Grave of 'America's First Professional Racist' in Mt. Hope Cemetery," *Talker of the Town*, June 28, 2020. https://talkerofthetown.com/2020/06/18/on-the-defacing-of-reflecting-in-nathaniel-square-and-restoring-the-grave-of-americas-first-professional-racist-in-mt-hope-cemetery/.

3. "Died," *New York Times*, May 20, 1896.

4. Zucchino, *Wilmington's Lie*.

5. Wiley and Rines, *United States*, 7:166; Reuter, *Mulatto in the United States*, 128, 188–89, 327; C. S. Davis, *Cotton Kingdom*, 225.

6. "Negro," in *Encyclopædia Britannica*, 17:320.

7. Chamberlain, *Foundations of the Nineteenth Century*; M. Grant, *Passing of the Great Race*; Stoddard, *Rising Tide of Color*.

8. On polygenism's decline, see Gossett, *Race*, 66–67, 145; Fredrickson, *Black Image*, 228–55. On parsing among white races, see Painter, *History of White People*, 212–27. For Van Evrie's critique, see Van Evrie, *Negroes and Negro "Slavery"* (1861 ed.), 44.

9. "Says God Wants Separation," *Indianapolis Star*, December 4, 1977.

10. Johnny Bananas, "Excellent Book," customer review at amazon.com, January 28, 2012, accessed August 12, 2025, www.amazon.com/Negroes-Negro-Slavery-Inferior-Condition/dp/1331354137/ref=monarch_sidesheet_title.

11. Harold Boulware, Robert L. Carter, Jack Greenberg, Oliver W. Hill, Thurgood Marshall, Louis L. Redding et al., "Brief for Appellants in Nos. 1, 2 and 4 and for Respondents in No. 10 on Reargument," 50–51, in Kansas: Topeka—Brown v. Board of Education (and Other Cases): 2nd Reargument—Legal Papers, 1953–55, Group II, Series B, Legal File, Schools, Papers of the NAACP, Part 03: The Campaign for Educational Equality, Series C: Legal Department and Central Office Records, 1951–55, ProQuest History Vault.

12. "Supplement to Brief: The Political, Social and Legal Theories Underlying the Fourteenth Amendment," 213–14, in Kansas: Topeka—Brown v. Board of Education (and Other Cases): 2nd Reargument—Legal Papers, 1954 (1), Group II, Series B, Legal File, Schools, Papers of the NAACP, Part 03: The Campaign for Educational Equality, Series C: Legal Department and Central Office Records, 1951–55, ProQuest History Vault.

13. Michael Powell, "'White Supremacy' Once Meant David Duke and the Klan. Now It Refers to Much More," *New York Times*, October 17, 2020.

14. Lyndon B. Johnson, "Special Message to Congress: The American Promise," March 15, 1965, The American Presidency Project, accessed August 11, 2025, www.presidency.ucsb.edu/documents/special-message-the-congress-the-american-promise.

15. On the importance of this conflict, see James Oakes, "Commentary: Conflict vs. Racial Consensus in the History of Antislavery Politics," in Hammond and Mason, *Contesting Slavery*, 291–303.

16. Douglass, *Claims of the Negro.*

Bibliography

Primary Sources

Manuscript Collections

Albany, NY
  New York State Library
    Horatio Seymour Papers
Arlington, TX
  Special Collections, University of Texas at Arlington
    "Siege of Puebla, Began Sept. 13th. Ended Oct. 12th. 1847"
Atlanta, GA
  Stuart A. Rose Manuscript, Archives, and Rare Book Library, Emory University
    Alexander H. Stephens Collection
Auburn, AL
  Auburn University Archives and Special Collections
    Samford-Wise Papers
Austin, TX
  Dolph Briscoe Center for American History, University of Texas at Austin
    Joseph E. Davis Papers
Baltimore, MD
  Maryland Center for History and Culture
    C. W. Jacobs Diary
Berkeley, CA
  Bancroft Library, University of California, Berkeley
    J. W. Leigh Letter: Puebla, Mexico, to Mrs. Benjamin Watkins Leigh, Richmond, Va., October 2, 1847
Bethlehem, PA
  Lehigh University
    Thomas Butler Gunn Diary
Bloomington, IN
  Lilly Library, Indiana University
    Joseph Lane Mss
Buffalo, NY
  Buffalo and Erie County Historical Society
    Millard Fillmore Papers
Cambridge, MA
  Baker Library, Harvard Business School
    R. G. Dun & Co. Credit Report Volumes

Houghton Library, Harvard University
Papers of Charles Sumner
Chapel Hill, NC
Wilson Library, University of North Carolina
W. Stump Forwood Papers
Charlottesville, VA
Albert and Shirley Small Special Collections Library, University of Virginia
Letters to Rufus Wilmot Griswold
Chicago, IL
Special Collections Research Center, University of Chicago
Stephen A. Douglas Papers
Durham, NC
Rubenstein Library, Duke University
W. Stump Forwood Papers
William W. Reavis Papers
Alexander H. Stephens Papers
Geneva, NY
Warren Hunting Smith Library, Hobart and William Smith Colleges
College History—Biographical Files
Hartford, CT
Connecticut Historical Society
Thomas Henry Seymour Papers
Jackson, MS
Mississippi Department of Archives and History
Quitman (John A.) and Family Papers
Kansas City, MO
National Archives Kansas City
Bankruptcy Act of 1841 Case Files, 1841–43 (RG 21)
Louisville, KY
Filson Historical Society
Madison Mills Diary
New Haven, CT
Beinecke Rare Book and Manuscript Library, Yale University
John W. Dodd Papers
Gen Mss Misc, Group 655
Gen Mss Misc, Group 1840
Gen Mss Misc, Group 1841
Manuscripts and Archives Repository, Yale University
Bacon Family Papers
New York City, NY
New York City Municipal Archives
John Van Evrie Certificate of Death (no. 8637)
Manuscripts and Archives Division, New York Public Library
Democratic Anti-Abolition State Rights Association of the City of New York Minutes
Rushmore G. Horton Papers
Charles O'Conor Letters and Documents

New-York Historical Society
David Francis Bacon Letters
Ralph Randolph Gurley Letters
Ottawa, Canada
Library and Archives Canada
Haldimand Papers
Land Petitions of Upper Canada, 1763–1865
Van Every Family Fonds
War of 1812: Upper Canada Returns, Nominal Rolls and Paylists
Paris, ON
County of Brant (ON) Public Library
Hiram Capron Account Book, 1828–31
Hiram Capron Collection
Hiram Capron Day Book Letter H, Account Book, 1833–41
Providence, RI
Hay Library, Brown University
Samuel Sullivan Cox Papers
Richmond, VA
Virginia Museum of History and Culture
Massie Family Papers
J. H. Van Evrie to Jefferson Davis, June 16, 1874
Rochester, NY
Rochester Genealogical Society
St. Luke and St. Simon Cyrene Episcopal Church, *Parish Register, Volume 1 (1820–1847)*
Rare Books, Special Collections, and Preservation, River Campus Libraries, University of Rochester
Anson Colman Papers
Edward Mott Moore Papers
Mt. Hope & Riverside Cemetery Records
Nathaniel Rochester Family Papers
Rochester Family Papers
Thurlow Weed Papers
Stanford, CA
Department of Special Collections and University Archives, Stanford University Libraries
David Morris Potter Papers
Syracuse, NY
Archives and Special Collections, Health Sciences Library, SUNY Upstate Medical University
Geneva Medical College Collection
Tucson, AZ
Special Collections, University of Arizona
"The Diary of Robert Hagan, Assistant Surgeon, United States Army with the 14th Infantry in the War with Mexico, 1847–1848"

Washington, DC
Folger Shakespeare Library
Autograph Letters Signed from R. G. Horton, New York, to William Winter, 1861
Manuscript Division, Library of Congress
American Colonization Society Records
Breckinridge Family Papers
Confederate States of America Records
DeButts-Ely Collection of Lee Family Papers
James H. Hammond Papers
Andrew Jackson Papers
Andrew Johnson Papers
Abraham Lincoln Papers
Manton Marble Papers
William L. Marcy Papers
George B. McClellan Papers
Alexander Hamilton Stephens Papers
National Archives
Records of the United States Senate (RG 46)
Domestic Letters of the Department of State, 1784–1906 (RG 59)
Letters of Application and Recommendation During the Administrations of James Polk, Zachary Taylor, and Millard Fillmore, 1845–53 (RG 59)
Records of the Adjutant General's Office, 1762–1894 (RG 94)
Records of the Public Buildings Service, 1801–2000 (RG 121)

Digital Databases and Records

The American Presidency Project
Ancestry.com
Canadian Census Collection
Civil War Muster Roll Abstracts
New York Wills and Probate Records, 1659–1999
Quebec, Vital and Church Records (Drouin Collection), 1621–1968
Record of Wills, Book No. 17, Monroe County, New York
US Federal Census Collection
US Passport Applications, 1867–73
Findagrave.com
Mcnygenealogy.com
National Park Service, Civil War Soldiers and Sailors System
ProQuest History Vault
Wikitree.com

Newspapers and Periodicals

Abbeville (SC) Press and Banner
Allen County Democrat (Lima, OH)
Alton (IL) Weekly Telegraph
American Agriculturist
American Citizen (Canton, MS)
American Railroad Journal
Anthropological Review
Anti-Slavery Bugle (New Lisbon, OH)

Arkansas Campaign Gazette (Little Rock)
Ashland (OH) Union
Atlanta Daily Sun
Atlas (Boston)
Aus der Heimath
Autauga Citizen (Prattville, AL)
Bangor (ME) Daily Whig and Courier
Bedford (PA) Gazette
Blue Hen's Chicken and Commonwealth (Wilmington, DE)
Boston Daily Advertiser
Boston Evening Transcript
Boston Herald
Boston Morning Post
Boston Post
Brandon (VT) Post
Bristol Mercury
British and Foreign Evangelical Review
Brooklyn Daily Eagle
Brooklyn Daily Times
Buffalo Courier
Buffalo Daily Gazette
Buffalo Daily Republic
Buffalo Evening Post
Burlington (VT) Daily Times
Cadiz (OH) Sentinel
California (MO) Weekly News
Camden (AL) Phoenix
Camden (SC) Weekly Journal
Canadian Casket
Cannelton (IN) Reporter
Central Missourian (California)
Central Transcript (Clinton, IL)
Charleston Courier
Charleston Daily News
Charleston Mercury
Chattanooga Daily Rebel
Chicago Tribune
Christian Ambassador
Cincinnati Enquirer
Clarksville (TN) Weekly Chronicle
Clearfield (PA) Republican
Columbus (GA) Daily Enquirer
Columbus (GA) Daily Enquirer-Sun
Commonwealth (Boston)
Confederate Union (Milledgeville, GA)
Confederate Veteran
Constitution (Washington, DC)
Cooper's Clarksburg (VA) Register
Courier-Journal (Louisville)
Crisis (Columbus, OH)
Daily Alabama Journal (Montgomery)
Daily Arkansas Gazette (Little Rock)
Daily Clarion (Jackson, MS)
Daily Cleveland Herald
Daily Constitution (Middletown, CT)
Daily Constitutionalist (Augusta, GA)
Daily Delta (New Orleans)
Daily Dramatic Chronicle (San Francisco)
Daily Evening Bulletin (San Franciso)
Daily Gate City (Keokuk, IA)
Daily Intelligencer (Atlanta)
Daily Iowa State Register (Des Moines)
Daily Louisville Democrat
Daily Missouri Republican (St. Louis)
Daily Ohio State Journal (Columbus)
Daily Picayune (New Orleans)
Daily Sentinel (Raleigh)
Daily Shreveport Times
Daily South Carolinian (Columbia)
Daily Sun (Columbus, GA)
Daily Union (Washington, DC)
Dallas Daily Herald
De Bow's Review
Defiance (OH) Democrat
Delaware (OH) Gazette
Delphi (IN) Weekly Times
Democrat (Huntsville, AL)
Democrat and Chronicle (Rochester, NY)
Democratic Advocate (Westminster, MD)
Democratic Enquirer (McArthur, OH)
Detroit Free Press
Donaldsonville (LA) Chief
Eastern Carolina Republican (New Bern, NC)
Eaton (OH) Democrat
Edgefield (SC) Advertiser
Episcopal Recorder (Philadelphia)
Evening Bulletin (San Francisco)
Evening Star (Washington, DC)
Fayetteville (NC) News
Fayetteville (TN) Observer

Flag of Freedom (Puebla, Mexico)
Frederick Douglass' Paper
Galaxy Advertiser
Gospel Magazine
Grand Haven (MI) News
Greenville (SC) News
Harper's Weekly
Hartford Daily Courant
Hillsdale (MI) Standard
Houston Tri-Weekly Telegraph
Idaho Tri-Weekly Statesman (Boise)
Independent (New York)
Indiana (PA) Democrat
Indiana State Sentinel (Indianapolis)
Indiana True Republican (Centreville, IN)
Indianapolis Star
Inter Ocean (Chicago)
Jeffersonian Republican (Stroudsburg, PA)
Kennebec Journal (Augusta, ME)
Knoxville Register
Lancaster (SC) Ledger
Leavenworth (KS) Daily Commercial
Lewisburg (PA) Chronicle
Liberator
Life Illustrated (New York)
Literary World
Long-Island Star (Brooklyn)
Louisiana Democrat (Alexandria, LA)
Loyalist Gazette
Macon (GA) Weekly Telegraph
Manchester Weekly Times and Examiner
M'Arthur Democrat (McArthur, OH)
Maumee (OH) Express
Memphis Daily Appeal
Memphis Evening Post
Methodist
Milwaukee Daily Sentinel
Mississippian (Jackson)
Mobile Register
Monroe Journal
Montgomery Daily Mail
Monthly Democratic Review
Moore's Rural New Yorker
Morning Express (Buffalo, NY)
Morning Post (London)
Morning Republican (Little Rock)
Moulton (AL) Advertiser
Nashville Daily Union
Natchez Daily Courier
Natchez Democrat
National Anti-Slavery Standard
National Era
New England Farmer (Boston)
New Hampshire Patriot and State Gazette (Concord)
New Hampshire Statesman (Concord)
New Haven Palladium
New Monthly Magazine
New Orleans Crescent
New York Day Book
New York Evening Post
New York Express
New York Freeman's Journal and Catholic Register
New York Herald
New York Merchant's Day Book
New York Spectator
New York Times
New York Tribune
New York Weekly Caucasian
Niles' Weekly Register
North American and United States Gazette (Philadelphia)
North Carolina Standard (Raleigh)
North Carolinian (Raleigh)
North Star
Norton's Literary Gazette and Publishers' Circular
Ohio Observer (Hudson)
Ohio Statesman (Columbus)
Old Guard
Orleans Independent Standard (Irasburgh, VT)
Oxford (NC) Mercury
Pennsylvania Freeman (Philadelphia)
Philadelphia Enquirer
Piston (PA) Gazette
Pittsburgh Daily Post
Plantation
Plymouth (IN) Weekly Democrat
Pomeroy's Democrat
Portland (ME) Daily Press

Poughkeepsie Journal
Princeton (NJ) Clarion
Quarterly Journal of Science
Racine County (WI) Argus
Raleigh Star, and North Carolina Gazette
Randolph County Journal (Winchester, IN)
Republican Banner (Nashville)
Revue Britannique
Richmond Dispatch
Richmond Enquirer
Rochester Gem and Ladies' Amulet
Roman Citizen (Rome, NY)
San Francisco Examiner
Saturday Evening Post
Savannah Republican
Scientific Mechanic (New York)
Scioto Gazette (Chillicothe, OH)
Semi-Weekly Mississippian (Jackson)
Semi-Weekly North Carolina Standard (Raleigh)
Shelby Guide (Columbiana, AL)
Southern Cultivator
Southern Literary Messenger
Southern Shield (Helena, AR)
Spirit of Missions (Burlington, NJ)
Spirit of the Age (Raleigh)
Spirit of the Age (Woodstock, VT)
Spirit of the South (Eufaula, AL)
St. Mary's Beacon (Leonard Town, MD)
Standard
Star of the North (Bloomsburg, PA)
Stark County Democrat (Canton, OH)
Staunton (VA) Spectator
Staunton (VA) Vindicator
Sugar Planter (West Baton Rouge, LA)
Sun (Baltimore)
Talker of the Town
Tarborough (NC) Southerner
Tasmanian (Launceston, Australia)
Tennessean (Nashville)
Times Literary Supplement
Times-Picayune (New Orleans)
Tri-Weekly Commercial (Wilmington, NC)
Tri-Weekly Kentucky Yeoman (Frankfort)
Tri-Weekly Messenger (Hannibal, MO)
True Democrat (Little Rock)
Una
Urbana (OH) Union
Van Buren (AR) Press
Vanity Fair
Vermont Patriot and State Gazette (Montpelier)
Vermont Watchman and State Journal (Montpelier)
Vicksburg Tri-Weekly Sentinel
Village Record (Waynesboro, PA)
Washington (AR) Telegraph
Washington (PA) Review and Examiner
Waverly Magazine
Weekly Advertiser (Montgomery)
Weekly Arkansas Gazette (Little Rock)
Weekly Champion and Press (Atchison, KS)
Weekly Columbus (GA) Enquirer
Weekly Indiana State Sentinel (Indianapolis)
Weekly National Intelligencer (Washington, DC)
Weekly North Carolina Standard (Raleigh)
Weekly Raleigh Register and North Carolina Gazette
Weekly Standard (Raleigh)
Weekly Underwriter
Weekly Vincennes (IN) Western Sun
Western Mirror (Cambridge City, IN)
Wheeling Daily Register
Wilmington (NC) Journal
Winfield (KS) Daily Telegram
Wisconsin Tribune (Mineral Point, WI)
Wyandot Pioneer (Upper Sandusky, OH)
York (PA) Democratic Press
York (PA) Gazette

Government Documents

Congressional Globe
House Documents 173, 26 Cong., 1 Sess. (Serial 366)
House Documents 1, 28 Cong., 2 Sess., Vol. 1 (Serial 463)

House Documents Ex. Doc. 3, 31 Cong., 1 Sess. (Serial 576)
House Documents Ex. Doc. 38, 31 Cong., 1 Sess. (Serial 576)
House Documents Ex. Doc. 88, 33 Cong., 1 Sess. (Serial 724)
House Documents Ex. Doc. 140, 34 Cong., 1 Sess. (Serial 864)
House Documents Ex. Doc. 29, 34 Cong., 3 Sess. (Serial 897)
House Miscellaneous Documents 5, 31 Cong., 2 Sess. (Serial 605)
House Miscellaneous Documents 2, 32 Cong., 1 Sess. (Serial 652)
House Report 648, 36 Cong., 1 Sess. (Serial 1071)
Senate Documents 22, 25 Cong. 1 Sess. (Serial 309)
Senate Documents 147, 26 Cong., 2 Sess. (Serial 377)

Published Primary Sources

Abolition and Secession, or, Cause and Effect: Together with the Remedy for Our Sectional Troubles. New York: Van Evrie, Horton & Co., 1862.

The Abolition Conspiracy to Destroy the Union; or, a Ten Years' Record of the "Republican" Party. New York: Van Evrie, Horton & Co., 1863.

Abolition Is National Death, or, the Attempt to Equalize Races the Destruction of Society. New York: Van Evrie, Horton & Co., 1866.

Adams, John Quincy. *An Eulogy on the Life and Character of James Madison*. Boston: American Stationers' Company, 1836.

The Administration Reviewed: Speech of Hon. John McKeon Before the Democratic Union Association, at Their Headquarters . . . October 29, 1862. New York: Van Evrie, Horton & Co., 1862.

The American Annual Cyclopaedia and Register of Important Events of the Year 1867. New York: D. Appleton, 1868.

Annual Report of the American Historical Association, 1941, Volume III. Washington, DC: Government Printing Office, 1943.

Avary, Myrta Lockett, ed. *Recollections of Alexander H. Stephens*. New York: Doubleday, Page, 1910.

Bacon, D. Francis. *Progressive Democracy: A Discourse, on the History, Philosophy, and Tendency of American Politics*. [New York]: Central Clay Committee, 1844.

Bacon, Leonard. *A Plea for Africa; Delivered in New-Haven, July 4th, 1825*. New Haven, CT: T. G. Woodward and Co., 1825.

[Bacon, Theodore.] *Delia Bacon: A Biographical Sketch*. Boston: Houghton Mifflin, 1888.

Bangs, Mrs. Bleecker. *Reminiscences of Old New Utrecht and Gowanus*. Brooklyn, NY: Brooklyn Eagle Press, 1912.

Banks, A. F. *Sharpe, the New York Detective*. New York: N. Munro, 1883.

Bentley, Wilbert Gorton. *Under the Search-Light: Address Delivered March 5, 1914, Before the Commandery of the State of Illinois Military Order of the Loyal Legion of the United States*. Chicago: Libby Company, 1914.

Bevan, H. *Thirty Years in India: or, a Soldier's Reminiscences of Native and European Life in the Presidencies, from 1808 to 1838*. 2 vols. London: Pelham Richardson, 1839.

Bowen, Eli. *The United States Post-Office Guide*. New York: D. Appleton, 1851.

Boyd's New York City Tax-Book. New York: William H. Boyd, 1857.

Caldwell, Charles. *Thoughts on the Original Unity of the Human Race.* New York: E. Bliss, 1830.

Campbell, John. *Negro-Mania: Being an Examination of the Falsely Assumed Equality of the Various Races of Men.* Philadelphia: Campbell & Power, 1851.

Carlyle, Thomas. *On Heroes, Hero-Worship, & the Heroic in History.* New York: D. Appleton, 1841.

Carnochan, Janet. *Names Only But Much More,* Niagara Historical Society No. 27. Niagara, ON: Niagara Historical Society, 1915.

Carroll, John. *My Boy Life.* Toronto: William Briggs, 1882.

Centz, P. C. [Bernard J. Sage.] *Davis and Lee: A Vindication of the Southern States, Citizens, and Rights, by the Federal Constitution and Its Makers.* New York: Van Evrie, Horton & Co., 1866.

Chamberlain, Houston Stewart. *Foundations of the Nineteenth Century.* 2 vols. Translated by John Lees. New York: John Lane Company, 1914.

Charter and Directory of the City of Rochester. Rochester, NY: Marshall & Dean Printers, [1834].

Circular and Catalogue of the Faculty and Officers of the Medical Institution of Geneva College. Auburn, NY: Oliphant & Skinner, [1834].

Cloquet, H. *A System of Human Anatomy.* Boston: Wells and Lilly, 1830.

Cockrell, Thomas D., and Michael B. Ballard, eds. *Chickasaw, a Mississippi Scout for the Union: The Civil War Memoir of Levi H. Naron.* Baton Rouge: Louisiana State University Press, 2005.

Coldham, Peter Wilson, ed. *American Loyalist Claims.* Vol. 1. Washington, DC: National Genealogical Society, 1980.

Colt, J. C. *The Science of Double Entry Book-Keeping.* 45th ed. New York: Lamport, Blakeman & Law, 1853.

Cooke, John Esten. *The Heir of Graymount: A Novel.* New York: Van Evrie, Horton & Co., 1870.

Crallé, Richard K., ed. *The Works of John C. Calhoun.* 6 vols. New York: D. Appleton, 1883.

Crist, Lynda Lasswell, Mary S. Dix, Kenneth H. Williams, and Suzanne S. Gibbs, eds. *The Papers of Jefferson Davis.* 14 vols. Baton Rouge: Louisiana State University Press, 1971–2015.

Dana, Charles A., ed. *Meyer's Universum or Views of the Most Remarkable Places and Object of All Countries.* 2 vols. New York: Herman J. Meyer, 1852.

Davis, Charles S. *The Cotton Kingdom in Alabama.* Montgomery: Alabama State Department of Archives and History, 1939.

[De Bow, James D. B.] *The Interest in Slavery of the Southern Non-Slaveholder.* Charleston, SC: Evans & Cogswell, 1860.

Dewees, William P. *A Treatise on the Diseases of Females.* Philadelphia: Carey & I. Lea, 1826.

Doggett's New York City Directory, for 1849–1850. New York: John Doggett Jr., 1849.

Doggett's New York City Directory, Illustrated with Maps of New York and Brooklyn, 1848–1849. New York: John Doggett Jr., 1848.

Douglass, Frederick. *The Claims of the Negro, Ethnologically Considered. An Address,*

Before the Literary Societies of Western Reserve College, at Commencement, July 12, 1854. Rochester: Lee, Mann & Co., 1854.
Drake, Daniel. *Practical Essays on Medical Education and the Medical Profession in the United States*. Cincinnati: Roff & Young, 1832.
Drake, Daniel. *A Systematic Treatise, Historical, Etiological, and Practical, on the Principal Diseases of the Interior Valley of North America*. 2 vols. Cincinnati: Winthrop B. Smith & Co., 1850.
Dred Scott Decision: Opinion of Chief Justice Roger B. Taney, in the Dred Scott Case. With an Introduction by Dr. J. H. Van Evrie, also, an Appendix on the Natural History of the Prognathous Race of Mankind, by Dr. S. A. Cartwright, of New Orleans. 2nd ed. New York: Van Evrie, Horton & Co., 1863.
Dred Scott Decision: Opinion of Chief Justice Taney, with an Introduction by Dr. J. H. Van Evrie. Also, an Appendix, Containing an Essay on the Natural History of the Prognathous Race of Mankind, Originally Written for the New York Day-Book *by Dr. S. A. Cartwright, of New Orleans*. New York: Van Evrie, Horton & Co., 1860.
Drew, Benjamin. *The Refugee: or the Narratives of Fugitive Slaves in Canada*. Boston: John P. Jewett, 1856.
Dunglison, Robley. *Human Physiology*. 2 vols. Philadelphia: Carey & Lea, 1832.
Durand, Charles. *Reminiscences of Charles Durand of Toronto, Barrister*. Toronto: Hunter, Rose Co., 1897.
"Early Records of St. Mark's and St. Andrew's Churches, Niagara." *Ontario Historical Society. Papers and Records Vol. III*. Toronto: Ontario Historical Society, 1901.
Encyclopædia Britannica: A Dictionary of Arts, Sciences and General Literature. 9th ed. 25 vols. Edinburgh, UK: Adam and Charles Black, 1884.
Exclusion of Newspapers from the Mail: A Plain Statement for a Candid Public. New York: Van Evrie, Horton & Co., 1861.
Farnham, Thomas J. *Life and Adventures in California*. New York: Wm. H. Graham, 1847.
Fernow, Berthold, ed. *Documents Relating to the Colonial History of the State of New York. Volume XV. State Archives*. Vol. 1. Albany, NY: Weed, Parsons, 1887.
Fitzhugh, George. *Sociology for the South, or the Failure of Free Society*. Richmond, VA: A. Morris, 1854.
Free Negroism, or, Results of Emancipation in the North and the West India Islands. New York: Van Evrie, Horton & Co., 1862.
Free Negroism, or, Results of Emancipation in the North and the West India Islands. 2nd ed. Revised and enlarged. New York: Van Evrie, Horton & Co., 1863.
Freehling, William W., and Craig M. Simpson, eds. *Secession Debated: Georgia's Showdown in 1860*. New York: Oxford University Press, 1992.
[Fuller, Hiram.] *Belle Brittan on a Tour, at Newport, and Here and There*. New York: Derby & Jackson, 1858.
Garrett, William. *Reminiscences of Public Men in Alabama, for Thirty Years*. Atlanta, GA: Plantation Publishing, 1872.
Geo. P. Rowell & Co's American Newspaper Directory. New York: Geo. P. Rowell & Co., 1869.
Geo. P. Rowell & Co's American Newspaper Directory. New York: Geo. P. Rowell & Co., 1872–79.

de Gobineau, A. *The Moral and Intellectual Diversity of Races*. Philadelphia: J. B. Lippincott & Co., 1856.

de Gobineau, Arthur. *The Inequality of Human Races*. Translated by Adrian Collins. New York: H. Fertig, 1976.

Gobright, J. C. & Co. *The New-York Hand Book and Merchants' Guide*. New York: Pudney & Russell, 1859.

Gourlay, Robert. *Statistical Account of Upper Canada*. 2 vols. London: Simpkin & Marshall, 1822.

Grant, Madison. *The Passing of the Great Race or the Racial Basis of European History*. New York: Charles Scribner's Sons, 1916.

Grayson, William J. *The Hireling and the Slave*. Charleston, SC: John Russell, 1854.

Greeley or Grant?: Speech of Hon. Charles Sumner, Intended to Be Delivered at Faneuil Hall, Boston, Sept. 3, 1872. Boston: Lee and Shepard, 1872.

Grund, Francis J. *The Americans in Their Moral, Social, and Political Relations*. 2 vols. London: Longman, Rees, Orme, Brown, Green & Longman, 1837.

Hammond, James Henry. *Gov. Hammond's Letters on Southern Slavery: Addressed to Thomas Clarkson, the English Abolitionist*. Charleston, SC: Walker and Burke, 1845.

Hay, Melba Porter, and Carol Reardon, eds. *The Papers of Henry Clay, Volume 10: Candidate, Compromiser, Elder Statesman, January 1, 1844–June 29, 1852*. Lexington: University of Kentucky Press, 1991.

Henderson, Thomas. *Hints on the Medical Examination of Recruits for the Army*. Philadelphia: Haswell, Barrington and Haswell, 1840.

Henderson, Thomas. *Hints on the Medical Examination of Recruits for the Army*. Rev. ed. Edited by Richard H. Coolidge. Philadelphia: J. B. Lippincott and Co., 1856.

Horton, R. G. *The Life and Public Services of James Buchanan*. New York: Derby & Jackson, 1856.

Horton, R. G. *Volks Geschichte des Grossen Bürgerkrieges in den Vereinigten Staaten, von 1861 bis 1865*. New York: Van Evrie, Horton & Co, 1867.

Horton, R. G. *A Youth's History of the Great Civil War in the United States, from 1861 to 1865*. New York: Van Evrie, Horton & Co., 1867.

Howard, Oliver Otis. *Autobiography of Oliver Otis Howard*. 2 vols. New York: Baker & Taylor Company, 1908.

Hunt, James. *The Negro's Place in Nature: A Paper Read Before the London Anthropological Society*. New York: Van Evrie, Horton & Co., 1864.

Hunt, James. *On the Negro's Place in Nature*. London: Trübner & Co., 1863.

Jackson, Samuel. *Principles of Medicine, Founded on the Structure and Functions of the Animal Organism*. Philadelphia: Carey & Lea, 1832.

Jacobs, Curtis M. *Speech of Col. Curtis M. Jacobs, on the Free Colored Population of Maryland*. Annapolis: Elihu S. Riley, 1860.

Jefferson, Thomas. *Notes on the State of Virginia*. 1785. Philadelphia: Prichard and Hall, 1788.

Journal of the Proceedings of the Senate of the State of Maryland, January Session, 1872. Annapolis: Wm. Thompson, 1872.

Journal of the Senate of Indiana, During the Thirty-Ninth Session of the General Assembly, Commencing Thursday, January 8, 1857. Indianapolis: Joseph J. Bingham, 1857.

Journals of the Senate and House of Commons of the General Assembly of the State of North Carolina, at Its Session of 1856-'7. Raleigh: Holden & Wilson, 1857.

Julian, George W. *Political Recollections, 1840 to 1872.* Chicago: Jansen, McClurg & Co., 1884.

The Kansas Struggle of 1856, in Congress, and in the Presidential Campaign; with Suggestions for the Future. New York: American Abolition Society, 1857.

Mackenzie, William L. *Sketches of Canada and the United States.* London: Effingham Wilson, 1833.

Manetta, Filippo. *La Razza Negra: Nel Suo Stato Selvaggio in Africa e Nella Sua Duplice Condizione di Emancipata e di Schiava in America.* Turin: Tipografia del Commercio, 1864.

Mayer, Brantz. *Mexico as It Was and as It Is.* New York: J. Winchester, New World Press, 1844.

Mayer, Brantz. *Mexico: Aztec, Spanish and Republican.* 2 vols. Hartford, CT: S. Drake, 1851.

McCaffrey, James M., ed. *"Surrounded by Dangers of All Kinds": The Mexican War Letters of Lieutenant Theodore Laidley.* Denton: University of North Texas Press, 1997.

McKivigan, John R., Julie Husband, and Heather L. Kaufman, eds. *The Speeches of Frederick Douglass: A Critical Edition.* New Haven, CT: Yale University Press, 2018.

Meriwether, Robert L., W. Edwin Hemphill, and Clyde N. Wilson, eds. *The Papers of John C. Calhoun.* 28 vols. Columbia: University of South Carolina Press, 1959–2003.

Minutes of the Proceedings of a Convention of Merchants and Others, Held in Augusta, Georgia, October 16, 1837. Augusta: Benj. Brantly, 1838.

Minutes of the Thirty-Eighth Annual Convention of the United Daughters of the Confederacy. Jacksonville, FL: n.p., 1931.

Miscellaneous Documents of the House of Representatives, During the First Session of the Thirty-Second Congress. Washington, DC: A. Boyd Hamilton, 1852.

Miscellaneous Documents Printed by Order of the House of Representatives, During the First Session of the Thirty-First Congress, Begun and Held at the City of Washington December 3, 1849. Washington, DC: Wm. M. Belt, 1850.

Mississippi in 1875. Report of the Select Committee to Inquire into the Mississippi Election of 1875, with the Testimony and Documentary Evidence. 2 vols. Washington, DC: Government Printing Office, 1876.

Morton, Samuel George. *Crania Aegyptiaca.* Philadelphia: John Penington, 1844.

Morton, Samuel George. *Crania Americana.* Philadelphia: J. Dobson, 1839.

Nevins, Allan, and Milton Halsey Thomas, eds. *The Diary of George Templeton Strong, Volume III: The Civil War, 1860–1865.* New York: Macmillan, 1952.

New York Mercantile Union Business Directory . . . Carefully Collected and Arranged for 1850–51. New York: S. French, L.C. & H. L. Pratt, 1850.

New York Weekly Caucasian. *The White Man's Paper.* New York: Van Evrie, Horton & Co., [1862].

Nott, J. C. "The Mulatto a Hybrid—Probable Extermination of the Two Races If the Whites and Blacks Are Allowed to Marry." *American Journal of the Medical Sciences* 6 (July 1843): 252–56.

Nott, Josiah C. *An Essay on the Natural History of Mankind, Viewed in Connection with Negro Slavery.* Mobile, AL: Dade, Thompson & Co., 1851.

Nott, Josiah C. *Two Lectures on the Connection Between the Biblical and Physical History of Man*. New York: Bartlett and Welford, 1849.

Nott, Josiah C. *Two Lectures, on the Natural History of the Caucasian and Negro Races*. Mobile, AL: Dade and Thompson, 1844.

O'Conor, Charles. *"Negro Slavery Not Unjust": Speech of Charles O'Conor, Esq., at the Union Meeting at the Academy of Music, New York City, December 19th, 1859*. New York: Van Evrie, Horton & Co., 1859.

Official Proceedings of the Democratic National Convention, Held in 1864 at Chicago. Chicago: Times Steam Book and Job Printing House, 1864.

Official Proceedings of the National Democratic Convention, Held at Baltimore, July 9, 1872. Boston: Rockwell & Churchill, Printers, 1872.

Oswandel, J. Jacob. *Notes of the Mexican War 1846–47–48*. Philadelphia: n.p., 1885.

Peace and Union, War and Disunion: Speech of John McKeon: Delivered Before the Democratic Union Association, at Their Headquarters, No. 932 Broadway, on Tuesday Evening, March 3. New York: Van Evrie, Horton & Co., 1863.

Peck, William Henry. *The Confederate Flag on the Ocean: A Tale of the Cruises of Sumter and Alabama*. New York: Van Evrie, Horton & Co., 1868.

Piersol, Mary Blackadar. *The Records of the Van Every Family, United Empire Loyalists*. Toronto: T. H. Best Printing, 1947.

Pike, James S. *The Prostrate State: South Carolina Under Negro Government*. New York: D. Appleton, 1874.

Pollard, Edward A. *The Lost Cause: A New Southern History of the War of the Confederates*. New York: E. B. Treat & Co., 1866.

Proceedings and Debates of the Constitutional Convention of the State of New York, Held in 1867 and 1868, in the City of Albany. 5 vols. Albany, NY: Weed, Parsons, 1868.

Proceedings of the Fourth Convention of Merchants and Others, Held in Charleston, S.C., April 15, 1839, for the Promotion of Direct Trade. Charleston, SC: A. E. Miller, 1839.

Proofs for Workingmen of the Monarchic and Aristocratic Designs of the Southern Conspirators and Their Northern Allies. Philadelphia: H. B. Ashmead, 1864.

Puritanism in Politics: Speech of Hon. S. S. Cox, of Ohio, Before the Democratic Union Association, January 13, 1863. New York: Van Evrie, Horton & Co., 1863.

Register of All Officers and Agents, Civil, Military, and Naval, in the Service of the United States, on the Thirtieth September, 1849. Washington, DC: Gideon and Co., 1849.

Register of All Officers and Agents, Civil, Military, and Naval, in the Service of the United States, on the Thirtieth September, 1851. Washington, DC: Gideon and Co., 1851.

Register of Officers and Agents, Civil, Military, and Naval, in the Service of the United States, on the Thirtieth September, 1853. Washington, DC: Robert Armstrong, 1853.

Register of Officers and Agents, Civil, Military, and Naval, in the Service of the United States, on the Thirtieth September, 1859. Washington, DC: William A. Harris, 1859.

Reid, William D. *Death Notices of Ontario*. 1980. Baltimore: Genealogical Publishing, 1997.

Resolves of the State of Maine from 1857 to 1860, Inclusive. Augusta: Stevens & Sayward, 1861.

Reuben Vose's Guide to New York City. New York: Reuben Vose, 1860.

Reuter, Edward Byron. *The Mulatto in the United States*. Boston: Richard G. Badger, 1918.

Richardson, James D., ed. *A Compilation of the Messages and Papers of the Presidents, 1789–1897*. 10 vols. Washington, DC: Published by Authority of Congress, 1899.

Richerand, Anthelme. *Elements of Physiology*. 5th ed. New York: W. E. Dean, 1833.

Riddell, William Renwick, ed. "Documents." *Journal of Negro History* 15 (January 1930): 115–16.

The Rights of the Citizen: Speech of Hon. D. W. Voorhees, on the Indemnity Bill, Delivered in the House of Representatives, February 18, 1863. New York: Van Evrie, Horton & Co., 1863.

Rowland, Dunbar, ed. *Jefferson Davis, Constitutionalist: His Letters, Papers, and Speeches*. 10 vols. Jackson: Mississippi Department of Archives and History, 1923.

Rutherford, Mildred Lewis. *Truths of History: A Fair, Unbiased, Impartial, Unprejudiced and Conscientious Study of History*. [Athens, GA]: n.p., 1920.

The Six Species of Men, with Cuts Representing the Types of the Caucasian, Mongol, Malay, Indian, Esquimaux and Negro. With Their General Physical and Mental Qualities, Laws of Organization, Relations to Civilization, &c. New York: Van Evrie, Horton & Co., 1866.

Smith, William R. *The History and Debates of the Convention of the People of Alabama*. Montgomery: White, Pfister & Co., 1861.

Smith, William Wye. *William Wye Smith: Recollections of a Nineteenth Century Scottish Canadian*. Edited by Scott A. McLean and Michael E. Vance. Toronto: Dundurn Press, 2008.

Smy, William A. *An Annotated Nominal Roll of Butler's Rangers, 1777–1784 with Documentary Sources*. St. Catharines, ON: Friends of the Loyalist Collection at Brock University, 2004.

The "Southern Trade": An Epitome of Commerce North and South. New York: E. K. Cooley, 1860.

Speech of Benjamin Wood of New York, on the State of the Union, in the House of Representatives, May 16th, 1862. New York: Van Evrie, Horton & Co., 1862.

Speech of Hon. Horatio Seymour, Before the Democratic Union State Convention, at Albany, September 10th, 1862, on Receiving the Nomination for Governor: Also, His Speech Delivered at the Albany Convention, Jan. 31st, 1861. New York: Van Evrie, Horton & Co., 1862.

Speech of Hon. J. C. Breckinridge, Delivered at Ashland, Ky., September 5th. New York: Van Evrie, Horton & Co., 1860.

Speeches of Hon. Horatio Seymour, and Hon. John Van Buren, at the Grand Ratification Meeting, at the Cooper Institute, October 13, 1862, with General Scott's Prophetic Letter. New York: Van Evrie, Horton & Co., 1862.

Speeches of the Hon. Jefferson Davis, of Mississippi, Delivered During the Summer of 1858. Baltimore: John Murphy & Co., 1859.

Stauffer, John, ed. *The Works of James McCune Smith, Black Intellectual and Abolitionist*. New York: Oxford University Press, 2006.

Stephens, Alexander H. *A Constitutional View of the Late War Between the States*. 2 vols. Philadelphia: National Publishing, 1868.

Stoddard, Lothrop. *The Rising Tide of Color Against White World-Supremacy*. New York: Blue Ribbon Books, 1920.

Stowe, Harriet Beecher. *Uncle Tom's Cabin; or, Life Among the Lowly*. 2 vols. Boston: John P. Jewett & Co., 1852.

Stowe, Nathan. *Sixty Years' Recollections of Milford*. Edited and revised by Newton Harrison. Milford, CT: n.p., 1917.

Strachan, James. *A Visit to the Province of Upper Canada in 1819*. Aberdeen: D. Chalmers & Co., 1820.

Table of Post Offices in the United States on the First Day of October, 1846. Washington, DC: John T. Towers, 1846.

Taylor, F. Jay, ed. *Reluctant Rebel: The Secret Diary of Robert Patrick, 1861–1865*. Baton Rouge: Louisiana State University Press, 1959.

Trow's New York City Directory. For the Year Ending May 1, 1884. New York: Trow City Directory Company, 1883.

Trow's New York City Directory. For the Year Ending May 1, 1885. New York: Trow City Directory Company, 1884.

Trow's New York City Directory. For the Year Ending May 1, 1886. New York: Trow City Directory Company, 1885.

Trow's New York City Directory. For the Year Ending May 1, 1889. New York: Trow City Directory Company, 1888.

Trow's New York City Directory. For the Year Ending May 1, 1890. New York: Trow City Directory Company, 1889.

The Two Proclamations: Speech of the Hon. James Brooks, Before the Democratic Union Association, Sept. 29th, 1862. New York: Van Evrie, Horton & Co., 1862.

Valuable Anti-Abolition Publications for General Circulation, Published by Van Evrie, Horton & Co. New York: Van Evrie, Horton & Co., 1863.

Van Evrie, J. H. *Negroes and Negro Slavery; The First, an Inferior Race—The Latter, Its Normal Condition*. Baltimore: J. D. Toy, 1853.

Van Evrie, J. H. *Negroes and Negro "Slavery"; The First, an Inferior Race—The Latter, Its Normal Condition*. New York: Day Book Office, 1853.

Van Evrie, J. H. *Negroes and Negro "Slavery": The First, an Inferior Race—The Latter, Its Normal Condition*. New York: Van Evrie, Horton & Co., 1861.

Van Evrie, J. H. *Negroes and Negro "Slavery": The First an Inferior Race; the Latter Its Normal Condition*. 3rd ed. New York: Van Evrie, Horton & Co., 1863.

Van Evrie, J. H. *White Supremacy and Negro Subordination; or, Negroes a Subordinate Race, and (So-Called) Slavery Its Normal Condition*. New York: Van Evrie, Horton & Co., 1868.

Van Evrie, J. H. *White Supremacy and Negro Subordination; or, Negroes a Subordinate Race, and (So-Called) Slavery Its Normal Condition*. 2nd ed. New York: Van Evrie, Horton & Co., 1868.

Van Evrie, J. H. *White Supremacy and Negro Subordination; or, Negroes a Subordinate Race, and (So-Called) Slavery Its Normal Condition*. New York: Van Evrie, Horton & Co., 1870.

Van Tyne, C. H., ed. *The Letters of Daniel Webster*. New York: McClure, Phillips & Co., 1902.

The War of the Rebellion: A Compilation of the Official Records of the Union and Confederate Armies. Washington, DC: Government Printing Office, 1880–1901.

Webster, Fletcher, ed. *The Private Correspondence of Daniel Webster*. 2 vols. Boston: Little, Brown, 1857.

White, Charles. *An Account of the Regular Gradation in Man*. London: C. Dilly, 1799.

Wiley, Edwin, and Irving E. Rines, eds. *The United States: Its Beginnings, Progress and Modern Development*. 10 vols. New York: American Educational Alliance 1913.

Wilson, H. *Trow's New York City Directory, for the Year Ending May 1, 1859*. New York: John F. Trow, 1858.

Wilson, H. *Trow's New York City Directory, for the Year Ending May 1, 1861*. New York: John F. Trow, 1860.

Wilson, H. *Trow's New York City Directory, for the Year Ending May 1, 1864*. New York: John F. Trow, 1863.

Winn, T. S. *Emancipation; or Practical Advice to British Slave-Holders*. London: W. Phillips, 1824.

Young, James. *Reminiscences of the Early History of Galt and the Settlement of Dumfries, in the Province of Ontario*. Toronto: Hunter, Rose, 1880.

Young Men's Fremont and Dayton Central Union, of the City of New York. *The New "Democratic" Doctrine*. New York: John W. Oliver, [1856].

Secondary Sources

Books

Abbott, Richard H. *For Free Press and Equal Rights: Republican Newspapers in the Reconstruction South*. Edited by John W. Quist. Athens: University of Georgia Press, 2004.

Albion, Robert Greenhalgh. *The Rise of New York Port, 1815–1860*. New York: Charles Scribner's Sons, 1939.

Anderson, Benedict. *Imagined Communities: Reflections on the Origin and Spread of Nationalism*. Rev. ed. London: Verso, 1991.

Andrews, J. Cutler. *The North Reports the Civil War*. Pittsburgh, PA: University of Pittsburgh Press, 1955.

Armstrong, F. H., H. A. Stevenson, and J. D. Wilson, eds. *Aspects of Nineteenth-Century Ontario: Essays Presented to James J. Talman*. Toronto: University of Toronto Press, 1974.

Asaka, Ikuko. *Tropical Freedom: Climate, Settler Colonialism, and Black Exclusion in the Age of Emancipation*. Durham, NC: Duke University Press, 2017.

Baker, Jean H. *The Politics of Continuity: Maryland Political Parties from 1858 to 1870*. Baltimore: Johns Hopkins University Press, 1973.

Balleisen, Edward J. *Navigating Failure: Bankruptcy and Commercial Society in Antebellum America*. Chapel Hill: University of North Carolina Press, 2001.

Baptist, Edward E. *The Half Has Never Been Told: Slavery and the Making of American Capitalism*. New York: Basic Books, 2014.

Barbuto, Richard V. *Niagara 1814: America Invades Canada*. Lawrence: University Press of Kansas, 2000.

Barnes, L. Diane., Brian Schoen, and Frank Towers, eds. *The Old South's Modern Worlds: Slavery, Region, and Nation in the Age of Progress*. New York: Oxford University Press, 2011.

Barrett, Walter. *The Old Merchants of New York City*. 5 vols. New York: Thomas R. Knox & Co., 1885.

Barreyre, Nicolas. *Gold and Freedom: The Political Economy of Reconstruction.* Translated by Arthur Goldhammer. Charlottesville: University of Virginia Press, 2015.

Baum, Bruce. *The Rise and Fall of the Caucasian Race: A Political History of Racial Identity.* New York: New York University Press, 2006.

Beckert, Sven. *The Monied Metropolis: New York City and the Consolidation of the American Bourgeoisie, 1850–1896.* New York: Cambridge University Press, 2001.

Behrend, Justin. *Reconstructing Democracy: Grassroots Black Politics in the Deep South After the Civil War.* Athens: University of Georgia Press, 2015.

Berlin, Ira, and Leslie M. Harris, eds. *Slavery in New York.* New York: New Press, 2005.

Bernstein, Iver. *The New York City Draft Riots: Their Significance for American Society and Politics in the Age of the Civil War.* New York: Oxford University Press, 1990.

Berwanger, Eugene H. *The Frontier Against Slavery: Western Anti-Negro Prejudice and the Slavery Extension Controversy.* Urbana: University of Illinois Press, 1967.

Biddiss, Michael D. *Father of Racist Ideology: The Social and Political Thought of Count Gobineau.* New York: Weybright and Talley, 1970.

Bilson, Geoffrey. *A Darkened House: Cholera in Nineteenth-Century Canada.* Toronto: University of Toronto Press, 1980.

Biographical Review . . . of the Leading Citizens of Delaware County New York. Boston: Biographical Review Publishing, 1895.

Biographical Sketch of Dr. Lewis A. Sayre. New York: Atlantic Publishing and Engraving, 1893.

Blackett, R. J. M. *The Captive's Quest for Freedom: Fugitive Slaves, the 1850 Fugitive Slave Law, and the Politics of Slavery.* New York: Cambridge University Press, 2018.

Blair, William A. *The Record of Murders and Outrages: Racial Violence and the Fight over Truth at the Dawn of Reconstruction.* Chapel Hill: University of North Carolina Press, 2021.

Blair, William A. *With Malice Toward Some: Treason and Loyalty in the Civil War Era.* Chapel Hill: University of North Carolina Press, 2014.

Blight, David W. *Frederick Douglass: Prophet of Freedom.* New York: Simon & Schuster, 2018.

Blight, David W. *Race and Reunion: The Civil War in American Memory.* Cambridge, MA: Harvard University Press, 2001.

Blondheim, Menahem. *News over the Wires: The Telegraph and the Flow of Public Information in America, 1844–1897.* Cambridge, MA: Harvard University Press, 1994.

Blue, Frederick J. *The Free Soilers: Third Party Politics, 1848–54.* Urbana: University of Illinois Press, 1973.

Bonner, Thomas Neville. *Becoming a Physician: Medical Education in Britain, France, Germany, and the United States, 1750–1945.* New York: Oxford University Press, 1995.

Bordley, James, III, and A. McGehee Harvey. *Two Centuries of American Medicine, 1776–1976.* Philadelphia: W. B. Saunders, 1976.

Bowes, John P. *Land Too Good for Indians: Northern Indian Removal.* Norman: University of Oklahoma Press, 2016.

Bradley, Mark. *Bluecoats and Tar Heels: Soldiers and Civilians in Reconstruction North Carolina.* Lexington: University Press of Kentucky, 2009.

Brandt, Nat. *The Man Who Tried to Burn New York.* Syracuse, NY: Syracuse University Press, 1986.

Brooke, John L. *"There Is a North": Fugitive Slaves, Political Crisis, and Cultural Transformation in the Coming of the Civil War.* Amherst: University of Massachusetts Press, 2019.

Brown, David. *Southern Outcast: Hinton Rowan Helper and* The Impending Crisis of the South. Baton Rouge: Louisiana State University Press, 2006.

Brown, Wallace. *The Good Americans: The Loyalists in the American Revolution.* New York: William Morrow, 1969.

Brown, Wallace, and Hereward Senior. *Victorious in Defeat: The American Loyalists in Exile.* New York: Facts on File Publications, 1985.

Broyld, dann J. *Borderland Blacks: Two Cities in the Niagara Region During the Final Decades of Slavery.* Baton Rouge: Louisiana State University Press, 2022.

Buford, Marcus Bainbridge. *A Genealogy of the Buford Family in America.* San Francisco: n.p., 1903.

Burge, Daniel J. *A Failed Vision of Empire: The Collapse of Manifest Destiny, 1845–1872.* Lincoln: University of Nebraska Press, 2022.

Burin, Eric. *Slavery and the Peculiar Solution: A History of the American Colonization Society.* Gainesville: University Press of Florida, 2005.

Burnett, Lonnie A. *Henry Hotze, Confederate Propagandist: Selected Writings on Revolution, Recognition, and Race.* Tuscaloosa: University of Alabama Press, 2008.

Burrows, Edwin G., and Mike Wallace. *Gotham: A History of New York City to 1898.* New York: Oxford University Press, 1999.

Caligiuri, Michael P., and Linton A. Mohammed. *The Neuroscience of Handwriting: Applications for Forensic Document Examination.* Boca Raton, FL: CRC Press, 2012.

Caniff, William. *History of the Settlement of Upper Canada (Ontario) with Special Reference to the Bay Quinte.* Toronto: Dudley & Burns, 1869.

Carmichael, Peter S. *The Last Generation: Young Virginians in Peace, War, and Reunion.* Chapel Hill: University of North Carolina Press, 2005.

Cassedy, James H. *Medicine and American Growth, 1800–1860.* Madison: University of Wisconsin Press, 1986.

Cecelski, David S. *The Fire of Freedom: Abraham Galloway and the Slaves' Civil War.* Chapel Hill: University of North Carolina Press, 2012.

Charvat, William. *The Profession of Authorship in America, 1800–1870: The Papers of William Charvat.* Edited by Matthew J. Bruccoli. Columbus: Ohio State University Press, 1968.

Cheathem, Mark R. *The Coming of Democracy: Presidential Campaigning in the Age of Jackson.* Baltimore: Johns Hopkins University Press, 2018.

Cheathem, Mark R. *Who Is James K. Polk?: The Presidential Election of 1844.* Lawrence: University Press of Kansas, 2023.

Cheng, Eileen Ka-May. *The Plain and Noble Garb of Truth: Nationalism and Impartiality in American Historical Writing, 1784–1860.* Athens: University of Georgia Press, 2008.

Clayton, Powell. *The Aftermath of the Civil War, in Arkansas.* New York: Neale Publishing, 1915.

Connelly, Thomas L., and Barbara L. Bellows. *God and General Longstreet: The Lost Cause and the Southern Mind.* Baton Rouge: Louisiana State University Press, 1982.

Craig, Gerald M. *Upper Canada: The Formative Years, 1784–1841.* London: McClelland and Stewart, 1963.

Crawford, George, and Robert M. Crawford, eds. *Memoirs of Iowa County Wisconsin: From the Earliest Historical Times Down to the Present.* 2 vols. n.p.: Northwestern Historical Association, 1913.

Crofts, Daniel W. *Lincoln and the Politics of Slavery: The Other Thirteenth Amendment and the Struggle to Save the Union.* Chapel Hill: University of North Carolina Press, 2016.

Cruikshank, Ernest. *The Story of Butler's Rangers and the Settlement of Niagara.* Welland, ON: Tribune Printing House, 1893.

Cullum, George W. *Biographical Register of the Officers and Graduates of the U.S. Military Academy. . . .* 2 vols. New York: D. Van Nostrand, 1868.

Cunliffe, Marcus. *Chattel Slavery and Wage Slavery: The Anglo-American Context, 1830–1860.* Athens: University of Georgia Press, 1979.

Curran, Andrew S. *The Anatomy of Blackness: Science & Slavery in an Age of Enlightenment.* Baltimore: Johns Hopkins University Press, 2011.

Curran, Robert Emmett. *American Catholics and the Quest for Equality in the Civil War Era.* Baton Rouge: Louisiana State University Press, 2023.

Cyclopedia of Eminent and Representative Men of the Carolinas of the Nineteenth Century. 2 vols. Madison, WI: Brant & Fuller, 1892.

Dain, Bruce. *A Hideous Monster of the Mind: American Race Theory in the Early Republic.* Cambridge, MA: Harvard University Press, 2002.

Daly, Christopher B. *Covering America: A Narrative History of a Nation's Journalism.* Amherst: University of Massachusetts Press, 2012.

Davies, Gareth, and Julian E. Zelizer, eds. *America at the Ballot Box: Elections and Political History.* Philadelphia: University of Pennsylvania Press, 2015.

Davis, Hugh. *Leonard Bacon: New England Reformer and Antislavery Moderate.* Baton Rouge: Louisiana State University Press, 1998.

Delbanco, Andrew. *The War Before the War: Fugitive Slaves and the Struggle for America's Soul from the Revolution to the Civil War.* New York: Penguin Press, 2018.

Dew, Charles B. *Apostles of Disunion: Southern Secession Commissioners and the Causes of the Civil War.* Charlottesville: University of Virginia Press, 2001.

Donald, David Herbert. *Charles Sumner and the Rights of Man.* New York: Knopf, 1970.

Dowling, David. *Capital Letters: Authorship in the Antebellum Literary Market.* Iowa City: University of Iowa Press, 2009.

Duffy, John. *From Humors to Medical Science: A History of American Medicine.* 2nd ed. Urbana: University of Illinois Press, 1993.

Dunlap, Leslie W. *American Historical Societies, 1790–1860.* Madison, WI: Cantwell Printing Co., 1944.

Earle, Jonathan H. *Jacksonian Antislavery & the Politics of Free Soil, 1824–1854.* Chapel Hill: University of North Carolina Press, 2004.

Early History of Michigan with Biographies of State Officers, Members of Congress Judges and Legislators. Lansing: Thorp & Godfrey, 1888.

Egerton, Douglas R. *The Wars of Reconstruction: The Brief, Violent History of America's Most Progressive Era.* New York: Bloomsbury, 2014.

Eisenhower, John S. D. *So Far from God: The U.S. War with Mexico, 1846–1848.* New York: Random House, 1989.

Elgersman, Maureen G. *Unyielding Spirits: Black Women and Slavery in Early Canada and Jamaica*. 1999. New York: Routledge, 2013.

Emberton, Carole. *Beyond Redemption: Race, Violence, and the American South after the Civil War*. Chicago: University of Chicago Press, 2013.

Escott, Paul D. *"What Shall We Do with the Negro?": Lincoln, White Racism, and Civil War America*. Charlottesville: University of Virginia Press, 2009.

Escott, Paul D. *The Worst Passions of Human Nature: White Supremacy in the Civil War North*. Charlottesville: University of Virginia Press, 2020.

Etcheson, Nicole. *The Emerging Midwest: Upland Southerners and the Political Culture of the Old Northwest, 1787–1861*. Bloomington: Indiana University Press, 1996.

Fabian, Ann. *The Skull Collectors: Race, Science, and America's Unburied Dead*. Chicago: University of Chicago Press, 2010.

Farrow, Anne, Joel Lang, and Jenifer Frank. *Complicity: How the North Promoted, Prolonged, and Profited from Slavery*. New York: Ballantine Books, 2005.

Faust, Drew Gilpin. *James Henry Hammond and the Old South: A Design for Mastery*. Baton Rouge: Louisiana State University Press, 1982.

Field, Phyllis F. *The Politics of Race in New York: The Struggle for Black Suffrage in the Civil War Era*. Ithaca, NY: Cornell University Press, 1982.

Fischer, Roger A. *Tippecanoe and Trinkets Too: The Material Culture of American Presidential Campaigns, 1828–1984*. Urbana: University of Illinois Press, 1988.

Fleming, Patricia Lockheart, Gilles Gallichan, and Yvan Lamonde, eds. *History of the Book in Canada, Volume One: Beginnings to 1840*. Toronto: University of Toronto Press, 2004.

Flint, David. *William Lyon Mackenzie: Rebel Against Authority*. Toronto: Oxford University Press, 1971.

Floyd, Barbara, ed. *Medicine on the Maumee: A History of Health Care in Northwest Ohio*. [Toledo, OH]: Ward M. Canaday Center for Special Collections, 2012.

Foner, Eric. *Reconstruction: America's Unfinished Revolution, 1863–1877*. New York: Harper & Row, 1988.

Foner, Philip S. *Business & Slavery: The New York Merchants & the Irrepressible Conflict*. 1941. New York: Russell & Russell, 1968.

Foos, Paul. *A Short, Offhand, Killing Affair: Soldiers and Social Conflict During the Mexican-American War*. Chapel Hill: University of North Carolina Press, 2002.

Forde, Kathy Roberts, and Sid Bedingfield, eds. *Journalism and Jim Crow: White Supremacy and the Black Struggle for a New America*. Urbana: University of Illinois Press, 2021.

Foster, Gaines M. *Ghosts of the Confederacy: Defeat, the Lost Cause, and the Emergence of the New South 1865 to 1913*. New York: Oxford University Press, 1987.

Fowler, Dorothy Ganfield. *Unmailable: Congress and the Post Office*. Athens: University of Georgia Press, 1977.

Fox, Louis H. *New York City Newspapers, 1820–1850: A Bibliography. The Papers of the Bibliographical Society of America, Volume Twenty-One, Parts One and Two*. Chicago: University of Chicago Press, 1927.

Fox-Genovese, Elizabeth, and Eugene D. Genovese. *Slavery in White and Black: Class and Race in the Southern Slaveholders' New World Order*. New York: Cambridge University Press, 2008.

Fredrickson, George M. *The Black Image in the White Mind: The Debate on Afro-American Character and Destiny, 1817–1914*. New York: Harper & Row, 1971.
Freehling, William W. *The Road to Disunion, Volume 1: Secessionists at Bay, 1776–1854*. New York: Oxford University Press, 1990.
Freehling, William W. *The Road to Disunion, Volume II: Secessionists Triumphant, 1854–1861*. New York: Oxford University Press, 2008.
Frost, Karolyn Smardz. *I've Got a Home in Glory Land: A Lost Tale of the Underground Railroad*. New York: Farrar, Straus, and Giroux, 2007.
Fryer, Mary Beacock. *King's Men: The Soldier Founders of Ontario*. Toronto: Dundurn Press, 1980.
Furniss, Jack. *Between Extremes: Seeking the Political Center in the Civil War North*. Baton Rouge: Louisiana State University Press, 2024.
Gallagher, Gary W., and Alan T. Nolan, eds. *The Myth of the Lost Cause and Civil War History*. Bloomington: Indiana University Press, 2000.
Gallagher, Gary W., and Rachel A. Shelden, eds. *A Political Nation: New Directions on Mid-Nineteenth-Century American Political History*. Charlottesville: University of Virginia Press, 2012.
Gallman, J. Matthew. *The Cacophony of Politics: Northern Democrats and the American Civil War*. Charlottesville: University of Virginia Press, 2021.
Gambill, Edward L. *Conservative Ordeal: Northern Democrats and Reconstruction, 1865–1868*. Ames: Iowa State University Press, 1981.
Gannon, Barbara A. *The Won Cause: Black and White Comradeship in the Grand Army of the Republic*. Chapel Hill: University of North Carolina Press, 2011.
Gellman, David N. *Emancipating New York: The Politics of Slavery and Freedom, 1777–1827*. Baton Rouge: Louisiana State University Press, 2006.
Gidney, R. D., and W. P. J. Millar. *Professional Gentlemen: The Professions in Nineteenth-Century Ontario*. Toronto: University of Toronto Press, 1994.
Goddard, M. E., and Henry V. Partridge. *A History of Norwich Vermont*. Hanover, N. H.: The Dartmouth Press, 1905.
Gómez, Laura E. *Manifest Destinies: The Making of the Mexican American Race*. New York: New York University Press, 2007.
González, Juan, and Joseph Torres. *News for All the People: The Epic Story of Race and the American Media*. London: Verso, 2011.
Gordon, George N. *The Communications Revolution: A History of Mass Media in the United States*. New York: Hastings House, Publishers, 1977.
Gossett, Thomas F. *Race: The History of an Idea in America*. New ed. New York: Oxford University Press, 1997.
Gould, Lewis L. *The Republicans: A History of the Grand Old Party*. New York: Oxford University Press, 2014.
Gould, Stephen Jay. *The Mismeasure of Man*. Rev. ed. New York: W. W. Norton, 2006.
Grant, John Webster. *A Profusion of Spires: Religion in Nineteenth-Century Ontario*. Toronto: University of Toronto Press, 1988.
Green, Patricia, Maurice H. Green, Sylvia Wray, and Robert Wray. *From West Flamborough's Storied Past: A Celebration of West Flamborough Township's Heritage*. n.p.: Waterdown-East Flamborough Heritage Society, 2003.

Greenberg, Amy S. *Manifest Manhood and the Antebellum American Empire*. New York: Cambridge University Press, 2005.

Greenberg, Amy S. *A Wicked War: Polk, Clay, Lincoln, and the 1846 U.S. Invasion of Mexico*. New York: Alfred A. Knopf, 2012.

Grossman, Lawrence. *The Democratic Party and the Negro: Northern and National Politics, 1868–92*. Urbana: University of Illinois Press, 1976.

Grover, Kathryn. *Make a Way Somehow: African-American Life in a Northern Community, 1790–1965*. Syracuse, NY: Syracuse University Press, 1994.

Guardino, Peter. *The Dead March: A History of the Mexican-American War*. Cambridge, MA: Harvard University Press, 2017.

Haller, John S., Jr. *Outcasts from Evolution: Scientific Attitudes of Racial Inferiority, 1859–1900*. Urbana: University of Illinois Press, 1971.

Hamilton, Holman. *Prologue to Conflict: The Crisis and Compromise of 1850*. 1964. New York: W. W. Norton, 1966.

Hammond, John Craig, and Matthew Mason, eds. *Contesting Slavery: The Politics of Bondage and Freedom in the New American Nation*. Charlottesville: University of Virginia Press, 2011.

Hansen, Marcus Lee. *The Mingling of the Canadian and American Peoples, Volume I: Historical*. New Haven, CT: Yale University Press, 1940.

Harris, D. W., and B. M. Hulse. *The History of Claiborne Parish, Louisiana*. New Orleans: W. B. Stansbury & Co., 1886.

Harris, Leslie M. *In the Shadow of Slavery: African Americans in New York City, 1626–1863*. Chicago: University of Chicago Press, 2003.

Harrold, Stanley. *Border War: Fighting over Slavery before the Civil War*. Chapel Hill: University of North Carolina Press, 2010.

Hatter, Lawrence B. A. *Citizens of Convenience: The Imperial Origins of American Nationhood on the U.S.-Canadian Border*. Charlottesville: University of Virginia Press, 2017.

Haynes, Sam W. *Unfinished Revolution: The Early American Republic in a British World*. Charlottesville: University of Virginia Press, 2010.

Headley, John W. *Confederate Operations in Canada and New York*. New York: Neale Publishing, 1906.

Heagerty, J. J. *Four Centuries of Medical History in Canada and a Sketch of the Medical History of Newfoundland*. 2 vols. Toronto: Macmillan of Canada, 1928.

Hébert, Keith S. *Cornerstone of the Confederacy: Alexander Stephens and the Speech That Defined the Lost Cause*. Knoxville: University of Tennessee Press, 2021.

Henkin, David M. *The Postal Age: The Emergence of Modern Communications in Nineteenth-Century America*. Chicago: University of Chicago Press, 2006.

Henle, Alea R. *Rescued from Oblivion: Historical Cultures in the Early United States*. Amherst: University of Massachusetts Press, 2020.

Hepburn, Sharon A. Roger. *Crossing the Border: A Free Black Community in Canada*. Urbana: University of Illinois Press, 2007.

Herschthal, Eric. *The Science of Abolition: How Slaveholders Became the Enemies of Progress*. New Haven, CT: Yale University Press, 2021.

Hickey, Donald R. *The War of 1812: A Forgotten Conflict*. 1989. Urbana: University of Illinois Press, 2012.

History of Hardin County, Ohio. Chicago: Warner, Beers & Co., 1883.

History of the County of Brant, Ontario. Toronto: Warner, Beers & Co., 1883.

History of Wages in the United States from Colonial Times to 1928, Bulletin of the United States Bureau of Labor Statistics No. 604. Washington, DC: United States Government Printing Office, 1934.

Hitsman, J. Mackay. *The Incredible War of 1812: A Military History*. Toronto: University of Toronto Press, 1965.

Hobart College General Catalogue of Officers, Graduates and Students, 1825–1897. Geneva, NY: W. F. Humphrey, 1897.

Hogarth, Rana A. *Medicalizing Blackness: Making Racial Difference in the Atlantic World, 1780–1840*. Chapel Hill: University of North Carolina Press, 2017.

Holt, Michael F. *The Election of 1860: "A Campaign Fraught with Consequences."* Lawrence: University Press of Kansas, 2017.

Holt, Michael F. *The Rise and Fall of the American Whig Party: Jacksonian Politics and the Onset of the Civil War*. New York: Oxford University Press, 1999.

Holzer, Harold. *Lincoln and the Power of the Press: The War for Public Opinion*. New York: Simon & Schuster, 2014.

Horn, Stanley F. *Invisible Empire: The Story of the Ku Klux Klan 1866–1871*. New York: Haskell House Publishers, 1968.

Horsman, Reginald. *Josiah Nott of Mobile: Southerner, Physician, and Racial Theorist*. Baton Rouge: Louisiana State University Press, 1987.

Horsman, Reginald. *Race and Manifest Destiny: The Origins of American Racial Anglo-Saxonism*. Cambridge, MA: Harvard University Press, 1981.

Houston, Susan E., and Alison Prentice. *Schooling and Scholars in Nineteenth-Century Ontario*. Toronto: University of Toronto Press, 1988.

Howe, Daniel Walker. *What Hath God Wrought: The Transformation of America, 1815–1848*. New York: Oxford University Press, 2007.

Huntzicker, William E. *The Popular Press, 1833–1865*. Westport, CT: Greenwood Press, 1999.

Huston, James L. *The Panic of 1857 and the Coming of the Civil War*. Baton Rouge: Louisiana State University Press, 1987.

Ignatiev, Noel. *How the Irish Became White*. New York: Routledge, 1995.

Jacobson, Matthew Frye. *Whiteness of a Different Color: European Immigrants and the Alchemy of Race*. Cambridge, MA: Harvard University Press, 1998.

Janney, Caroline E. *Remembering the Civil War: Reunion and the Limits of Reconciliation*. Chapel Hill: University of North Carolina Press, 2013.

Jasanoff, Maya. *Liberty's Exiles: American Loyalists in the Revolutionary World*. New York: Alfred A. Knopf, 2011.

Jewett, Clayton E., ed. *The Battlefield and Beyond: Essays on the American Civil War*. Baton Rouge: Louisiana State University Press, 2012.

Johannsen, Robert W. *To the Halls of the Montezumas: The Mexican War in the American Imagination*. New York: Oxford University Press, 1985.

John, Richard R. *Spreading the News: The American Postal System from Franklin to Morse*. Cambridge, MA: Harvard University Press, 1995.

Johnson, Guion Griffis. *Ante-Bellum North Carolina: A Social History*. Chapel Hill: University of North Carolina Press, 1937.

Johnson, Timothy D. *A Gallant Little Army: The Mexico City Campaign*. Lawrence: University Press of Kansas, 2007.

Jordan, John W., and James Hadden, eds. *Genealogical and Personal History of Fayette and Greene Counties Pennsylvania*. 3 vols. New York: Lewis Historical Publishing, 1912.

Jordan-Lake, Joy. *Whitewashing* Uncle Tom's Cabin: *Nineteenth-Century Women Novelists Respond to Stowe*. Nashville: Vanderbilt University Press, 2005.

Karsten, Peter. *Patriot-Heroes in England and America: Political Symbolism and Changing Values over Three Centuries*. Madison: University of Wisconsin Press, 1978.

Kaufman, Martin. *American Medical Education: The Formative Years, 1765–1910*. Westport, CT: Greenwood Press, 1976.

Kendi, Ibram X. *Stamped from the Beginning: The Definitive History of Racist Ideas in America*. New York: Nation Books, 2016.

Keyssar, Alexander. *The Right to Vote: The Contested History of Democracy in the United States*. Rev. ed. New York: Basic Books, 2009.

Kidd, Colin. *The Forging of Races: Race and Scripture in the Protestant Atlantic World, 1600–2000*. New York: Cambridge University Press, 2006.

Kielbowicz, Richard B. *News in the Mail: The Press, Post Office, and Public Information, 1700–1860s*. New York: Greenwood Press, 1989.

Klein, Milton M., ed. *The Empire State: A History of New York*. Ithaca, NY: Cornell University Press, 2001.

Kousser, J. Morgan, and James M. McPherson, eds. *Region, Race, and Reconstruction: Essays in Honor of C. Vann Woodward*. New York: Oxford University Press, 1982.

Kraditor, Aileen S. *Means and Ends in American Abolitionism: Garrison and His Critics on Strategy and Tactics, 1834–1850*. New York: Pantheon Books, 1969.

Lander, Ernest McPherson. *Reluctant Imperialists: Calhoun, the South Carolinians, and the Mexican War.* Baton Rouge: Louisiana State University Press, 1980.

Lanzendörfer, Tim., ed. *The Routledge Companion to the British and North American Literary Magazine*. New York: Routledge, 2022.

Latimer, Jon. *1812: War with America*. Cambridge, MA: Belknap Press of Harvard University Press, 2007.

Lee, Alfred McClung. *The Daily Newspaper in America: The Evolution of a Social Instrument*. New York: Macmillan, 1937.

Lemire, Elise. *"Miscegenation": Making Race in America*. Philadelphia: University of Pennsylvania Press, 2002.

Leonard, Thomas C. *News for All: America's Coming-of-Age with the Press*. New York: Oxford University Press, 1995.

LeSueur, William Dawson. *William Lyon Mackenzie: A Reinterpretation*. Edited by A. B. McKillop. Toronto: Macmillan of Canada, 1979.

Lewis, Kay Wright. *A Curse upon the Nation: Race, Freedom, and Extermination in America and the Atlantic World*. Athens: University of Georgia Press, 2017.

Livingstone, David N. *Adam's Ancestors: Race, Religion, and the Politics of Human Origins*. Baltimore: Johns Hopkins University Press, 2008.

Lott, Eric. *Love and Theft: Blackface Minstrelsy and the American Working Class*. New York: Oxford University Press, 1993.

Lundberg, James M. *Horace Greeley: Print, Politics, and the Failure of American Nationhood*. Baltimore: Johns Hopkins University Press, 2019.

Lurie, Edward. *Louis Agassiz: A Life in Science*. Chicago: University of Chicago Press, 1960.

Luskey, Brian P. *On the Make: Clerks and the Quest for Capital in Nineteenth-Century America*. New York: New York University Press, 2010.

Maddex, Jack P., Jr. *The Reconstruction of Edward A. Pollard: A Rebel's Conversion to Postbellum Unionism*. Chapel Hill: University of North Carolina Press, 1974.

Magdol, Edward, and Jon L. Wakelyn, eds. *The Southern Common People: Studies in Nineteenth-Century Social History*. Westport, CT: Greenwood Press, 1980.

Maizlish, Steven E. *A Strife of Tongues: The Compromise of 1850 and the Ideological Foundations of the American Civil War*. Charlottesville: University of Virginia Press, 2018.

Marten, James. *Sing Not War: The Lives of Union and Confederate Veterans in Gilded Age America*. Chapel Hill: University of North Carolina Press, 2011.

Maxwell, W. J., comp. *General Alumni Catalogue of the University of Pennsylvania*. [Philadelphia: University of Pennsylvania General Alumni Society,] 1917.

Mayfield, John. *Rehearsal for Republicanism: Free Soil and the Politics of Antislavery*. Port Washington, NY: Kennikat Press, 1980.

McCaffrey, James M. *Army of Manifest Destiny: The American Soldier in the Mexican War, 1846–1848*. New York: New York University Press, 1992.

McCalla, Douglas. *Planting the Province: The Economic History of Upper Canada, 1784–1870*. Toronto: University of Toronto Press, 1993.

McCardell, John. *The Idea of a Southern Nation: Southern Nationalists and Southern Nationalism, 1830–1860*. New York: W. W. Norton, 1979.

McCurry, Stephanie. *Confederate Reckoning: Power and Politics in the Civil War South*. Cambridge, MA: Harvard University Press, 2012.

McGovern, Bryan P. *John Mitchel: Irish Nationalist, Southern Secessionist*. Knoxville: University of Tennessee Press, 2009.

McKay, Ernest A. *The Civil War and New York City*. Syracuse, NY: Syracuse University Press, 1990.

McKelvey, Blake. *Rochester: The Water-Power City, 1812–1854*. Cambridge, MA: Harvard University Press, 1945.

McKenna, Thomas P. *From Vicksburg to Cedar Creek: The 22nd Iowa Volunteer Infantry in the Civil War*. Iowa City, IA: Camp Pope Publishing, 2014.

McPherson, James M. *Battle Cry of Freedom: The Civil War Era*. New York: Oxford University Press, 1988.

Mélonio, Françoise. *Tocqueville and the French*. Translated by Beth G. Raps. Charlottesville: University Press of Virginia, 1998.

Mendelberg, Tali. *The Race Card: Campaign Strategy, Implicit Messages, and the Norm of Equality*. Princeton, NJ: Princeton University Press, 2011.

Merrill, Georgia Drew, ed. *History of Androscoggin County, Maine*. Boston: W. A. Fergusson & Co., 1891.

Miner, Craig. *Seeding Civil War: Kansas in the National News, 1854–1858*. Lawrence: University Press of Kansas, 2008.

Mitchell, Stewart. *Horatio Seymour of New York*. Cambridge, MA: Harvard University Press, 1938.

Mohr, James C. *The Radical Republicans and Reform in New York During Reconstruction*. Ithaca, NY: Cornell University Press, 1973.

Moore, John W. *Roster of North Carolina Troops in the War Between the States*. 4 vols. Raleigh: Ashe & Gatling, 1892.

Morrison, Chaplain. *Democratic Politics and Sectionalism: The Wilmot Proviso Controversy*. Chapel Hill: University of North Carolina Press, 1967.

Morrison, Michael A. *Slavery and the American West: The Eclipse of Manifest Destiny and the Coming of the Civil War*. Chapel Hill: University of North Carolina Press, 1997.

Mushkat, Jerome. *Fernando Wood: A Political Biography*. Kent, OH: Kent State University Press, 1990.

Mushkat, Jerome. *The Reconstruction of the New York Democracy, 1861–1874*. Rutherford, NJ: Fairleigh Dickinson University Press, 1981.

Napton, William Barclay. *Past and Present of Saline County Missouri*. B. F. Bowen & Co., 1910.

Neely, Mark E., Jr. *The Boundaries of American Political Culture in the Civil War Era*. Chapel Hill: University of North Carolina Press, 2005.

Neely, Mark E., Jr. *The Fate of Liberty: Abraham Lincoln and Civil Liberties*. New York: Oxford University Press, 1992.

Neely, Mark E., Jr. *Lincoln and the Democrats: The Politics of Opposition in the Civil War*. New York: Cambridge University Press, 2017.

Nicoletti, Cynthia. *Secession on Trial: The Treason Prosecution of Jefferson Davis*. New York: Cambridge University Press, 2017.

Nimura, Janice P. *The Doctors Blackwell: How Two Pioneering Sisters Brought Medicine to Women and Women to Medicine*. New York: W. W. Norton, 2021.

Notes on Niagara, 1759–1860, No. 32. Niagara, ON: Niagara Historical Society, [1919].

Nye, Russel Blaine. *Fettered Freedom: Civil Liberties and the Slavery Controversy, 1830–1860*. East Lansing: Michigan State College Press, 1949.

Oakes, James. *The Radical and the Republican: Frederick Douglass, Abraham Lincoln, and the Triumph of Antislavery Politics*. New York: W. W. Norton, 2007.

Oakes, James. *The Scorpion's Sting: Antislavery and the Coming of the Civil War*. New York: W. W. Norton, 2014.

Olney, James H. *A Genealogy of the Descendants of Thomas Olney, an Original Proprietor of Providence, R.I., Who Came from England in 1635*. Providence, RI: E. L. Freeman and Son, 1889.

Osofsky, Gilbert. *The Burden of Race: A Documentary History of Negro-White Relations in America*. New York: Harper & Row, 1967.

Osterhammel, Jürgen. *The Transformation of the World: A Global History of the Nineteenth Century*. Translated by Patrick Camiller. Princeton, NJ: Princeton University Press, 2014.

Owen, Thomas McAdory. *History of Alabama and Dictionary of Alabama Biography*. 4 vols. Chicago: S. J. Clarke Publishing, 1921.

Owens, Deirdre Cooper. *Medical Bondage: Race, Gender, and the Origins of American Gynecology*. Athens: University of Georgia Press, 2017.

Ownby, Ted, Charles Reagan Wilson, Ann J. Abadie, Odie Lindsey, and James G. Thomas Jr., eds. *The Mississippi Encyclopedia*. Jackson: University Press of Mississippi, 2017.

Painter, Nell Irvin. *The History of White People*. New York: W. W. Norton, 2010.

Parfait, Claire. *The Publishing History of* Uncle Tom's Cabin, *1852–2002*. New York: Routledge, 2007.

Parsons, Elaine Frantz. *Ku-Klux: The Birth of the Klan During Reconstruction*. Chapel Hill: University of North Carolina Press, 2015.

Pasley, Jeffrey L. *"The Tyranny of Printers": Newspaper Politics in the Early American Republic*. Charlottesville: University of Virginia Press, 2001.

Paulus, Carl Lawrence. *The Slaveholding Crisis: Fear of Insurrection and the Coming of the Civil War*. Baton Rouge: Louisiana State University Press, 2017.

Perman, Michael. *Struggle for Mastery: Disfranchisement in the South, 1888–1908*. Chapel Hill: University of North Carolina Press, 2001.

Perrin, W. H., J. H. Battle, and G. C. Kniffin. *Kentucky: A History of the State*. 6th ed. Louisville: F. A. Battey, 1887.

Petrie, George. *William F. Samford, Statesman and Man of Letters. Transactions of the Alabama Historical Society*, Reprint No. 23. Montgomery: n.p., 1904.

Polgar, Paul J. *Standard-Bearers of Equality: America's First Abolition Movement*. Chapel Hill: University of North Carolina Press, 2019.

Porter, Glenn, and Harold C. Livesay. *Merchants and Manufacturers: Studies in the Changing Structure of Nineteenth-Century Marketing*. Baltimore: Johns Hopkins University Press, 1971.

Portrait and Biographical Album of Lancaster County, Nebraska. Chicago: Chapman Brothers, 1888.

Portrait and Biographical Album of Muscatine County, Iowa. Chicago: Acme Publishing, 1889.

Portrait and Biographical Record of Kalamazoo, Allegan, and Van Buren Counties, Michigan. Chicago: Chapman Brothers, 1894

Portrait and Biographical Record of Lafayette and Saline Counties, Missouri. Chicago: Chapman Brothers, 1893.

Potter-MacKinnon, Janice. *While the Women Only Wept: Loyalist Refugee Women in Eastern Ontario*. Montreal: McGill-Queen's University Press, 1993.

Pred, Allan R. *Urban Growth and the Circulation of Information: The United States System of Cities, 1790–1840*. Cambridge, MA: Harvard University Press, 1973.

Prince, K. Stephen. *Stories of the South: Race and the Reconstruction of Southern Identity, 1865–1915*. Chapel Hill: University of North Carolina Press, 2014.

Quigley, David. *Second Founding: New York City, Reconstruction, and the Making of American Democracy*. New York: Hill and Wang, 2004.

Quigley, Paul. *Shifting Grounds: Nationalism and the American South, 1848–1865*. New York: Oxford University Press, 2012.

Rable, George C. *But There Was No Peace: The Role of Violence in the Politics of Reconstruction*. Athens: University of Georgia Press, 1984.

Rafuse, Ethan S. *McClellan's War: The Failure of Moderation in the Struggle for the Union*. Bloomington: Indiana University Press, 2005.

Rao, Gautham. *National Duties: Custom Houses and the Making of the American State*. Chicago: University of Chicago Press, 2016.

Rapport, Mike. *1848: Year of Revolution*. New York: Basic Books, 2009.

Remini, Robert V. *Daniel Webster: The Man and His Time*. New York: W. W. Norton, 1997.

Richards, Leonard L. *"Gentlemen of Property and Standing": Anti-Abolition Mobs in Jacksonian America*. New York: Oxford University Press, 1970.
Richards, Leonard L. *The Slave Power: The Free North and Southern Domination, 1780–1860*. Baton Rouge: Louisiana State University Press, 2000.
Richardson, Heather Cox. *The Death of Reconstruction: Race, Labor, and Politics in the Post–Civil War North, 1865–1901*. Cambridge, MA: Harvard University Press, 2011.
Riddell, William Renwick. *The Slave in Canada*. Washington, DC: Association for the Study of Negro Life and History, 1920.
Risley, Ford. *Civil War Journalism*. Santa Barbara, CA: Praeger, 2012.
Roberts, Timothy Mason. *Distant Revolutions: 1848 and the Challenge to American Exceptionalism*. Charlottesville: University Press of Virginia, 2009.
Robinson, Michael D. *A Union Indivisible: Secession and the Politics of Slavery in the Border South*. Chapel Hill: University of North Carolina Press, 2017.
Roediger, David R. *The Wages of Whiteness: Race and the Making of the American Working Class*. London: Verso, 1991.
Rogers, Molly. *Delia's Tears: Race, Science, and Photography in Nineteenth-Century America*. New Haven, CT: Yale University Press, 2010.
Rogers, William Warren, Jr. *Reconstruction Politics in a Deep South State: Alabama, 1865–1874*. Tuscaloosa: University of Alabama Press, 2021.
Rosen, Hannah. *Terror in the Heart of Freedom: Citizenship, Sexual Violence, and the Meaning of Race in the Postemancipation South*. Chapel Hill: University of North Carolina Press, 2009.
Ross, Earle Dudley. *The Liberal Republican Movement*. New York: Henry Holt, 1919.
Rothert, Otto A. *A History of Muhlenberg County*. Louisville: John P. Morton, 1913.
Rothstein, William G. *American Physicians in the Nineteenth Century: From Sects to Science*. Baltimore: Johns Hopkins University Press, 1972.
Rubbinaccio, Michael. *Abraham Oakey Hall: New York's Most Elegant and Controversial Mayor*. Seattle: Pescara Publishing, 2011.
Russel, Robert R. *Economic Aspects of Southern Sectionalism, 1840–1861*, University of Illinois Studies in the Social Sciences 11. Urbana: University of Illinois Press, 1924.
Rutkow, Ira. *Seeking the Cure: A History of Medicine in America*. New York: Scribner, 2010.
Sachsman, David B., ed. *After the War: The Press in a Changing America, 1865–1900*. New Brunswick, NJ: Transaction Publishers, 2017.
Sachsman, David B., ed. *A Press Divided: Newspaper Coverage of the Civil War*. New Brunswick, NJ: Transaction Publishers, 2014.
Savitt, Todd L. *Medicine and Slavery: The Diseases and Health Care of Blacks in Antebellum Virginia*. Urbana: University of Illinois Press, 1978.
Savitt, Todd L. *Race and Medicine in Nineteenth- and Early-Twentieth-Century America*. Kent, OH: Kent State University Press, 2007.
Saxton, Alexander. *The Rise and Fall of the White Republic: Class Politics and Mass Culture in Nineteenth-Century America*. London: Verso, 1990.
Schermerhorn, Calvin. *The Business of Slavery and the Rise of American Capitalism, 1815–1860*. New Haven, CT: Yale University Press, 2015.
Schiller, Dan. *Objectivity and the News: The Public and the Rise of Commercial Journalism*. Philadelphia: University of Pennsylvania Press, 1981.

Schott, Thomas E. *Alexander H. Stephens of Georgia: A Biography.* Baton Rouge: Louisiana State University Press, 1988.

Schudson, Michael. *Discovering the News: A Social History of American Newspapers.* New York: Basic Books, Inc., 1978.

Sewell, Richard H. *Ballots for Freedom: Antislavery Politics in the United States, 1837–1860.* New York: Oxford University Press, 1976.

Shelden, Rachel A. *Washington Brotherhood: Politics, Social Life, and the Coming of the Civil War.* Chapel Hill: University of North Carolina Press, 2013.

Sheldon, George W. *The Story of the Volunteer Fire Department of the City of New York.* New York: Harper & Brothers, 1882.

Sheppard, Si. *The Partisan Press: A History of Media Bias in the United States.* Jefferson, NC: McFarland, 2008.

Shick, Tom W. *Behold the Promised Land: A History of Afro-American Settler Society in Nineteenth-Century Liberia.* 1977. Baltimore: Johns Hopkins University Press, 1980.

Shryock, Richard Harrison. *Medicine and Society in America, 1660–1860.* New York: New York University Press, 1960.

Siddali, Silvana R. *From Property to Person: Slavery and the Confiscation Acts, 1861–1862.* Baton Rouge: Louisiana State University Press, 2005.

Silbey, Joel H. *A Respectable Minority: The Democratic Party in the Civil War Era, 1860–1868.* New York: W. W. Norton, 1977.

Silbey, Joel H. *Storm over Texas: The Annexation Controversy and the Road to Civil War.* New York: Oxford University Press, 2005.

Silverman, Jason H. *Unwelcome Guests: Canada West's Response to American Fugitive Slaves, 1800–1865.* Millwood, NY: Associated Faculty Press, 1985.

Slap, Andrew L. *The Doom of Reconstruction: The Liberal Republicans in the Civil War Era.* New York: Fordham University Press, 2006.

Smedley, Audrey. *Race in North America: Origin and Evolution of a Worldview.* Boulder, CO: Westview Press, 1993.

Smith, Culver G. *The Press, Politics, and Patronage: The American Government's Use of Newspapers, 1789–1875.* Athens: University of Georgia Press, 1977.

Smith, H. Shelton. *In His Image, But . . . : Racism in Southern Religion, 1780–1910.* Durham, NC: Duke University Press, 1972.

Smith, John A., comp. *The History of Maumee: 1748–1926.* Toledo, OH: Henry M. Schmit, 1924.

Smith, Michael Thomas. *The Enemy Within: Fears of Corruption in the Civil War North.* Charlottesville: University of Virginia Press, 2011.

Smithers, Gregory D. *Science, Sexuality, and Race in the United States and Australia, 1780s–1890s.* New York: Routledge Press, 2009.

Snodgrass, Mary Ellen. *The Underground Railroad: An Encyclopedia of People, Places, and Operations.* New York: Routledge, 2008.

Solomos, John, and Les Back. *Racism and Society.* Basingstoke: Macmillan, 1996.

Spann, Edward K. *Gotham at War: New York City, 1860–1865.* Wilmington, DE: S. R. Books, 2002.

Spann, Edward K. *The New Metropolis: New York City, 1840–1857.* New York: Columbia University Press, 1981.

Sperber, Jonathan. *Karl Marx: A Nineteenth-Century Life*. New York: Liveright Publishing, 2013.

Stampp, Kenneth M. *The Era of Reconstruction, 1865–1877*. New York: Vintage Books, 1965.

Stampp, Kenneth M., and Leon F. Litwack, eds. *Reconstruction: An Anthology of Revisionist Writings*. Baton Rouge: Louisiana State University Press, 1969.

Stanton, William. *The Leopard's Spots: Scientific Attitudes Toward Race in America, 1815–59*. Chicago: University of Chicago Press, 1960.

Starr, Paul. *The Creation of the Media: Political Origins of Modern Communications*. New York: Basic Books, 2004.

Stauffer, John, and Zoe Trodd, eds. *The Tribunal: Responses to John Brown and the Harpers Ferry Raid*. Cambridge, MA: Belknap Press of Harvard University Press, 2012.

Stein, Melissa N. *Measuring Manhood: Race and the Science of Masculinity, 1830–1934*. Minneapolis: University of Minnesota Press, 2015.

Stepan, Nancy. *The Idea of Race in Science: Great Britain, 1800–1960*. London: Macmillan, 1982.

Stevens, George A. *New York Typographical Union No. 6: Study of a Modern Trade Union and Its Predecessors*. Albany, NY: J. B. Lyon Company, 1913.

Stockwell, Mary. *The Other Trail of Tears: The Removal of the Ohio Indians*. Yardley, PA: Westholme Publishing, 2014.

Stott, Richard B. *Workers in the Metropolis: Class, Ethnicity, and Youth in Antebellum New York City*. Ithaca, NY: Cornell University Press, 1990.

Stouffer, Allen P. *The Light of Nature and the Law of God: Antislavery in Ontario, 1833–1877*. Baton Rouge: Louisiana State University Press, 1992.

Summers, Mark W. *The Plundering Generation: Corruption and the Crisis of the Union, 1849–1861*. New York: Oxford University Press, 1987.

Summers, Mark W. *The Press Gang: Newspapers & Politics, 1865–1878*. Chapel Hill: University of North Carolina Press, 1994.

Summers, Mark Wahlgren. *A Dangerous Stir: Fear, Paranoia, and the Making of Reconstruction*. Chapel Hill: University of North Carolina Press, 2009.

Sussman, Robert Wald. *The Myth of Race: The Troubling Persistence of an Unscientific Idea*. Cambridge, MA: Harvard University Press, 2014.

Sweeney, Matthew. *The Lottery Wars: Long Odds, Fast Money, and the Battle over an American Institution*. New York: Bloomsbury, 2009.

Talman, James J., ed. *Loyalist Narratives from Upper Canada*. Toronto: The Champlain Society, 1946.

Taylor, Alan. *The Civil War of 1812: American Citizens, British Subjects, Irish Rebels, and Indian Allies*. New York: Alfred A. Knopf, 2010.

Taylor, Joe Gray. *Louisiana Reconstructed: 1863–1877*. Baton Rouge: Louisiana State University Press, 1974.

Taylor, Paul. *"The Most Complete Political Machine Ever Known": The North's Union Leagues in the American Civil War*. Kent, OH: Kent State University Press, 2018.

Thomas, John L. *The Liberator: William Lloyd Garrison*. Boston: Little, Brown, 1963.

Towns, W. Stuart. *Enduring Legacy: Rhetoric and Ritual of the Lost Cause*. Tuscaloosa: University of Alabama Press, 2012.

Tunnell, Ted. *Crucible of Reconstruction: War, Radicalism and Race in Louisiana, 1862–1877.* Baton Rouge: Louisiana State University Press, 1984.

Turner, Wesley B. *The Astonishing General: The Life and Legacy of Sir Isaac Brock.* Toronto: Dundurn Press, 2011.

Tuttle, Roger W., ed. and comp. *Biographies of Graduates of the Yale Law School, 1824–1899.* New Haven, CT: Tuttle, Morehouse & Taylor Company, 1911.

Voegeli, V. Jacque. *Free but Not Equal: The Midwest and the Negro During the Civil War.* Chicago: University of Chicago Press, 1967.

Waggoner, Clark, ed. *History of the City of Toledo and Lucas County, Ohio.* New York: Munsell & Co., 1888.

Wang, Xi. *The Trial of Democracy: Black Suffrage and Northern Republicans, 1860–1910.* Athens: University of Georgia Press, 1997.

Ware, Norman. *The Industrial Worker, 1840–1860: The Reaction of American Industrial Society to the Advance of the Industrial Revolution.* 1924. Gloucester, MA: Peter Smith, 1959.

Watson, Harry L. *Liberty and Power: The Politics of Jacksonian America.* New York: Hill and Wang, 2006.

Watson, Ritchie Devon, Jr. *Grand Emporium, Mercantile Monster: The Antebellum South's Love-Hate Affair with New York City.* Baton Rouge: Louisiana State University Press, 2023.

Watson, Ritchie Devon, Jr. *Normans and Saxons: Southern Race Mythology and the Intellectual History of the American Civil War.* Baton Rouge: Louisiana State University Press, 2008.

Watt, Gavin K. *The Burning of the Valleys: Daring Raids from Canada Against the New York Frontier in the Fall of 1780.* Rev. ed. Toronto: Dundurn Press, 1997.

Weber, Jennifer L. *Copperheads: The Rise and Fall of Lincoln's Opponents in the North.* New York: Oxford University Press, 2006.

Weitz, Mark A. *The Confederacy on Trial: The Piracy and Sequestration Cases of 1861.* Lawrence: University Press of Kansas, 2005.

Wells, Jonathan Daniel. *Blind No More: African American Resistance, Free-Soil Politics, and the Coming of the Civil War.* Athens: University of Georgia Press, 2019.

Wells, Jonathan Daniel. *The Kidnapping Club: Wall Street, Slavery, and Resistance on the Eve of the Civil War.* New York: Bold Type Books, 2020.

Wert, Jeffry D. *From Winchester to Cedar Creek: The Shenandoah Campaign of 1864.* Carbondale: Southern Illinois University Press, 2010.

White, Randall. *Ontario, 1610–1985: A Political and Economic History.* Toronto: Dundurn Press, 1985.

Williams, Kidada E. *I Saw Death Coming: A History of Terror and Survival in the War Against Reconstruction.* New York: Bloomsbury, 2023.

Willoughby, Christopher D. E. *Masters of Health: Racial Science and Slavery in U.S. Medical Schools.* Chapel Hill: University of North Carolina Press, 2022.

Wilson, Charles Reagan. *Baptized in Blood: The Religion of the Lost Cause, 1865–1920.* Athens: University of Georgia Press, 1980.

Wilton, Carol. *Popular Politics and Political Culture in Upper Canada, 1800–1850.* Montreal: McGill-Queen's University Press, 2000.

Winders, Richard Bruce. *Mr. Polk's Army: The American Military Experience in the Mexican War.* College Station: Texas A&M University Press, 1997.
Winks, Robin W. *The Blacks in Canada: A History.* New Haven, CT: Yale University Press, 1971.
Wish, Harvey. *George Fitzhugh, Propagandist of the Old South.* Baton Rouge: Louisiana State University Press, 1943.
Wood, Forrest G. *The Arrogance of Faith: Christianity and Race in America from the Colonial Era to the Twentieth Century.* New York: Alfred A. Knopf, 1990.
Wood, Forrest G. *Black Scare: The Racist Response to Emancipation and Reconstruction.* Berkeley: University of California Press, 1968.
Woods, Michael E. *Arguing Until Doomsday: Stephen Douglas, Jefferson Davis, and the Struggle for American Democracy.* Chapel Hill: University of North Carolina Press, 2020.
Wyatt-Brown, Bertram. *Lewis Tappan and the Evangelical War Against Slavery.* 1969. New York: Atheneum, 1971.
Yacovone, Donald. *Teaching White Supremacy: America's Democratic Ordeal and the Forging of Our National Identity.* New York: Pantheon Books, 2022.
Zaeske, Susan. *Signatures of Citizenship: Petitioning, Antislavery, and Women's Political Identity.* Chapel Hill: University of North Carolina Press, 2003.
Zucchino, David. *Wilmington's Lie: The Murderous Coup of 1898 and the Rise of White Supremacy.* New York: Atlantic Monthly Press, 2020.

Articles

Akingbade, Harrison. "The Liberian Settlers and the Campaign Against the Slave Trade 1825–1865." *Africa* 38 (September 1983): 339–68.
Baehre, Ranier. "*The Medical Profession in Upper Canada* Reconsidered: Politics, Medical Reform, and Law in a Colonial Society." *Canadian Bulletin of Medical History* 12 (1995): 101–24.
Barth, Alan. "Synthetic Misanthrope." *New Republic* 108 (May 17, 1943): 676–77.
Bean, W. G. "Anti-Jeffersonianism in the Antebellum South." *North Carolina Historical Review* 12 (April 1935): 103–24.
Bohde, Cheryl D. "'Magazines as a Powerful Element of Civilization': An Exploration of the Ideology of Literary Magazines, 1830–1850." *American Periodicals* 1 (Fall 1991): 34–45.
Bolster, Paul. "Georgia Plays the Numbers: A History of Lotteries in Georgia." *Atlanta Historical Journal* 29 (1985): 95–104.
Corner, Betsy C. "Early Medical Education in Western New York, Geneva and Rochester Areas, 1827 to 1872." *New York State Journal of Medicine* 55 (November 1955): 3156–64.
Downs, Gregory P. "The Mexicanization of American Politics: The United States' Path from Civil War to Stabilization." *American Historical Review* 117 (April 2012): 387–409.
Duncan, Louis C. "Medical History of General Scott's Campaign to the City of Mexico in 1847." *Military Surgeon* 47 (October 1920): 436–70.
Earnhart, Hugh G. "*West and South*: Its Struggle Against the Tide." *Filson Club History Quarterly* 42 (April 1968): 150–56.

Fleming, Walter L. "The Buford Expedition to Kansas." *American Historical Review* 6 (October 1900): 38–48.

Freidel, Frank. "The Loyal Publication Society: A Pro-Union Propaganda Agency." *Mississippi Valley Historical Review* 26 (December 1939): 359–76.

Gara, Larry. "Slavery and the Slave Power: A Crucial Distinction." *Civil War History* 15 (March 1969): 5–18.

George, Joseph, Jr. "'A Catholic Family Newspaper' Views the Lincoln Administration: John Mullaly's Copperhead Weekly." *Civil War History* 24 (June 1978): 112–32.

Haller, John S., Jr. "The Negro and the Southern Physician: A Study of Medical and Racial Attitudes, 1800–1860." *Medical History* 16 (July 1972): 238–53.

Heath, Andrew. "'The Producers on the One Side, and the Capitalists on the Other': Labor Reform, Slavery, and the Career of a Transatlantic Radical." *American Nineteenth Century History* 13 (June 2012): 199–227.

Hochschild, Jennifer L., and Brenna M. Powell. "Racial Reorganization and the United States Census 1850–1930: Mulattoes, Half-Breeds, Mixed Parentage, Hindoos, and the Mexican Race." *Studies in American Political Development* 22 (Spring 2008): 59–96.

Holley, Bradley L. "I Shall Never Be a White Man Again: Race and Junior Officers in the Mexican War." *War & Society* 35 (October 2016): 259–74.

Hubbell, Jay B. "Charles Chauncey Burr: Friend of Poe." *Publications of the Modern Language Association* 69 (September 1954): 833–40.

Hutter, W. H., and Ray H. Abrams. "Copperhead Newspapers and the Negro." *Journal of Negro History* 20 (April 1935): 131–52.

Irey, Thomas R. "Soldiering, Suffering, and Dying in the Mexican War." *Journal of the West* 11 (April 1972): 285–98.

Kelly, Wayne Edward. "Race and Segregation in the Upper Canada Militia." *Journal of the Society for Army Historical Research* 78 (Winter 2000): 264–66.

Luse, Christopher A. "Slavery's Champions Stood at Odds: Polygenesis and the Defense of Slavery." *Civil War History* 53 (December 2007): 379–412.

McNairn, Jeffrey L. "Towards Deliberative Democracy: Parliamentary Intelligence and the Public Sphere in Upper Canada, 1791–1840." *Journal of Canadian Studies* 33 (Spring 1998): 39–60.

Oakes, James. "Capitalism and Slavery and the Civil War." *International Labor and Working Class History* 89 (Spring 2016): 195–220.

Peck, Gunther. "Labor Abolition and the Politics of White Victimhood: Rethinking the History of Working-Class Racism." *Journal of the Early Republic* 39 (Spring 2019): 89–98.

Rice, C. Duncan. "The Anti-Slavery Mission of George Thompson to the United States, 1834–1835." *Journal of American Studies* 2 (April 1968): 13–31.

Riddell, W. R. "The Slave in Upper Canada." *Journal of Negro History* 4 (October 1919): 372–95.

Riddell, William Renwick. "Notes on Slavery in Canada." *Journal of Negro History* 4 (October 1919): 396–411.

Roberts, Julia. "'A Mixed Assemblage of Persons': Race and Tavern Space in Upper Canada." *Canadian Historical Review* 83 (March 2002): 1–28.

Rogers, William Warren. "C. Chauncey Burr and The Old Guard." *Proceedings of the New Jersey Historical Society* 73 (July 1955): 168–81.

Rugemer, Edward B. "Robert Monroe Harrison, British Abolition, Southern Anglophobia, and the Annexation of Texas." *Slavery & Abolition* 28 (August 2007): 169–91.

Sale, Maggie. "Critiques from Within: Antebellum Projects of Resistance." *American Literature* 64 (December 1992): 695–718.

Shelden, Rachel A. "The Politics of Continuity and Change in the Long Civil War Era." *Civil War History* 65 (December 2019): 319–41.

Shelden, Rachel A., and Erik B. Alexander. "Dismantling the Party System: Party Fluidity and the Mechanisms of Nineteenth-Century U.S. Politics." *Journal of American History* 110 (December 2023): 419–48.

Siebert, Wilbur H. "The Temporary Settlement of Loyalists at Machiche, P.Q." *Proceedings and Transactions of the Royal Society of Canada* 8 (1914): 407–14.

Skidmore, Joe. "The Copperhead Press and the Civil War." *Journalism Quarterly* 16 (December 1939): 345–55.

Taylor, George Rogers. "Gaslight Foster: A New York 'Journeyman Journalist' at Mid-Century." *New York History* 58 (July 1977): 297–312.

Taylor, George Rogers. "Wholesale Commodity Prices at Charleston, South Carolina, 1796–1861." *Journal of Economic and Business History* 4 (1931–32): 848–68.

Toplin, Robert Brent. "Between Black and White: Attitudes Toward Southern Mulattoes, 1830–1861." *Journal of Southern History* 45 (May 1979): 185–200.

Wallace, W. S. "The Periodical Literature of Upper Canada." *Canadian Historical Review* 12 (March 1931): 4–22.

Wallis, Brian. "Black Bodies, White Science: The Slave Daguerreotypes of Louis Agassiz." *Journal of Blacks in Higher Education* 12 (Summer 1996): 102–6.

Wells, Jonathan Daniel. "Inventing *White Supremacy*: Race, Print Culture, and the Civil War Draft Riots." *Civil War History* 68 (March 2022): 42–80.

Wharton, V. L. "The Race Issue in the Overthrow of Reconstruction in Mississippi." *Phylon* 2 (4th Quarter 1941): 362–70.

Wigmore, Gregory. "Before the Railroad: From Slavery to Freedom in the Canadian-American Borderland." *Journal of American History* 98 (September 2011): 437–54.

Winders, Richard B. "Puebla's Forgotten Heroes." *Military History of the West* 24 (Spring 1994): 1–23.

Woods, Michael E. "'The Indignation of Freedom-Loving People': The Caning of Charles Sumner and Emotion in Antebellum Politics." *Journal of Social History* 44 (Spring 2011): 689–705.

Dissertations and Theses

Alexander, Erik Benjamin. "'A Revival of the Old Organization': Northern Democrats and Reconstruction 1868–1876." PhD diss., University of Virginia, 2011.

Bodson, Robert Louis. "A Description of the United States Occupation of Mexico as Reported by American Newspapers Published in Vera Cruz, Puebla, and Mexico City, September 14, 1847, to July 31, 1848." EdD diss., Ball State University, 1971.

Gardner, John Cooper. "Winning the Lower South to the Compromise of 1850." PhD diss., Louisiana State University, 1974.

Huff, Lawrence. "Joseph Addison Turner: A Study in the Culture of Ante-Bellum Middle Georgia." PhD diss., Vanderbilt University, 1958.

Ruehlen, Christopher Ronald. "The Specter of Subversion: Fears, Perceptions, and Reactions to Dissent in the Civil War North, 1861–1865." PhD diss., University of Florida, 2015.

Warner, Lee Howland. "The Silver Grays: New York State Conservative Whigs, 1846–1856." PhD diss., University of Wisconsin, 1971.

Index

www.ingramcontent.com/pod-product-compliance
Lightning Source LLC
LaVergne TN
LVHW100815200826
845923LV00028B/197